Teaching in the Secondary School

W9-BNG-652

18,617

Teaching in the
secondary school

DATE DUE

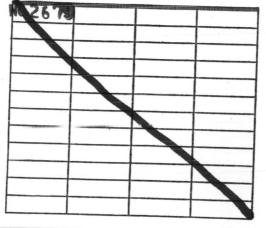

Teaching in the secondary school: planni

LB2609.T4   18617

Callahan, Joseph F.
VRJC/WRIGHT LIBRARY

LB 1737 .A3 T43 1977

Teaching in the secondary school : planning for
competence.

18617

Planning for Competence

Teaching in the Secondary School

Joseph F. Callahan

Leonard H. Clark

Jersey City State College

Macmillan Publishing Co., Inc.
New York

Collier Macmillan Publishers
London

Copyright © 1977, Macmillan Publishing Co., Inc.

Printed in the United States of America

All rights reserved. No part of this book may be reproduced or transmitted in any form or by any means, electronic or mechanical, including photocopying, recording, or any information storage and retrieval system, without permission in writing from the Publisher.

Macmillan Publishing Co., Inc.
866 Third Avenue, New York, New York 10022

Collier Macmillan Canada, Ltd.

ISBN 0–02–318250–4

Printing: 2 3 4 5 6 7 8   Year: 7 8 9 0 1 2 3

To Jane E. Callahan *and* Maria A. Clark

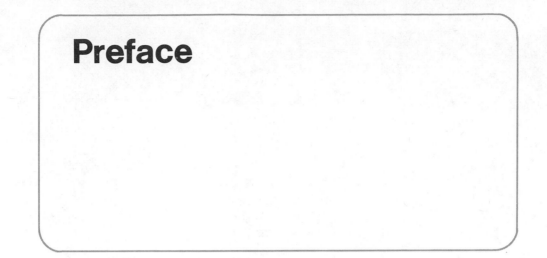

Preface

This volume is an attempt to provide a basic self-instructional text on teaching methods. In preparing this material, the authors have attempted to explain the rationale for various methods and techniques in teaching and to show how to carry out these methods and techniques in the classroom. To facilitate these objectives the authors have prepared a series of learning modules that should make it possible for students to learn the basic understandings and skills necessary for carrying out these methods and techniques on their own. To this end they have provided in their modules specific objectives, learning activities, textual explanation, self-administered and self-corrected tests, and instructions for studying.

Of course, expertise in methods and techniques comes from practice, particularly guided practice and experience. No one ever became truly expert simply by studying a book and carrying out learning activities. But it is expected that these modules will give the student the necessary background and basic know-how that will make early teaching practice and experience more profitable. The modules should serve as effective springboards for laboratory experiences in teaching. The editors believe that instructors using the modules in methods courses can depend on them to provide the basic instruction so that they can individualize instruction and devote their time to higher learning and laboratory activities.

J. F. C.
L. H. C.

Contents

Teaching in the Secondary School

To the Student

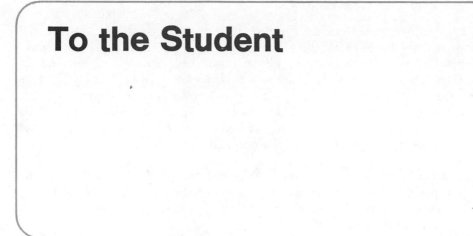

Welcome to an adventure in learning.

Now that you have begun to think seriously about a career in teaching, it is our guess that you will find adventures of this sort very helpful in planning to meet the challenges that await you in the classroom. It seems safe to predict that not only will you increase your background in educational theory and methodology as you work your way through these modules, but also you will improve your chances of becoming an effective teacher when the time arrives to put theory learned into practice.

Probably you have not encountered many books organized as this one, calling for such active participation on your part. From this point forward, you are expected to become a sensitive, self-motivated learner engaged in making frequent and sound judgments about your learning. You will be the one to control the rate of progress through the various modules and you will decide when you have mastered the knowledge presented in each. We have tried to help by (1) listing the objectives of each module, (2) providing a comprehensive set of questions to test your mastery at the end of each module, and (3) providing an answer key for your use in evaluating progress. Those with little time to spend on study can move through the various modules and finish quickly so long as they study attentively and demonstrate the mastery called for on each test. Slower-paced individuals, who wish to ponder and probe various areas and who decide to read extensively from the selected readings listed in each module, can establish a pace that suits their purposes.

It is not intended that any student will be able to prepare himself for a teaching career solely by completion of this kind of study program. Teaching is a human activity. It deals with people, with children, parents, and fellow professionals. It involves various kinds of knowledge, judgments, and decision making; it requires communications skills, human relations techniques, and a host of other attributes for the cultivation of which human interaction and professional expertise are necessary. But faithful and zealous use of this learning tool will add depth and meaning to your classroom sessions in education courses. Mastery of these modules will carry you beyond the initial steps of preparation so that you may place into context more of the campus lectures about education which you hear, and ask questions about schools and students that go beyond the layman's level of significance.

The sections of the book are called modules, for essentially they are self-contained units that have cognitive values by themselves. Each module contains a rationale, a list of objectives, a post test, an answer key, and a list of selected readings. The rationale attempts to establish the purpose of each module and, in some cases, the link with other aspects of pedagogical knowledge. The objectives inform you very specifically what you should know and be able to do as a consequence of your study of the module. The test and the key inform you of your progress toward module mastery. The general study plan recommended is as follows:

1. Read the rationale to acquaint yourself with the task you are addressing and, if possible, with how this module fits among the others that you will study.
2. Examine carefully the module objectives. Find out what will be expected of you upon completion of your study.
3. Read through the module, checking back from time to time to see how well you are mastering the objectives. Review what you do not understand.
4. Take the Post Test. Evaluate your success by using the answer key. Where your answer differs from that of the author, search out the sentence or paragraph in the text that confirms your answer or his.
5. If you score less than 85 per cent on any test, reread and retake the test until your mastery improves.
6. Try out your knowledge by exposing yourself to some of the suggested reading. Your progress should accelerate as you bring more and more knowledge to each book that you read.
7. Engage in interaction with fellow students, professors, and members of your family on the topics studied, whenever possible.
8. Enjoy the experience. The profession needs zealous seekers of knowledge who enjoy learning and who, in the process, develop a capacity for infecting other people with the same "felicitous virus."

Planning: General Principles

Leonard H. Clark

Jersey City State College

module 1.1

Importance of Planning / Two Essential Elements / Objectives and Planning / Plan for Action / Evaluating the Plan / Resources for Planning / Teacher-Pupil Planning / Team Planning

INTRODUCTION

Careful planning is a critical skill for a teacher. A well-developed plan for teaching will not guarantee the success of the lesson or unit or even the over-all effectiveness of the course, but the lack of a well-developed plan will almost certainly result in failure. There are almost as many different methods and variations of methods as there are teachers who use them. The same holds true for planning. There is not any one lesson plan form or unit plan form that will insure that you will *reach* your class. The form of the plan is insignificant; it is the substance of the plan by which you will succeed or fail in reaching your objectives.

This module deals with this key area of planning. For convenience, it has been divided into five subsections. The first of these will present some general principle of planning; the second will closely examine behavioral objectives; a third will explain how to construct a course plan; the fourth will concern the unit plan, the framework upon which the daily lessons rest; and the last will concentrate on the daily lesson plan and the day-by-day development of skills and knowledge.

GENERAL PRINCIPLES

Rationale

In the introduction, we pointed out that good planning is imperative if there is to be good teaching. If education is to succeed, we must plan good curricula, good courses, good units, and good lessons. Planning takes care and skill. The fact that principles in all educational planning are pretty much the same makes the necessary planning skills somewhat easier to master. In this section we shall try to set forth these principles clearly for you to give you a good base for your actual classroom teaching.

Specific Objectives

Specifically, we expect that at the end of your study of this section, you will be able to

1. Explain why planning is so absolutely essential to good teaching.
2. Explain the dangers of ad lib teaching.
3. Describe the essential elements in any plan, deciding what one hopes to accomplish and how to accomplish it.
4. Describe the purposes of general and specific objectives.
5. Describe and illustrate the most common ways of writing both general and specific objectives.
6. List the essential elements of a good objective.
7. Describe the relationship between learning activities (learning experiences) and the objectives.

8. Describe the criteria that one should use in selecting learning activities (experiences) to include in one's plans.
9. Explain how each of the following may be used as a resource for planning:
   (a) curriculum guide,
   (b) syllabus,
   (c) course of study,
   (d) textbook,
   (e) curriculum bulletin, and
   (f) resource unit.
10. Explain the procedures recommended in this module for conducting teacher-pupil planning.

MODULE TEXT

Importance of Planning

Planning is a large part of every teacher's job. He is responsible for planning at three levels: the planning of courses, the planning of units, and the planning of lessons. In this module, we define a course as a complete sequence of instruction which presents to the pupils a major division of subject matter or a discipline. A unit is a major subdivision of a course, comprising planned instruction about some central theme, topic, issue, or problem for a period of several weeks. A lesson is a subdivision of a course to be taught in a single period or, on occasion, two or three successive periods. Courses may be laid out for a year, a semester, a quarter, or, in the case of mini-courses, a few weeks. Units are shorter than courses ordinarily; a mini-course is in effect a free-standing unit and should be treated as a unit as far as planning is concerned. In many school systems, teachers as members of curriculum committees and workshops also participate in the planning of the entire curriculum.

It would be difficult to overestimate the importance of planning for professional teachers. It is absolutely essential for effective teaching. It helps create good discipline, a purposeful class atmosphere, and well-organized lessons. It points the instruction and subject matter in the courses, unit, or lesson toward the learning. It helps to insure that the teacher knows his subject, for, when one plans carefully, he is forced to become master of his material and the methods of teaching it. No one can know all there is to know in the subject matter of any course, but careful planning keeps one from fumbling through half digested, not clearly understood content, and from making mistakes. It is likely to make classes more lively, more interesting, more accurate, more relevant, and to the point. Teachers who do not plan carefully are asking for trouble. Roy Meadows says that *ad lib* teaching, which he says is teaching with little or no written preparation, is "the chief weakness of the high school" because in ad lib teaching "the teacher has not zeroed in on the topics to be presented, the examples to be used for illustration, or the work to be assigned" and, as a result, tends to teach the same old stuff in the same old way day after day and year after year.[1] To be brutally frank, teaching without adequate

---

[1] Roy Meadows, "Adverse Effects of Ad Lib Teaching," *School and Community,* **51**:26–27 (May 1965).

written planning is usually sloppy. It tends to be ineffective because the teacher has not thought out exactly what he wants to accomplish and how he proposes to accomplish it.

Two Essential Elements

These two elements—deciding what one wishes to accomplish and how one wishes to go about accomplishing it—are the essential elements in any planning. They require that you, as teacher, and perhaps your pupils as well, ask yourself such questions as

1. What do I want to accomplish?
2. How can I accomplish it?
3. Who is to do what?
4. When and in what order should things be done?
5. What resources are available?
6. What materials and equipment are needed?
7. How will I get things started?
8. How shall I follow up?
9. How can I tell whether I have accomplished my goals?

Review these questions. Why are they important? What other questions do you think you should ask yourself when getting ready to lay out a course, unit, or lesson plan? There is at least one important question missing from the list. That question is "why?" Why should pupils learn the content? Why do you want them to achieve these objectives? It is important that you ask yourself "why?" often. When a pupil asks you, "Why do I have to learn this stuff?" you should have at the tip of your tongue a legitimate reason that you have thought out long before. All too frequently, teachers do not have the slightest idea why students should study the content of their courses. That is why so much teaching is irrelevant to the lives and needs of the pupils and to the needs of the community.

Select a topic in your field of major interest and determine just what you would want the pupils to know or be able to do as a result of studying it. Then ask yourself why any pupil should know or be able to do what you have set forth. Be honest. Are your reasons really convincing? Take your field as a whole. Really, why should the pupils study it?

Objectives of Planning

Just as it is difficult to overestimate the importance of planning, it is also difficult to overestimate the importance of good objectives. In one sense, it is impossible to do any real planning until you have decided what to do. In teaching, deciding on the objectives means deciding what you hope the pupils will learn: what facts? what concepts? what skills? what attitudes? what appreciations? what ideals? The objectives are the foundation on which one builds his plan of action. They provide the basis for your decision regarding the choice of content, material, and methods and techniques which comprise your strategy for teaching the course, unit, or lesson.

A commonplace example will illustrate our meaning. Let us suppose that you are in New York City and want to go to San Francisco. Having this objective in mind, you could then decide on a plan of action. You might decide to leave on Monday, or Wednesday, or Friday, or maybe next month. You might decide to drive, or go by train, bus, or airplane. You might decide to go by the shortest route possible or take the long scenic route, or even to go by way of the Panama Canal. All of these alternatives would bring you to your objective, San Francisco, but if you did not have that objective, none of the alternatives would be of any value to you.

As another example closer to the teaching profession, let us suppose your objective in a history course is to teach pupils basic concepts underlying democratic freedom. In this situation, you must decide which course of action would best serve your purpose: pupil understanding of the basic concepts of democratic freedom. You might conclude that for this purpose your content should include the Magna Charta, the Bill of Rights, and similar documents. Or you might decide that to concentrate on modern examples of freedom and fairness, and of rights and responsibilities would be more effective. You might decide that it would be best to lecture, to show films, to use role playing, to use free discussion, or perhaps to combine several methods. You might decide that the pupils ought to study original documents, scholarly discussions, popular reading, textbooks, or learning activity packets. When it comes to deciding what to do to achieve a teaching objective, an effective teacher's options are almost limitless, but they all must be based on achieving that objective.

When one selects objectives and strategies for teaching, there are several things one needs to consider in order to make reasonable decisions. One, of course, is the curriculum. Another is the nature of the learners: are they bright or slow, mature or immature, advantaged or disadvantaged? What are their interests, goals, and general tendencies to behavior? A third consideration is what you have to work with: materials, equipment, software, texts, and reading materials. Another consideration is the nature of the community and community expectations. And a final consideration is the nature of the subject matter or discipline to be taught.

Assume that you are teaching a ninth-grade course in your major field. What would you need to know about the curriculum, students, resources, and the like in order to plan the course? Try to be as specific as you can. Talk over your solution with your friends to find out their reactions to your thinking. (Remember that plans go askew if they do not fit the situation.)

One hears a lot about making teaching relevant. What does one have to know if he wants to make his teaching relevant? Relevant to what? Argue this one out with your friends.

Generally, educators speak of two broad classes of objectives: general objectives and specific objectives. These are discussed in detail in Module 1.2. You should remember that the general objectives are broad concepts, skills, attitudes, appreciations, and ideals; such as understanding the scientific method. Specific objectives are narrow objectives, the achievement of which will bring about the general objectives. For example, at the conclusion of the unit, you (the pupil) will be able to demonstrate three techniques for checking the validity of a hypothesis. Course plans are usually built around broad objectives, lesson plans around specific objectives, and unit plans around a combination of the two. The specific objectives set for the lessons and units should be so designed that their combined impact will bring about the general unit and course objectives. When a general objective is listed in a lesson plan, it is understood that it is an over-all unit or course goal to which a number of lessons contribute.

Try to identify a broad, general objective that you might make one of your major objectives when teaching a course in your field of major interest. Now, try to select ten specific goals, the achievement of which would contribute to attaining the general objective.

Teachers can state objectives in a number of ways. One way is to prepare a statement or descriptive phrase in which you describe the skill, concept, appreciation, attitude, or ideal to be learned. For example:

Concept (or Generalization)—Weather affects nearly all of man's enterprises.
Skill (or Ability)—The ability to recognize the difference in spelling of the masculine and feminine of French nouns and adjectives. Or, the ability to find synonyms in Roget's Thesaurus quickly and easily.
Attitude—An attitude of respect toward people of other races. Or, the United States is a nation of immigrants. Or, because of its great agricultural potential in a densely populated region, Southeast Asia is an area of strategic importance.

Another way to state an objective is to describe the behavior that you hope will result from the learning. For example:

As a result of the study of this course, the pupil will refrain from making final conclusions until he has carefully examined the data; or, the student will treat members of other races with respect and consideration; or, the student will listen to classical recordings on his own volition. This type of objective will be examined in some detail in Module 1.2.

A common way to write objectives is to use an infinitive phrase such as the following: To discover the common cause of accidents in the home; to appreciate the contribution of immigrants to American life; to encourage good citizenship; or, to develop skill in the use of the micrometer. Usually objectives written in this form are very general. For this reason their use is discouraged by many authorities on the subject. There is no reason why they should not be used for general objectives, however; careful writers can couch very specific objectives in such infinitive phrases.

Plan for Action

As we have already noted, the bulk of any plan consists of the content and procedures that one decides to use to bring about the objectives. The essential element is that the content and teaching procedures be so designed that they really contribute to the achievement of the goal. For instance, if your goal is to teach your pupils to be skillful in thinking scientifically, then you must design course content and procedures that actually give pupils training and practice in thinking. Memorizing formulas and learning the textbook by heart will not achieve that goal because they will not give him a chance to learn to think. Similarly, if you wish to teach pupils to learn to express themselves well in writing, you must provide them training and practice in writing. Learning rules of grammar may help, but it will not do the entire job. Sometimes teachers seem to forget this basic fact: if you want pupils to learn something, your content and procedures must be appropriate for what you want them to learn.

Suppose you want to teach pupils to be good citizens. What types of things would you want them to do? Make a list of ten specific things that you think would actually help make them good citizens.

Of course, in selecting your procedures and content there are a number of other important considerations you should keep in mind. Among them are degrees of difficulty, interest levels, suitability for pupils' backgrounds, and feasibility.

Evaluating the Plan

Effective teachers find it helpful to evaluate their plans so as to find out in what ways they succeeded and in what ways they failed. By saving the good plans and the good parts of mediocre plans and by revising (or discarding) the poor plans or poor parts of mediocre plans, they build up a collection of sound plans and a repertory of effective teaching procedures.

Resources for Planning

The planning of courses, units, and lessons is hard, time-consuming work, even if not really difficult. Fortunately, you will not have to do it entirely from scratch, alone and unassisted. You can make your beginning years in the classroom easier by getting together a file of material and ideas for teaching while you are still in college. In addition to the training and practice during your teacher preparation program, when you get on the job, department heads, supervisors, and other teachers are usually ready to give you a helping hand and to give you the benefit of their experience. Many school systems have worked out curriculum guides, courses of study, and syllabuses for the courses offered in their schools. These documents usually suggest topics to be included in courses, general objectives for courses, general and specific objectives for units, materials and methods that might be used, and a helpful bibliography. Use them. In some school systems, teachers are expected to follow them closely. In others, probably most, the guides, courses of study, and syllabuses are suggestions that you may or may not use as you please. You should study them and use what seem to be good for your purposes. Some school systems have adopted standardized curriculums which include prepackaged texts, material for study, exercises, assignments, and audio-visual materials and the like. When these are provided, much of your planning has been taken care of. These materials, however, will not teach. Many teachers have found it necessary to change and adapt them. When this is so, supervisors, department heads, and other teachers will undoubtedly advise you. Some school systems have published resource units for particular units of study. These are usually rich in suggestions for teaching the unit. You will find in them, as in courses of study, suggestions for objectives, content, methods, readings, audio-visual, and other materials.

Some systems provide no guide, syllabus, or course of study. In that case, the neophyte has several options he can follow. One is to use curriculum guides, syllabuses, courses of study, and resource units of other school systems. If you do not use them slavishly, they can be just as helpful to you as to the teachers in the school system for which they were designed. These can usually be found in the central office or curriculum centers of city, regional, or county school systems, or school administrative districts, and at the curriculum libraries of teacher preparation institutions. Other sources usually available in curriculum libraries are the curriculum bulletins and curriculum materials on various topics, published by state departments of education, large city school systems, professional organizations, the federal government, and commercial publishing houses. Some of the resource units published by organizations and governmental agencies are especially helpful. The more of these resources you have available to you, the better off you will be. Therefore, if you can, become familiar with the curriculum and teaching resources at your college or in the district where you live now. And begin to collect materials for the day when you will need them in your own classroom.

Study several curriculum guides, resource units, state curriculum bulletins, and other materials described in this module. What do they include? How might they be useful to you in planning lessons, units, and courses?

Teacher-Pupil Planning

Pupils should enter into the planning of units, lessons, and courses. But no matter how much pupils enter into planning, the responsibility for the plan is the teacher's.

There are two approaches to teacher-pupil planning. In one, the basic planning is done by the teacher in such a way that the pupil has many options. The pupil, then, plans his own work by selecting those options he will undertake. In the other approach, the class participates in the formulating of the original plan. They may go so far as to select the goals, the content, the procedures, the sequences, and the materials to be studied, although usually they do not have that large a role. There are also various combinations of these two approaches.

The simplest form of the pupil option approach is the standard practice of encouraging pupils to select and carry out, in their own way, projects, reports, outside reading, and similar independent activities. Another form is the type of unit plan in which pupils must select what they will do from a study guide that lists required and optional activities. That approach is illustrated by the following description of a class, planned and conducted almost entirely by pupils in a Massachusetts high school.

In a social studies classroom a group of junior high school pupils were conducting a lesson. This lesson consisted of a series of committee reports on research projects just completed and a class discussion of the implications and significance of each of the reports under the quite capable direction of the young lady in charge.

This young lady was a ninth-grader. The lesson, the culmination of several weeks' work, had been organized and conducted by the pupils under her chairmanship. Three or four weeks before, the pupils had selected their topic from a short list of alternatives suggested by the teacher as one naturally following from their previous unit. In a group discussion they had decided the various facets of the topic they thought ought to be the most important to investigate. Committees were formed to look into the various aspects of the topic to be investigated and to report to the group what they had learned. But before letting the committees start their work, the class as a whole had set up a set of standards to guide them in their research and to use in evaluating their success. Now they had come to the last step.

Almost every activity in this unit had been planned by the pupils under the surveillance of the teacher. At no time had the teacher dictated to them what they must or must not do. Neither had she ever left them without support or guidance. She was always there to remind them of the essentials, to suggest alternatives, to point out untapped resources, to correct errors, to question unwise decisions. This sort of teaching is teacher-pupil planning at its best. To do it well requires great skill, much forbearance, and the careful training of one's pupils.

It also requires careful preparation by the teacher. Since cooperative planning may take the group off in any one of several directions, the teacher-pupil planning situation often necessitates the teacher's having several possible plans ready to suggest so that he can provide the pupils with guidance no matter which direction they take.[2]

To carry out teacher-pupil planning of this type requires that the teacher be well versed in planning techniques and well supervised. Pupils cannot become expert in their roles in cooperative planning overnight. We recommend that you use the following procedures for introducing teacher-pupil planning.

1. Initiate teacher-pupil planning in small steps.
   a. Ask the pupils' advice about coming assignments: Would they prefer to have the test Tuesday or Wednesday? Or would they prefer to study this unit or that unit next?
   b. Allow them to choose which activities they will do from a list of alternatives.
   c. Give the pupils a study guide or learning packet and allow them to plan how they will carry out the activities suggested and solve the problems proposed.
2. Gradually give the pupils more responsibility.
   a. Work out cooperatively with the pupils what they should learn in a unit and a plan for learning it.
   b. Increase the responsibility until pupils can take a major share in planning a course or unit.
   c. Help pupils to establish reasonable standards by which to guide their own work.
3. Finally, plan courses cooperatively with the pupils.[3]

Procedures for cooperative course planning will be discussed in Module 1.3.

Team Planning

In many schools teacher teams plan together. Planning procedures in these teams, except for the fact that the team members plan together, are about the same

---

[2] Leonard H. Clark and Irving S. Starr, *Secondary School Teaching Methods,* 3rd ed. (New York: Macmillan Publishing Co., Inc., 1976), p. 103.

[3] Leonard H. Clark, *Teaching Social Studies in Secondary Schools* (Macmillan Publishing Co., Inc., 1973), p. 59.

as in any other planning. After the team has completed its planning, each teacher must plan specifically for his role in the team teaching or for his segment of the over-all plan. The advantage of team planning is that it makes it easier for teachers to coordinate their teaching activities.

POST TEST

1. Name two dangers of ad lib teaching.

_____

_____

_____

_____

2. What are the two most important decisions in planning, according to this module?

_____

_____

3. Name four questions you should ask yourself when planning, according to this module.

_____

_____

_____

_____

4. Much teaching is irrelevant. What seems to be the reason for this, according to this module?

_____

_____

5. Name four considerations important in the selecting of objectives when planning.

_____

_____

_____

6. What is the most important criterion for the selection of content for a course, unit, or lesson, according to this module?

_____

7. A broad objective, such as to understand the scientific method, is called a _____ objective.

8. It has been said that each lesson plan should list a general objective that it is expected the pupils will achieve in that lesson. Do you agree or not?

_____

9. Planners sometimes write objectives as infinitive phrases and sometimes as statements describing the learning product (the skill, concept, attitude, appreciation, or ideal to be learned). Which of the two is preferable for specific objectives, according to this module?

_____

_____

_____

_____

10. If you were to test the adequacy of certain subject matter for inclusion in a particular course, unit, or lesson, what should be your chief criterion?

_____

11. What would you expect to find in a course of study?

_____

_____

_____

_____

_____

12. What is the advantage of team planning?

_____

_____

Planning: Behavioral Objectives

Leonard H. Clark

Jersey City State College

module 1.2

What Is a Behavioral Objective? / Covert versus Overt Behavior / General and Specific Objectives / Terminology / Criterion-Referenced and Simple Behavioral Objectives / Domains / Writing Objectives / Putting It All Together / Pupil Goals

RATIONALE

In any endeavor it is important that one know what he is trying to do or where he is trying to go. Aimless behavior seldom pays off in any desirable way. Teaching is no different from other human activities in this respect. Unless it is well aimed, it is ineffectual, because the teachers and pupils do not know what they are trying to do. It is absolutely essential, therefore, that teachers learn to set clear objectives for themselves and their pupils.

In the past, teachers' objectives have often been vague, general, and meaningless. In truth, as often as not, neither teachers nor pupils knew what they were doing or why. This condition has led to a considerable amount of ineffective teaching. It has also led to ineffective measurement and evaluation of teaching and learning. When teachers have only vague ideas about what it is they are trying to teach, it is really difficult to measure how well the teaching has succeeded. This fact has considerable importance in the present age of educational accountability. Teachers, the community believes, should be rated, paid, and rehired only on the basis of how well the pupils learn those things the teacher was supposed to teach—no "ifs," "ands," or "buts"—so we must know what we should be expected to teach.

Behavioral objectives have been invented as a device by which the objectives of teaching and learning can be made more definite and precise. If teachers are to be held accountable for what pupils learn, they need precise statements of what pupils are supposed to have learned so they know what they will be rated against. Furthermore, teachers need precise objectives so that they know what learning to strive for and how to tell whether the pupil has or has not reached the objectives. The pupil also needs to have definite objectives so that he knows what he is supposed to accomplish and so that he can direct his efforts and judge his own progress. The only way one can judge what pupils have learned and how well they have learned is to see how well they perform with behavioral objectives, which describe what and how well pupils are expected to perform as a result of their learning.

Behavioral objectives have since become extremely popular. They are used to give precision to instruction and to evaluation both of instruction and of pupil progress. They are essential elements in schemes for assessing teacher accountability and the adequacy of school curricula. No teacher today can count himself competent unless he understands behavioral objectives and how they work. Consequently, this module will be devoted to an attempt to teach you to understand and use behavioral objectives. It is hoped that at the conclusion of this module you will be able to perform the general and specific behaviors called for in the list of objectives that follows.

Specific Objectives

1. At the conclusion of your study of this module you should understand what behavioral objectives are. You should be able to
   a. Given a list of nonbehavioral and behavioral objectives, distinguish the behavioral objectives from the nonbehavioral objectives with 100 per cent accuracy.

    b. Define accurately the terms *behavioral objective, terminal behavior, criterion-referenced objective, performance objective.*

    c. Distinguish good behavioral objectives from lesser ones in a test provided.

    d. Describe the advantages and disadvantages of using behavioral objectives in teaching.

    e. Explain the significance of the three hierarchies of educational objectives.

    f. Describe the types of behavioral goals sought at each level of the hierarchy of goals in the cognitive, affecting, and psychomotor domains.

2. You should be able to distinguish the various orders of behavioral objectives from each other.

    a. Define accurately each of the following: General objective, aim, goal, specific objective, educational objective, instructional objective, performance objective, simple behavioral objective, criterion-referenced objective, covert objective, overt objective.

    b. Given a list of general and specific objectives, distinguish the specific from general behavioral objectives.

    c. Given a list of behavioral objectives, pick out overt and covert objectives.

3. You should be able to write acceptable behavioral objectives.

    a. Given a list of verbs, identify verbs that describe overt behavior and those that describe covert behavior.

    b. Write general behavioral objectives.

    c. Generate and write precise subordinate specific behavioral objectives supportive of the general objectives.

    d. Write satisfactory criterion-referenced objectives.

    e. Write behavioral objectives in all three of the domains: cognitive, affective, and psychomotor.

    f. Write acceptable behavioral objectives for each of the various levels of the cognitive and affective domains.

    g. Tell how to use the taxonomies as a way of ensuring satisfactory behavioral objectives.

MODULE TEXT

What Is a Behavioral Objective?

A behavioral objective is a statement that describes what the pupil will do, or be able to do, it is hoped, once the instruction has been completed. It is a learning product that the teacher hopes will result from the instruction, whether in a lesson, unit, course, or curriculum. It is the terminal behavior expected from the pupils at the conclusion of a period of learning.

Note that in this definition the behavioral objective describes the behavior of the pupil that results from the instruction. In that sense, the behavior described is terminal behavior for it is the behavior that is expected when the instruction terminates. It is not terminal in the sense that all learning stops at that point. The terminal behavior resulting from one unit of instruction may well be the jumping-off-point for the learning of new or different behavior in the next unit.

Note also that the behavior described is the terminal behavior of the *pupil*. It is not teacher behavior. Behavioral goals do not describe what the teacher is going to do. They describe what the teacher or the school authorities expect the pupil to do or be able to do as a result of being taught. In this sense, behavioral goals are teacher goals. Pupil goals may also be behavioral, but we shall discuss pupil goals later.

Behavioral goals, then, are descriptions of the pupil terminal behavior that it is expected will result from the instruction. If we assume the formula for writing a behavioral objective to consist of these basic words, *At the end of the instruction* (lesson, unit, course, or school curriculum), *the pupils will* (or will be able to) . . . you can easily distinguish behavioral from nonbehavioral objectives. If we examine the following list of objectives, we could easily determine that some describe what pupils will be able to do at the end of the instruction, and some do not. Those that describe terminal behavior of the pupils are behavioral objectives. It does not matter what type of behavior they describe as long as they describe a terminal behavior. One source of confusion is that many writers of behavioral objectives use the present tense rather than the future tense. One would think that objectives would always be written in the future tense, because, after all, an objective is something one hopes to achieve in the future, but educational practices are not always logical.

These objectives were prepared by college juniors for their practicum experience. Which ones describe terminal behavior of pupils and therefore are behavioral objectives?

1. The pupils will understand that the basic issue that resulted in secession was the extension of slavery.
2. Digestion is the chemical change of foods into particles that can be absorbed.
3. To explain what an acid is and what an acid's properties are.
4. Introduction to vector qualities and their use.
5. The pupils will be able to convert temperatures recorded in Celsius scale to Fahrenheit.
6. The pupils will understand that vibrating bodies provide the source of all sounds and sound waves.
7. At the end of the lesson, the pupils will be able to read a bus schedule well enough to determine at what time buses are scheduled to arrive and leave at designated stations, with at least 90 per cent accuracy.
8. Given a number of quadratic equations in one unknown, the pupil solves the equations correctly in 80 per cent of the cases.
9. The pupils will appreciate the problems faced by those who emigrated from Europe to America.
10. A study of the external features and internal organs of the frog through dissection.
11. To discuss the reasons why the field of philosophy was so well developed by the Ancient Greeks.
12. Animals' physical adaption to their environment.

If you understand the principle that a behavioral objective is one that describes pupil terminal behavior, the following becomes obvious:

Objective 1 is a behavioral objective. Understanding is a kind of behavior and, in this case, understanding that slavery was the basic issue that brought about secession is the terminal behavior the teacher expects of the pupils.

Objective 2 is not a behavioral objective. It is a description of a concept. It does not describe terminal behavior.

Objective 3 is not a behavioral objective. It describes teacher behavior rather than pupil terminal behavior. It is more a teaching procedure than an objective.

Objective 4 is not a behavioral objective. It is a topic or title. It is not an objective of any type.

Objective 5 is a behavioral objective. It describes what the pupils will be able to do at the end of the lesson; it describes the pupils' terminal behavior.

Objective 6 is also a behavioral objective. Understanding is a kind of terminal behavior. The objective is very broad, but it is still behavioral.

Objective 7 is a behavioral objective. It describes pupil terminal behavior somewhat more specific than that described in Objective 6.

Objective 8 is also a behavioral objective. It is similar to Objective 7 except that it uses the present tense to describe the pupil terminal behavior.

Objective 9 is a behavioral objective. The terminal behavior described is vague and general, but it is terminal behavior.

Objective 10 is not a behavioral objective. Rather, it is the title of a topic. It describes no behavior of any kind.

Objective 11 is not a behavioral objective. It is not an objective at all, but a description of the teaching procedure to be used.

Objective 12 is not a behavioral objective. It is a title of a topic. It describes no behavior and no objective.

Covert versus Overt Behavior

You noticed that certain of the behavioral objectives called for the pupils to "understand" or "appreciate" at the conclusion of the instruction. Although such objectives describe terminal behavior, they call for a quite different type of behavior than did the behavioral objectives that require pupils to solve problems, to read the bus schedule correctly, or to convert from one scale to another. Understanding and appreciating are types of behavior that cannot be observed directly. When one understands, he does it inside his head. He may understand perfectly without giving any outward sign. Such behavior is covert. Behavioral objectives that call for covert behavior that cannot be observed directly are called covert objectives.

Behavioral objectives that call for pupils to solve problems, to convert from one scale to the other, and to read bus schedules are talking about overt behavior that anyone can see. To judge whether a person can read a bus schedule successfully, all we must do is to give him a bus schedule and see if he can read it. The behavior itself is directly observable. This type of behavior is called overt behavior, and objectives that call for overt terminal behavior are called overt behavioral objectives.

Both overt and covert behavioral objectives are useful in education. Each has its drawbacks, however. One cannot observe covert behavior directly. Therefore, the only way in which one can judge how well a pupil has progressed toward

VERNON REGIONAL
JUNIOR COLLEGE LIBRARY

achieving a covert behavioral objective is to observe overt behavior that indicates whether or not the pupil has reached the covert behavioral objective. For any covert behavioral objective to be useful in a specific teaching and learning situation, one must generate from it overt behavioral objectives that he can use as a basis for determining how well pupils have achieved the covert behavioral objective.

For instance, if the objective is, "Upon completion of this unit, the pupils will understand why North Africa and the Middle East are rapidly changing in today's world," one cannot observe directly how well the pupils have achieved the objective, or how well they understand. However, one can estimate how well they understand by measuring their achievement of such overt objectives as, "The pupils will be able to explain the impact that the discovery and exploitation of the Middle East oil fields has had on the development of the area." Frequently, several overt behavioral objectives are needed in order to get a good sampling of the behavior encompassed by the covert behavioral objectives.

The trouble with covert behavioral objectives, then, is that one cannot observe them directly. The trouble with overt behavioral objectives often is that in an effort to find objectives that are readily observable, teachers dredge up trivial objectives. After all, it is difficult to write overt behavioral objectives that adequately describe major cognitive or affective goals. Consequently, writers of objectives tend to concentrate on the less important details and forget the big picture. This tendency to emphasize the unimportant at the expense of the important has been true of teaching throughout all history. That is why in every period of history we find that teachers have concentrated on isolated, unrelated facts rather than on ideas, appreciations, and attitudes. The search for easily observable and easily measurable objectives has made this tendency even stronger. Some lists of behavioral objectives reveal an emphasis on petty and inconsequential learning. We shall discuss this problem again later.

Overt behavioral objectives describe observable action. Therefore, they use action verbs. We have seen examples in the overt behavioral objectives of such verbs as *solve, convert, read, explain,* and *describe.* Covert objectives use less active verbs such as *understand, appreciate, feel, think,* and *believe.* The test by which one determines whether behavior is overt or covert is to check whether or not the verb describes action that can be observed directly. See if you can pick out the verbs used in overt behavioral objectives from the list that follows. It is possible, of course, that, sometimes because of different contexts, a verb may be used in both overt and covert behavioral objectives.

apply	design	select
appreciate	enjoy	solve
comprehend	explain	state
compute	identify	summarize
create	know	understand
define	outline	
demonstrate	predict	

Of this list, only *appreciate, comprehend, enjoy, know,* and *understand* were covert; all the rest were overt action verbs. Remember the verbs in this list and which verbs are covert and which are overt action verbs. The information may come in handy later on.

Overt objectives are sometimes called performance objectives.

VERNON REGIONAL
JUNIOR COLLEGE LIBRARY

General and Specific Objectives

As you have seen, some behavioral objectives are more general than others. Some objectives describe what it is hoped will be the ultimate goals of the entire educational programs. For example:

As a result of their schooling, American youth will
be good citizens;
think clearly and rationally;
use their leisure time worthily;
live a healthful life;
earn a good living at their vocations;
appreciate beauty in art, music, nature, and the community.

Nothing could be more general than these objectives which are paraphrases of commonly cited major educational objectives. On the other hand, some behavioral objectives are astoundingly specific:

He will be able to recite from memory without error the first stanza of A. E. Housman's "Loveliest of Trees."
Given a topographical map of the area, he will be able to find the altitude of the block house on Signal Mountain to the nearest five feet.

Nothing could be much more specific than these objectives. Most teaching objectives fall somewhere between these extremes, for, in teaching, objectives fall in a continuum from the very general to the very specific. A fairly general objective might be relatively specific compared to a major objective to which it was subordinated. For example:

Major—He is a good citizen.
Subordinate—He understands his duties and responsibilities as a citizen.
Subordinate—He understands the legislative process and how it works.
Subordinate—He takes an active part in community affairs.

In thinking of general and specific objectives, it is good to remember that it is not so much a matter of general and specific goals as it is that some goals are more general or more specific than others (Figure 1.2-1).

As a rule, general objectives are a combination of more specific objectives. By achieving several specific objectives, we achieve a more general objective, which in turn contributes to the accomplishment of a still more general objective. Thus, the specific objectives of several lessons may combine to accomplish a unit objective,

Most General	General	Specific	Most specific

Continuum showing range of objectives from the most general to the most specific

Figure 1.2-1

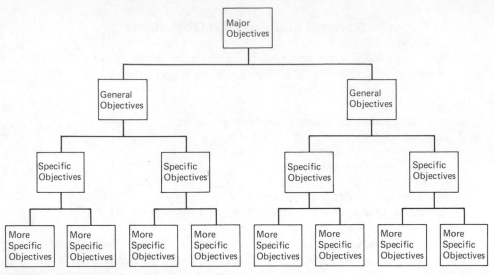

Figure 1.2-2   *General and Specific Objectives.*

and several unit objectives combine to accomplish a course objective. Sometimes the more general objectives are covert behavioral objectives that can be accomplished only by achieving several more specific overt behavioral objectives (Figure 1.2-2). For example, in a unit, one of the general objectives might be the following:

> The pupil understands the difference between common and proper nouns.

Subordinate, specific objectives whose achievement would result in attaining this general objective might be

> 1. The pupil can define both proper and common nouns.
> 2. The pupil can pick out the proper and common nouns in a passage with 90 per cent accuracy.
> 3. The pupil capitalizes proper nouns but not common nouns when he writes.

In practice, it is best to set one's general objectives first and then generate a sampling of subordinate specific objectives that together would accomplish the major objectives. It may then be necessary to build a sampling of still more specific objectives to accomplish the specific objectives which then become lower-level general objectives.

For example, you might select the following as a unit objective:

> The pupils will understand the difference between the two temperature scales: Fahrenheit and Celsius (centigrade).

You might decide that a good way to get the pupils to understand the difference between the two scales would be to teach them to convert from one scale to another and to interpret the meaning of readings on the two scales. You then set up the following subordinate goals:

1. The pupils will be able to convert from Fahrenheit to Celsius.
2. The pupils will be able to convert from Celsius to Fahrenheit.
3. The pupils will be able to give the formulas for converting from Celsius to Fahrenheit and from Fahrenheit to Celsius.
4. The pupils will be able to interpret verbally the temperature as indicated on either a Celsius or Fahrenheit scale.

If you have chosen these subordinate goals well, presumably the pupils will have achieved the understanding you seek once they have reached the subordinate objectives.

To be sure that you understand, try to set up a sequence of objectives from most general to most specific in which every specific objective supports a more general objective.

On the continuum from most general to most specific, where would you put each of the following objectives?

1. The pupil will appreciate the problems faced by those who emigrate to the United States.
2. The pupil will demonstrate the scientific attitude.
3. The pupil will understand that various species of birds have different types of beaks and that these differences in type of beak are related to what the birds feed on.
   a. The pupils will be able to identify from pictures the beaks of (1) woodpeckers, (2) birds of prey, (3) ducks, (4) seed eaters (finches, grosbeaks), (5) insect eaters, (6) pelicans, (7) herons, (8) crossbills, (9) sandpipers.
   b. The pupils will be able to explain the functions of each type of beak listed.

Obviously, in this list, Objective 2 is very general; Objective 1 is quite general; Objective 3 is fairly specific, and its subordinate objectives are more specific.

Terminology

We have taken some time to point out that objectives may be extremely general or extremely specific, or somewhere in between. We have done so because it is so easy to get confused by the terminology. The most general objectives of education are sometimes called the *aims of education, goals,* or *educational goals.* The more specific goals of particular units and lessons are often referred to as *instructional objectives.* Objectives so extremely specific that they seem petty and trivial have been termed *drill objectives* by some educators. Such limited objectives should not be used except in rare cases. It is important to remember this terminology when reading educational literature, if you are to understand it. One should be cautious when interpreting any pedagogical literature, however, because the various writers in the field do not use the terms consistently. Figure 1.2-3 is an attempt to portray the relationships among the terms.

Most General	General	Specific	Most Specific
	Instructional Objectives		
Aims			Drill
Goals			Objectives
Educational	General Objectives		
Objectives		Specific	
		Objectives	
Education,	Course	Unit	Lessons
School District			

Figure 1.2-3 *Relationships of Objectives.*

Criterion-Referenced and Simple Behavioral Objectives

"At the end of the lesson, the pupil will be able to read a bus schedule" is a behavioral objective. It describes pupil terminal behavior, but it does not tell us how well the pupil can perform. To indicate just what terminal behavior would be satisfactory and to aid in measurement, educators have invented the criterion-referenced behavioral objective. When writing a criterion-referenced objective, the teacher states not only the terminal behavior expected, but also what standards of performance the pupil should attain, as in the following example:

"At the end of the lesson, the pupil will be able to read a bus schedule well enough to determine at what time buses are scheduled to arrive and leave designated points, with at least 90 per cent accuracy."

The criterion-referenced objectives may also give the conditions under which the pupil is expected to meet the standard required, as in the following:

"Given an interurban bus schedule at the end of the lesson, the pupil will be able to read the schedule well enough to determine at what times buses are scheduled to arrive and leave designated points, with at least 90 per cent accuracy."

Notice that the conditions and, consequently, the severity of the standards of this criterion-referenced objective differ from the conditions set forth in the following example:

"Given excerpts from a bus schedule, the pupil will be able to read the schedule well enough to determine at what time buses are scheduled to arrive and leave the points contained in the excerpts, with at least 90 per cent accuracy."

Presumably, reading excerpts from the bus schedule would not be as difficult as reading the bus schedule itself.

Obviously, criterion-referenced behavioral objectives call for much more specific terminal behavior than do simple behavioral objectives. They are more useful for test building, evaluation, diagnosis, and feedback than are other types of objectives because they provide the test builder and evaluator a definite standard by which to judge pupil performance. This type of objective has become quite popular with educational experts, particularly those whose interests center on tests and evaluation, programming, and systematizing instruction. This is the type of objective referred to as an *instructional objective.*

Criterion-referenced objectives (or instructional objectives) set forth at least three essentials: some observable and therefore measurable behavior that the pupil will be able to perform at the completion of instruction; the standard at which the pupil is expected to perform; and the conditions under which he is expected to do them in order to meet the standard. Some critics think that these three essentials tend to make the objectives too trivial so that instruction is likely to emphasize bits and pieces of information at the expense of large understandings and appreciations. No doubt this is true, but the wary teacher can avoid such pitfalls. With care, teachers can make the performance standards and conditions broad and strong. Furthermore, understandings, appreciations, and attitudes are made up of clusters of smaller behaviors. By selecting a good sampling of subordinate instructional (criterion-referenced) objectives for each understanding, attitude, and appreciation that we wish to teach and by achieving them, we can attain the larger goals and tell when we have done so. For these reasons, the specific objectives that we use in our teaching probably should be criterion-referenced behavioral objectives.

Of the following, which examples are criterion-referenced behavioral objectives?

1. The pupil will be able to solve equations in one unknown.

2. Given examples of the type $\dfrac{X^5}{X^3}$, the pupil will solve the examples correctly by subtracting exponents in at least nine out of ten cases.

3. The pupil will be able to describe the difference between the policies followed by Lincoln and Johnson and those followed by the Radical Republicans in Congress.

4. Given a paper triangle, the pupil will be able to determine the center of gravity of the triangle by the paper-folding technique.

5. The pupils will be able to spell correctly each of the common contractions: *doesn't, wouldn't, he's, you're, isn't, aren't, I'd, what's, hadn't, there's, they're, hasn't, you'll, don't.*

6 Given a new and strange situation, the pupil usually attempts to examine all the available relevant data before making a conclusion.

7. He can accurately define both common and proper nouns.

8. Given an unassembled machine gun, he can quickly and unhesitatingly assemble it.

9. He can run a hundred yards in twelve seconds.

10. Given a dozen examples of rocks, he can identify each of them without making more than three errors.

Of the ten sample objectives you should have concluded (a) that items 2, 9, and 10 are unequivocally criterion-referenced; (b) that items 6, 7, and 8 are also criterion-referenced although the criteria, *usually, accurately, quickly,* and *unhesitatingly,* are subjective and liable to interpretation; (c) that items 4 and 5 are not criterion-referenced unless the writer means that the goal is 100 per cent errorless performance; and (d) that items 1 and 3 are not criterion-referenced.

Domains

Generally, educational objectives fall into three major categories or domains: the cognitive domain, the affective domain, and the psychomotor domain. Bloom and his associates have attempted to formulate taxonomies of educational objectives for both the cognitive and affective domains. The cognitive goals were arranged into classifications from the highest to the lowest mental processes, according to the complexity of skills and abilities and to the objectives required. The affective domain was arranged into categories from highest to lowest according to the degree of internalization each of the objectives required. They did not create a hierarchy of categories for the psychomotor domain. Since then, others have done so, notably Elizabeth Jane Simpson,[1] who based her taxonomy on the principle of complexity and difficulty, and Anita J. Harrow whose categories are included in this module.

Theoretically, the taxonomies are arranged so that it would be necessary for learners to achieve each lower level before one could get to the higher levels. How-

Table 1.2-1 Cognitive Domain*

KNOWLEDGE

1.00 Knowledge
1.10 Knowledge of Specifics
1.11 Knowledge of Terminology
1.12 Knowledge of Specific Facts

1.20 Knowledge of Ways and Means of Dealing with Specifics
1.21 Knowledge of Conventions
1.22 Knowledge of Trends and Sequences
1.23 Knowledge of Classifications and Categories
1.24 Knowledge of Criteria
1.25 Knowledge of Methodology

1.30 Knowledge of the Universals and Abstractions in a Field
1.31 Knowledge of Principles and Generalizations
1.32 Knowledge of Theories and Structures

INTELLECTUAL ABILITIES AND SKILLS

2.00 Comprehension
2.10 Translation
2.20 Interpretation
2.30 Extrapolation

3.00 Application

4.00 Analysis
4.10 Analysis of Elements
4.20 Analysis of Relationships
4.30 Analysis of Organizational Principles

5.00 Synthesis
5.10 Production of a Unique Communication
5.20 Production of a Plan, of Proposed Set of Operations
5.30 Derivation of a Set of Abstract Relations

6.00 Evaluation
6.10 Judgments in Terms of Internal Evidence
6.20 Judgments in Terms of External Criteria

* Reprinted by permission from Benjamin S. Bloom, ed. *Taxonomy of Educational Objectives, Handbook I: Cognitive Domain* (New York: David McKay Co., Inc., 1956).

[1] Elizabeth Jane Simpson, "The Classification of Educational Objectives in the Psychomotor Domain," *The Psychomotor Domain,* Vol. 3 (Highland Park, N.J.: Gryphon House, 1972).

ever, this theory probably does not hold in practice, particularly in the affective domain in which categories overlap greatly (see Table 1.2-2). Attempts to arrange instruction so that pupils move in order up through the categories are likely to be self-defeating. However, the taxonomies are important in that they point out the various levels to which instruction should aspire. If education is to be worthwhile, teachers must aim at and achieve objectives in the higher levels of the taxonomies as well as in the lower ones. If the teacher aims at these higher objectives, his teaching will not be trivial. Most writers of objectives do not include enough objectives in the higher categories of the domains.

The categories are shown in Tables 1.2-1, 1.2-2, and 1.2-3.

To what category does each of the following objectives belong? If you do not agree with the key, turn back to the taxonomy and study it again. Then if you still disagree, discuss the matter with your instructor. These classifications are sometimes ambiguous. It may be that your answer is as right as that in the key.

The examples are all in the cognitive domain:

1. The pupil will be able to detect faulty logic in advertising propaganda.
2. The pupil will be able to differentiate fact and opinion in news stories.
3. Given the facts of a political situation, the student will be able to draw reasonable hypotheses concerning the causes of the situation.
4. The student can devise a workable plan for investigating a social phenomenon.
5. The pupil will be able to write clear directions.
6. At the end of the lesson, the pupils will perceive the moods of melancholy and retreat in Byron's *The Ocean*.
7. You will be able to define corporation in your own words.
8. Given the requisite tools and materials, electric drill and bit, knife, screwdriver, ruler, soldering gun, wire strippers, solder, and flax, the pupil will be able to construct a portable testing device for repair of motors and cooled in units.
9. Given a list of five solids, five liquids, and five gases, pupils will be able to describe the physical and chemical properties of each.
10. You will be able to devise a method to prove a ray to be the bisector of an angle.

According to our classification, the general category to which each of these belong is as follows:

1.	6	(6.2)
2.	4	(4.1)
3.	5	(5.3)
4.	5	(5.2)
5.	5	(5.1)
6.	2	(2.2)
7.	2	(2.1)
8.	3	(3.00)
9.	1	(1.23)
10.	5	(5.2)

Do you agree?

Table 1.2-2 Affective Domain*

1.0 Receiving (Attending)
1.1 Awareness
1.2 Willingness to Receive
1.3 Controlled or Selected Attention
2.0 Responding
2.1 Acquiescence in Responding
2.2 Willingness to Respond
2.3 Satisfaction in Response
3.0 Valuing
3.1 Acceptance of a Value
3.2 Preference for a Value
3.3 Commitment
4.0 Organization
4.1 Conceptualization of a Value
4.2 Organization of a Value System
5.0 Characterization by a Value or Value Complex
5.1 Generalized Set
5.2 Characterization

* Reprinted by permission from David R. Kratwohl, Benjamin S. Bloom, and Bertram B. Masia, *Taxonomy of Educational Goals, Handbook II: Affective Domain* (New York: David McKay Co., Inc., 1964).

Table 1.2-3 Psychomotor Domain*

1.00 Reflex Movements
    1.10 Segmental Reflexes
    1.20 Intersegmental Reflexes
    1.30 Suprasegmental Reflexes
2.00 Basic-Fundamental Movements
    2.10 Locomotor Movements
    2.20 Non-Locomotor Movements
    2.30 Manipulative Movements
3.00 Perceptual Abilities
    3.10 Kinesthetic Discrimination
    3.20 Visual Discrimination
    3.30 Auditory Discrimination
    3.40 Tactile Discrimination
    3.50 Coordinated Abilities
4.00 Physical Abilities
    4.10 Endurance
    4.20 Strength
    4.30 Flexibility
    4.40 Agility
5.00 Skilled Movements
    5.10 Simple Adaptive Skill
    5.20 Compound Adaptive Skill
    5.30 Complex Adaptive Skill
6.00 Non-Discursive Communication
    6.10 Expressive Movement
    6.20 Interpretive Movement

* Reprinted by permission from Anita J. Harrow, *A Taxonomy of the Psychomotor Domain* (New York: David McKay Co., Inc., 1972), pp. 1–2.

Try to write an objective for each of the major categories listed in the following:

Cognitive Domain
1. Knowledge or memory
2. Comprehension
3. Application
4. Analysis
5. Synthesis
6. Evaluation

Affective Domain
1. Receiving
2. Responding
3. Valuing
4. Organization
5. Characterization

Try to write objectives for the following:

Psychomotor Domain
1. Reflex movements
2. Basic fundamentals
3. Perceptual abilities
4. Physical abilities
5. Skilled movements
6. Nondiscursive communication

Perhaps the list in Table 1.2-4 will help you with this assignment.

Writing Objectives

Criterion-referenced Objectives. To write good criterion-referenced behavioral objectives is difficult, so difficult, in fact, that some critics feel that writing them is not worth the effort. However, they do make for precise objectives, especially as a basis for evaluation and feedback. Perhaps we should always use them for specific objectives of units and lessons. We can use other types of objectives for larger units perhaps, although criterion-referenced objectives may serve there too. If we keep the taxonomy of educational objectives before us and bear in mind the need for some objectives from the higher categories of all of the three domains, we can avoid criterion-referenced objectives that make the teaching content petty and trivial.

As we have seen, a complete criterion-referenced behavioral objective consists of a statement that tells us

1. Who will perform the behavior.
2. The overt behavior that will be performed. (Some authorities divide this into two categories, the act or behavior and the product. Thus the will to write would be the behavior and the book the product. We think combining the two is preferable.)
3. The standard of performance expected.
4. The conditions under which the behavior will be performed.

Therefore, in writing out the criterion-referenced objectives, first you must designate the person who is going to do the performing called for by the objectives. That is the pupil, student, learner, or candidate (see examples, p. 27). If the objective is addressed to the learner, use "you." Even when the words are not written down, one should assume that every objective begins, "At the conclusion of the instruction, the pupil (or you). . . ." If you wish, there is no reason that you cannot use the plural, pupils, learners, students, if the instruction is not going to be individualized.

Table 1.2-4 Instrumentation of the Taxonomy of Educational Objectives: Cognitive Domain*

	KEY WORDS	
TAXONOMY CLASSIFICATION	EXAMPLES OF INFINITIVES	EXAMPLES OF DIRECT OBJECTS
1.00 Knowledge		
1.10 Knowledge of Specifics		
1.11 Knowledge of Terminology	to define, to distinguish, to acquire, to identify, to recall, to recognize	vocabulary, terms, terminology, meaning(s), definitions, referents, elements
1.12 Knowledge of Specific Facts	to recall, to recognize, to acquire, to identify	facts, factual information, (sources), (names), (dates), (events), (persons), (places), (time periods), properties, examples, phenomena
1.20 Knowledge of Ways and Means of Dealing with Specifics		
1.21 Knowledge of Conventions	to recall, to identify, to recognize, to acquire	form(s), conventions, uses, usage, rules, ways, devices, symbols, representations, style(s), format(s)
1.22 Knowledge of Trends, Sequences	to recall, to recognize, to acquire, to identify	action(s), processes, movement(s), continuity, development(s), trend(s), sequence(s), causes, relationship(s), forces, influences
1.23 Knowledge of Classifications and Categories	to recall, to recognize, to acquire, to identify	area(s), type(s), feature(s), class(es), set(s), division(s), arrangement(s), classification(s), category/categories
1.24 Knowledge of Criteria	to recall, to recognize, to acquire, to identify	criteria, basics, elements
1.25 Knowledge of Methodology	to recall, to recognize, to acquire, to identify	methods, techniques, approaches, uses, procedures, treatments
1.30 Knowledge of the Universals and Abstractions in a Field		
1.31 Knowledge of Principles, Generalizations	to recall, to recognize, to acquire, to identify	principle(s), generalization(s), proposition(s), fundamentals, laws, principal elements, implication(s)
1.32 Knowledge of Theories and Structures	to recall, to recognize, to acquire, to identify	theories, bases, interrelations, structure(s), organization(s), formulation(s)
2.00 Comprehension		

Table 1.2-4 (Continued)

Taxonomy Classification	Key Words	
	Examples of Infinitives	Examples of Direct Objects
2.10 Translation	to translate, to transform, to give in own words, to illustrate, to prepare, to read, to represent, to change, to rephrase, to restate	meaning(s), sample(s), definitions, abstractions, representations, words, phrases
2.20 Interpretation	to interpret, to reorder, to rearrange, to differentiate, to distinguish, to make, to draw, to explain, to demonstrate	relevancies, relationships, essentials, aspects, new view(s), qualifications, conclusions, methods, theories, abstractions
2.30 Extrapolation	to estimate, to infer, to conclude, to predict, to differentiate, to determine, to extend, to interpolate, to extrapolate, to fill in, to draw	consequences, implications, conclusions, factors, ramifications, meanings, corollaries, effects, probabilities
3.00 Application	to apply, to generalize, to relate, to choose, to develop, to organize, to use, to employ, to transfer, to restructure, to classify	principles, laws, conclusions, effects, methods, theories, abstractions, situations, generalizations, processes, phenomena, procedures
4.00 Analysis		
4.10 Analysis of Elements	to distinguish, to detect, to identify, to classify, to discriminate, to recognize, to categorize, to deduce	elements, hypothesis/ hypotheses, conclusions, assumptions, statements (of fact), statements (of intent), arguments, particulars
4.20 Analysis of Relationships	to analyze, to contrast, to compare, to distinguish, to deduce	relationships, interrelations, relevance, relevancies, themes, evidence, fallacies, arguments, cause-effect(s), consistency/consistencies, parts, ideas, assumptions
4.30 Analysis of Organizational Principles	to analyze, to distinguish, to detect, to deduce	form(s), pattern(s), purpose(s), point(s) of view(s), techniques, bias(es), structure(s), theme(s), arrangement(s), organization(s)
5.00 Synthesis		
5.10 Production of a Unique Communication	to write, to tell, to relate, to produce, to constitute, to transmit, to originate, to modify, to document	structure(s), pattern(s), product(s), performance(s), design(s), work(s), communications, effort(s), specifics, composition(s)

Table 1.2-4   (Continued)

| | KEY WORDS | |
TAXONOMY CLASSIFICATION	EXAMPLES OF INFINITIVES	EXAMPLES OF DIRECT OBJECTS
5.20 Production of a Plan, or Proposed Set of Operations	to propose, to plan, to produce, to design, to modify, to specify	plan(s), objectives, specification(s), schematic(s), operations, way(s), solution(s), means
5.30 Derivation of a Set of Abstract Relations	to produce, to derive, to develop, to combine, to organize, to synthesize, to classify, to deduce, to develop, to formulate, to modify	phenomena, taxonomies, concept(s), scheme(s), theories, relationships, abstractions, generalizations, hypothesis/hypotheses, perceptions, ways, discoveries
6.00 Evaluation		
6.10 Judgments in Terms of Internal Evidence	to judge, to argue, to validate, to assess, to decide	accuracy/accuracies, consistency/consistencies, fallacies, reliability, flaws, errors, precision, exactness
6.20 Judgment in Terms of External Criteria	to judge, to argue, to consider, to compare, to contrast, to standardize, to appraise	ends, means, efficiency, economy/economies, utility, alternatives, courses of action, standards, theories, generalizations

* Robert J. Kibler, Donald J. Cegala, Larry L. Barker, and David T. Miles, *Objectives for Instruction and Evaluation* (Boston: Allyn & Bacon, Inc., 1974), pp. 189–194. Reprinted by permission.

The next thing to do is to describe what the behavior or performance will be. To do this you will need an action verb and its object, such as the following: will write a poem; will describe the plan; will run the mile; will build a desk. In this type of behavioral objective, the verb must be an action verb that describes overt action which can be observed and measured. Action that is covert is useless to you.

You then describe the conditions under which the behavior will occur. These conditions include the information, tools or equipment, and material and supplies the pupil will have available when he performs; the things that he will not have available; limitations as to time and space; and other restrictions that may be applicable. In writing this portion of the objective, it would be wise to try to visualize what conditions would be present in a "real life" performance and to try to duplicate them as nearly as you can in the objective.

Examples include such introductory phrases as in a 30-minute written multiple choice test; given a ruler and protractor; given excerpts from the interurban bus schedule; completing without notes; in a new and strange situation; or from a set of pictures. These conditions should be clear enough so that conditions are standard for everyone. If they are vague and fuzzy, one pupil may have a considerably more difficult task to perform than another, although the basis for behavior and standards set may be the same.

The standard of performance is the last part of the objective to write, in which

Table 1.2-5 Instrumentation of the Taxonomy of Educational Objectives: Affective Domain*

| | KEY WORDS | |
TAXONOMY CLASSIFICATION	EXAMPLES OF INFINITIVES	EXAMPLES OF DIRECT OBJECTS
1.0 Receiving		
1.1 Awareness	to differentiate, to separate, to set apart, to share	sights, sounds, events, designs, arrangements
1.2 Willingness to Receive	to accumulate, to select, to combine, to accept	models, examples, shapes, sizes, meters, cadences
1.3 Controlled or Selected Attention	to select, to posturally respond to, to listen (for), to control	alternatives, answers, rhythms, nuances
2.0 Responding		
2.1 Acquiescence in Responding	to comply (with), to follow, to commend, to approve	directions, instructions, laws, policies, demonstrations
2.2 Willingness to Respond	to volunteer, to discuss, to practice, to play	instruments, games, dramatic works, charades, burlesques
2.3 Satisfaction in Response	to applaud, to acclaim, to spend leisure time in, to augment	speeches, plays, presentations, writings
3.0 Valuing		
3.1 Acceptance of a Value	to increase measured proficiency in, to increase numbers of, to relinquish, to specify	group membership(s), artistic production(s), musical productions, personal friendships
3.2 Preference for a Value	to assist, to subsidize, to help, to support	artists, projects, viewpoints, arguments
3.3 Commitment	to deny, to protest, to debate, to argue	deceptions, irrelevancies, abdications, irrationalities
4.0 Organization		
4.1 Conceptualization of a Value	to discuss, to theorize (on), to abstract, to compare	parameters, codes, standards, goals
4.2 Organization of A Value System	to balance, to organize, to define, to formulate	systems, approaches, criteria, limits
5.0 Characterization by Value or Value Complex		
5.1 Generalized Set	to revise, to change, to complete, to require	plans, behavior, methods, effort(s)
5.2 Characterization	to be rated high by peers in, to be rated high by superiors in, to be rated high by subordinates in	humanitarianism, ethics, integrity, maturity
	and	
	to avoid, to manage, to resolve, to resist	extravagance(s), excesses, conflicts, exorbitancy/ exorbitancies

* Robert J. Kibler, Donald J. Cegala, Larry L. Barker, and David T. Miles, *Objectives for Instruction and Evaluation* (Boston: Allyn & Bacon, Inc., 1974), pp. 193–194. Reprinted by permission.

			Adjustment	Value	Attitudes	Appreciation	Interest
1.0 Receiving	1.1 Awareness						
	1.2 Willingness to receive						
	1.3 Controlled or Selected Attention						
2.0 Responding	2.1 Acquiescence in Responding						
	2.2 Willingness to Respond						
	2.3 Satisfaction in Response						
3.0 Valuing	3.1 Acceptance of a Value						
	3.2 Preference for a Value						
	3.3 Commitment						
4.0 Organization	4.1 Conceptualization of a Value						
	4.2 Organization of a Value System						
5.0 Characterize by a Value Complex	5.1 Generalized Set						
	5.2 Characterization						

Figure 1.2-4

you state what will be the level of behavior you will accept as satisfactory. Your criterion may be the minimum number acceptable ("at least five reasons," "all ten reasons"); the per cent or proportion acceptable (with 90 per cent accuracy, in eight out of ten cases); acceptable limits of tolerance (within ±5 per cent); acceptable limits of time (within a period of fifteen minutes); or some other standard. Usually, this standard is set rather arbitrarily on the basis of one's experience and expectations.

In the following objectives, identify the parts of the objectives:
Objective 1—You will write a 500-word account of the battle between the forces of Gondor and its allies against those of Mordor and its allies, as related in *The Lord of the Rings,* completely from memory. This account will be accurate in all basic details and include all the important incidents of the battle.
Objective 2—Given an interurban bus schedule, at the end of the lesson the pupil will be able to read the schedule well enough to determine at what time buses are scheduled to leave randomly selected points, with at least 90 per cent accuracy.

The parts of Objective 1 are (a) you; (b) will write a 500-word account of the battle between the forces of Gondor and its allies against those of Mordor and its allies, as related in *The Lord of the Rings;* (c) completely from memory; (d) this account will be accurate in all basic details and include all the important incidents of the battle.

The parts of Objective 2 are (a) the pupil; (b) will be able to read the schedule; (c) given an interurban bus schedule; (d) well enough to determine.

Now try to make up some criterion-referenced objectives for each of the following hypothetical situations:

1. You are a teacher of typewriting. You think that by the end of the semester each pupil should be able to type at least 40 words per minute with no more than one error per minute.

2. You are teaching map reading, and you hope that at the end of the unit your pupils will be able to locate places on the practice globe by giving latitude and longitude to the nearest degree ± 3 degrees in at least 75 per cent of the examples you set for them as a test.

3. You are teaching English literature. At the end of the unit you hope that at least half of your pupils will like Shakespearean comedy enough so that they will read some on their own.

4. You are teaching mathematics. You expect that at the end of the unit each person will be able to do simple multiplications and division on the slide rule with reasonable accuracy at least nine-tenths of the time.

5. You are teaching French. You expect all your pupils to be able to read and translate simple high-school level-three French prose at the end of the semester.

Simple Behavioral Objectives. Simple behavioral objectives are much easier to formulate than criterion-referenced objectives. You must state what has to be done and who has to do it. The procedure for writing simple behavioral objectives is the same as that for writing criterion referenced behavioral objectives except that steps three and four are omitted and you may use the less active verbs such as *know, understand, apprehend, appreciate,* and *enjoy.* Remember that simple behavioral objectives may be covert objectives; criterion-referenced objectives may not!

Now try to make up some simple behavioral objectives for each of the hypothetical situations described in the preceding exercise.

Putting It All Together

As we have seen, behavioral objectives must be (a) overt or covert, (b) general or specific, (c) simple or criterion-referenced. Also, in some cases these categories tend to overlap (for example, some general objectives are more general than other general objectives), and the categories may be combined in a number of ways (for example, a general objective may be either overt or covert and either simple or criterion referenced.

In what ways can we combine the behavioral objectives? Answer each of the following Yes or No.

1. Can an overt objective also be both simple and criterion-referenced?
2. Can a covert objective be a simple objective?

   3. Can a simple objective be overt?
   4. Can a simple objective be both covert and general?
   5. Can a criterion-referenced objective be covert?
Your answers should have been: (1.) No. (2.) Yes. (3.) Yes. (4.) Yes. (5.) No. If you disagree, read over the sections concerned.

   You will have to use all the possible combinations of characteristics in the behavioral objectives you will need to prepare for your courses, units, and lessons when you teach.

   When you write the objectives for your courses, units, and lessons, you will want to follow a procedure similar to the following:

1. Set up your course objectives. Usually, these will have to be quite general; therefore, you will probably need to make them simple, and in many cases you will find it easier and more rewarding to make them covert. Can you see why general, simple, covert behavioral objectives may be most useful as over-all course objectives? Overt objectives and criterion-referenced objectives may also be useful. In some cases criterion-referenced objectives are a necessity. This is particularly likely to be so in skill subjects and under accountability systems.
2. Once the course objectives have been formulated, you should set up the general objectives for each of your units. When doing so, be sure that these unit objectives, together, make up the course objectives. No necessary ingredient should be left out or short-changed. These objectives may be overt or covert, simple or criterion-referenced, depending upon *your* evaluation of what is most desirable.
3. Now you need to set the specific objectives for the unit. These may be objectives for specific lessons if the unit is organized on a day-by-day lesson basis, or they may be simply unit subdivisions if you are using the laboratory or module approach. In any case, these objectives should all add up to the learning products called for in the general objectives. Remember, the specific examples can only be a sampling of all the subordinate objectives that combine to make up the general objectives. The general objectives can be broken down into many specific objectives, but you can select only a limited number, so you must try to get a good sampling of specific objectives for each and every general objective. Usually you will want to make these specific objectives both overt and criterion-referenced. However, simple objectives may seem preferable at times. Covert objectives are seldom useful for specific objectives.

   When you write your objectives, you should attempt to get a good spread among the various categories of the three domains: cognitive, affective, and psychomotor. It is much too easy to get caught up with trivia. To build specific, criterion-referenced behavioral objectives that call for use of the higher mental processes and affective responses is particularly difficult. Perhaps the list of action verbs compiled by Kibler, Cegala, Barker, and Miles, included in Tables 1.2-4 and 1.2-5, will help you as you try to write specific objectives that call for important learnings.

   Following are some general objectives taken from a high school social studies unit. Each of the objectives selected is elementary enough in nature so that any college student should be informed on it. However, unless you are a sociologist, we expect you to answer only on the basis of common knowledge and common sense rather than sociological principles. For each of these objectives, write two or three specific objectives. Try to make your objectives nontrivial and, if possible, criterion-referenced. Discuss your solutions to this exercise with your instructor and friends. It is not easy.

1. Generalizations.
   The pupil will understand that (a) social problems have many causes; (b) man is a social animal who lives in groups; (c) solutions to social problems involve effecting changes in society and in the individual.
2. Skills.
   The pupil (a) attacks problems in a rational manner; (b) gathers information effectively; (c) organizes and analyzes information and draws conclusions.
3. Attitudes.
   The pupil (a) is skeptical of panaceas; (b) values human dignity; (c) is committed to the free examination of social attitudes and data; (d) has a sense of responsibility for taking informed action about problems confronting the nation.

Recapitulation. When writing behavioral objectives you should remember to:

1. State each general behavioral objective as a statement that describes the behavior sought, in general terms such as understands, comprehends, knows, appreciates.
2. Each behavioral objective, general or specific, should describe pupil performance rather than teacher performance.
3. Each behavioral objective, general or specific, should describe the terminal behavior of the pupil rather than subject matter, learning process, or teaching procedure.
4. Each behavioral objective should be stated at the proper level of generality.
5. Each general behavioral objective should be defined by a sampling of specific behavioral objectives that describe terminal behavior and thus show when the objective has been reached.
6. Provide a sufficient sampling of relevant specific behavioral objectives to demonstrate that each of the more general objectives has been achieved.
7. Behavioral objectives should include the complex, high-level cognitive and affective goals that are so frequently omitted because they are so difficult to write.
8. Each specific behavioral objective should include only one learning product rather than a combination of learning products.

Pupil Goals

Although so far in this module we have talked only of the objectives formulated by teachers, these objectives are likely to be fruitless unless the pupils adopt the same or similar ones. Pupils act not to fulfill the teacher's objectives but their own objectives. Therefore, you must take steps to ensure that pupils adopt objectives that will lead them to your objectives. One way to do this is to inform the pupils early in the course, unit, or lesson of what you hope they will learn. If they consider these learnings to be desirable and decide to accept them as goals for which they will work, you will be well on your way toward success. For that reason, it may be wise for you to select goals that are attractive and also to try to sell them as worthwhile to your pupils. In addition, in many courses, pupils have a good notion of what learning they would enjoy and profit from most. Research indicates that pupil participation in the selection of objectives can be highly motivating. Knowing the goals set for courses and having good feedback concerning one's progress toward these goals are strong motivating devices. When the pupils know clearly what they are supposed to do, and why, and can see that they are making progress, they will usually try. That is why, if teachers set clear behavioral objectives that seem reasonable, pupils will accept them as their own objectives and work toward them.

POST TEST

1. Which of the following are behavioral objectives? Which are not behavioral objectives?
   a. The pupils will realize that Romanticism was and is sentimental.
   b. You will be able to read altitudes by the use of contour lines on a topographical map.
   c. To encourage pupils to be neat and accurate in their work.
   d. To discuss the reasons for the Protestant Reformation.
   e. In this course we will examine the great works of Renaissance art.
   f. An appreciation of modern music.
   g. To cultivate the scientific attitude.
   h. The pupils will be able to type at least thirty words a minute with no more than five errors.

   _____

   _____

2. Define a criterion-referenced behavioral objective.

   _____

   _____

3. Give two arguments for using behavioral objectives.

   _____

   _____

   _____

   _____

4. Define terminal behavior.

_____

_____

5. What is a covert objective?

_____

_____

6. Of the following, which describe overt behavior and which covert behavior?
  a. Appreciate.   **b.** Comprehend.
  c. Define.   **d.** Estimate.
  e. Identify.   **f.** Organize.
  g. Predict.   **h.** Realize.
  i. Recognize.   **j.** Solve.
  k. Understand.   **l.** Write.

_____

_____

7. Which of the following are general objectives? Which are specific objectives?
  a. You will be able to speak French well enough to carry on a simple conversation.
  b. The pupil will develop salable vocational skills.
  c. Given an appropriate sample of verse, the pupil will be able to identify the alliteration in it.
  d. The pupil will appreciate the role economics plays in our national life.
  e. The pupil will be able to define ionization.
  f. The pupil will be able to convert yards to meters.
  g. The pupil will speak correct idiomatic English.

_____

_____

8. Which of the following objectives are covert? Which are overt?
  a. The pupils will realize the contributions of the various ethnic groups.
  b. The pupils will enjoy listening to good music.
  c. You will be able to identify correctly the tools in an ordinary woodworking laboratory.
  d. The pupils will be able to use the card catalog easily and accurately.

_____

_____

9. Rank the following in correct order from lowest to highest.
   a. Analysis.
   b. Application.
   c. Comprehension.
   d. Evaluation.
   e. Knowledge.
   f. Synthesis.

_____

10. What is the value of a taxonomy of educational objectives?

_____

_____

_____

11. A complete criterion-referenced objective consists of four parts. What are they?
   a. _____

   b. _____

   c. _____

   d. _____

12. Are the following complete criterion-referenced objectives?
   a. You will be able to write an accurate summary of the plot of *The Wife of Bath*.
   b. Given a diagram of an internal combustion engine, the student will be able to label at least 80 per cent of the components.
   c. You will be able to list the steps for troubleshooting a Tecumseh motor without error.
   d. Given a right triangle with the length of sides indicated, the student will specify the sine of one of the acute angles as a fraction in four out of five cases.

_____

_____

_____

_____

Planning: Course Planning

Leonard H. Clark

Jersey City State College

module 1.3

Basic Principles / Selecting the Objectives / Planning the Sequence of Topics / Continuous Progress Course Planning / Cooperative Course Planning

RATIONALE

The responsibility for what goes on in your course is yours as teacher. In some schools, as you know, you will be provided with courses of study, syllabuses and curriculum guides that provide suggestions concerning course objectives, content, sequences, procedures, and materials of instruction. In some schools, you will be expected to give pupils a major role in charting the course. In others, you will be left alone to cope as best you can. No matter which policy the school follows, the responsibility for the course and what the pupils learn from it is still yours.

Even when the course plans are rigidly laid out by the school authorities, it is the teacher who determines what is really taught. As teacher, you determine emphases, interpretations, and methods of presentation. It is also you who adapts the course so that it suits the pupils. You put your stamp on the course by such procedures as changing the unit sequence, modifying the time to be spent on topics, using different teaching methods, supplementing the prescribed content, and providing for individualized projects and papers. Even such a simple thing as the way you field questions makes a difference in what you teach in your course.

This section will discuss some of the principles of course planning and a procedure for planning a course.

Specific Objectives

At the conclusion of your study of this submodule, it is expected that you will be able to perform the following:

1. Describe the basic steps in planning a course.
2. Explain what is meant for a course to be psychologically organized.
3. Describe the five principles of course organization set forth in this submodule.
4. Explain what steps one can take in course planning so as to increase the course's value for retention and transfer.
5. Explain a procedure for selecting course objectives.
6. Outline a procedure for a setting up a sequence of topics or units.
7. Describe a procedure for building a plan for a continuous progress course.
8. Describe a procedure for using cooperative planning in planning a course.

MODULE TEXT

Basic Principles

The procedures for planning a course are not difficult. In general, they consist of the following basic steps:

1. Determine the course objective, what it is you hope the pupils will learn.

2. Determine what content to incorporate into the course in view of your objectives. This step includes selecting the topics to be studied, arranging them into an appropriate sequence, and deciding how much emphasis to place on each topic.
3. Decide how much time to spend on each topic.
4. Determine your approach including basic strategies, major assignments, references, texts, and so on, in view of the goals and topics you have selected.

In carrying out these steps one should keep in mind several important principles:

1. The course should be psychologically organized.
   a. Its organization should be based on the nature of the pupils and how they learn.
   b. It should pick up pupils at their own levels of maturity and be relevant to their present needs, interests and concerns.
   c. It should allow for the differences in pupils, recognizing that pupils do not all have the same needs, interests, and concerns. Neither are an individual's needs, interests, and concerns constant. Consequently, the effective teacher not only tries to select topics that have intrinsic interest for the pupils, if he can, but he also tries to provide variation for individuals within the topics by providing ways in which pupils may skip, add, or substitute topics if it should seem desirable.
   d. It should be selective. It does not try to cover all of the subjects, which no course could really do, but it includes the content most valuable and relevant to the student and to the goals, and leaves out content not necessary for those purposes.
   e. It should encourage the development of logical memory as opposed to rote memory, skill in the use of the tools of learning, and the ability to think and solve problems. Its teaching approaches guidance of learning and inquiry rather than instructional exposition.
   f. It uses a combination of both vicarious and direct learning experiences in proportions suitable to the ability levels of the learners. Ordinarily, younger, less able, less experienced, and less sophisticated pupils will profit more from direct experiences, and older, more able, more experienced, and more sophisticated students learn well from vicarious experiences, such as lectures and reading. In any case, the course does not limit itself to book learning.
2. The course should be compatible with the resources available. If you do not have, or cannot get, the things you need to carry out your plans, they will be fruitless.
3. The course content organization and approach should be selected because of their value in securing transfer and retention. Unless the content stays with the learner and can be used by him in new situations, it is not of much value. Retention and transfer are most likely when
   a. The learner sees the value of the learning and how it can be used by him in other situations and the learning situation is similar to the using situation.

   b. The learning is thorough.
   c. The learning is reviewed by frequent use in which the learner applies what he has learned and adds the new learning to previous learning.
   d. The learner draws generalizations that help him see the application of the learning to new situations. To encourage retention and transfer, effective teachers try to plan courses that meet these conditions.
4. The course content, organization, and instructional approaches should contribute to achieving the course objectives. This is such an obvious requirement that it seems hardly worth repeating, but teachers often ignore it. You must plan your course so that it contributes to your objectives. For example, if your objective is to create skill in writing, your course must give plenty of practice in writing. Practice in reading may be excellent for some things but it cannot take the place of writing if the goal is excellence in writing. It is surprising how many courses contain content that has nothing to do with what the teachers claim to be their objectives.
5. The course content, organization, and teaching strategies must reflect the nature of the discipline or subject matter. Not all subject matter can be learned in the same way. The structures of disciplines and portions of discipline differ. In planning courses, it is necessary to respect these differences and reflect the structures of the disciplines we teach in the organization of our courses and the strategies for teaching them.

Selecting the Objectives

   In many school districts, the course objectives are established by the school authorities in a course of study, curriculum guide, or syllabus. When this is true, the teacher should make use of the objectives provided. But even so, you must think out what it is you would like the pupil to learn. It may be that you want them to master certain subject matter, and feel that other subject matter is relatively expendable. Or it may be that you feel that the most important goal should be the development of certain skills or attitudes. The important thing is that you should know what *you want the pupils to learn* and *why you want them to learn it.* All too often what we teach in school has absolutely no value to the learners. (This fact has always been true; the Roman philosopher Seneca complained about it in Nero's time.)

   Your over-all course objectives should be, and of necessity will be, quite general. This is not the time to make up specific objectives, although some general objectives may refer to rather specific criteria. Specific objectives should be used for the planning of units and lessons. What form the course objectives should take is not so very important at this point, either. Whether or not they should be behavioral or criterion-referenced is a matter for your individual decision. Ordinarily, general descriptions of the learning will suffice.

   Following are a few examples of course objectives gleaned from courses of study:

   To develop reading and writing skills (in French) to the point that the student can read and write anything he can express orally.

To develop the ability to recognize, define, and use English derivations from Latin encounter during Level I.

To foster an appreciation of the English language.

Examine the course objectives listed. How much guidance does each give the teacher who is about to plan the sequence of topics, subject matter content, and instructional approaches?

Examine some courses of study. What are the objectives? What objectives would you think most desirable for these courses? Specify what you consider to be the ten most important general concepts that pupils should learn in a course you might teach.

For a course in your major field, decide exactly what the course objectives should be.

Planning the Sequence of Topics

After you have decided on the objectives for the course, it becomes necessary to select the basic content and teaching approaches. Probably the best way is to outline the content and divide the course into broad topics that you expect can be covered in two to four weeks. Then arrange these topics into a logical, psychological sequence and allocate the amount of time to be given to each. At this time you should also decide on the general teaching approach you expect to use for the topics. This is important because your teaching approach may make a considerable difference in the amount of time you will need for teaching the topic. In setting up the time schedule for the course, you should give yourself a leeway of ten days or so to allow for assemblies, examinations, storms, miscalculations, and so forth. You should also decide on any major assignments, such as term papers and projects, so that you can provide time for them in your calendar.

Of course, the basic criterion in deciding the sequence of topics and approaches is whether or not they contribute to the course objectives. You must also consider other criteria such as transfer value, interest level, and relevance. These topics are, in effect, the titles of the unit that will make up the course.

As a neophyte you will find that you need assistance in setting up a sequence of topics. You can usually find all the assistance you need in courses of study, curriculum guides, syllabuses, or teacher's manuals. A teacher's manual for Pennsylvania's Introduction to Social Science course, for example, outlines the following sequence of units, with commentary on how each unit should be taught: A general introduction to social science; sociology: its history, subject matter, and point of view; the language of sociology; a sociological method; a general introduction to anthropology; the culture concept; anthropology and the modern world; a general introduction to psychology; scientific method in psychology; psychoanalysis; a general introduction to political science; field research in political science; the perspective of the political scientist; a general introduction to economics; economics as a science; careers in social studies.

Many schools and districts do not provide outlines or, if they do, do not suggest time allocations in them. If you do not have such an outline provided by your own school or district, do not hesitate to consult the courses of study of other school districts. Another aid is the table of contents of a good textbook. Following a textbook has the advantage of giving you a carefully built structure on which to lean until you become more expert and confident. If you elect to go this route, however, you should remember that all the topics (chapters or units) included in the text are probably not equally important and that to follow a text too closely reduces your chances to make your course creative, flexible, innovative, and relevant to your pupils' needs. It seldom pays to "marry" the text. If you find that you have to plan this way at first, you should try to divorce yourself from it as soon as you can. It is particularly important to remember that it is not necessary to cover everything just because it is in the text. Remember, to cover everything in a subject is impossible.

Map out a sequence of topics for a course in your major field. Be sure that (a) all the topics necessary for fulfilling your course objective are covered; (b) enough time is allocated for each topic (assume a 180-day school year); (c) the sequence of topics makes sense logically and psychologically.

Take your time with the assignment. It may take some juggling before it satisfies you. Then have your friends criticize it. Will it really do what you want it to do?

You should also keep in mind that all course plans are of necessity tentative. Therefore, make your plans in outline. You can and should fill in the details later when you plan your units. However, if you plan to order films or similar aids you ought to have firm dates in order to get them when you need them.

Continuous Progress Course Planning

The only difference between preparing a continuous progress, individualized course and an ordinary course is that one must divide the course into modules and give the pupils self-instructional packets or learning activity packets so they can guide their own learning. The procedure we recommend for teaching such courses is as follows:

1. Divide the course into modules and try to make the modules of equal length.
2. Prepare behavioral objectives with standards of competence performance.
3. Prepare a learning activity packet for each module. Each packet should contain (1) the rationale for studying the module; (2) the objective of the module stated as behavioral objectives; (3) the materials necessary for the pupil to have as he works on the module, or directions for getting the materials and equipment he needs; and (4) the directions he needs for carrying out the activities called for in the module.
4. Prepare a plan for evaluating the pupils' learning for each module. This plan should provide for pretest, progress tests, and final mastery tests. Provisions should be made so that pupils can "test out" of modules or parts of modules in which they are already competent.
5. Set pupils to work on their modules in laboratory fashion.
6. Supervise the pupils as they work on the modules.
7. Determine when the pupils are ready to move on from one module to another. Each pupil who fails to achieve the standards of performance in

the mastery test should be asked to restudy the module and take another mastery test until he can meet the standard. For this reason it is wise to give each pupil a diagnostic pretest before he begins each module. Note that the mastery tests should be criterion-referenced but do not need to be written tests. Often performance tests are more satisfactory. Note also that in many instances there is no need for pupils to follow the same sequence. Pupils should be allowed to select which module they will do and when they will do it, as long as you agree that their selection is a reasonable one and will allow them to meet the criteria set by you in step 2.

Work with individuals as they progress through the module. Pupils should not have to stand around waiting to find out what they should do next; neither should they have to struggle along trying to do work they do not understand. When pupils need help, they need help and should get it! Consequently, plan to give all your class time to supervising and guiding while pupils are working on the modules. In order to save time, it may be helpful to gather pupils, who are having the same or similar problems or who are doing the same activities in a particular module, for small group instruction.

In such a sequence, pupils can work through the modules at their own speed, selecting or omitting modules, under guidance, as seems most desirable. This freedom makes it possible for each person to have, in effect, his own curriculum.

Cooperative Course Planning

Courses can and should be planned cooperatively by teachers and students. However, successful teacher-pupil planning of courses and units is rather difficult. We recommend that you adopt the following procedure:

1. Begin by introducing the pupils to the course and to the notion that it is to be planned cooperatively.
2. Set up limits:
   a. The course will be limited to major problems of the United States, particularly problems having to do with government.
   b. We may consider any topics that really concern the class as long as (1) they are important problems of American democracy, and (2) the resources for studying them are available.
   c. During part of the year, we must study certain aspects of local and state government as required by school regulations.
3. Set up criteria for selection of the topics.
   a. Conduct buzz sessions in which each buzz group makes a short list of criteria to present to the class.
   b. Conduct a whole class session in which all the criteria recommended by the groups are listed on the chalkboard and discussed.
   c. By common consensus, develop a final list of criteria.
4. Select the topics.
   a. For homework, pupils individually make lists of the topics they would like to suggest.
   b. In class discussions, the pupils decide on a list of topics.
   c. Before the class makes its final choice, committees should check the

availability of materials for the various topics proposed and compile a
bibliography.

d. Choices should be made by consensus. Never take a formal vote if you
can help it before a consensus of opinion seems evident; if you do, you
can split the group into armed camps or be forced to accept a topic
palatable to only a bare majority.

5. Use a similar plan to select specific areas to be studied in the various units:

a. Have pupils make lists of what they would like to learn about. You will
have to give them help, because they may not know enough to realize
the possibilities. These can be listed as a series of questions from which
pupils can choose the areas they particularly wish to learn. At this point,
it is very important for you to help the pupil fix clearly in his mind what
he is trying to do. If his understanding of his task is not clear, probably
the understandings he gleans from his study will not be clear either.

b. Use discussion and consensus procedures to make the final selections.

An Example of Cooperative Unit Planning. An approach to teacher-pupil
planning used in a unit conducted by a teacher in Massachusetts calls for less
participation in the over-all planning. In this school, the teacher was working with
a preselected unit prescribed by the course of study. The teacher also had carefully
worked out an overview and objective. In her introduction, she asked the pupils
to develop the kind of things they would like to learn about most in the unit. On
the basis of this discussion, a list of questions was drawn up and the class was
divided into committees to prepare a bibliography of available material for use in
answering the various questions. The committees then proceeded to investigate
the topics and to prepare plans for reporting their findings and conclusions. For a
few meetings, the class met as a club with a pupil presiding to make decisions about
the scheduling and reporting phase of the plan. An ad hoc committee, selected
by the pupils in their club meeting, worked out the details. Each committee planned
its own reporting technique in accordance with the general plan proposed by the
ad hoc committee and approved by the class. After the presentations, the class
discussed the presentations both as to technique and to content.[1]

POST TEST

1. Who is responsible for what is actually taught in a course?

_____

2. According to this module there are four basic steps in planning a course. What
are they?

_____

_____

_____

_____

[1] Leonard H. Clark, *Teaching Social Studies in Secondary Schools:* A Handbook (New
York: Macmillan Publishing Co., Inc., 1973), pp. 60–61.

3. Basically, what does it mean to organize a course psychologically?

_____

_____

_____

_____

_____

4. Unless a course plan facilitates pupils' retention and transfer of what is studied in it, it will be unsuccessful. In general, what can you do in planning the course to aid retention and transfer? You should be able to name at least three possibilities.

_____

_____

_____

5. Is it better to make over-all course modules general or specific, according to this module?

_____

6. In setting up a time schedule for a full year's course, you should make an allowance of ten days or so. Why?

_____

_____

_____

_____

7. In what way is the use of a textbook in planning a course advantageous?

_____

8. What is the most common danger in using a textbook when mapping out and teaching a sequence of units?

_____

_____

9. Outline the procedure recommended for building a continuous progress course.

_____

_____

_____

_____

_____

10. Outline the procedure recommended for cooperative planning of courses.

_____

_____

_____

_____

_____

_____

Planning: Unit Planning

Leonard H. Clark

Jersey City State College

module 1.4

Definition / Preparing a True Unit / Introductory Phase / Laboratory Phase / Sharing Phase / Evaluating Phase / Organization of a Unit Plan / Planning the Unit / Selecting the Topics / Planning the Unit of Work / The Study Guide / Developing a Scheme for Evaluation / Planning a Learning Packet / Planning a Learning Contract

RATIONALE AND OBJECTIVES

The unit is the major subdivision of most courses.

This submodule attempts to explain how to plan several types of units. As a result of studying it, you should understand the basic characteristics of the four types of units presented and how to plan to teach with them. Specifically, when you have completed this module, you should be able to do the following:

1. Describe the distinguishing characteristics of each of the four types of units.
2. Outline the steps one goes through when planning each of the four types of units.
3. Prepare a study guide for (a) a true unit, and (b) a learning packet.
4. Prepare a contract.
5. Explain what considerations one should keep in mind when selecting (a) goals, (b) activities, (c) content, (d) materials, (e) evaluating materials and devices.

Some of these learnings will be a cumulation of what you have learned in Modules 1.1, 1.2, and 1.3, plus your application of that learning to the various types of learning units.

MODULE TEXT

Definition

A unit is the planned study of a topic, theme, or a major concept over a period of weeks. In effect it is a long assignment. During these weeks the activities or lessons all focus on the central topic. From our point of view they can be organized in four basic ways:

1. An ordinary unit that is a series of lessons centered on a topic, theme, major concept, or block of subject matter.
2. A true unit.
3. A learning packet or module.
4. A learning contract.

Preparing the Ordinary Unit. To prepare a unit of the first type is quite simple. The procedure consists of the following steps:
1. Selecting a topic, such as the Civil War, *A Tale of Two Cities,* or Water. Since your course is probably already divided into topics, this is probably easy enough to do.
2. Select general and specific objectives representing what you hope the pupils will learn about the topic.
3. Concoct a sequence of daily lesson plans that will cause pupils to reach

your objectives. You do not have to build the lessons in their entirety now, but you should note what you expect their content and procedure to be.

4. Decide on any major activities, projects, or other assignments, and schedule them.
5. Prepare some sort of scheme or instrument(s) for evaluating the pupils' progress.

Pick a topic. Outline a sequence of daily lessons that would be adequate for that topic.

Preparing a True Unit

A true unit differs from an ordinary unit in that it is much more cohesive and, at the same time, allows for much more individualization. Most of the teaching takes place in an individualized, problem-solving, laboratory fashion rather than in daily lessons. The bulk of the teaching is of the inquiry rather than of the expository type. Not all of the activities and experiences are required of each pupil. Some of them are, but in addition, there are a number of optional activities which pupils can choose to do or not as they please in view of their interests, needs, and goals. The required activities or experiences we shall call *core* or *basic activities*. The optional activities we shall call *optional related* activities. In this type of unit the pupils do a considerable amount of the planning themselves. So that they can have freedom to proceed at their own speed and in their own directions, the pupils are provided with a study guide that allows them to begin and to carry out activities, under supervision, without being tied to the teacher. Perhaps a description of a unit in action will clarify teaching of a true unit.

A Unit in Action

Mr. Jones teaches Problems of Democracy at Quinbost High School. In his course outline he has listed a unit on minority groups. Mr. Jones always tries to make his course interesting and challenging, stimulating and motivating his students. On the day he was to begin the unit, he came to the classroom seemingly in an angry mood, tossed his books on the desk, and glared at the class. He then began a tirade on a particular minority group, telling the class of something that a member of this group had done to him the day before, and concluding by saying that all members of that particular group were alike.

Immediately, his class began to challenge him, disagreeing, telling him he was unfair to generalize about one incident and that he shouldn't talk like that. Seizing upon this reaction, Mr. Jones then asked the class whether or not they had ever expressed such feelings toward any group. As the animated discussion continued, the class members began to see what the teacher was doing. Almost as one body they said that they wanted to discuss minority groups as a class topic.

The stage had been set! The teacher had fired their interest; the students' desire to study the topic was keen. He, then, set the class to discussing what subject matter should be discussed and what outcomes there should be. This led to general teacher-pupil planning. Soon pupils were choosing committees and projects on which to work. Then, with the aid of study guides and their committee and project assignments, individual pupils completed tentative plans for their roles in the unit.

The study guide they used consisted of three parts:

1. The first part noted questions and problems for which everyone was to find answers and also suggested where the pupils might look to find these answers.

2. The second part listed a number of readings and activities that the pupils might find interesting. All were expected to do some of these, but no one had to do any particular one. These activities were optional. In none of these activities or the required problems and questions was the pupil held to any prescribed reading or procedure. All he was asked to do was to carry out the activity, solve the problem, or find the information; he had free choice of ways and means.

3. The third part of the study guide was a bibliography.

Once the teacher and pupils had finished the planning, they began to work. Except for two periods that Mr. Jones used for motion pictures, the next two weeks were devoted to laboratory work. The committees met, the researchers investigated; the pupils carried out their plans.

Then the committees and researchers began to report. Some of the groups presented a panel discussion. Another group presented a play. Another conducted a question-and-answer game. In all of these activities pupils tried to bring out what they had learned. In between these reports, Mr. Jones and the pupils discussed the implications of the findings and other points they thought pertinent and important.

Finally, the unit ended with everyone's setting down his ideas concerning the treatment of minority groups, and with a short objective test, based on the teacher's objectives as shown in the questions of the study guide.[1]

Thus, after a little over three weeks, the unit was finished.

A close examination of this unit will show you that it was actually divided into four phases. First, Mr. Jones introduced the unit to his students and tried to "fire their interest" in it. Second, the pupils worked individually and in small groups in laboratory fashion. Third, the committees and individual researchers reported on what they had accomplished and discussed their findings. Finally, Mr. Jones tried to assess the pupils' growth by means of evaluative devices and evaluative procedures. These four phases we shall call (1) the introductory phase; (2) the laboratory phase; (3) the sharing phase; and (4) the evaluating phase. The phases of the unit may appear in order or they may not. The most effective teachers usually evaluate pupil progress continually as they observe them at work from the beginning of the unit to the end. When a unit is successfully individualized, all the phases of the unit may be going on at once.

As you read Dean Starr's description of Mr. Jones's class and the Problems of Democracy unit, you probably realized the purpose of the various phases and, if you reflected, could see how they might apply to your own teaching.

Introductory Phase

In the introductory phase your purpose is to get the unit off to a good start. If your introductory activities work well, they should arouse the pupils' interest; inform the pupils of what the unit is about; help you learn more about your pupils, their interests, their abilities, and their present knowledge; show how the unit relates to earlier units and courses; and provide an opportunity for the pupils to plan how they will study the unit. The introductory unit should be well done because it

---

[1] Leonard H. Clark and Irving S. Starr, *Secondary School Teaching Methods,* 3rd ed. (New York: Macmillan Publishing Co., Inc., 1976), pp. 114–115.

NAME_____ CLASS_____

UNIT _____ DATE _____

Activities I plan to do

Committees I plan to work with

Materials I plan to read

Things I plan to make

Figure 1.4-1   *A Form for a Work Plan.*

sets the tone for the whole unit. A bright, breezy, stimulating start may make a the difference. Therefore, the teacher should strive to find introductory activiti that will challenge the pupils' curiosity, arouse their interest, and set them to thi ing. Since it is expected that pupils will plan their work cooperatively, the tea r must see to it that the pupils have the necessary backgrounds. Introductory tea er talks, moving pictures, recordings, and tapes may give pupils just the orient on they need. For the actual planning of their own activities, probably the est methods are to give out a study and activity guide or lists of possible activiti and let the pupils choose and organize for themselves under your guidance. On they have decided what to do, individual pupils could fill out a plan such as tha hown in Figure 1.4-1.

The Laboratory Phase

During the laboratory phase, the pupils carry out the plans they ve made, both the required activities and the optional activities they have selec d. Most of the work in this phase is done individually or in small groups, at the pupil's own speed and in his own way. Nevertheless, the teacher reserves class t e for whole class activities that may be necessary or seem advantageous. Some nes, pooling and sharing activities are interspersed through the laboratory pha . During this phase, most of the pupils' direction for carrying out their learning activities comes from their study and activity guides and from special study guides provided for optional, related activities. Although the pupils will not all do the same activities in the same way during the laboratory phase, the pupils will learn the same things, the learning products set forth in the objectives. For this reason, the required activities are usually set up as problems that all pupils must attempt to solve in one way or another, and the optional activities are related to them. In this way, pupils should achieve the same objectives although they do not read or study the same books, and solve the problems in different ways.

Sharing Phase

The pooling and sharing of experience phase consists of opportunities for pupils to pool what they have learned. This does not mean a series of reports although there should be some reporting. Since the activities have all been aimed at the same set of objectives, the pupils' learning should have much in common. Therefore, there should be much meat for group discussion and debate on the problems in which pupils pool their ideas and share what they have found out. In addition, the pupils might share their experiences through panels, dramatizations, demonstrations, exhibits, class newspapers, jury procedures, and similar techniques.

Evaluating Phase

Effective teachers evaluate continually, as we have said. Nevertheless, the end of the unit makes an excellent occasion for taking stock. At this point, the teacher needs to know how well the pupils have done so as to estimate the success of the unit, to prepare for whatever remedial follow-up seems necessary, and to move smoothly into the next unit. To be of most practical value, the measurement devices you use in the evaluation should be diagnostic.

Organization of a Unit Plan

The plan for a unit of this type contains the following elements:

1. Introduction, including topic, time duration, course title, grade level, justification, and place in the course or curriculum.
2. The general objective, often written as an overview, telling what the unit is about and what pupils are expected to learn.
3. The specific objectives, skills, understandings, attitudes, ideals, and appreciations it is expected that the pupils will learn. These should be expressed as learning products or as behavioral objectives. Current opinion seems to favor behavioral objectives.
4. The unit of work or unit assignment, the required and optional related activities in which your pupils engage. Frequently, these activities are categorized as introductory activities, developmental activities, and culminating activities. The introductory activities are used, of course, in the introductory phase, the developmental activities in the laboratory and sharing phases, and the culminating activities in the sharing and evaluating phases. Note that the activities of the sharing phase can be either developmental or culminating. Culminating activities are activities that tie things together and bring the unit to an end in high style. Activities in which pupils pool and share experiences and learning are excellent for this purpose; so is an end-of-unit test. The idea is for the unit of work to start with a boom and end with a bang. A calendar, scheduling when various activities and films are to occur, is a handy tool for implementing the unit of work.
5. The study and activity guide, which will contain the instructions for carrying out the core activities to be done individually and in small groups.
6. Special study and activity guides, which contain the instructions for carrying out the optional, related activities and special activities, such as field trips.

7. Procedures and instruments for measuring and evaluating pupil progress and the success of the unit. These should adequately test both the general and specific objectives.
8. A list of readings for the pupils to use.
9. A list of the materials needed.
10. A short bibliography for the teacher's use.

Some teachers also include an outline of the subject matter content.

Planning the Unit

When you are planning a unit, it is recommended that you use the following general procedure:

1. Select the topic theme to be studied.
2. Determine the general objective for pupils.
3. Determine specific objectives that will lead to the general objective.
4. Determine a sequence of pupil-teacher activities by which to attain the specific and general objectives.
5. Build a study guide for pupils to use in their study.
6. Develop a scheme and instrument for assessing each pupil's progress toward attaining the objectives.
7. Decide what materials of instruction, supplies, and equipment will be necessary for the unit.

Selecting the Topics

The topic of the unit is, for all practical purposes, the name of the unit. It is usually a section of subject matter, but it might be a problem or a theme. Ordinarily, it is one of the topics in the sequence already outlined in the course plan. To be usable it should center around some major understanding, problem, issue, or theme; fit the course objectives and further the course plan; be relevant to pupils' lives and to the society in which they live; be manageable, not too difficult, too big, or too demanding of time and resources; and be suitable to pupils' abilities and interests.

Writing the Unit Objectives. The general objective can be written as an overview describing the major concept that the pupils should learn. For example:

The overview for Mr. Jones' unit on minority groups was that:
Every citizen should understand what our minority problems are. Citizens should analyze their feelings about different minority groups. All should evaluate the contributions of each of these groups to the development of America. We must try to understand the importance of cooperation among all the groups.

Other examples of unit overviews follow.

Overview: The learning products sought for each pupil are (1) the ability to make a screwdriver involving the use of those common hand tools peculiar to the machine shop; the ability to operate the engine lathe, drill press, and milling machine with the dividing or indexing head; (2) some understanding and appreciation of the source, characteristics, and properties of tool steel (water quench), machinery steel, and hard maple from the standpoint of the consumer; (3) some understanding and appreciation of the place of the metalworking industry in present-day civilization from the standpoint of materials and processes employed, products produced, and the effect of these materials, processes, and products on the worker and on the consuming public; and (4) some understanding and appreciation of the work performed by those employed in a variety of occupations in the metalworking industries and related shops from the standpoint of the opportunities and requirements for employment in these industries.

Overview: Well-written adventure stories appeal to seventh-grade readers because of their exciting, suspenseful plots, their heroic characters, and interesting settings.

It may be simpler and just as effective to prepare a list of generalizations such as those in Module 1.2. The purpose of the overview or general objectives is to give the unit a focus point (examples of overviews can be found in the objective or rationale sections of many of the modules in this series). In addition, the general objectives section of the unit should list the general skills, attitudes, appreciations, and ideals that it is hoped pupils will acquire from studying the unit.

The specific learning products can be written as descriptions of the concepts, attitudes, or skills to be learned, or as behavioral objectives, such as in the following example:

Concept to be learned—The guilt for starting World War I was shared by many nations.

Behavioral objectives—The pupils will be able to determine the perimeter of (a) triangles, (b) squares, (c) rectangles, (d) parallelograms, (e) trapezoids, and (f) general polygons.

The important concerns are that the specific goals must contribute to your larger goal, and that they must be specific enough and clear enough for you, the teacher, and the pupils to understand what the goals are. In addition, the objectives must be achievable in the time allotted and with the resources available; be worthwhile in the eyes of the pupils and, in fact, be neither too difficult nor too easy to achieve; and allow for differences in pupils' abilities, interests, needs, and goals. Teachers seem to find it helpful to list the different categories of specific objectives separately, as follows:

Concept—Immigrants find it difficult to adapt and progress in their new country because they are not familiar with the language and means of getting along.

Skill—The pupils will become skillful in the interpretation of statistical tables showing population shifts.

Attitudes—The pupils will learn to treat immigrants respectfully.

Appreciation—The pupils will appreciate the fact that many immigrants made great progress against great odds.

Planning the Unit of Work

Once the objectives are ready, it is time to prepare the activities for the unit of work. The first step in this procedure is to identify potentially good activities. To gather activities that might be useful, search curriculum guides, curriculum bulletins, textbooks, books on teaching in the field, and professional periodical literature. Then the activities must be culled. Are they really suitable for the objectives? If not, can they be adapted so as to make them suitable? Are they feasible in view of the time, material, equipment, and other resources available? Are they worth the time and effort? Are they too difficult or too easy? Which will do the job best? At this point, it would be good to check the resources available and list them. The list should include audio-visual media, library resources, equipment, and supplies. It is embarrassing after concocting elaborate plans to find that you don't have the materials and supplies you need.

Now divide the activities into two categories: those that should be required of all pupils and those that should be optional. In each unit there should be enough optional work to give every pupil a chance to do something he can enjoy and do well. Next decide how to introduce the unit. Try to find introductory activities that will tell the pupils what the unit is about and arouse their interest. If you intend to have pupils cooperate in planning, include cooperative planning in your introductory activities.

Next plan the developmental activities and culminating activities. These should include (1) provisions for committee and individual problem-solving laboratory types of work; (2) opportunities for pupils to share what they have learned with each other; and (3) whole class activities, such as films, guest speakers, and field trips. Schedule activities that need scheduling for definite, even if tentative, times. In your scheduling, remember to allow pupils enough time to complete both their required and optional work.

Then prepare a study guide for the pupils to follow during the laboratory phases when they are working alone or in small groups. In addition to using this study guide in the laboratory phase, the pupils will find it helpful in the introductory phase for their personal planning. Finally, plan how you will evaluate the pupils' work. Build tests, quizzes, rating scales, and other instruments and devices that you will need in your evaluating.

The following is an excerpt from the unit of work designed for the industrial arts unit, for which the overview was presented earlier in this module.

Unit of Work: (Tentative time allotment, five forty-four-minute periods per week for five weeks. Four periods each week are given to manipulative and observational experiences in the machine shop; one period each week to witnessing demonstrations, listening to brief lectures and illustrated talks, participating in discussions, and in other forms of individual and group activity in the industrial arts related laboratory.)

    A. Introduction: Illustrated lecture, discussion, test, and demonstration.

        1. Explain the threefold nature of the unit of study: (a) to learn how to make a useful and practical screwdriver from both wood and steel in preparation for doing more advanced work which permits the learner to select, under the guidance of the instructor, those projects which best meet immediate and anticipated needs of the students; (b) to learn about the various branches of the metalworking industry, related industries, and their services to society (through readings and through visual aids, such as the films, "The Tool and Diemaker," "The Drama of Steel," "Grits that Grind," "Magnesium," and "Files on Parade"; (c) to learn how to buy and care for the tools and products of metalworking and related industries.

2. Demonstrate the correct and safe use of each tool and machine in the elementary situations in which the pupils will use it.
3. Give a test of multiple-response, completion, matching, and identification questions to discover what the pupils already know about the meanings and insights to be developed.
4. Hand out the "List of Readings and References" and activity guide (Job Breakdown) for the Screwdriver Ferrule, and explain the uses of the list of readings and references and the more detailed activity guides (Job Breakdowns) to follow.

B. Laboratory work.
  *1. Make a useful screwdriver with a wooden handle as per assembly print to be furnished by the instructor.
    *a. Study the sample screwdriver, completed component parts, and the assembly print submitted by the instructor, and develop the necessary working detail sketches, scale of two to one, of the screwdriver ferrule, blade, and handle. (Ask the teacher for a special study and activity guide showing good sketches and giving suggestions for making them.)
    *b. After the sketches for the screwdriver have been completed and initiated by the instructor, prepare a bill of materials needed for making the project (ask the teacher for a special study guide and activity guide for making out a bill of materials.) Figure how much the article will cost to produce. Get the teacher's approval on your bill of materials and estimated cost.
    *c. Select and cut to length on the power hacksaw the stock which you will need for making the screwdriver (ask for the special study and activity guide).
    *d. Machine the stock to over-all finished length and break all sharp edges (ask for the special study and activity guide or breakdown).
    *e. Machine and fabricate screwdriver ferrule, and blade to blueprint (B/P) specifications (ask for the special study and activity guides or job breakdowns).

The Study Guide

The purpose of the general unit study and activity guide is to give the pupils the information they need to do the required activities and to select the optional activities they want to pursue. The activities should be largely of the problem-solving or inquiry type. The instructions should be explicit enough so that the pupils can guide themselves through the activities without undue dependence on the teacher. They are useful because they give the pupil (1) a source to which he can refer if he forgets his assignment; (2) a picture of what activities he might want to do so that he can pick his choice of activities and the order in which he wishes to do them; (3) a definite assignment so that he can go ahead to new activities on his own without waiting for a new assignment from the teacher; and (4) definite instructions which should eliminate misunderstandings about assignments and excuses for incomplete or unattempted assignments.

The following are excerpts from a general study guide accompanying a unit on adventure stories, for which the overview was presented earlier in this module.

---

* All items marked with asterisks will be mimeographed as a general study and activity guide or job breakdown.

1. Read Jack London's story, "The Lost Poacher" (1:312–321). [Read thusly: pages 312–321 of the first reference appearing at the end of the study guide.] What chance has "Bub" Russell to become a hero in the eyes of his mates? What makes a person a hero? Study the questions appearing in 1:380–381 as a basis for class study.
3. Read Jeannette Eaton's story of David Livingstone's life (1:176–186). As you read, think how Livingstone's life differs from that of "Bub" Russell. If you could change places with either of these people, which would you prefer to be? Write a short paragraph explaining why. Be prepared to discuss the story using the questions appearing in the study guide.
5. Read "Old Slewfoot" from *The Yearling* by Marjorie Kennan Rawlings (2:109–120). What sort of person is Penny to the other people and animals in the story?
6. Prepare an adventure poem to recite to the class as a committee. Part of the poem might be recited in chorus. Examples of poems your committee might recite are "Casey at the Bat," "Clara Barton," "The Cremation of Sam McGee," and "The Highwayman." Be prepared to show why the poem is a good adventure poem.
8. Read "Treasure," by Mark Twain (1:65–75) and "Mafatu Stout Heart," by Armstrong Sperry (1:91–100). Which had the more exciting existence, Mafatu or Tom Sawyer? Back up your answer with evidence from the story.
10. Read "One Minute Longer," by Albert Payson Terhune (1:240–249). How does Mr. Terhune build up suspense in this story?
11. Read Stephen Meader's "Escape From the River of the Wolves" (1:250–260). Notice how the excitement is carried through the story. How does the author maintain this excitement?

Developing a Scheme for Evaluation

Because the evaluating of pupil progress must take place continually throughout the unit, it is necessary to incorporate evaluating procedures and devices into the unit of work. Reports, papers, classwork, and progress tests are among the types of activities that make up this continual evaluation. In addition, probably each unit should culminate in a diagnostic test. Such a culmination will help tie together the various threads in the unit and to learn how well you have achieved your teaching goals. It is essential for determining what you should do next.

Planning a Learning Packet

To prepare a learning packet (also called a learning activity packet or instructional packet), one follows about the same procedures as for other types of units. The principal differences is that the learning packet is designed for independent, individual self-instruction. The process consists of the following five basic steps:

1. Assuming that the course has already been divided into a sequence of topics or modules as described in Module 1.3, the first step is to set up the module objectives. The process is essentially the same as in any other unit. The general objectives can be presented as an overview, commonly called the Rationale, in which you give a general description of (a) the terminal be-

havior to result from studying the modules; (b) why anyone should study the module; (c) the relationship of the module to other modules and courses; and (d) any other information that you think necessary for the pupils' orientation and motivation. The specific objectives are usually expressed as behavioral objectives. They may be either simple or criterion-referenced, depending upon your preference and the exigencies of the situation. They, of course, should be pertinent to the general objectives. Because these objectives will be used by the students as guides in their studying, it is usually helpful to write these goals in the second person, as follows:

At the conclusion of your study of this unit, you should be able to construct a learning packet with reasonable ease and effectiveness.

2. Select the content activities to be included in learning packets. These include all the readings, problems, and exercises that the pupil will do in the module. Take care that the activities and content are pertinent to the goals.

3. Develop a plan for evaluating the pupils' progress. Ordinarily this plan should include self-correcting tests—pretests, progress tests, and post tests. The pretest can be used by pupils to ascertain their present strengths and weaknesses, what they know and what they do not know. They can also be used by pupils to prove that they have already learned what is in the module and so should be excused from studying it at this time. The progress tests can be used by pupils to evaluate their progress as they move through the module. The post test can be used to measure the students' final progress. Probably this should be a teacher-corrected criterion-referenced test to be practical in the elementary and secondary schools.

4. Gather all the materials that have not yet been gathered and assemble them.

5. The final step is to prepare the study guide and packet. These should be carefully prepared. Directions should be written so that the pupils will know exactly what to do and how to do it. They should make clear just where the pupil will find the information and materials he needs. In many packets, it will be advantageous or essential to include the material needed as part of the study guide. The guide should include

a. Topic.

b. Rationale, including the general objectives and reasons the learning is worthwhile.

c. The specific objectives stated as specific behavioral objectives, and addressed to the pupil in this form: "At the end of this module, you should be able to locate the principal oceanic streams on the globe." Sometimes, provisions are made by which the pupil can check off each of these behavioral objectives when he feels he has mastered the required behavior.

d. Directions for the pupil to follow while completing the module. These directions should include:

(1) General directions: agenda, time limits (if any), and options.

(2) Specific directions; that is, the directions and explanations for specific activities. For example,

(a) Problem to be solved: What the problem is, what the background of the problem is, what requirements must be met to solve the problem successfully.

(b) Reading: Purpose of the reading, what information is to be

learned, what is to be done with the information, questions on
the reading, exact citations.

    (c) Information to be learned: Possible sources of the information.

  (3) Where to go for materials and information.

e. Bibliography.

f. Instructional materials that you have prepared for the module. (These
may be included with the study guide or distributed separately.)

g. Self-correcting and other testing and evaluating materials. These should
include both pretest and posttest material and perhaps intermediate
progress tests. These may be included with the study guide or distributed
separately. Note, however, that teacher-corrected mastery tests should
be distributed separately as needed, not in the original packet. Mastery
tests should be administered separately under supervision and corrected
by the teacher. Progress tests are more useful when they are self-correcting.

Planning a Learning Contract

The contract is still another variation of the unit. The procedure for a plan for
a contract is about the same as that for any other unit except that in the learning
contract plan the pupil agrees to fulfill certain requirements in return for a certain
grade or mark. The essential difference between a learning contract and any other
unit of work is the element of *quid pro quo.*

The basic procedure for planning a contract is as follows:

1. Set up objectives and activities whereby pupils may achieve the objectives.
2. Decide what activities will be required.
3. Decide which activities will be required and which will be optional.
4. Decide what the requirements will be for the different grade levels (A, B,
C, D).
5. Provide a written study and activity guide describing the activities.
6. Let each pupil decide how he will meet the requirements.
7. On the basis of these decisions have the pupil make out a contract in writing.

An example of a contract is shown on the next page.[2]

An easier system for planning a contract is to decide what activities and quality
of work will be required for each of the grade levels A, B, C, and D, and specify
these requirements on the study guide. For example:

To pass with a D, you must complete activities 1–10 and pass the post test.

For the grade of C, you must complete activities 1–10, receive at least a C on
the post test, and do two optional, related activities satisfactorily.

For the grade of B, you must complete activities 1–10 plus four of the optional,
related activities, and receive a grade of at least B on the post test.

For a grade of A, you must complete activities 1–10 plus six of the optional
activities, and receive a grade of at least B on the post test.

[2] Ibid., p. 126.

```
┌─────────────────────────────────────────────────────────────┐
│                        CONTRACT                             │
│                                                             │
│   Susan Q                           To be completed by Nov. 1│
│            During this unit I will                          │
│                 1.  Read Chapter III of the text.           │
│                 2.  Do the problems on Worksheet A.         │
│                 3.  Participate in the panel on the Panama Canal.│
│                 4.  Pass the unit test with a mark of at least C.│
│                 5.  Demonstrate that I can perform all the requirements│
│                     in group C.                             │
│                                                             │
│            Satisfactory completion of this contract will be awarded by a unit│
│    mark of C.                                               │
│                                                             │
│                               signed     PUPIL              │
│                                                             │
│                               approved   TEACHER            │
└─────────────────────────────────────────────────────────────┘
```

POST TEST

1. According to this module, there are at least four kinds of unit plans. What are they?

_____

_____

_____

_____

2. In preparing the objective for an ordinary unit, what types of objectives should you use, general or specific?

_____

3. Is is necessary to set up a time schedule when planning a unit?

_____

4. Should a plan for an ordinary unit contain provisions and other major assignments?

_____

5. Should the specific objectives for the true unit be written as statements describing the learning products or as behavioral objectives?

_____

_____

6. If I were to write a general overview of what I hope the pupils would learn in a true unit rather than listing the general objectives, would it be acceptable (providing I did a good job)?

_____

7. Name four criteria for the topic of a unit.

_____

_____

_____

_____

8. What are four criteria for good, specific unit objectives?

_____

_____

_____

_____

9. Ordinarily, what type of activities would you hope to find in the introductory phase of a true unit?

_____

_____

_____

10. What is the purpose of each of the phases of the true unit?

_____

_____

_____

_____

_____

_____

11. Why do study guides consist largely of problem-solving activities in the true unit?

_____

_____

_____

_____

_____

12. Do all the required activities in the unit have to be done by all pupils
    a. at the same time?
    b. in the same way?

_____

_____

_____

13. What is the principal difference between a learning packet and a true unit?

_____

_____

14. What are the essential differences between writing objectives for a unit and a learning packet; for a unit and a contract plan?

_____

15. What is the simplest way to set up a learning contract in a contract plan?

_____

16. What would you expect to find in a study guide for a true unit?

_____

_____

_____

_____

_____

17. What would you expect to put in a learning packet you constructed?

_____

_____

_____

_____

_____

_____

Planning: The Daily Lesson Plan

William J. Meisner

Jersey City State College

module 1.5

Planning a Daily Lesson / Constructing a Daily Lesson Plan / Components of a Daily Lesson Plan / Examples of Lesson Plans

RATIONALE

Few teachers have the experience or skill to step before a class, without preparation, and teach a lesson that is meaningful, has objectives to justify it, is interestingly and logically presented, and from which the students will develop a clear understanding of the knowledge, skills, or concepts underlying its inclusion in the curriculum. Admittedly, not all teachers have elaborate written plans for teaching a lesson; some have no written plans at all. This is not to say, necessarily, that a great deal of thought and planning has not gone into what they do in the classroom. Certain assumptions must be made about planning from the outset:

1. Not all teachers need extensive written plans.
2. Not all teachers follow a particular format in lesson planning.
3. Some subject matter fields require more planning than do others.
4. Some experienced teachers have clearly defined goals and objectives in mind, but have not written them into lesson plans.
5. *All effective teachers* have a *planned* pattern of introduction, whether that plan is written or not.

These are assumptions which the prospective teacher must keep clearly in mind when considering planning in the broadest sense. This module is designed to acquaint the prospective teacher with the basic components necessary to develop an effective daily lesson plan, and includes both examples and suggestions. Ultimately, however, it will fall upon you, the teacher, to adapt, alter, modify, and adjust these suggestions to meet the needs of your students and to find a lesson plan style that is comfortable and usable in your classroom.

SPECIFIC OBJECTIVES

Specifically, we expect that at the end of your study of this section, you will be able to
1. List the basic components that make up a daily lesson plan.
2. Define each subsection of the daily lesson plan as it relates to the plan as a whole.
3. Write general objectives for a daily lesson plan.
4. Write specific objective for a daily lesson plan.
5. Arrange content in a daily lesson plan so as to maximize its effective use during a lesson.
6. Develop a daily lesson plan, using at least two different formats.
7. Select the key point or points in the material you are presenting to the class.
8. Reinforce this key point in the conclusion of your lesson.
9. Select the appropriate answers in the accompanying post test with a maximum of three errors.

MODULE TEXT

Planning a Daily Lesson

Good teachers are in a constant state of planning. They plan the scope and sequence of courses, develop the content within each course of study, develop units within courses of study and topics within units, and develop the activities to be used and the tests to be given. Teachers familiarize themselves with textbooks, resource materials, and innovations in their fields. Yet, despite all of this planning, the daily lesson plan is still the pivotal aspect of the process.

Lesson plans should be clearly written, simply stated and, above all, flexible. Nothing gives the beginning teacher more confidence or a greater sense of security than a well-developed lesson plan. The following simple rules should apply to lesson plans: (1) the teacher should be able to teach from it; (2) someone else (a substitute) who knows the field should be able to teach from it; (3) it should be useful as a basis for planning the lesson if it is taught again in the future.

With a carefully prepared plan, the beginning teacher can walk into a classroom with the confidence that he has developed, in some organized form, a sensible framework for that day's instruction. For this reason, beginning teachers should expect to make considerably detailed lesson plans. Naturally, this will require a great deal of work for at least the first year or two, but the reward of knowing that you have prepared and presented an effective lesson easily compensates for the effort. Since most teachers plan their daily lessons no more than a day or two ahead, you can expect a busy first year of teaching.

Some prospective teachers are concerned with being seen using a written plan in class, as it may suggest that the teacher has not mastered the field. On the contrary, a lesson plan is a visible sign of preparation on the part of the teacher. There can be no excuse for a teacher's appearance before his class without some evidence of previous preparation. Lesson planning is essentially the careful and meaningful organization of the wide range of activities and materials available on a particular topic. Good planning also requires that these activities and materials be divided into manageable segments for use within class periods.

Experienced teachers do not require plans as detailed as those necessary for beginning teachers. Likewise, with experience, the teacher develops short cuts to lesson planning without sacrificing effectiveness. Lesson planning is a continual process. Even the experienced teacher should see the need for constantly keeping his material and plans current. No two classes are ever exactly the same and the lesson plan should be tailored to meet the needs of the group to which it is directed. Furthermore, the content of a course may change as new developments occur or new theories are introduced. Perhaps the objectives of the students, of the school, and of the staff will change over the years.

It is for these reasons that lesson plans should be in a constant state of revision. Once the basic framework is developed, however, the task of updating and modifying becomes minimal. The daily lesson plan should be flexible and provide a tentative outline of the class period. A carefully worked out plan may have to be set aside because unforeseen circumstances, such as a delayed school bus, an impromptu assembly program, or a fire drill, interfere with its implementation. A planned lesson covering six aspects of a given topic may result in only three of those points being considered. These occurrences are natural in the school setting, and the teacher and the plans should be flexible enough to accommodate them.

The lesson plan should provide enough materials and activities to consume the entire class period. Since exact planning is a skill that only very experienced teachers master, it is wiser for the beginning teacher to over-plan rather than run the risk of running short. The beginning teacher may find that he has lost control of the class and that discipline problems are developing when his lesson plans do not provide enough activity to take up the class period. Students are very perceptive when it comes to a teacher who has finished his plan for the period and attempts to bluff his way through the last ten minutes.

Note: Should you ever be unfortunate enough to get caught short, as most teachers do at one time or another, one suggestion that avoids the embarrassment of giving a study period or letting the class begin its homework is to tell the class that you have completed all the *new* material planned for today, and now you would like to review the material considered during the past thirty minutes or past several days.

Constructing a Daily Lesson Plan

Each teacher may and perhaps should develop his own system of lesson planning. The best rule of thumb is to develop a plan that works for you. It may be difficult for a beginning teacher to work from so vague a framework, and it is for that reason that this module includes some suggestions as to format. Whatever form is used, however, should be written out in an intelligible style. There is some reason to question teachers who assert that they have no need for written plans since they have their lessons planned "in their heads." The distinction should also be made between a lesson plan and the plan book that many schools require teachers to submit a week in advance. A plan book is most assuredly not a daily lesson plan. It provides a small, lined box for each day of the week. Usually there is just enough room to place the topic for the day and the homework assignment. The only function this serves is to assist the substitute if the teacher is absent. There is serious question that it even serves this function adequately. The plan book is not a daily lesson plan, and the teacher who asserts that it is or that he is using it as such is only deluding himself.

Let us consider now some of the basic elements or components that go into the construction of a daily lesson plan. All lesson plans might not lend themselves to the inclusion of each of these components. For the beginning teacher, however, it might be wise to consider the suitability of each before attempting to construct a plan.

Components of a Daily Lesson Plan

1. Name of course and grade level.
2. Name of unit.
3. Topic to be considered within the unit.
4. General objective for the lesson (may be the same for the entire unit).
5. Specific objective for the lesson (daily).

6. Introduction of the lesson.
   a. Review of previous day's work.
   b. Review of old vocabulary.
   c. Review of concepts developed.
7. Content to be considered.
   a. New material to be introduced.
   b. Questions to be discussed.
   c. Discussion of divergent views.
   d. Activities to be engaged in.
8. Method or methods to be used.
9. Materials to be used and skills to be developed.
10. Key point or points (if any).
11. Conclusion.
12. Assignment.
13. Evaluation.

It should be noted that this list does not represent a rank order, and some of the basic components might be more effectively used if the order were changed.

Let us now consider in somewhat more detail each of these basic components.

1. Name of course and grade level are self-explanatory, merely serve as headings for the plan, and facilitate orderly filing of plans. Examples follow:

   United States History I   Grade 11
   Biology   Grade 10

2. Name of the unit facilitates the orderly control of the hundreds of lesson plans a teacher constructs and makes it easier to locate a plan.

   United States History I   Grade 11
   Unit: The Civil War

3. Topic to be considered with the unit includes the following:

   United States History I   Grade 11
   Unit: The Civil War
   Topic: Main Causes for the War

4. General objectives relate to the broader aims that the teacher has for a unit. Sometimes there are general objectives for two or three days' work rather than for a two- or three-week unit. A beginning teacher should state general objectives in the daily lesson plan to insure that he keeps his specific goals consistent with his major over-all goals. General objectives are usually not stated in behavioral terms and are more closely related to concept development. Examples follow:
   a. To develop an understanding of the reasons for the division between the strict constructionist and loose constructionist points of view at the Philadelphia Convention in 1787.
   b. To appreciate the effect that the life style of Edgar Allan Poe had on his writing.
   c. To understand the differences between the laws of probability and random choice.

5. Specific objectives deal with the specific aims of the lesson for the day. The teacher should briefly indicate the major aims of the daily lesson plan. These goals must be specific enough for accomplishment within the class period. Teachers should consider outcomes, understandings, appreciations, attitudes, special abilities, skills, and facts. Both teacher and student objectives should be included. Frequently, specific objectives are stated in behavioral terms, but this should not preclude the teacher from striving for attitudinal change. There has been a great educational war raging for a number of years that

JUNIOR COLLEGE LIBRARY

has resulted in a swing toward behavioral objectives which are more easily measured in terms of performance than are the objectives that deal with attitude and opinion. The beginning teacher might consider his own philosophical bent when developing such specific objectives as the following:

a. The student will be able to add, subtract, multiply, and divide two-digit numbers using the slide rule. (Behavioral).

b. The student will be able to identify the major internal organs of a common pond frog. (Behavioral).

c. The student will appreciate the symbolism in *Lord of the Flies*.

d. The student will understand the underlying cause of the Civil War as it relates to the stated causes.

6. Introduction of the lesson means that like any good performance, a lesson needs an effective introduction. In many respects the introduction sets the tone for the rest of the lesson. It alerts the class to the fact that the business of learning is to begin. If it is an exciting, interesting, or innovative introduction, it can set a mood for the class. It is difficult to develop an exciting introduction for each lesson, but it suffices as a solid indication that a teacher is thoroughly prepared. Although an introduction is necessary, there are a variety of options available. One might begin by briefly reviewing yesterday's lesson. This serves the twofold purpose of introducing today's work and reinforcing yesterday's. A second possibility is to review vocabulary words from previous lessons and possibly introduce new vocabulary. A teacher might review a concept developed in the previous day's lesson. Another possibility, which will be discussed in more detail later, is to use the key point of the lesson as an introduction and then again as the conclusion of the same lesson.

a. "As we have seen by yesterday's demonstration, the gravitational pull on the earth's surface affects the tides . . . Today we will consider different types of tide . . ."

b. "Johnny, what is meant by factor?"
"Suzy, what do we mean when we say interpolate?"

c. "We have seen that despite the claims of national unity, the period of the 1820s was actually a time of great regional rivalry."

7. Content to be used generally must be the most flexible area in the daily lesson plan. This section embodies the heart of what the teacher plans for the class period. If he is going to introduce new material, using the lecture method, he will want to outline the content. It should be noted here that the word *outline* is not used casually. The teacher should not have pages of notes to sift through nor should he read declarative statements to the class. The teacher should be familiar enough with the content that an outline (in detail if necessary) will be sufficient to carry on the lesson. If the teacher intends to conduct the lesson through discussion, he should write the discussion questions. It is presumptuous to assume that one can remember all aspects of a topic while in the midst of responding and reacting to student discussion. If there are varying sides to topics, the pros and cons of each should be noted in order to prompt student discussion. If activities, such as a debate or simulation, are to be engaged in, then the details of the activity should be spelled out as in the following examples:

I. Causes of Civil War.
   A. Primary Causes.
      1. Economics.
      2. Abolitionist pressure.

**VERNON REGIONAL
JUNIOR COLLEGE LIBRARY**

  3. Slavery.
  4. _____.
 B. Secondary causes.
  1. North-South friction.
  2. Southern economic dependence.
  3. _____.
II. What do you think Golding had in mind when he wrote *Lord of the Flies?* What did the conch shell represent? Why did the other boys resent Piggy?
III. Capital Punishment.

Pro	*Con*
A. Deterrent.	A. Not a deterrent.
B. Saves money.	B. Rehabilitation.
C. Eye for eye.	C. Morally wrong.

IV. Simulation: War and Peace.
 A. Read directions.
 B. Break class into nation groups.
 C. Elect spokesman.
 D. Read directions for Phase I.
 E. Begin Phase I.

8. Method to be used means that the teacher should note the procedure he intends to use to achieve his goals. Examples follow.
 a. Teacher introduction (10 minutes).
 b. Class discussion (15 minutes).
 c. Review (10 minutes).
 d. Go over homework assignment.

9. Materials to be used should be noted as a reminder to the teacher. It is not a big task, and it often reminds the teacher that he must obtain a projector, or remind students to bring a particular book to class, or to put certain materials on the board. An example follows.
 Materials: Chalkboard, opaque projector, pictures from *Rise and Fall of Rome*, pp. 29, 47, 137, 540.

10. Key Point—Not every lesson has a key point. The teacher must ask himself if he had to select one thing in the lesson that he most wanted the students to retain, could he identify it. If not, then there is no need to include this component in the plan. On the other hand, if there is a key pivotal point around which the entire lesson centers, he may wish to identify it, not only for himself but for the class as well. This key point could be effectively used as an introduction or as a conclusion. It could also be emphasized in the content of the lesson. Examples follow:
 Key Point: Although there were many causes, primary and secondary, for the Civil War, the main cause for this as for all wars was economics.
 Used as an introduction:
 Today we shall see that. . . .
 Used as a conclusion:
 Today we have seen. . . .

11. Conclusion—It is as important to an effective lesson to have a clear-cut conclusion as it is to have a strong introduction. The lesson does not conclude when the bell rings and the students get up and walk out while you are still talking. It is important to note that students will learn within a day or two if you will dismiss them or if they will dismiss themselves when the bell sounds. It is wise to establish early that the bell is a signal for you and not for them. That is not to say that you should ramble on for one or two minutes after the

bell sounds. A sound conclusion can be delivered in five or ten seconds after the bell rings and do no disservice to the time they need to pass to the next class. Examples follow:

1. Today we have seen how the plot is developed in a novella. Tomorrow we will consider character development.
2. Restatement of the key point.
3. Consider for tomorrow what you would do if you were in Harry S. Truman's position in 1945 upon the death of President Roosevelt.

12. Assignment—If a homework assignment is to be given, the teacher should be certain to include it somewhere in his lesson plan. It is optional as to when it is presented to the class, except it should never be an afterthought as the students are leaving. Some teachers prefer to place the assignment on the board at the beginning of the class and to draw the students' attention to it early. Some prefer to wait until the end. Either method is acceptable; however, doing it at the beginning of a class period minimizes the chance of your forgetting it. An example follows:

Assignment: Read pp. 234–239, and answer questions 1, 5, 8.

13. Evaluation—This component is reserved for the teacher to make any notes or comments regarding the lesson. It is particularly useful if you use the plan again. When you take it out the following year or two, it is unlikely that you will recall if the lesson was dull, or if you had too much material, or your over-all reaction to it. If you jot down a few notes such as the following, it may help to make the second presentation more effective than the first.

1. Evaluation: Fairly good, dragged near end, and kids got bored.
2. Evaluation: Bombed out, too technical, pep it up.
3. Evaluation: Fantastic, into the national archives with it.

Summary

The preceding pages attempt to outline, in some logical order, the fundamental components that go into the development of a daily lesson plan. It must be emphasized again that there is no single best way to prepare a daily lesson plan; no fool-proof formula that will insure a teacher of an effective lesson nor guarantee that students will absorb the materials or concepts that are being considered. Each teacher will, with experience and increased competence in the field, develop his own style, his own methods of implementing that style and his own formula for preparing a "teaching map." This teaching map charts the course, places markers along the trails, pinpoints danger areas, highlights places of interest and importance along the way, and ultimately brings the journeyer to the successful completion of the objective. Metaphorically, this is what the daily lesson plan is about.

It is important for the beginning teacher to note the various aspects of the daily lesson plan as mentioned in this module. Some components will bear more strikingly on different subject matter fields. Some can be modified to relate more specifically to a given subject, topic, or even different intelligence levels. The key point to remember, however, is that a daily lesson plan should be a flexible instrument that can be used by the classroom teacher. It is valueless if it is simply prepared to meet an obligation to the administration that plans be prepared and filed in the main office. Similarly, it is valueless if it is prepared so rigidly that departures are impossible.

Examples of Lesson Plans

LESSON PLAN #1

Algebra I, Grade 9
1. Course: Algebra I.
             9th grade.
             Average group.
2. Topic: Factoring polynomials having common factors.
3. Vocabulary: Old: Factor, product, polynomial, monomial.
                New: Common factor, greatest common factor.
4. Concepts: Old: Distributive law.
              New: Factoring polynomials that have common factors is the inverse process of multiplying a polynomial by a monomial.
5. Skills: Old: Using the distributive law, multiplying a polynomial by a monomial.
            New: Finding the greatest common factor.
6. Method of presentation: Teacher-pupil discussion.
    Time Schedule: 10 min.—review homework.
                    15 min.—present new material.
                    15 min.—supervised study.
    Assignment: Read pp. 244–245, p. 245, 1–29 all odd numbers.

Procedure:
  1. Review: a. What is a product?
              b. What is a factor:
  2. Given the problem: $3a + 4b$ what are the factors?
                         $\times\ 4a$ how do we find the products?
                                 what is the product?
  3. Can we write this problem another way?
     $4a(3a - 4b) = 12a^2 - 16ab$.
     What gives us the right to do the problem this way? (Dist. Law).
     What is the Distributive Law?
  4. Give examples: $2a(m + 3n)$, $3x(2x - 1)$, $a^2(a^2 + b^2)$.
  5. $a(x + y + z) = ax + ay + az$.
     What law is this?
     When multiplying a polynomial by a monomial, what may be said about the product? (The monomial is seen in each term of the product.)
     We may say that a is what to each term in the product? (common).
  6. In $2ax + 2ay =$ what is the comon factor? (2a).
                      Where do you think we would put the common factor?
                      What do we do to each term in the product? (divide it by the common factor and put quotient in parenthesis).
                      Just as division is the inverse of multiplication, what can we say the relationship between factoring polynomials and the process of multiplying a polynomial by a monomial is? (the inverse).

7. $6m + 6n = 6(m + n)$.　　　$\left[\begin{array}{l}\text{What is the common factor?}\\ \text{Where do I put it?}\\ \text{What do I do to each term in the product?}\end{array}\right.$
   $mn_2 + m1 = m(n + 1)$.
   $3a_2 - 3a = 3a(a - 1)$.

8. $4a + 12a = 4a(a + 3)$.
   Could I write $4a^2 + 12a = 4(a^2 + 3a)$? Why?
   What is $4a$ called? (greatest common factor).
   What is the greatest common factor in these problems?

9. $6xy - 3x^2 = 3x(2y - x)$.　　$\left[\begin{array}{l}\text{What is G.C.F.?}\\ \text{Where do I put it?}\\ \text{What do I do to each term in product?}\end{array}\right.$
   $2\pi r - 2\pi R = 2\pi(r - R)$.
   $2a + 4ab + 2ac = 2a(1 + 2b + c)$.

10. Given the example: $6a^2b - 15ab^2 = ?$　$3ab(2a - 5b)$.
    This check would still be valid if G.C.F. had not been chosen, ex. $3a$ instead of $3ab$. Therefore, what should we do to check for G.C.F.? (Inspect each term in the polynomial to make sure no single number or letter is seen in each term.)

LESSON PLAN #2

Social Studies II:　United States History and Problems.
Unit:　"Evolving A Foreign Policy."
Topic:　The Changing Relationship of Puerto Rico to the United States in the Twentieth Century.

Objective:　To assist pupils to do the following:
1. Understand the evolution of the political and economic ties between Puerto Rico and the United States.
2. Listen and read analytically for information.
3. Appreciate the unique role of Puerto Rico in current inter-American affairs.
4. Relate current problems to their historical antecedents.

Procedure:
1. Conclude some unfinished business: an oral report comparing life in Maryland suburbia with life in the rural Dakotas.
2. Review by means of puzzle.
3. Establish purposes for listening to oral reports by offering listening guide questions.
   Present reports sequentially to trace the changing relationship of Puerto Rico to the United States.
   a. "The Island of Puerto Rico Before 1898."
   b. "Political and Economic Change, 1898–1940."
   c. "Luis Muñoz Marin and Operation Bootstrap."
   d. "Puerto Rico: The Cultural Bridge Between the Americas."
   e. "Teodoro Moscoso and the Alliance for Progress."
4. Summarize by means of a special assignment, which the pupils will copy from the chalkboard upon entering the classroom.

Assignment:　Read "Crisis in Latin America," a speech made by the Governor of Puerto Rico. Keep these questions in mind:
1. Why does the author caution us about the use of political "labels"?
2. In what ways is the term "Latin America" really an unsuitable expression?
3. What are the particular problems which Latin America faces?
4. In the Alliance for Progress, what role does the author hope the United States will play?

5. Why is there stress on the phrase "Operation Seeing-Is-Believing"?
6. What unique function does the Governor feel his own island can play in the Alliance for Progress?

LESSON PLAN #3

Sophomore Biology Class, Advanced
The Microscope and Its Use
Objective: To learn the parts and the proper use of the microscope.

Procedure:
1. Assign one microscope to every two students, and record the microscope numbers.
2. Inform the class of the proper manner in which to carry and hold a microscope so as not to damage it.
3. Show the prepared diagrams of the microscope on the overhead projector, and point out the various parts and their functions.
4. Point out the parts on the prepared diagrams and have the students locate the parts on their microscopes.
5. Pass out the mimeographed material on the proper use of microscopes. This information is as follows:

Skill in using the microscope can be developed only by following all steps correctly. Read and perform each step in the order given.
   a. Place the microscope on the table with the arm toward you and with the back of the base about one inch from the edge of the table.
   b. Adjust your position and tilt the microscope so that you can look into the eyepiece comfortably.
   c. Wipe the top lens of the eyepiece, the lens of the objectives, and the mirror with lens paper.
   d. Turn the disk to the largest opening so that the greatest amount of light i admitted.
   e. Turn the low-power objective in line with the body tube.
   f. Place your eye to the eyepiece and turn the mirror toward a source light, but never directly toward the sun. Adjust the mirror until a unifo circle of light without shadows appears. This is a field. The microscope now ready for use.
   g. When you receive the prepared slide, place it on the stage, clip it into pla and move the slide until the object is in the center of the stage opening.
   h. Watching the bottom lens, turn the low-power objective down as far a t will go, using care not to touch the slide.
   i. Place your eye to the eyepiece, and as you watch the field, turn the c e adjustment slowly toward you, raising the body tube. Watch for the ma- terial to appear in the field.

Go through each step with the class, making sure that the students understand the procedure of using low magnification.
Ask for volunteers to describe the slides they are examining.
When they have grasped the procedure of using low-power magnification, instruct the class to turn the high-power objective in line with the body tube, and use the fine adjustment slowly until the object comes into the field. Go around the room and help individuals who are having difficulty.
Ask for volunteers to compare the differences between low power and high power.
Instruct the students to place the microscopes in the cabinets and prepare for leaving.

Materials: Microscopes, lens paper, overhead projector, prepared diagrams of the microscope and labeled parts, mimeographed information on the proper use of the microscope, and prepared slides on insects.

Notes: Be sure to instruct the class as to the proper technique of handling slides. Caution them that they are responsible for damaged slides.

Assignment: Know the parts of the microscope and their functions in preparation for a short quiz at the next meeting.

A Final Comment. The preceding daily lesson plans were reprinted from *Secondary School Teaching Methods,* second edition, by Leonard H. Clark and Irving Starr. They are included in the module to give the beginning teacher some alternative formats for lesson planning. You can see, however, that many of the components discussed in the module are included in these plans.

As we have said, there is no standard or essential format for lesson plans. Not all of the information included in our outline is essential, although it is usually handy to have. Nor is it absolutely essential to write everything out. The only reasons for writing lesson plans are to ensure that you know what you want to do and how you propose to do it, and that when the time comes, you remember to do it. When you are conducting laboratory teaching in a well-planned unit, your daily plan may be simply to continue the committee and individual work already commenced. When teaching certain store-bought curricula or continuous progress courses, your plan may be simply to have the pupils follow the exercises and procedures prescribed by the authors for the module, or to continue with their learning activity packets. On the other hand, if you plan to conduct a discussion, a discovery lesson, a talk, or an open-book recitation, your plan may have to be very detailed indeed.

SUGGESTED READING

Alcorn, Marvin D., James S. Kinder, and Jim R. Schunert. *Better Teaching in Secondary Schools,* 3rd ed. New York: Holt, Rinehart & Winston, Inc., 1970.

Armstrong, Robert J., et al. *The Development and Evaluation of Behavioral Objectives.* Belmont, Calif.: Wadsworth Publishing Co., Inc., 1970.

Clark, D. Cecil. *Using Instructional Objectives in Teaching.* Glenview, Ill.: Scott, Foresman and Company, 1972.

Gronlund, Norman E. *Stating Behavioral Objectives for Classroom Instruction.* New York: The Macmillan Publishing Co., Inc., 1970.

Hoover, Kenneth H. *The Professional Teacher's Handbook.* Boston: Allyn & Bacon, Inc., 1973.

Kibler, Robert J., Donald J. Cegala, Larry L. Barker, and David T. Miles. *Objectives for Instruction and Evaluation.* Boston: Allyn & Bacon, Inc., 1974.

Mager, Robert F. *Preparing Instructional Objectives.* Palo Alto, Calif.: Fearon Publishers, 1962.

McAshan, H. H. *Writing Behavioral Objectives.* New York: Harper and Row, Publishers, 1970.

Noar, Gertrude. *Teaching and Learning the Democratic Way.* Englewood Cliffs, N.J.: Prentice-Hall, Inc., 1963.

Samalonis, Bernice L. *Methods and Materials for Today's High Schools.* New York: Van Nostrand Reinhold Company, 1970.

Tanner, Daniel. *Using Behavioral Objectives in the Classroom.* New York: Macmillan Publishing Co., Inc., 1972.

Zapf, Rosalind M. *Democratic Processes in the Secondary Classroom.* Englewood Cliffs, N.J.: Prentice-Hall, Inc., 1959.

POST TEST

TRUE-FALSE   *If you consider the statement false, explain why.*

1. _____ A good daily lesson plan insures a good lesson.

2. _____ All teachers, regardless of their experience, should have daily lesson plans.

3. _____ It is quite acceptable for beginning teachers who are firm in their grasp of subject matter to keep their lesson plans in their heads.

4. _____ Each teacher should develop his own style of lesson planning that is appropriate for his needs.

5. _____ Students should never see a teacher using his lesson plan.

6. _____ Most teachers develop the knack of perfect timing after severa' months, that is they can bring a class right up to the bell with a lesso plan.

7. _____ Lesson plans should be in a constant state of revision.

8. _____ Lesson plans are the single most important element in all th' .an- ning a teacher does.

9. _____ General objectives usually refer to larger goals than just those sought after in the daily lesson.

10. _____ A lesson begins when the bell rings and ends when the bell rings.

11. _____ A teacher should never use the same plan twice.

12. _____ Formats for lesson plans should be tailored to meet student and teacher goals.

13. _____ If the lesson plan falls short of the time limit, giving the class a study hall is the best remedy.

14. _____ A lesson plan should be flexible: it should lend itself to sudden unforeseen occurrences.

15. _____ A strong introduction to a lesson sometimes sets the tone for the entire class period.

Motivation, Discipline, and Control

William B. Fisher

Leonard H. Clark

Jersey City State College

module 2

Getting to Know Your Pupils / Motivation / Achieving Classroom Control / Classroom Management

RATIONALE

The aspect of teaching that worries beginning teachers most is maintaining discipline and control in their classes. And they have good cause to be concerned. Even more experienced teachers find discipline and control difficult, particularly at the junior high school and high school levels where teachers have so many pupils each day that it is difficult to know them well and where so many pupils have been turned off by unfortunate school experiences in earlier years.

The key to discipline and control is motivation. Motivation is also the key to effective classes. Pupils who are well motivated to learn usually do learn if lessons are reasonably well designed. If pupils' attitudes are antagonistic toward school, school learning, or classes, teachers' efforts are not likely to be fruitful. Therefore it behooves teachers to persuade pupils that learning well in their classes is the thing to do. One has a better chance of persuading them if he knows the individual pupils well enough to adapt the lessons and courses to their needs and interests and to tempt them by making the course seem valuable to them personally.

Specific Objectives

In this module we shall attempt to show you some methods and techniques that will help you as you try to learn to know your pupils, to make their motivation favorable to your course work, and to gain good discipline and control in your classes.

Specifically, by the completion of this unit, you should be able to do the following:

1. Describe resources and devices teachers can use to know more about pupils so that they can adjust their teaching to individuals. Specifically, you should be able to tell how to use the cumulative record, observation, pupil conferences, parent conferences, pupil assignments, questionnaires, and test results.
2. Describe a dozen general procedures for improving students' motivation toward their school work.
3. Describe how one might use principles of reenforcement for school motivation.
4. Describe the modern concept of good discipline.
5. Define permissiveness, democratic discipline, and self-discipline.
6. Explain several strategies and tactics that should help self-discipline in your pupils.
7. Show how each of the following contributes to good classroom control: a positive approach, well-planned classes, a good start, classroom rules, enforcement of rules, correcting misbehavior, and classroom management.

8. Describe specific procedures for establishing the conditions and carrying out the actions necessary to establish and maintain classroom control pertinent to each of the headings listed in Objective 7.

MODULE TEXT

Motivation, discipline, and control are all facets of the same teaching problem. If pupils' motivation is favorable to your classes and teaching, then their behavior will also be favorable, and y͏ classes will be well disciplined and effective. If pupils' motivation is not fav͏ ͏le, the chances are that your control and your effort to teach will also fail. ͏ ͏iously, then, you should do whatever you can to see to it that pupils are favo͏ ͏ly motivated toward your classes and their content. You can carry out this go͏ ͏ore successfully if you know the pupils in the classes well enough so that you͏ ͏ adjust your teaching content and teaching method so as to catch their interes͏ ͏nfortunately, it is difficult to learn to know pupils well in secondary schools ͏ ͏use there are so many of them. The high school teacher is quite likely to ͏ ͏e 100 or more pupils to teach each day. Therefore, in this section of the ͏ ͏ule, we shall try to point out some ways in which one can learn to know his p͏ ͏s better.

Think back over your own h͏ ͏school days. Which courses and teachers do you remember as being interestin͏ ͏d worthwhile? Why were they so? What was there about them that caused yc͏ ͏ be motivated favorably toward them? Now think of courses that have turne͏ ͏u off completely. What was there about them that caused your motivation to b͏ ͏negative?

Getting ͏ Know Your Pupils

Obviously, the best way t͏ ͏ow anyone is to spend a lot of time with him, to talk together, to socialize to͏ ͏er, and to work together. Since any real intimacy is virtually impossible in the ͏ ͏nary school situation, teachers who wish to get to know their pupils must de͏ ͏ upon a variety of information-gathering devices and techniques. Among the m͏ ͏useful of these are the following:

1. Cumulative record fo͏ ͏. These will give you all sorts of information about the pupils' academi͏ ͏ackground, standardized test scores, and extracurricular activities.
2. Observation. Watching the pupils in class, on the playing field, and at lunch may give you information about their personalities and potentialities. Often you find the uninterested, uninteresting, lackadaisical student is a red hot fireball on the playing field. At times, if you can use a checklist as you observe pupils, you will find that your observation will be more productive.
3. Conferences. Conferences with the pupils are usually the best way to find out pupils' interests, ambitions, problems, hopes, and other things that would help you to individualize instruction for them. As a rule, you can

learn more information from short, informal conversations. In any conference, you should observe the following rules:

   a. Ask only open-ended questions. Encourage the pupil to talk freely. Listen to what he says.

   b. Don't moralize, judge, or condemn, but accept a pupil's opinions and values as what they are, his opinions and values.

   c. Record at once points you should remember. Otherwise, you will forget them or mix them up.

4. Parent conferences. Parent conferences can tell you a lot about the pupil, his interests, abilities, and goals.

5. Utilize such assignments as autobiographies, themes, reading reaction sheets, and value sheets.

6. Use questionnaires such as the following:

   a. Interest finder. An interest finder asks such questions as, What type of television programs do you like best? Do you like sports? Which sport do you like the most? Figure 2-1 is an interest finder made by a senior interne. How could it be used in your teaching? Could you make a better one?

   b. Autobiographical questionnaires. Autobiographical questionnaires can give you many ideas about how to tailor assignments for individual pupils. Include such questions as the following:

     (1) What do you plan to do when you finish high school?

     (2) Do you have a job? If so, what is it? Do you like it?

     (3) How do you like to spend your leisure time?

     (4) Do you like to read? What do you like to read?

     (5) Do you have a hobby? What is it?

7. Use test results of both standardized and teacher tests. They will help you match the learning activities to present knowledge and capabilities of the pupils. Diagnostic tests are especially useful for this purpose. Many excellent ones are available commercially. However, it is quite possible to build useful diagnostic tests of your own. Unit tests should almost always be diagnostic, unless they are end-of-term tests. To build a diagnostic test, proceed as follows:

   a. Establish the specific learning products, information, concepts, skills, attitudes, ideas, and appreciations for which you wish to test. Probably these will be most useful if they are written as specific behavioral objectives.

   1. When talking to your friends in the cafeteria, what do you usually discuss?

   2. Do you like to read?

   3. What kind of books do you read in your spare time?

   4. Do you read the daily newspaper?

   5. If so, which section do you read the most?

   6. What kind of movies do you enjoy seeing?

   7. Do you watch television very often?

   8. If so, what type of programs do you like?

   9. Do you have any hobbies?

   10. If you had your choice, would you take a course in American History or Political Science?

Figure 2-1 *Interest Finder.*

Objective	Item	Abel	Bill	Charles	David	Ellen	Etc.
	1	√	0	√	√	√	
1	2	√	0	√	√	√	
	3	√	0	√	√	√	
	4	0	0	0	0	0	
2	5	0	√	0	0	0	
	6	√	√	0	0	0	
	7	√	√	√	√	0	
3	8	√	0	0	√	0	
	9	√	√	√	√	√	

Etc.

√ = correct answer   0 = incorrect answer

Figure 2-2   *Sample Item Analysis.*

b. Write test items that test each of these objectives.

To utilize such tests for diagnostic purposes, it is necessary to analyze the test results so as to find where the pupils do well and where they do not. This can be done by inspection sometimes, but often it is essential to use some form of test analysis, as in the item analysis illustrated in Figure 2-2. In this type of analysis, simply check off which items each pupil answered correctly and which he answered incorrectly. If you find that a pupil answered the items having to do with an objective correctly, you can assume that he has learned that, but if he did not, you can assume that he has not.

Exercise:

Assuming that the small sample of an item analysis in Figure 2-2 is typical of the entire analysis, what, if anything, needs to be retaught? Do any of the pupils need any remedial work? If so, what?

8. Use sociometric devices. Sociometry is "the measurement of attitudes of social acceptance or rejection through expressed preferences among members of a social group."[1] By the use of sociometric devices, it is possible to learn much about the social structure of a class and the interrelationship among the individual pupils in the class. During the past years, social scientists have developed a number of sociometric instruments that can be used in school. In this module we shall discuss only two of them, the sociogram, and the Guess Who Test.

a. Sociogram. A sociogram is a diagrammatic representation of the structure of a group. By examining a sociogram, one should be able to find clues to group leaders, isolates, cliques, friendships, and the like. A procedure recommended for constructing a sociogram follows.

[1] The Random House Dictionary of the English Language, unabridged ed. (New York: Random House, Inc., 1966).

(1) Ask the pupils to answer in secret such questions as, Which two pupils would you like to work with on a topic for an oral report? If we should change the seating plan, whom would you like to sit beside? Or, with whom would you most like to work on a class committee in planning? Sometimes one might also ask, With whom would you rather not work?

(2) Tabulate the choices of each pupil. Keep the boys and girls in separate columns.

(3) Construct the sociogram.

    (a) Select a symbol for boy and another for girl.

    (b) Place the symbols representing the most popular pupils near the center of the page, those of the less popular farther out, and those of the least popular on the fringes. It may be helpful to place the boys on one side of the page and the girls on the other.

    (c) Draw lines to represent the choices. Show the direction of the

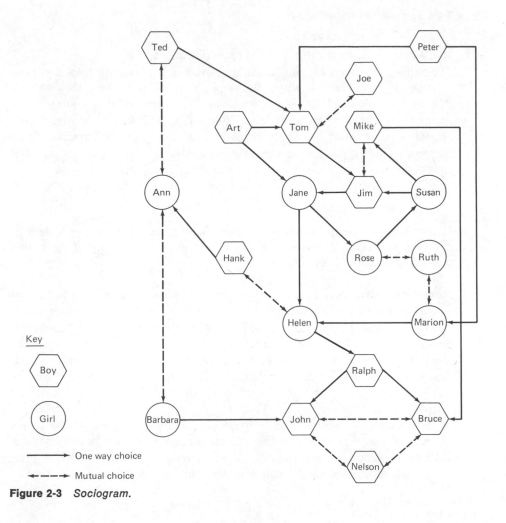

Figure 2-3 *Sociogram.*

choice by an arrow. Show mutual choices by a double arrow. Dislike may be shown by using dotted or colored lines.[2]

An example of a sociogram built by this method appears as Figure 2-3. Some authorities recommend more complex sociograms, but probably this type of sociogram will suffice for all your needs in the classroom.

Exercise:

Construct a sociogram from the information in Table 2-1. Then, interpret the sociogram appearing as Fig. 2-3.

Table 2-1 Sociogram

Students listed in the left-hand column have chosen to work with students in the right-hand columns. Make a sociogram of the group. Interpret the sociogram.

	FIRST CHOICE	SECOND CHOICE
Barbara	Agnes	Elaine
Mary	Helen	Barbara
Helen	Mary	Carol
Pat	Mary	Helen
Carol	Bill	Tom
Agnes	Barbara	Elaine
Elaine	Agnes	Barbara
James	Paul	Tom
Paul	Carol	James
Bill	Tom	Carol
Tom	James	Paul

b. The Guess Who Test. Guess Who Tests can be used to find leads concerning such things as pupils' habits, interests, friendships, hobbies, and problems. These tests are easy to construct. All that is necessary is to make up a series of statements such as the following:

(1) This person likes to read.

(2) This person is always worrying.

(3) This person has lots of dates.

Then ask the pupils in the class to identify the classmates each of the statements describes.

Exercise:

Complete this Guess Who Test.

1. This person is always reading.

2. This person is crazy about baseball.

3. _____

[2] Leonard H. Clark and Irving S. Starr, *Secondary School Teaching Methods,* 3rd ed. (New York: Macmillan Publishing Company, Inc., 1976) p. 346.

A Couple of Examples. Following is an excerpt from a case study of a high school pupil prepared by a student teacher.

If you were to teach Mike, what more information would you want to have? What sources could you use to get this information?

Case Study of A Pupil

The student I studied was a 16-year-old Negro boy. He is 5 feet, 8 inches tall weighs about 145 pounds, and is a very neat dresser. He has one brother and two sisters, and lives in the downtown area of _____. His father is a service station mechanic and his mother works part-time as a waitress. He has a very active mind and can't stay interested in one thing too long, but once something does interest him, he becomes very inquisitive. Most of the time he is very well mannered.

Mike is in the second period American History class, which is a slow group with a few discipline problems in this section. Mike is passing history through his efforts in class and his performance on tests. Speaking to Mike before class one day, I asked what he wants to do after he graduates, and he told me that he wants to join the army and make it his career. I asked why he wanted to join the army, and he said he thought a soldier's life was very exciting and filled with adventure. I said I certainly agreed with him and I wished him success in attaining his goal. At least Mike has some sort of constructive aspiration for his future and seems determined to achieve his goal. Most people his age are confused and undecided about what they really want to be in life.

Observations of Mike:

4/16—I went to the cafeteria to buy a container of orange juice, and I found out that Mike helped out in the cafeteria before the lunch session starts. When he saw me in the teacher's cafeteria he asked if I ate alone, and I told him I ate in the teacher's room with the other teachers. He was glad when I told him this, for he said the teachers around here are too snobby to new people to sit at their tables. I thought he was being very thoughtful to ask and decided to make him the student I would do my case study on because he has a very interesting personality.

4/17—I was giving out answer papers for the test the students were about to take, and Mike was the only student to say thank you after I handed him a piece of paper. After the test the teacher asked for the answers to the homework questions, and Mike was exceptionally anxious to answer the questions.

4/21—This wasn't a good day for Mike. Mike didn't have any paper to write answers to reference questions with, and he was clowning around so much that the teacher had to scold him. He asked me a question about the slave issue in the South when the answer was right in the textbook, but he said he could not find it. Then he made a paper airplane and the teacher found it on his desk and accused him of being the one who was throwing paper airplanes around the classroom two weeks ago. He said he made it a month ago and just found it in his book now. The teacher took it from him and threw it away.

4/23—Mike had no homework because he was absent the day the assignment was given. The teacher asked why he did not come to him for the questions, but Mike had no excuse. He had no cover on his text so the teacer told him to get the book covered for the following day or penalties will be dealt to him and to others who did not cover their books.

Mike didn't fail any subjects the past marking period, and he received a C in history, and that is what he was working for.

My opinion of Mike is that he wants to learn but his mind is too active and he is unable to direct his thinking in a scholastic direction. In order to teach Mike, you must always make your lectures and discussion periods very exciting and interesting.

The following information concerns a twelfth-grade chemistry student. The information was gathered by talks with his teachers, his guidance counselor, and the health office.

Subject: Caucasian, male, 5′10″, blonde hair.
Birth: 1/13/52   in Philadelphia, Pennsylvania.
Father's Name: James.   Home: Washington, D.C.
Mother's Name: Joan.   Home: Atlanta, Georgia.
Father's Occupation: Warehouseman.
I.Q. Result: 93.
Health Record: 19– 58/59   Poor teeth.
                       59/60   Large tonsils.
                       60/61   Very large tonsils, poor teeth.
                       61/62   Infected tonsils.
                       62/63   Enlarged tonsils.
Favorite Hobbies: Girls, models, movies, hunting, swimming.
Plans upon graduation: Go to college.
What do you eventually hope to do?: Go to college.
Activities: Boy Scouts, High School Band.
Tests: Grade Equivalent-Word Knowledge,   10.
                            Reading,   8.3.
         Otis Gamma I.Q.,   103.
Guidance comments on test results: Unsatisfactory growth in reading.
                            Poor achievement in mathematics.

Teachers: English   Jones.
            U.S. History   Smith.
            Ac. Chemistry   Anderson.
            Geometry   Peattie.
            Spanish II   Bartlett.
            Phys. Ed.   Schwann.
Teacher Comments: A. Immature but hard worker.
                    B. He is quiet, never volunteers, and is failing the course.
Guidance Counselor comments: He seems average. His work may be poor because he didn't work hard enough at the beginning of the year and now has to work hard to catch up. He is worried about his size and therefore may see himself as unable to compete and achieve. His friends seem to be both active and quiet, sort of balanced. Possibly he is actually quite alone. He may be older and heavier, possibly even self-conscious. He does well in gym but shouldn't if he is really self-conscious. He lives in a town which is considered a slum area. I believe that his parents are concerned about his education.
Excerpt from Observation Report:

If I had more data, I believe I could make a better judgment than that which I shall make with what is available. The boy seems either bored by the classwork or sees no need to learn certain subjects. He just sits in class, not talking to anyone. In three weeks, the most he said was no when answering a teacher's question. I checked other classes and again none of his classmates spoke to him. He sat with his notebook open and pencil in hand but never took notes. At least I would expect him to draw or doodle with the book open and 50 minutes to write anything down. He just seemed to come in like the tide and go out the same way. I never observed him speaking to any friends that the guidance counselor spoke of.

Problem:

⌐If you were this boy's teacher, how could you use this information? What other information would you like to have in order to help this pupil? How would you get it? How would you use it?

Motivation

A primary objective of the effective teacher is to so motivate pupils that they will endeavor to use their own resources in their learning rather than relying on spoon-feeding from their teacher. Pupils who can attain such intellectual independence can go on to educate themselves when they have left school and no longer have a teacher to fall back on. Pupils who have been spoon-fed cannot.

The experienced teacher knows that if he is to motivate his pupils he must teach many things beside book studies. In our public schools, there will always be some pupils who have not learned to read with understanding, and without comprehension, there is no interest. Such pupils must depend upon the teacher for the interest they take in school. There are many ways for the teacher to supply this interest. The *silent demonstration, role playing, games,* and *simulation* are but a few examples of the kind of devices which can be used. These are described in other modules.

If the teacher is patient enough and willing to explore, he may discover that each pupil has a special proclivity. On the surface, this may appear unrelated to the subject matter being taught. Yet, with some ingenuity on the teacher's part, it may well be the means by which to involve the pupil. For example, in one science class at the secondary level, a teacher became aware of John's dawdling in the back of the classroom. After an informal conversation, the teacher learned that John loved to draw. The teacher gradually drew John out by having him make charts for the class. These charts were displayed prominently. Drawing them helped John to better understand what the class was learning, and the fact that he was playing such an important role in what they were doing gave him the recognition and feeling of adequacy for which he thirsted. This incident is but one example of how boredom and apathy can be turned into enthusiasm and motivation for further inquiry. It is important to keep in mind that this is a most critical period of the pupils' lives, the potential turning-off period in their education. Whatever impression is made upon them now may be final. If pupils become disgusted with the boredom and confinement of school and associate learning with pain and repulsiveness, injury done to their attitudes toward education may be irreparable. If, on the other hand, the teacher is really skillful, and excites in pupils a spirit of inquiry and curiosity, leading them to observe, to think, to explore and to feel that school is a stimulating experience, all will be enriched in the process.

Some general suggestions that you might use to help you foster proper motivation include the following:

1. Provide a supportive atmosphere. Let the pupils know that you are seeing them do their best. Do not put them down. Give them time. Support their attempts. Award their successes and honest attempts. Especially avoid punishing a pupil who tried but did not succeed. After all, we all make mistakes, don't we?

2. Be sure the learnings and activities seem worthwhile. Show the pupil how what they are studying can be useful to them now! Provide an assortment of activities, materials, and content that will appeal to the variety of tastes and interests present in the class. Find special things for special individuals to do. Encourage pupils to cooperate with you in the planning of their own learning activities. Above all, select content that is relevant to their lives and to the needs of the community, and be sure they know why it is important and relevant for them personally. Never start them off on an activity without being sure they know why they should do it!

3. Keep things lively. Do not let them drag. Keep the pupils informed of their progress. Involve them in their own learning. Utilize active activities rather than passive ones. Be sure the work is difficult enough to be challenging, but not too difficult. Do not baby pupils, but do not frustrate them either.

4. Be sure the pupils know what to do and how to do it. If they don't know what to do, when to do it, and how to do it, how can you expect them to do it? So be sure your directions, assignment, and time schedule are clear. Teach and show them what to do, and how to do it, and set standards so that they will know when they are doing well.

5. Take advantage of the pupils' motives. Use their interests, ideals, goals, and attitudes. Appeal to their curiosity, pride, desire for fun, need for achievement, and social interests.

6. Try to run a happy ship. Make the classroom atmosphere as pleasant as possible. Try to make what you have to teach seem attractive. A little fun or humor once in a while seldom hurts.

7. Introduce variety and novelty. Too many classes are humdrum repetitions of the same sort of stuff done in the same old way. Boredom seldom motivates pupils to study well, so vary your approach and the kinds of materials and content you use. Bring in new material, change the seating arrangement, put up new displays on the bulletin board, use unusual activities, play music, show pictures—in short, do anything that will make your class sprightly and profitable, and avoid the deadly rehashing of the text day after day, so common in schools.

8. Reinforce the type of activity you want to encourage. Try not to reinforce untoward behavior. We shall explain this advice later in the module.

9. Be enthusiastic about what you teach, and show your enthusiasm in your teaching. If you are enthusiastic, your enthusiasm may rub off on the pupils.

10. Personalize your teaching. Treat the pupils as individuals. Call them by

name, chat with them about their personal interests, and extracurricular life. Compliment them when they look good or do well, both in class and out. Follow their lives outside class as much as you can. Try to build up their self-concepts, show them that you are interested in them and respect them, and aim your teaching at their individual needs, interests, and goals by adjusting your courses and lessons for them and providing special experiences for individual pupils. Try your best never to let any pupil get lost in the crowd.

11. Try to build pupils' trust in you. Careful preparation, hard work, good teaching techniques, empathy, respect for your pupils, fairness, and justice will help you here. Trust is something you cannot create unless you deserve it. Try to earn it.

12. Try to use interesting strategies and tactics. Examples of the many different teaching methods that can be used to arouse interest and sharpen productive motivation are as follows:

   a. Special projects, both individual and group.
   b. Real-life situations in which pupils do real things.
   c. Simulations and role playing.
   d. Games (adaptations of "Hollywood Squares" and "Jeopardy").
   e. Value clarification techniques.
   f. Problem solving and action (attempts to solve a real community problem).
   g. Building real things.
   h. Use of overhead projector, maps, globes, charts, pictures, and other audio-visual aids, and media.
   i. Real discussions on real topics.

Prepare a list of specific techniques by which the teacher could have made classes more interesting to you.

Reinforcement Theory and Motivation. One of the theories of modern psychology holds that people tend to behave in ways that have paid off in some sort of reward that they find valuable. This is called reinforcement theory because it is based on the belief that rewards or gratifying results strengthen a tendency to behave in a certain fashion, and lack of reward weakens the tendency to act in that fashion. For instance, if a pupil is allowed free time for his own purposes when he works well for a certain period, the pupil may work for that reward and develop higher standards for work in the future. This theory seems to hold many implications for the motivation and control of student behavior.

Unfortunately, this theory has been honored in the breach in all too many cases. Frequently, teachers unintentionally reinforce the wrong behavior. When the pupil who is seeking attention misbehaves, we reward him by reprimanding him, thus giving him the attention he craves, but when he behaves well, we ignore him. We reinforce the bad behavior and neglect the good behavior and, as a result, strengthen his tendency to misbehave and weaken his inclinations to behave well.

There are several types of rewards that can be used to reinforce desirable student behavior. Among them are tangible rewards (such as athletic passes), social rewards (such as being assistant coach or teacher), activities (preparing a bulletin board or doing free reading), and intrinsic rewards (deriving pleasure from doing the activity). List examples of rewards in each category that would be suitable for a course you might teach.

Observe a class or think back over your own classroom experience. What behaviors were rewards? What were not? Do you find examples of pupils being rewarded for being quiet, for being cooperative, and so on? Do you find examples of pupils being rewarded for misbehaving? Remember, sometimes a punishment can be a reward. Can you think of examples when this is so? Sometimes success or doing an activity is its own reward. Can you think of an example when this is so? What specific examples of reinforcement do you see in your own classes?

Following are some principles of reinforcement that may be helpful to you in motivating and controlling pupils.

REINFORCEMENT PRINCIPLES:

1. Try to reinforce new behavior by rewarding it every time it occurs.
2. Then, when the behavior has been established fairly consistently, gradually reduce the frequency of reinforcement until finally the reinforcement occurs only occasionally at haphazard intervals. Such intermittent reinforcement is much more effective for maintaining an established behavior than frequent or regular reinforcement.
3. At first, reward the behavior as soon as it occurs. Then, as the pupil becomes more confident, you may delay the reward somewhat.
4. Try to use rewards that are suitable for each pupil. Remember that what is rewarding for one pupil may be punishing to another. (Also, what may be a punishment for one pupil, or what you may think to be a punishment may be rewarding to another.) Remember also that performing the act or improving one's competency may be its own reward. Probably a mix of tangible rewards, social rewards, rewarding activities and feedback, and success activities will prove the most satisfactory. If possible, try to see to it that the performance itself is rewarding.

   It is, of course, advantageous if the pupils can select their own rewards. For this purpose, the reinforcement menus described in a later section of this module can be very helpful.
5. In using rewards with recalcitrant pupils, it is wise to start small. Sometimes, it is very hard to find anything really commendable in a pupil's work at first. Therefore, you should reward such pupils when they do better and keep rewarding small improvements until the pupil achieves the behavior desired.
6. Utilize contingency contracts.

CONTINGENCY CONTRACTS. Contingency contracts were first developed by L. E. Homme[3] from the common practice that he calls Grandma's law: if first you do this, then you can do that, or have that. Most of us remember this law as, "You don't get any ice cream until you finish eating your vegetables." Clarizio describes contract categories as follows:

In the school setting, the contract specifies that the student can engage in an enjoyable high preference task, for example, art activities, or will receive a very de-

---

[3] L. E. Homme, *How to Use Contingency Contracting in the Classroom* (Urbana, Ill.: Rescard Press, 1969).

sirable tangible or social reward, if he first engages in a low preference task, for example, a math assignment. To be effective, the contract must offer a reward that is, (a) highly attractive and (b) not obtainable outside the conditions of the contract.[4]

When the pupils find it difficult to meet the terms of the contingency contract or it becomes evident that their motivation is slipping, teachers should feel free to re-negotiate the contract.

Set up a contingency contract that you could use in your course. Use rewards that you could offer in the course or classroom without impinging on the time or prerogatives of other teachers.

REINFORCEMENT MENUS. The reinforcement menu is a close cousin of the contingency contract. It consists of a list of activities a pupil can do if he completes a certain assignment according to certain conditions. These activities may be purely recreational or strictly educational, but they must be of high value to the pupils if they are to be effective. Reading a comic book might be a useful activity for this purpose.

Complete the following reinforcement menu:
1. Read a comic book.
2. _____.
3. _____.
4. _____.
5. _____.
6. _____.
7. _____.

Modeling. Pupils of school age learn most of their behavior by imitating others. If we can provide them with good prestigious models that they will pattern themselves after, we shall do much to achieve the kind of behavior we seek. For this reason, you should try to be a good model. It may also be possible to harness pupils' admiration for older students, highly regarded pupils, natural peer group leaders and such admired personalities as stars of sports, screen, television, or world figures. Unfortunately, such personages are not always available or reliable. However, fictional and historical characters are always available in books and other media. It may be possible to use such characters to great advantage.

What characters in television might one harness as models for creating the type of behavior you wish in your classes? What could you do to harness these models?

During a model United Nations assembly debate, a matter came up that, according to the UN rules, can only be decided by Security Council vote. Pupils, representing countries not in the Security Council, protested because they felt they should be allowed to vote. They argued that to forbid them the right to vote just because the countries they represented were not members of the Security Council was ridiculous.

How would you handle this situation?

[4] Harvey F. Clarizio, *Toward Positive Classroom Discipline* (New York: John Wiley & Sons, Inc., 1971), p. 42.

Discipline and Control

Presumably, if we are successful in eliciting strong motivation in our students favorable to our courses and teaching, we shall have nothing to worry about as far as the pupils' behavior in our classes is concerned. However, we should probably examine much more carefully and extensively some of the ways we can encourage desirable pupil behavior and discourage undesirable pupil behavior. This we shall do in this section of the module. First, however, a word about what good discipline is.

In the schools of today, the classroom atmosphere is more likely to be, in the words of the lyricist, "more free and easy," and teachers, "more bright and breezy" than they were in the days of our grandparents when "reading and writing and 'rithmetic" were "taught to the tune of a hickory stick." Nevertheless, this swing toward pleasantness and permissiveness does not mean that teachers can abdicate. Even though silence is no longer a *sine qua non* and repressive classes are considered taboo, every teacher is charged with the responsibility of seeing to it that the classroom atmosphere is favorable to learning. Learning does not usually occur in disorderly, noisy classes. The degree of quiet and kind of order necessary depends somewhat on the type of class. Laboratory sessions allow for a great amount of conversation and movement; lecture sessions require quiet attention; and discussions, purposeful conversation. Work sessions in schoolrooms resemble work sessions in business or industry, periods in which many things are happening, most of which it is hoped, will be productively directed toward the job at hand.

Sometimes, beginning teachers misunderstand the new philosophy of classroom atmosphere and assume that the permissive classroom atmosphere means that anything goes. Such teachers are way off base; the pupils will soon tag them out. Orderliness is essential. Permissiveness, as used in this context, merely means that the teaching should support the pupil in his efforts to learn and not clamp him down tightly in a pattern that would keep him from thinking for himself. In a permissive class, pupils are encouraged to seek out and express their own ideas without fear of reprisals because of honest mistakes. In a permissive class, misbehavior should not be tolerated any more than it would be in a traditional class.

Another belief that seems to confuse young teachers is that correction and strict control will be harmful to the mental health of pupils. Quite the contrary is true. Pupils evidently benefit from the maintenance of high standards and strict discipline; laissez-faire teaching, in contrast, can be downright harmful. Evidently, mental health is best fostered by democratic teaching in strictly controlled classes. This is known as democratic discipline.

Self-discipline. The best discipline is self-discipline. If one can teach pupils to take over the responsibility for their own learning and to carry out this responsibility, he has done much. Some of the ways teachers work to help pupils become self-disciplined include the following:

1. Help pupils establish a code of conduct for themselves. Doing so has the advantage of acquainting pupils with what acceptable behavior is and why such behavior is necessary for the success of the group or of society. This code should not be dictated by the teacher, but worked out together to the mutual satisfaction of all concerned if it is to be successful.

2. Help pupils improve their own standards of conduct. This must be a slow process. It is done by making pupils aware of the advantages to them of high standards and the disadvantages of the lower standards. Techniques such as value-clarifying questions and discussions should be helpful in the process.

3. Use the enforcement of rules as a tool. Sometimes, enforcing rules helps pupils learn to discipline themselves. Proper enforcement of rules and making pupils follow the rules tend to make desirable behavior habitual. Teachers also have had good success by talking out behavior problems with the pupils so they can see why the behavior is unacceptable, what the pupil should do about it as penance, and the remedy to the fault. In some classes pupils enforce many of the rules themselves. This procedure may work well for mature groups, but it is likely to throw too much burden on the pupils. Probably it is best for the teacher to assume all the responsibility for rule enforcement.

Achieving Classroom Control

Why Pupils Misbehave. Pupils misbehave for many reasons. One is the sheer deviltry of it. Classroom situations are somewhat unnatural, restrictive situations, so pupils like to relieve the tension. Other reasons for misbehavior may stem from their family and community backgrounds or their emotional life. Some misbehavior is simply the outburst of the restlessness, rowdiness, and exuberance of youth. But much of pupil misbehavior is school-caused and teacher-caused. Classes are tedious and boring. The curriculum seems worthless and irrelevant to anything that is important to youth. When their schooling is often so far removed from the pupils' lives, it is no wonder that they lose interest, become inattentive, and direct their energies into, what to them, seem more productive, fulfilling activities. Furthermore, many teachers and their classes are unpleasant, repressive, and abrasive. Irrelevance, tedium, unpleasantness, repression, and boredom all contain the seeds of misbehavior.

A Positive Approach. To accentuate the positive is a good motto for teachers who are seeking to establish and maintain control of their classes. Teachers who foster a pleasant, positive atmosphere in their classes find discipline much less a problem than teachers whose classes seem harsh and repressive. Therefore, in your teaching try to emphasize the do's, not the don'ts; the rewards, not the punishment; the joy of learning, not the pain of studying or the fear of failure.

The first ingredient for creating a productive classroom atmosphere is a pleasant teacher whose classroom personality is characterized by "empathy, warmth and genuineness"[5] and who does not take himself too seriously. Self-centered teachers, who worry about how they will appear and how classroom incidents will affect them, are much more likely to have difficulty than teachers whose interests center on their pupils and on how classroom incidents will affect their pupils. Therefore, go in there and teach the best you can. Act with confidence but without arrogance, and everything will probably go well. If you concentrate on teaching well and if your plans and procedures are reasonably good, discipline

---

[5] Duane Brown, *Changing Student Behavior: A New Approach to Discipline* (Dubuque, Iowa: William C. Brown Company, Publishers, 1971), p. 12.

may take care of itself. Also, you would do well to develop an active interest in your pupils, a friendly attitude, an interesting personality, and a sense of humor if you wish to avoid discipline problems. Above all, show that you enjoy teaching, studying, and working with pupils. Attitudes are contagious. If you show that you are enthusiastic about what you teach and teach joyously, your pupils may become enthusiastic too. Approach your teaching with pleasure and with confidence. If you concentrate on teaching in a businesslike, confident manner, you will probably be well on the road to having the kind of classroom control you desire.

Although every teacher should be friendly with his pupils, it does not pay to become too chummy with them. Avoid entangling alliances, teacher's pets, and boon companionship. Teachers should be adults, behave as adults, and socialize with adults. Pupils will like them better that way, and then there is no danger of playing favorites or of pupils attempting to take advantage of friendship.

In the final analysis, what we are trying to say is that the teacher should set a good example. If the pupils realize that a teacher is trying his best to serve them well and that he really cares for them as people, they will probably respond well to his teaching.

Well-Planned Classes. Good planning can prevent many problems of discipline and control. Poorly planned classes that wander, or in which pupils have nothing to do, or that seem worthless, or that are dull and drab, have the seeds of discipline problems in them. As we pointed out earlier, *ad lib* teaching is sloppy teaching, and sloppy teaching leads to control problems. To prevent or minimize problems of this sort, the teacher should take care in planning. The following suggestions should help:

1. Furnish the pupils with sufficient purposeful activities to keep them busy and active. The devil makes work for idle hands, so be sure the pupils have plenty of worthwhile things to do.
2. Beware of scheduling too much time for lectures or teacher talk. One fifth of the class time is usually about all of the time that should be given to such activities. Most classes get restless after more than twenty minutes of straight lecture. If you must lecture, and sometimes it may be the only practicable procedure, then plan to lighten your lecture with key questions, audio-visual aids, or some other interest-catching tactic.
3. Provide for individual differences in your planning. Be sure pupils know what to do and how to do it. If necessary, provide instruction in how to study the lesson, how to use the equipment or reference, and how to do the assignment. Plan the lesson so that it keeps the class moving quickly with no deal spots. Furnish plenty of all the necessary materials. Be sure they are ready for use at the time they can be used. Allow for pupils' predispositions. Let your plan fit the nature of the pupil but, if for some reason his mood is not what you expected, be ready to adjust your plan to meet the occasion if it seems necessary. Any plan that combats the natural inclinations of the pupils is likely to go down in defeat. Unreasonable expectations, such as absolute quiet from an excited student body, will lead only to complications.
4. Provide for good motivation. The lesson plan should seem interesting, challenging, and valuable to the pupils. Avoid planning classes that repeat

the same deadly routine day after day after day. This is the type of class that so often results from ad lib teaching.

5. Routinize the organizational and administrative details of classroom manner so as to eliminate dead spots and to avoid disorderly breakdowns in classroom decorum. The routines should be part of your plan.

6. Spice up your assignments. Be sure that you tell the pupils clearly what to do and how to do it. It may be necessary to go into great detail, give examples, and demonstrate proper procedures to make everything clear. When pupils are not clear on what they should do or how to do it, they tend to give up easily. In addition, the assignment should seem worthwhile, interesting, relevant, and challenging.

Criticize the following assignment, and rewrite it to meet your specifications: Assignment: Finish Chapter 18, paying special attention to the Radical Reconstruction Program as compared to President Johnson's.

Getting Off to a Good Start. A good beginning may make all the difference in preventing disrupting control problems. Therefore, you should appear at the first class as well prepared and as confident as possible. Undoubtedly, you will feel nervous and apprehensive, but being well prepared will probably help you at least look confident. Then if you proceed in a businesslike, matter-of-fact way, things will probably go well.

Until you gain complete confidence in your control abilities, it is best to be quiet strict and to keep movement in the classroom to a minimum. It is also a good idea to have an alternate plan ready in the event the original plan fails. A written assignment is often a good change for a restless class.

One of the first things you should do is to learn the names of the pupils as soon as you can prepare a seating chart. (See Figure 2-4.) A good technique for making a chart is to prepare slips of paper bearing the names of the pupils, and then as you call the roll, place the name slips into the proper spots in a pocket-type seating chart. If the school does not provide pocket-type charts, you can make them

			Ross Bernard		Chinsky Christine
	Westerman Kathaleen	Healy Thomas	Ghirlanda Ann		Casey Noreen
	Anderson Keith	Wyles Henry	Gallagher Maureen	Matta Theodore	Bush Eleanor
	Pear Constance	Donovan Gayle	Gaffney Edward	Dobrowolski Maryann	Wozniak Helene
	Szper Richard	Kubrak James	Foley Patricia	Debski Christine	Berriz Carmen
	Niedzinski Michael	Adamkiewicz Geraldine	Eyles Janette	Donahue Richard	O'Donnell Sharon

FRONT OF ROOM

ROOM NO. __33__ PERIOD __1st__

TEACHER __J. Sullivan__ SUBJECT __W History__

Figure 2-4 *Seating Chart.*

very easily. You can also make a blank seating chart on which you write in the names during roll call or when the pupils are doing seat work. Then work at learning names and faces just as soon as you can. While pupils are working at their seats, some teachers spend the time trying to associate names and faces and fixing them in their memory. Addressing pupils by name every time you speak to them will help you remember their names.

Classroom Rules. Earlier we spoke about the salutory effect of enforcing rules. Even, just, compassionate but objective enforcement of rules will improve the tenor of your classes if the rules seem reasonable. But sometimes the rules can be a cause of trouble. To avoid this difficulty, you should set up only a few rules. Too many rules may confuse pupils and make the classroom atmosphere too repressive. Ordinarily, these rules should be quite definite and specific so that pupils will know just what is acceptable and what is not. However, a few general principles such as, "rowdy behavior which interferes with other people will not be acceptable," may serve just as well. Whatever rules you select, it is best not to make them too rigid at first. Rigid rules, particularly when there are too many of them, seem to encourage misbehavior. Besides, they may compel you to enforce rules when you really do not think it wise. By sticking to a few rules or principles, you can leave yourself a little room for maneuvering.

Obviously, the rules you decide on should be reasonable ones. Not many people, young or old, will comply with rules that seem unreasonable to them, except under duress, but they will usually accept rules that seem to be reasonable. One of the key words in this statement is *seem*. Pupils will resist reasonable rules if they do not seem to be reasonable. Rules that do not seem reasonable create tension and dissension when one tries to enforce them. For this reason, it may be wise to talk over the reasons for establishing and enforcing these particular rules. At this time, and in this way, one can also make sure that the pupils understand just what abiding by the rules entails.

Make up a list of rules that you feel you should insist on when you teach.

Enforcing Rules. We have already mentioned the fact that reasonably strict enforcement of rules can have a salutory effect on the class and the classroom atmosphere. One reason for this is that enforcement has a ripple effect. When pupils see that you take swift, firm action against infractions by other pupils, they are less likely to misbehave. The ripple effect is especially powerful when you show that you can control pupils who have high status in their peer group. Conversely, when pupils see that others are getting away with breaking the rules, they lose respect for the rules and for the teacher. To gain the most advantage of the ripple effect, teachers should start a policy of strict enforcement on the very first day. Being lax in the beginning is to court disaster. It is much easier to relax a policy of strict enforcement later than it is to turn a class around.

Other important points in rules enforcement are consistency and fairness. Fairness and consistency in enforcement does not mean mindless conformity to an enforcement pattern. Sometimes justice should be tempered with mercy, and sometimes the nature of the punishment should be adjusted to the nature of the offender as well as to the nature of the offense.

On the whole, positive methods of rule enforcement art preferable to negative means. Methods of enforcement that are not effective and that should be avoided include the following:

NAGGING. Continual or unnecessary scolding or criticizing of a pupil succeeds only in upsetting the pupil and arousing the resentment of other pupils.

HARSH PUNISHMENT. Flogging, beating, tongue lashing, and humiliation are seldom effective. Although it may well be that occasionally some pupils need to be told off, hurting or humiliating them may do much more harm than good.

THREATS AND ULTIMATUMS. Once you have made a threat or ultimatum, you are stuck with it if the pupils call you. In maintaining discipline, threats become promises. Once made, they must be carried out, or you will lose control. If pupils learn that your threats are impotent, they will disregard them and you.

Correcting Misbehavior. The goal of classroom control is to so motivate and shape the pupils that they do not create discipline problems. Positive motivation is a preventative measure that is the real key to classroom control. When pupils are working well, control and discipline take care of themselves. Nevertheless, even in the best of classes, the behavior of some pupils is less than desirable and needs to be turned into new directions.

Theoretically, there are four basic ways to stop anyone from behaving in an undesirable way. One is by satiation which means to keep the offender at it until he gets sick of it. A second is make sure that the undesirable behavior is not rewarded in any way and so dies out. A third approach is to provide an alternative that is incompatible with the undesirable behavior, and to see to it that the alternate behavior is rewarded but the undesirable behavior is not. The fourth method is to create an aversive situation which the person can relieve only by giving up the undesirable behavior. The principles on which these methods are based are called, respectively, the satiation principle, the extinction principle, the incompatible alternative principle, and the negative reinforcement principle. A fifth principle calls for punishment or results supposedly so unpleasant that the person will not willingly repeat the misbehavior again.

Satiation and extinction are seldom practicable measures for correcting unseemly behavior. Therefore, teachers can depend only on incompatible alternatives, negative reinforcement, and punishment to correct misbehavior. The incompatible alternative and the negative reinforcement are likely to be more successful than is punishment.

In the incompatible alternative method, the teacher sets up an alternative behavior which is so rewarding that the pupil forsakes the misbehavior. To find extremely strong, usable rewards suitable to the classroom situation may be difficult, but they do exist, as we pointed out in the discussion of the reinforcement menu. The catch, of course, is that the reward for the alternative behavior must be very powerful so as to overshadow the reward derived from the misbehavior.

Assume that one of the girls in your class is a continual talker. Can you think of a high-status reward activity that might cause her to keep quiet?

The negative reinforcement method is much more subtle. In this method, the teacher sets up an aversive situation, designed to plague the pupil as long as he misbehaves. As soon as he stops misbehaving, then the plaguing stops. The pupil who stops misbehaving is rewarded by relief from pain or annoyance. This approach is a much more effective way to correct student misbehavior than is punishment.

At times it is necessary to fall back on punishment in attempts to cure a malefactor. When this time comes, a teacher should attempt to make the punishment appropriate to the misdeed and also swift, sure, and impressive. The pupil should have no doubt that he is being punished, why he is being punished, and the types of behavior that will prevent his being punished again. Among the punishments often used are isolation, reprimands, extra work, deprivation of privileges, and detention. None of them is very effective in the long run. In the short term, however, they may shake up the pupil enough so that more positive measures can be used with greater chances of success.

What is the principal difference between negative reinforcement and punishment? Give examples of each.

Classroom Management

Good classroom management makes good classroom discipline and control easier to maintain. After all, classroom management is simply the process of keeping things neat and orderly.

Appearance of the Classroom.   A pleasant, neat, comfortable, and bright classroom helps to provide an atmosphere favorable to good discipline. When things look nice, you usually do not wish to mess them up. Therefore, it pays to keep the classroom as attractive as possible. It is surprising how much you and your pupils can do to make even the most drab classroom a pleasant place if you put your minds to it.

The first things to do to improve the classroom's appearance and pupil attitudes is to keep the classroom neat and orderly. Provide a place for everything and try to keep everything in its place. Tidy up, clean up, and put things away after using them. Improve the classroom atmosphere by brightening it up. Use displays, murals, bulletin boards, posters, and pictures. If you lack tack boards or display areas, extemporize. Use the new adhesives that allow you to fasten things directly to the wall without marring it, or cover the wall with murals drawn on wrapping paper. Cover the walls with wrapping paper and let your grafitti artists decorate them (be sure not to use paint or ink that will stain through and injure the wall). Use lots of pictures. Preferably, these should all be pertinent to what you are teaching, and should be changed every few weeks so as to keep the classroom bright and interesting.

Pay attention to the light, heat, and ventilation. A hot, stuffy classroom can kill motivation and control. So can classrooms that are too dark or in which pupils are facing a glare.

Most college classrooms are quite drab. Plan how you could brighten up a drab classroom in your school to make it more attractive.

Clarifying by Routinizing. Routinizing the humdrum day after day tasks is another aid to establishing good motivation and discipline. Pupils are more likely to do things without argument or disruption when they are used to doing them and doing them in a certain way. If you set up routines for various everyday functions, pupils will always know what to do. In this way, you can reduce fuss and confusion. Just what routine you select does not really matter, as long as it seems reasonably efficient. Among the common tasks that need routinizing are taking attendance, issuing equipment and supplies, collecting and passing papers, starting class, and stopping class.

Two examples of problems in motivation and planning follow.

Mrs. Jones taught twelfth graders in an American History II class. No lesson plan was used, and a problem arose during a unit dealing with the Eisenhower Administration. Mrs. Jones doesn't even write out general goals to be accomplished. The teacher distributed as a homework assignment mimeographed copies of an article by Archibald MacLeish discussing the "Swing Right." There were seniors in the class, some about to leave for a work-study program, and only about five were interested in what Archibald MacLeish had to say about conservatism in America. Mrs. Jones tried to start a discussion, and when, in frustration, she asked how many had read the article, only two students raised their hands. After about five minutes of scolding, she said that she would attempt to carry on a discussion with the two who had read the article.

How could Mrs. Jones have avoided this fiasco? What could she have done to salvage the situation?

We have a young person—small, different from the rest of the class—who tends to monologue. The other children seem to dislike her. She wants to answer all the questions. When she does, the other pupils make remarks to each other and make faces. The student teacher does not interrupt her because he is afraid of hurting her feelings. Neither does he speak to the other pupils. This is an eighth-grade class.

How would you handle this girl and others in the class?

SUGGESTED READING

Brown, Duane. *Changing Student Behavior: A New Approach to Discipline.* Dubuque, Iowa: Wm. C. Brown Co., Publishers, 1971.

Clarizio, Harvey F. *Toward Positive Classroom Discipline.* New York: John Wiley & Sons, Inc., 1971.

Davis, Jean E. *Coping with Disruptive Behavior,* "What Research Says to the Teacher" series. Washington, D.C.: National Education Association, 1974.

Frymier, Jack R. *Motivation and Learning in School.* Bloomington, Ind.: Phi Delta Kappa Educational Foundation, 1974.

Jessup, M., and M. Kelley. *Discipline: Positive Attitudes for Learning.* Englewood Cliffs, N.J.: Prentice-Hall, Inc., 1971.

Kounin, Jacob S. *Discipline and Group Management in the Classroom.* New York: Holt, Rinehart & Winston, Inc., 1970.

Krumboltz, John D., and Helen B. Krumboltz. *Changing Children's Behavior.* Englewood Cliffs, N.J.: Prentice-Hall, Inc., 1972.

Madsen, Charles H., Jr., and Clifford K. Madsen. *Teaching Discipline.* Boston: Allyn & Bacon, Inc., 1974.

Marx, Melvin H., and Tom N. Tombaugh. *Motivation: Psychological Principles and Educational Implications.* San Francisco, Calif.: Chandler Publishing Co., 1967.

Meacham, Merle L., and Allen E. Wiesen. *Changing Classroom Behavior,* 2nd ed. Scranton, Pa.: Intext Educational Publishers, 1974.

Sloane, Howard N., Jr., and Donald A. Jackson. *Guide to Motivating Learners.* Englewood Cliffs, N.J.: Educational Technology Publications, 1974.

Wiener, Daniel N. *Classroom Management and Discipline.* Itasca, Ill.: F. E. Peacock Publishers, Inc., 1972.

POST TEST

1. What would you expect to find in a cumulative record folder?

_____

_____

_____

2. In a pupil conference, is it usually preferable to ask open-ended or closed questions?

_____

3. What is the purpose of an interest finder?

_____

4. In a sociogram you noticed the following:

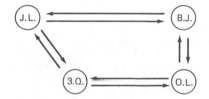

(In this sociogram circles indicate girls)

What would you interpret this as meaning?

_____

5. In a sociogram a large number of arrows point to /m\. What does this probably mean?

_____

6. List five general suggestions for encouraging pupil motivation favorable to your class work.

_____

_____

_____

_____

_____

7. According to reinforcement theory, which is usually preferable, to reward or to punish?

   _____

8. When using rewards in early reinforcement, which is preferable, immediate or deferred reward?

   _____

9. What is a reinforcement menu?

   _____

   _____

10. Plutarch, the Roman writer, tried to build character in boys by providing models for them to imitate. According to modern theory, was his basic idea sound?

    _____

    _____

11. Why do we advise teachers to avoid laissez-faire teaching?

    _____

    _____

    _____

12. Name one strategy that might help pupils to improve their own standards of conduct.

    _____

    _____

    _____

13. What is probably the most common cause of pupil misbehavior?

    _____

14. A new teacher was told never to smile in her classes until she has established firm control. Is this sound advice?

    _____

    _____

15. Would you advise a new teacher to set up a long list of rigid rules?

    _____

    _____

16. According to this module, which is the better technique: to be very strict at first and then relax when you have established control, or to be relaxed at first and become strict later if pupils misbehave?

_____

_____

_____

17. What is negative reinforcement?

_____

_____

_____

18. What is the incompatible alternative method of control?

_____

_____

Lecture, Questioning, and Practice Techniques

William B. Fisher

Jersey City State College

module 3

Lectures and Lecturing / Questioning / Drill and Practice / Memorization / Reviews and Reviewing

INTRODUCTION AND RATIONALE

Every teacher, before he begins the work of instruction, should have some definite idea of what constitutes education; otherwise, he may work to very little purpose. The painter, who would execute a beautiful picture, must have beforehand a true and clear conception of beauty in his own mind. The same may be said of a sculptor. The crude block of marble, unsightly to the eyes of others, contains the godlike form, the symmetrical proportion, the lifelike attitude of the finished and polished statue; and before the chisel has its purpose, the intended form is clear to the artist's mental eye. Not a blow is struck that is not guided by consummate skill; not a chip is removed that does not develop the ideal of the artist. When the once unsightly marble, as if by miraculous power, stands before the astonished spectator in all the perfection of beauty, it is to the artist the realization of his own conception.

Now let the same astonished and delighted spectator, with the same instruments, attempt to produce another statue from a similar block. On one side, he scores too deeply; on the other, he leaves a protuberance; here, by carelessness, he encroaches upon the rounded limb; there, by accident, he hews a chip from off the nose; from want of skill one eye does not match the other; one hand is distorted; the other is paralyzed. Such would be his signal of failure. It would be a strange surprise if in a thousand efforts he would succeed once.

Two significant factors differentiate the artist from the spectator. One is the ability to formulate a plan based upon objectives, and the other is the technical skill required to execute the plan. In this module, we shall concentrate on some of the technical skills one must conquer to become a master teacher.

Today, teachers have entered a period of "professional competency." As professionals they know what they want and ought to do and how to do it. Therefore, if you are to become a professional, it is all-important that you have well-defined educational goals at which to aim. Basically, those aims should be to arouse each pupil to think for himself and to awaken his power to observe, to remember, to reflect, and to combine.

To achieve these basic objectives, you must develop skill in teaching because, in spite of clichés, most master teachers are made, not born. Aptness for teaching, the cliché tells us, is a native endowment, a sort of instinct—an interest such as that which guides the robin, though hatched in an oven, to build a perfect nest just like that of its parent without ever having seen one. Nonsense! Instincts in man are rare. Ability to teach, as the ability to do anything else, is usually an acquired power derived from a correct knowledge of what is to be done. If there are exceptions to this rule, they are very uncommon. Of course, teachers vary in their ability to execute instructional plans effectively, and to some extent these variations derive from differences in innate skills. However, seeming variations in innate ability are more likely the product of the personal skills and personality traits that a teacher has developed during the normal course of growing up. Therefore, the only safe way for most humans to become master teachers is to study carefully the how and why of the educational processes and to practice diligently, according to the best theory. Each teacher can most effectively harness whatever innate skills and character traits he may possess only through careful definition of objectives, thoughtful planning, and effective execution of his plans.

Knowledge of these procedures can be learned. And so it is imperative that you master the skills required for preparing and giving interesting, informative lectures, for using questions to build concepts and to stimulate thinking, and for carrying out lessons that will both drive concepts home and increase pupils' skills.

In this module, we shall consider the fact that there is no phrase more popular in works on methodology than "learning by discovery." Both John Dewey, the progressive, and William C. Bagley, the essentialist, advocated teaching by discovery. Bagley wrote in 1905 that

The pupil is not to be told, but led to see. Whatever the pupil gains, whatever thought connections he works out, must be gained with consciousness, that he, the pupil is the active agent—that he is, in a sense at least, the discoverer.[1]

Similarly, Jerome Bruner has pointed out that discovery is its own reward, thereby reinforcing the learning that has taken place and stimulating the learner to new efforts in discovery.

Although basic, "learning by discovery" is not achieved by a single, all-purpose method. Indeed, it takes about as many methods and techniques as the teacher can contrive to cause students to learn inductively and thus arrive at conceptual understanding. At the conclusion of your study of this module, you should be able to demonstrate how various methods, specifically, the lecture, the question, the practice activities, and the recitation, can be used to help pupils learn by discovery and to further the basic educational aims: to arouse the pupil to think for himself and to awaken his power to observe, to remember, to reflect, and to combine.

SPECIFIC OBJECTIVES

More specifically, upon the completion of this module, it is expected that you will be able to do the following:

1. Demonstrate how to use the lecture method.
2. Explain the steps to take in planning a lecture.
3. Explain why experts recommend that teachers keep their use of the lecture minimal.
4. Describe at least a half dozen techniques one can use to make the lecture effective.
5. Show how to develop a lesson by the Socratic method.
6. Describe how to conduct an open-book recitation.
7. Show how to use the clarifying-response technique.
8. List seven guidelines for conducting practice activities.
9. Demonstrate the recall method of memorizing.
10. State at least five principles basic to reviewing.

[1] William C. Bagley, *The Education Process* (New York: Macmillan Publishing Co., Inc., 1905), p. 262.

11. Name at least five techniques to use in reviewing.
12. List at least five techniques that should be useful for motivating classes.
13. Develop questions with emphasis upon "how" and "why" questions.
14. Develop questions that require the pupils to compare and contrast.
15. Develop questions that will bring about speculation as to the outcome.
16. Develop questions that will help determine cause and effect.
17. Develop questions that will bring about certain assumptions and the ability to defend those assumptions.
18. Develop questions so that pupils will be able to apply learnings in special context.
19. Develop key questions so that pupils will respond with expected answers which should be heard and acknowledged.
20. Develop questions that will elicit inquiring questions from the pupils.

MODULE TEXT

There are many and varied techniques that are used by teachers in the process of learning. Some, of course, are more effective than others; however, there is no single technique that is most effective with all pupils and all varied disciplines. The teacher must select the best technique for his particular group.

Lectures and Lecturing

In the lecture method the teacher tries to give to the learner by word of mouth knowledge he possesses but the learner does not. This statement applies just as much to short, informal teacher talks as it does to the formal classroom lecture so familiar to college students. Although this definition is true as far as it goes, it is something of an oversimplification. The lecture, when done well, is not only a matter of the teacher's telling learners things they do not know. Skillful lecturers use it to arouse pupil interest, to set pupils to thinking and wondering, to open up new vistas, to tie together loose facts and ideas, to summarize and synthesize quickly, and to review.

Unfortunately, few lecturers are skillful. As a consequence, pupils usually do not learn much from lectures and retain even less. The reasons for this failure are that (1) most lecturers are not good lecturers, and (2) the nature of the lecture tends to make the learner passive. Although physical passivity does not necessarily indicate mental inactivity, all too often desirable mental activity does not result from situations in which one sits and listens. The lecture situation seldom gives pupils a chance to interact or explore. Instead of leading to depth study, lectures too often result in pupils' superficially receiving and accepting knowledge. Other shortcomings of lectures are (1) they provide little reinforcement; (2) pupils seldom really listen unless the lecture is exceptional, one reason why ad lib lecturing is so ineffective; (3) the teacher in the secondary school seldom has time to construct a really stimulating lecture.

Planning the Lecture. The lecture is a presentation developed by the lecturer in a manner which best suits the situation and the level of the audience to whom it is addressed. It must and can be used effectively. A great deal depends upon the personality of the lecturer and the amount of preparation involved in developing the discourse. The lecture should be well planned. As the lecturer, you must determine what you want to say and how to say it. It must be arranged in a manner that will demand instant recall at some later time, rather than act as a lullaby to a passive and inactive audience. To that end, the lecturer's plan should

1. Clearly state the purpose and major theme or themes of the lecture.
2. Develop the lecture in a logical fashion that the pupils can follow.
3. Include clues that point out the logical development of the concepts step by step.
4. Avoid attempting too much. The lecture is the quickest way to present material that cannot be given in writing or by film, but if the lecture rushes on too fast, its impact will be lost. To include only a few important points is usually quite enough. Too often, especially with the inexperienced teacher, lecturing consists of pouring into the pupils every fact that occurs to him. His lectures are focused on bringing to the pupils as many facts as possible in a limited time. Such lecturing is analogous to forced-feeding which can cause resistance and loathing for the food. As in forced-feeding, stuffing educational content into the pupils may result in resistance, loathing, lack of receptiveness, and the turning off of pupils' intellectual curiosity and self-discovery.
5. Begin with some interest-catching device. Often, experienced lecturers say, it is good to puzzle the listeners a little at first in order to catch their interest and to entice them to listen carefully.
6. Provide for the repetition of important points. Repetition is about the only means of reinforcement available to the lecturer.
7. Provide for questions, both real and rhetorical, to check pupils' understanding and to revive their interest at strategic points.
8. Make the lecture as short as you reasonably can.
9. Include humor and the excitement of the unexpected.
10. Provide concrete examples.
11. End with some sort of summarizing device.
12. Finally, follow the advice in the old cliché: First tell them what you are going to tell them, then tell them, and finally tell them what you have told them.

Giving the Lecture. During the lecture, the transfer of knowledge should produce an exhilarating experience. It should develop in the learner a sense of putting things together. To produce this feeling, the skillful lecturer learns to read his audience, feel its reaction, and adjust himself to the response. Therefore, when you lecture you should

1. Be alert to signs of restlessness, boredom, or confusion, and provide some sort of change of pace when such signs occur.
2. Include recapitulation as an aid to the pupil.

3. Point out clues that will help the listener follow the steps in the development of the concept.

4. Use your voice to emphasize and dramatize. Remember that the teacher who lectures is on stage and must use any device that will captivate his audience.

5. Use other methods to complement the lecture. Study guides and outlines that the pupils may follow during the lecture may help, for instance. Any device that you can use to capture your pupils' attention and put across your concepts is legitimate. On occasion, you may wish to use a silent demonstration to bolster your lecture presentation, as in the following example: For a lecture on the relationship of gas volume to temperature change, a lecturer prepared a system consisting of a Bunsen burner heating a retort to which a balloon had been attached. He did not explain the purpose of this system. However, as he lectured on the concept that the heating of a gas tends to increase its volume, the size of the balloon attached to the heated retort increased until finally the balloon burst. By this technique, the lecturer hoped to give the pupils a visual example of the concept he was developing verbally. This technique not only concretized the concept, but also dramatized it. The bursting of the balloon particularly brought forth a strong class response to what might otherwise have been an obscure abstraction.

6. Use incomplete outlines that the pupils complete as the lecture goes on so as to make an active learning situation out of a passive one.

7. Throw in a question, real or rhetorical, from time to time to whet pupils' interest and to start them thinking.

8. Whenever feasible, use audio-visual aids. The use of the chalkboard, the overhead projector, pictures, maps, and graphs not only adds life to your lectures, but usually also makes your ideas clearer. It is easier to understand what you can both see and hear than what you can only hear.

9. Keep your language clear, concise, and as simple as you reasonably can. Avoid pomposity.

10. Try to keep to the point. Digressions, reminiscences, and trivia obscure the message.

11. To be sure that your message is getting across, ask a few check questions once in a while.

12. In your lecture notes, mark those things that you wish to stress by writing them in capital letters, by underlining, or by placing a large star in the margin.

13. Above all, try to excite a spirit of inquiry and create in each pupil a desire to know and, when possible, to discover by himself. Therefore, you must not think for the pupil or give him results before the pupil has been given the opportunity to explore the concepts himself. A teacher who does that makes the mind of the pupil into something resembling a two-gallon jug into which he can pour two gallons, but no more. The mind, so far as retention is concerned, will act as the jug; that is, what is poured in today will be diluted by a part of that which is forced in tomorrow, and that again will be partially displaced and partially mixed with the next day's pouring until, at the end, there will be nothing characteristic left. The jug may be as good after such use as before, but the mind suffers by every

unsuccessful effort to retain in this manner. This process of lecturing pupils into torpidity is altogether too frequently practiced, and it is hoped that intelligent teachers will pause and inquire before they pursue it further.

Following up the Lecture. Because the lecture method is so often a matter of the pupils' passively receiving what the teacher says, it is imperative that you follow up your lectures with other related activities. Hold the pupils responsible for the content of the lecture. Make sure that they take notes and study them. Check their notes and check their knowledge. Utilize follow-up discussions, projects, themes, tests, quizzes, and other activities. Have someone summarize the main points in the next class session. It does not matter so much what you do as long as you do something that will help pupils to fix the important ideas in their heads and build these ideas into larger concepts through thought and inquiry.

When to Use the Lecture. Lectures have limited usefulness in secondary school classes. They are even less useful at the middle and elementary school levels, but considerably more useful at the college, graduate school, and adult levels. They give pupils little opportunity to inquire or explore. They are not very effective for changing attitudes. They seldom exercise pupils' higher mental faculties or lead pupils directly to the attainment of the higher cognitive goals.

Yet, lectures do have many uses, and you should learn to use them to (1) establish a general point of view; (2) run over facts quickly; (3) arouse interest (if you are a good lecturer); (4) fill in background information; (5) introduce new units, assignment, or content; (6) summarize; and (7) provide information otherwise not available to the pupils.[2]

A Reprise. As a summary and review, consider each of the following questions. If you cannot answer any of them readily, you should turn back and review the pertinent section.

1. The lecture, although a useful technique, should not be overused in junior and senior high school classes. Why is it not as useful as some other techniques? For what might you use the lecture?
2. What can a lecturer do to arouse and maintain interest in his lecture?
3. How can one encourage the inquiry process when he lectures?
4. What principles should you keep in mind when planning a lecture?
5. What can you do to make your lecturing successful?

The answers to these questions can all be found in this module. In brief, they all point out that you should make your lectures short, interesting, and pointed and that you can arouse and maintain interest in your lecture by such techniques as the following:

1. Open with a challenging question, problem, or fact.
2. Puzzle them a little.
3. Tell them what you intend to do.
4. Relate the content to things they already know and like.

[2] Leonard H. Clark, *Teaching Social Studies in Secondary Schools: A Handbook* (New York: Macmillan Publishing Co., Inc., 1973), p. 84.

5. Use questions (both real and rhetorical).
6. Use demonstrations, projectors, flannel boards, and other instructional aids.
7. Utilize humor.
8. Give plenty of examples—the more specific and concrete the better.[3]

Questioning

Questioning is probably the key technique in most teaching. It can be used for so many purposes that it is hard to see how a teacher can persevere unless he is a skillful questioner. Therefore, you, as a new teacher, should learn the rationale for different questioning techniques and should practice these techniques.

As we have already noted, questions may be used for many purposes. Among them are the following:

1. To find out something one did not know.
2. To find out whether someone knows something.
3. To develop the ability to think.
4. To motivate pupil learning.
5. To provide drill or practice.
6. To help pupils organize materials.
7. To help pupils interpret materials.
8. To emphasize important points.
9. To show relationships such as cause and effect.
10. To discover pupil interest.
11. To develop appreciation.
12. To provide review.
13. To give practice in expression.
14. To reveal mental processes.
15. To show agreement or disagreement.
16. To establish rapport with pupils.
17. To diagnose.
18. To evaluate.
19. To obtain the attention of wandering minds.[4]

The effective teacher tries to adapt the type and form of each question he asks to the purpose for which he asks it. Consequently, the question he asks to find out whether a pupil knows something may differ considerably from a question designed to start pupils thinking.

Questions may be either narrow or broad. Narrow questions usually call for recall of fact or specific correct answers. The answer may consist of a single word or phrase. Broad questions seldom can be answered in a single word; neither do they often have correct answers. Rather, they usually require considerable thought, often can be answered only by an extended explanation, and always allow the answerer to arrive at his own conclusion. Real learning is more likely to come from

[3] Ibid., p. 84.
[4] Leonard H. Clark and Irving S. Starr, *Secondary School Teaching Methods,* 3rd ed. (New York: Macmillan Publishing Co., Inc., 1976), p. 218–19.

broad questions than from narrow questions, because they intend to broaden the scope of the learning situation and to cause interaction and involvement amongst the pupils.

Questions can also be categorized as cognitive memory questions, convergent questions, divergent questions, and evaluative questions.[5] According to this classification, cognitive memory questions are those which tests one's memory. They are narrow rather than broad and require little or no thinking—just remembering. Convergent questions are also quite narrow. In answering this type of question, the pupil should come up with the correct answer. The question may require quite a lot of thinking but, once thought out, there is a correct answer and usually only one correct answer. For example, the question, "If the radius of a circle is 10 feet, what is the circumference of the circle?" requires one to come up with a specific correct answer even though he may have to do some thinking. Many questions in logic call for quite complicated thinking and close analysis, but can result in only one correct answer if one accepts the premises. In convergent questions then, the correct answer can be predicted.

Try to formulate some convergent questions that would be appropriate for your subject field. Remember that you are trying to ask questions that require considerable thinking but have a predictable correct answer.

Divergent questions are wide-open questions. No one can predict exactly what the answers will, or should, be. Divergent questions do not have correct answers. They are the type of questions that open pupils up, that get them to thinking and imagining. Some examples follow. Supposing that the thirteen American colonies had not separated themselves from England, what would the map of North America look like today? or What steps might the United States Government take to improve the economic situation? What course would you advise the government to take?

Try to prepare a few divergent questions that would be suitable for a course you might teach.

The fourth category, evaluative questions, asks the pupil to put a value on something. In a sense, this is a special case of the divergent question because, as a rule, values are very subjective. As the Romans used to say, "There is no accounting for taste." However, some evaluative questions may be convergent, because if we start with similar assumptions, presumably we should all arrive at the same or similar conclusions. Examples of evaluative questions are (1) Which do you consider to be the better practice? (2) Should Mr. Nixon have been impeached? (3) What kind of a character was Othello?

Try to construct some evaluative questions suitable for classes you might teach.

In discussing the various categories of questions, one should remember that one must allow pupils to arrive at their own answers to convergent, divergent, and evaluative questions. If you have given pupils ready-made answers which they cough up on call, your questioning is not convergent, divergent, or evaluative, but is the cognitive memory type.

You should also remember that in your teaching you will have to use all of the types of questions. There will be times when your questions should be broad and times when they should be narrow. There will be times when you should use

---

[5] James J. Gallagher and Mary Jane Aschner, "A Preliminary Report of Analyses of Classroom Interaction," *The Merrill-Palmer Quarterly of Behavior and Development,* **9**:183–194 (July 1963).

memory questions and times when you should use convergent questions just as there will be times when you should use divergent or evaluative questions. The point is that you should always try to use the type of question best suited to your purpose. Usually, this means that you should use divergent and evaluative questions much more frequently than most teachers do.

Obviously, the teacher should have a well-digested plan of operation and one that he knows beforehand he can successfully execute. If the teacher thinks of the concepts he wishes to develop, then he can easily select his texts and, with appropriate orchestration, he can keep his pupils constantly on inquiry and observation. A useful tool in this pursuit is the divergent question described earlier. This type of question inquires "how" rather than "what" and encourages greater inquiry. Avoid asking leading questions which the pupils can barely fail to answer, just as you should avoid lecturing. Similarly, avoid the regurgitative and the pouring-in process. Let your objective be to excite inquiry by using a question that pupils cannot answer without thought and observation. Questioning is a dynamic process. We can compare it to a chemical reaction. If we start with two reactants, the movement is to the right and the reaction starts moving toward the left. Eventually the reaction reaches an equilibrium and is moving in both directions. There is reaction and there is movement. Questions cause the movement of information from pupil to teacher, from teacher to pupil, and, it is hoped, from pupil to pupil. All participants become involved and interaction occurs. Real learning comes from interaction and involvement.

Guidelines for Questioning Techniques. To develop good skill in questioning is not difficult, but it does require attention to detail. Perhaps the following guidelines will prove useful as you try to build your skill in questioning.

The following are guidelines for forming questions:

1. Questions should be clear.
2. Questions are to be used to stimulate thinking and to produce an extended answer.
3. A question should not contain the answer.

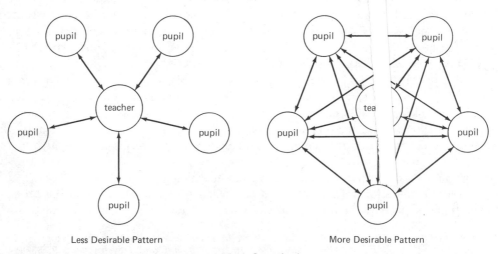

Less Desirable Pattern   More Desirable Pattern

Figure 3-1 *Patterns of Classroom Interaction, Questioning.*

4. Questions should not suggest the correct answer.
5. Questions should rarely call for a simple yes or no answer.
6. Questions should lead pupils toward the development of the concept.

Here are guidelines for presenting questions:

1. Ask the question first, and then call on some pupil to answer it.
2. Ask the question and provide time for thought. Do not use the machine gun approach.
3. If a partial answer is given, pose another question to expand the answer.
4. Involve as many pupils as possible. Do not fall into the habit of calling on only those who you know will give the answer.
5. Praise a good answer. Do not use sarcasm for a wrong answer. The teacher should rephrase the question in such a way that might lead the pupil to arrive at the correct answer or at least at a partially correct answer. Further questioning may help the pupil to view the question and the answer from another perspective. Reinforce the correct part of partially correct answers.
6. Encourage pupils not to accept an answer that they feel to be incorrect. This calls for listening and thinking.
7. Evaluate your own questions as to clarity, level, and relevancy.

Some examples of questions follow. Note whether they are (1) narrow or broad, and (2) cognitive memory, convergent, divergent, or evaluative.

1. Do you agree with Mary, John?
2. Do you believe that argument will hold up in the case of Switzerland?
3. What must I multiply by in order to clear the fractions in this equation?
4. How does the repetition in the Bolero affect you?
5. Did O'Henry's trick ending make the story more interesting?
6. How would you end the story?
7. Who came out of the door, the lady or the tiger?
8. How do the natural resources of the United States compare with those of the U.S.S.R.?
9. If you were setting up the defense of the colonies, where would you put the forts?
10. In view of all the information we have, do you feel that the union's sending out 70,000 letters asking voters to defeat the six assemblymen was justified?
11. What difference will an Equal Rights Amendment make?
12. Who was Otto Jespersen?
13. Should a teacher who earns $15,000 a year be entitled to unemployment benefits during the summer months when school is not in session and when he does not get paid?
14. What would you do in this situation if you were the governor?
15. What would have happened if Washington had decided to attack New Brunswick rather than Quebec?
16. What would happen if you used H_2SO_4 instead of HCl?
17. How would you set up the equation?
18. Why did you like this poem better?

Note learning situations that are likely to occur in a course you expect to teach in which you would use cognitive memory questions; convergent questions; divergent questions; and evaluative questions.

Build some questions for situations of each type.

Handling Pupil Questions. To create the proper atmosphere for interaction and involvement, you must be careful not only how you ask questions, but also how you handle pupils' questions and answers. There is an old proverb that says, "What I hear, I forget. What I see, I remember. What I say and do, I understand." What pupils say and do can also cause them to think in an inquiring manner. They may question each other; they may question the teacher, who should be able to respond with other questions that can guide the pupil in the right direction. This approach should help the pupil come to some conceptual conclusion.

The question of how far the teacher should help the pupil and how far the pupil should be required to help himself is a persistent dilemma. The nature of teaching would seem to indicate that the pupil should be taught to depend mainly on his own resources. Whatever is learned should be so thoroughly learned that the next higher step may be comparatively easy. The questioning approach must be such as to reveal to the teacher that the class has the necessary understanding of the fundamentals and is ready to move on to a more difficult concept. It may not be wise to have the pupils acquire the habit of running to the teacher as soon as a slight difficulty presents itself to request him to remove it. Some teachers may send the pupil to his seat with a reproof, and others may answer the question as the shortest way of getting rid of it. In general, both these courses are wrong. The inquirer should never be frowned upon because this may discourage him. On the other hand, a pupil should not be relieved from his work as this will diminish his self-reliance without his having gained by discovery. Unless the problem is closely studied, it will leave a feeble impression and soon be forgotten. The best way is to neither discourage inquiry nor answer the question. Refer the pupil to the principles which he previously has learned and of which he now may have lost sight. Perhaps call his attention to some rule or explanation previously given to the class. Go just so far as to enlighten him enough to put him on the track. Then leave him to achieve the victory himself. There is a great satisfaction in discovering a difficult thing for one's self. The teacher should simply be suggestive but should never take the glory of victory from the pupil by doing his work for him, at least not until the pupil has given it a thorough trial.

Some additional hints on handling pupil questions and promoting pupil interaction might include the following:

1. Always be courteous and kind.
2. Use pupil questions as springboards for further questions and discussion.
3. Consider all relevant questions that pupils ask. Some you may answer yourself; others you may refer to the class or to specific classmates; others you may have to look up or have someone look up.
4. Encourage pupils to ask questions that challenge the text or other pupils' statements, such as "What was the authority or basis for that statement?" or "Can you prove that to be true?"
5. Turn off trivial and irrelevant questions kindly and courteously, but firmly.

6. Avoid allowing particular pupils to dominate. Counsel pupils who dominate. Counsel pupils who take up too much time privately.

Socratic Questioning. The Ancient Greek philosopher, Socrates, used questions in an orderly fashion to try to get his pupils to think. Socrates' idea was that he should never tell a pupil what to think but that by means of questioning he should act as a midwife assisting at the birth of pupils' ideas. In general, the procedure for Socratic questioning is to

1. Elicit from your pupils a statement of belief or opinion. This can be done by using some sort of simple expository statement or one of the various springboard techniques, or by asking pupils to express their belief or opinion.
2. Examine this situation, belief, or opinion by the use of probing questions. In your questioning you should
   a. Try to bring out certain answers.
   b. Challenge pupils to examine their own ideas and beliefs.
   c. Ask your questions in a logical sequence.
   d. Attempt to aid pupils to develop their own idea as a result of your questioning.
   e. Lead the pupils to your predetermined goal concept or belief.

Open-Book Recitation. One technique that exemplifies the philosophy behind the use of broad questions is the open-book recitation. In this technique, pupils discuss the topic under consideration with their texts and notebooks open. The general procedure is to ask the pupils broad questions which they discuss freely. Opinions, theories, facts, and evidence are passed around the class as pupils attempt to arrive at general conclusions or at least an airing of differences and a sharing of ideas. In the discussion, pupils are encouraged to turn to their books or notes to check on facts and to back up their arguments.

This technique has many advantages. It frees the class from fact remembering and opens it up to thinking. Pupils realize that facts are means to ends—the ends being concepts, ideas, understanding, and the ability to think—rather than ends themselves. It gives pupils practice in checking and documenting, and, it is hoped, shows them the importance of getting facts straight. All in all, this procedure is an excellent means of teaching pupils to use their higher mental faculties. In using this method, the basic technique is to use broad divergent and evaluative questions and to bounce follow-up questions around the class until the group takes the bait and begins to discuss the question freely.

Drill and Practice

Sometimes we learn things quite thoroughly in one attempt. More frequently, repetition is needed if learning is to be thorough or lasting. That is why we must count on drill and practice to master skills and to increase understanding. Use them to consolidate, clarify, strengthen, and refine what pupils have already learned and to give them additional opportunities to learn thoroughly.

When using drill and practice activities, do the following:

1. Give clear instructions.
2. Keep the practice as real as possible.
3. Supervise carefully.
4. Take difficult portions out of context to work on separately, if necessary, but concentrate on practicing the whole operation.
5. Individualize. Adjust each person's practice to his skills and abilities. Use self-administering, self-correcting material if possible.
6. Incorporate practice in your regular teaching activities. Do not make a big deal of practicing. Use the regular classroom materials as much as is feasible.
7. Use a variety of materials.[6]

Memorization

Sometimes pupils just have to memorize things. There is even a time for memorization without understanding. For example, in the study of chemistry, it would be advantageous to know the symbols and valences of the common elements. These symbols must be memorized. They are tools. In mathematics, certain assumptions must be memorized before other concepts can be developed. In fact, in all of the disciplines there are always some basic points that we must memorize so that we can understand other concepts.

What in your discipline must be memorized before one can move on to the development of other concepts?

When teaching through memorizing, remember that memorization is really a special case of practicing. In general, the techniques suggested for conducting practice sessions hold for memorizing sessions. Nevertheless, perhaps the following five guidelines will prove to be of service:

1. Avoid overuse of memorizing. Have pupils memorize only those things it is essential that they memorize.
2. Be sure there is a purpose for the memorizing and that the pupils see what that purpose is.
3. If possible, have pupils study for meaning before memorizing. As we have seen, some things we must learn, meaningful or not, such as German word order, or Cyrillic or Greek letters, which do not have any real reason for being as they are. They just are as they are, so we must memorize that Σ is sigma and that in mathematics it stands for the sum of. These are tools of the trade and we must master them.
4. When pupils are memorizing long pieces, they should use the part-whole method. Otherwise, it is probably better to memorize by whole units. The part-whole method consists of learning parts separately and then incorporating them in learning the whole, just as in practicing you work on the hard parts and then practice the whole operation.
5. Utilize the recall method. Pupils should study and then try to recall without prompting.

[6] Clark, op cit., pp. 86–87.

Reviews and Reviewing

In the development of learning within any class of pupils, frequent reviews are necessary. This is so because memory is aided by repetition and by association, but also understanding is improved by review. In the sciences, for instance, many concepts cannot be fully understood in isolation. Neither can all the scientific terms be fully appreciated until they are seen in the context of later topics. Frequently, notions that were understood only dimly the first time they were studied become much clearer when "re-viewed" later in connection with later topics.

In conducting reviews, the teacher must be aware of the character of the pupils and of the discipline being pursued. In mathematics, where so much depends upon every link in the great chain, very frequent reviews are generally necessary. It is profitable to recall, almost daily, some principles which were previously studied. In several disciplines, where the parts have less intimate connection, as in geography and some others, the reviews may be given at greater intervals, although daily review helps to keep pupils on their toes.

Here again, the techniques of questioning come into play. As far as possible, the review should lead from facts to concepts and principles applied to practical life. Experience in thinking is often more profitable than the knowledge itself.

It is always advantageous to have a general review at the close of any particular study. This enables you to detect any false conceptions that the pupil entertained during the original process. You now can present the subject as a whole, and view one part in the light of another. In physiology, much more understanding is gained about the process of growth after one has studied absorption and secretion. Similarly, the economy of respiration is much clearer when viewed in connection with the circulation of the blood.

A general review is an enlightening process and is always profitable, with perhaps one exception: when the review is instituted solely as preparation for a written examination. Then, review may degenerate into a mere device for getting by at exam time. The object of reviewing should be to master the subject for its own sake, not for the purpose of being able to talk about it on one special occasion.

In summary, a review is an opportunity for the pupils to look at a topic again. It is a "re-view" or second look. It is not the same as drill or practice, although sometimes one can use the same methodology. Review is useful every day as a means for tying the day's lesson to preceding lessons. At this time you can summarize the points that should have been made and establish relationships with past and future lessons. End-of-unit and end-of-term reviews are also useful, but it is usually unwise to put off reviewing for such a long time. Frequent reviews are more effective. Besides, end-of-unit and end-of-term reviews tend to become preparations for examinations.

Almost any technique can be used in review classes, although the common oral quiz in which the teacher asks fact question after fact question is not much good. Among the tactics that you might profitably use are pupil summaries, re-teaching the lesson, quiz games, dramatizations, pupil-constructed test questions, application problems, discussion, and broad questioning.

Techniques that require pupils to use what they should have learned are good because they may not only serve as review but also open up new vistas for the pupils.

For Your Consideration

Teaching is primarily the ability to develop awareness. In each of the following three statements, identify and elaborate the concept relevant to the educational process in view of what we have discussed.

1. No man can reveal to you aught but that which is half asleep in the dawning of your knowledge.[7]
2. If the teacher is wise, he does not bid you enter the house of wisdom, but rather leads you to the threshold of your own mind.
3. Find that the vision of one man lends not its wings to another man.

The concepts about teaching just mentioned are frequently quoted to teachers. The words have had little effect upon the behavior of many teachers. Why?

Explain why students do not often understand what college professors are talking about.

SUGGESTED READING

Alcorn, Marvin D., James S. Kinde, and Jim R. Schurest. *Better Teaching in Secondary Schools,* 3rd ed. New York: Holt, Rinehart, & Winston, Inc., 1970.

Callahan, Sterling G. *Successful Teaching in Secondary Schools,* 2nd ed. Chicago: Scott, Foresman and Company, 1970.

Clark, Leonard H. and Irving S. Starr. *Secondary School Teaching Method,* 3rd ed. New York: Macmillan Publishing Co., Inc., 1976.

Dale, Edgar. "The Art of Question". *The Newsletter* **34:**1–4 (Dec. 1968).

Grambs, Jean D., John C. Carr, and Robert M. Fitch. *Modern Methods in Secondary Education,* 3rd ed. New York: Holt, Rinehart & Winston, Inc., 1970.

Grossien, Philip. *How to Use the Fine Art of Questioning.* Englewood Cliffs, N.J.: Teachers Practical Press, 1964.

Hamachek, Don E. "Motivation in Teaching and Learning," *What Research Says to the Teacher* No. 34. Washington, D.C.: Association of Classroom Teaching, 1968.

Hyman, Ronald T. *Ways of Teaching.* Philadelphia: J. B. Lippincott Co., 1970.

Raths, Louis E., Merrill Harmen, and Sidney B. Simon. *Values and Teaching.* Columbus, Ohio: Charles E. Merrill Publishers, 1966.

Raths, Louis E., et al. *Teaching for Thinking.* Columbus, Ohio: Charles E. Merrill Publishers, 1967.

Sanders, Norris M. *Classroom Questions* New York: Harper and Row, Publishers, 1966.

POST TEST

I. Check the appropriate columns for each question, and use the following code letters to indicate your reasons:

[7] Kahlil Gibran, *The Prophet* (New York: Alfred A. Knopf, Inc., 1923, 1968).

X—Indicates poor, fair, or good.

A—Calls for no answer and is a pseudo question.

B—Asks for recall but no thinking.

C—Challenging, stimulating, or discussion provoking type of question that calls for thinking and involves reasoning and problem solving.

Questions	Poor	Fair	Good	Why?
1. In what region are major earthquakes located?				
2. According to the theory of isostasy, how would you describe our mountainous regions?				
3. What mineral will react with HCl to produce carbon dioxide?				
4. What kind of rock is highly resistant to weathering?				
5. Will the continents look different in the future and why?				
6. Who can describe a continental shelf?				
7. What caused the Industrial Revolution?				
8. What political scandal involved President Harding?				
9. This is a parallelogram, isn't it?				
10. Wouldn't you agree that the base angles of an isosceles triangle are congruent?				
11. In trying to determine the proof of this exercise, what would you suggest we examine at the outset?				
12. What conclusion can be drawn concerning the points of intersection of two graphs?				
13. Why is pure water a poor conductor of electricity?				
14. How do fossils help explain the theory of continental drift?				
15. If Macbeth told you about his encounter with the apparitions, what advice would you have offered?				
16. Who said, "if it were done when 'tis done, then 'twere well if it were done quickly"?				
17. In the poem, "The Sick Rose," what do you think Blake means by "the invisible worm"?				
18. Should teachers censor the books which students read?				
19. Explain the phrase, "Ontogeny recapitulates philogeny."				
20. What are the ten life functions?				
21. What living thing can live without air?				
22. What is chlorophyll?				

Questions	Poor	Fair	Good	Why?

23. Explain the difference between RNA and DNA.

24. Who developed the periodic table based on the fact that elements are functions of their atomic weight?

II.

1. Why is the lecture considered to be one of the least effective methods of teaching secondary school pupils?

_____

_____

_____

_____

2. Name six suggestions for the lecturers' plan made in the module.

_____

_____

_____

_____

_____

_____

3. What can the lecturer do to excite a spirit of inquiry in his students?

_____

_____

4. Name five of the more important uses of the lecture.

_____

_____

_____

_____

5. What are the distinguishing characteristics of cognitive memory questions, convergent questions, divergent questions, and evaluative questions?

_____

_____

_____

_____

6. What does the module recommend that you do when the pupil answers your question incorrectly or superficially?

7. Should you encourage pupils to ask questions that challenge the text?

8. What is the basic principle in Socratic questioning?

9. Is it ever permissible to allow pupils to use their books during a class recitation or discussion?

10. When pupils practice a skill, is it better to provide special materials or the regular materials they would ordinarily use?

Discussion and Small Group Techniques

Louise E. Hock

New York University

module 4

Total Class As a Group Enterprise / Various Techniques of Interaction / Role of the Teacher / Means and Ends / Analysis of Roles / Desirable Outcomes / Some Concepts to Be Explored

RATIONALE

In recent years, as in earlier ones of this century, many theorists and practitioners have attempted to make what goes on in the classroom more consonant with the reality of the world outside the classroom. They urge us to give greater recognition to the various skills needed to function in society as human being, worker, citizen, consumer, and parent to develop a more sophisticated awareness of the uses of knowledge, and to become concerned not only with knowing about but also in knowing how.

These theorists and practitioners also urge us to accept the principle that learning is an active process. The goals of education, they tell us, encompass not only the acquisition of knowledge but also the guidance of the individual to his fullest potential. The latter involves the development of a multitude of skills—skills of critical thinking, of independent inquiry, of group participatory behavior, for instance. They also urge us to consider the role of the school as a humanizing experience and to move toward more openness in the educative process—openness of objectives, of curriculum, of methodology, of evaluation, of environment. In many ways, these twin currents of openness and humanism can be traced to an earlier era when some progressive educators were suggesting that the educational experience is not preparation for life, but rather that learning is living here and now.

As these progressive ideas have gained new support and fresh interpretation, the nature of teaching itself has undergone critical scrutiny with a resultant broadening of the processes, techniques, and procedures used by many teachers, as they try to cope with new priorities among vastly expanded objectives. Illustrative of this trend to mesh process with goals is a growing interest in developing skills of active participation in group endeavors and of active involvement with others in life's ongoing activities. It is obvious to all that life is not a solitary existence but must be lived in and with the company of others. Group living is a fact of life and a realistic aspect of existence.

Even cursory reflection reveals the extent to which group activity is prevalent in one's life—in the circles of one's family and friends, as well as in the civic, religious, economic, governmental, and social recreational realms. In one way or another, at one time or another, we are all involved in activities with others, either as participants or observers. To call the roll of such activities would be to cite, among others, legislative committee operations, collective negotiations in business and labor, radio and television talk shows, discussion and round-table sessions, religious and club activities, various symposia, panels, and Town Hall meetings on the cultural circuit, and many more.

It is readily evident that participants in such group activities assume multiple roles, depending upon the nature and purpose of the activity and the personal predilection of individual participants. In addition to the obvious leader-follower dichotomy, participants' roles in group activity include those as questioner, clarifier, problem solver, compromiser, advocate, facilitator, catalyst, evaluator, and synthesizer.

The past dozen years have seen a growing awareness of the need for more and more sophisticated skills in participatory behavior and deeper insights into such phenomena. We have only to witness the proliferation of human relations workshops, group dynamics training sessions, encounter groups, sensitivity training, and similar efforts to recognize the drive for increased skill in human interaction.

Such efforts are vivid testimony to the fact that group participatory skills are learned skills, not innate skills. As a result of this and other testimony, it is increasingly evident that the school has a role to play in the development of social skills, both by encouraging cognitive awareness and analysis and by experiential approaches. More and more teachers, therefore, are adding to their repertoire of instructional strategies a variety of techniques and procedures that provide students with opportunities to interact with one another. Such procedures also provide experience in analysis of group behavior and human interaction, and the development of individual skills along those lines. The range of possibilities is wide and varied; to name only a few, there are debates, forums, panels, symposia, committee work, buzz sessions, small group activities and role playing.

The task of the prospective teacher is threefold: (1) to acquire skills of functioning in such participatory endeavors oneself; (2) to comprehend the principles and theory underlying effective use of such activities; and (3) to develop skill in the use of such group experiences with learners and ability to guide students toward effective functioning in and understanding of participatory activities.

SPECIFIC OBJECTIVES

The techniques and procedures described in this module are ones that teachers can use, whatever the character of their educational enterprise. In other words, teachers in relatively traditional classroom situations would find them useful as part of their over-all instructional repertoire, and teachers in more innovative, open educational settings would find them especially appropriate to the participatory nature of such learning situations.

In studying this module, your goal is to become familiar with the wide range of possibilities for student participation in the learning process through discussion and group experiences. You should be able to identify those most relevant to your subject area and to conceive of various possible uses of them. The following objectives should guide your study of and reading for this module.

Upon conclusion of your study of this module, it is expected that you will be able to do the following:

1. Comprehend the variety of techniques for discussion and group work available for instructional purposes.
2. Analyze the advantages and disadvantages of each.
3. Distinguish among the various roles that participants play in group activities.
4. Analyze your own participation in discussion or other group activities, especially your own role performance.
5. Create classroom situations requiring the use and application of group skills by learners.

6. Select the specific discussion or other group work technique appropriate to your specific purposes and content.
7. Diagnose strengths, weaknesses, and needs of learners vis-à-vis group participatory behavior.
8. Gain an appreciation of the interactive nature of the communicative process.
9. Apply the basic principles of group dynamics to classroom use of participatory activities.
10. Become familiar with a number of ways of evaluating learner growth in discussion and group processes.

MODULE TEXT

The American school has long accepted as a major function the socializing of the human being—the guidance of the child from a self-centered, immature, dependent state to that of a mature, self-directive, interdependent individual able to live and work with others in responsible fashion. This function assumes greater significance as participatory democracy becomes a pervasive characteristic of all phases and segments of our society. The increased sophistication of such participation requires the use of highly developed skills of communication, cooperation, self-direction, critical judgment, and problem-solving. Such skills can and should be taught in our schools.

Fortunately, the teacher has at his disposal a wide and varied range of techniques of a participatory nature. These procedures can be formal or informal. The purposes can be of an information-giving nature or can be opinion-sharing or value-clarifying in character. The participants can number two or many times that number. The time involved can vary from a few minutes to many sessions continuing over a period of days or weeks.

List the types of activities of a participatory nature that you can remember. See end of module for listing of some of the activities you might have included in your list. Consider how you would go about conducting such activities in your own class.

Total Class As a Group Enterprise

Perhaps the most helpful way to start thinking about processes of participation and group interaction is to view the total class as a group. In their efforts to provide discussion and group experiences for learners, teachers frequently overlook the opportunity to make the total class sessions more interactive in nature. A teacher should not find it difficult to move from a relatively typical recitation, lecture, or teacher-dominated type of classroom to one involving various discussion approaches.

Consider for a moment some readily evident characteristics of the two instructional approaches. The stereotypic, yet still prevalent, recitation-type strategy suggests (1) teacher-led and teacher-dominated sessions; (2) a questioning approach of a relatively superficial information-seeking nature; (3) repeating or restating (re-citing) that which was learned, studied, memorized; (4) the "hearing" of lessons to detect right and wrong answers; (5) teacher checking to see if students have done their work; (6) a one-to-one relationship between the questioner and hearer and the teller and answerer; (7) all decision-making in the hands of the teacher regarding purposes, content, process, and participation.

A flow chart of participation in such a session would probably reveal a significant number of tallies for the teacher, with a smaller number distributed over a relatively small number of students selected by the teacher to participate. The major mode of operation would tend to be question and answer with occasional comment relative to accuracy or character of student response. There might be occasional lecture or minilecture.

On the other hand, consider the possibilities inherent in the concept of such total class activity viewed as genuine discussion, with student interactive participation and the focus not on hearing lessons but on inquiry and discovery. When viewed this way, class sessions are characterized by (1) the probing exploration of ideas, concepts, and issues; (2) building upon student responses in a developmental flow; (3) interaction among all participants; (4) shifting leadership among participants; (5) questioning, sharing, differing, conjecturing on the part of all; (6) student participation in decision-making; (7) hypothesizing and problem-solving.

The essential difference between the two types of classroom is that the first seems to view knowledge as consisting of a series of correct answers, whereas the latter tends to view knowledge as the product of creative inquiry and active student participation in the learning process. Only through genuine student involvement and interaction can hypotheses be tested, views expressed, questions raised, controversy examined, and insights developed, along with other desirable cognitive processes.

A helpful way to begin analyzing the differences between the two approaches is to use an interaction analysis system, such as the Flanders approach or the Amidon-Hunter Verbal Interaction Category System or other similar ones. These

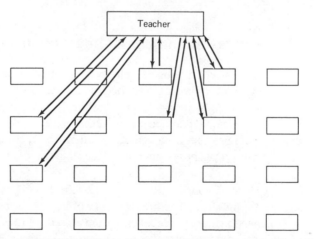

Figure 4-1 *Diagram Showing the Type of Flow of Interaction Found in a Typical Recitation.* Note that the interaction is between the teacher and individual pupil only. There is no cross flow between pupil and pupil at all.

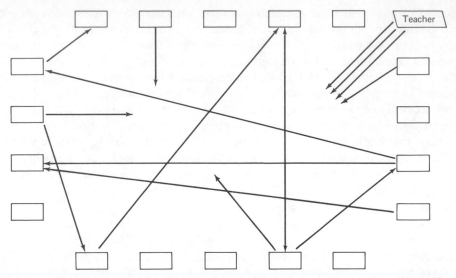

Figure 4-2 *Diagram Showing the Type of Flow Interaction in a Whole Class Discussion.* In this class, pupils have been arranged in a hollow square. Arrows pointing to the center of the square indicate that the person was speaking to the group as a whole. Arrows pointing to individuals indicate the person the speaker was addressing. Note that the conversation includes much cross talk between pupil and pupil, and much talk addressed to the group as a whole. The teacher has kept his role in the discussion minimal.

systems attempt to record in easily recognizable and quantifiable ways the nature of classroom interaction, providing a clear indication of the relative proportion of teacher-talk and student-talk, along with varying degrees of analysis of the nature of the interaction and exchange. Any teacher wishing to move toward more participatory discussion might well start with such analysis to determine the present character of his classroom sessions. Steps can then be taken to improve the amount and quality of student involvement. See Module 12 for a brief discussion of the Verbal Interaction Category System (VICS).

Various Techniques of Interaction

In addition to total class discussion, teachers have at their disposal a varied repertoire that provides many opportunities for students to participate actively in the learning process. The tactics and strategies can be broadly classified into two types: (1) the relatively formal, planned, short-term presentation-type technique; and (2) those group strategies that involve more student interaction and work of a long-term nature with varied purposes, including the analysis of the group process itself.

Presentation-type Techniques. The first category of group discussion techniques includes the use of panels, symposia, debates, forums, round-table discussions and similar ways of involving students in their own learning. All these possibilities provide opportunities for student presentation of ideas, opinions, and information and for the expression of differing viewpoints. They all involve a degree of structure and the need for some planning. However, they vary in the degree of formal preparation involved.

Symposia, debates, and forums require thoughtfully prepared and well-organized material, whether in the form of written papers or outlines, or in the form of well-conceived remarks. Panels and round-table discussions, while usually benefiting by advance preparation, can be utilized along more informal lines, permitting the chance for spontaneous exchange of views, free-flowing exposition of ideas, even rap sessions of a wide-open character.

Such techniques are widely adaptable to a variety of subject areas. As you read these examples of the varying uses of these methods in various subjects, try to think of how you could utilize these or similar tactics in courses you expect to teach. A symposium might be held in a science class to present and discuss various current developments of a scientific nature or to present differing viewpoints on certain controversial issues. In a home economics class or home and family living course, a panel of students could discuss views on family roles and responsibilities. A variation on this could have each student reacting in a particular role, as parent, child, peer group friend, or non-parental adult. Or a panel might consist of a group of invited participants, parents, community leaders, and law enforcement representatives, who would exchange views on the meaning and character of family life today.

In a social studies class, students could engage in a panel discussion of the causes and manifestations of racism in society and in their own lives and experience. Or a symposium could examine the problem of racism from several aspects, historically, economically, socially, morally, and ethically. Or a debate could be held on a topic such as, "There is less racism in the 1970s than there was in the 1960s."

An interesting variation of such approaches is that of adapting a "Meet the Press" or "Face the Nation" format for exploration of important ideas and developments. Students could take turns playing the expert, or the instructor, or the interviewers; the entire class could be involved in the questioning as well.

Other examples should come readily to mind for English and foreign language classes, as well as other areas of the curriculum. There are manifold opportunities throughout the instructional program for the use of such techniques for student participation.

It should be pointed out that all of these techniques also permit development of some specific skills, such as exposition, discussion, or analysis. For example, debates require skills of critical analysis, the art of persuasion, rapid rebuttal skills, and the ability to suspend judgment until all points are heard. Panels, forums, and symposia provide opportunity for learning how to organize material, as well as the listening and communication skills necessary to any informal interaction following the original presentation. Round-table discussions provide experience in effective exchange of ideas, opinions, and viewpoints, active listening and responding, and rapid, spontaneous, and responsive interaction.

These techniques are helpful one-shot approaches to be used whenever appropriate to the given content and purposes. Teachers should not take for granted that students know how to handle such procedures. The skills involved in individual preparation and presentation are acquired and can be taught, as should the skills of working with others in such enterprises. Students need to be taught how to gather information, take notes, select major points, organize material, present a position succinctly and engage in dialogue and debates with one another. These are skills that can be taught by the teacher, sometimes in class sessions as a whole, sometimes with individual guidance, as students begin to participate in a variety of such activities. The use of such techniques helps students learn to avoid verbatim copying of material and memorization of presentations, which should be eliminated from the classroom.

Sociodrama and Role Playing. Another type of experience in participation and interaction is that of sociodrama and role playing. Examples of this type of activity include mock trials and portrayals of town meetings, United Nations sessions, Congressional hearings and similar types of civic portrayals. A more imaginative form of dramatic involvement would be acting out "You Are There" types of scenes in which students portray various figures from history or fiction. Reference has already been made to the possibilities of role-playing adaptations of various television programs, such as "Meet the Press."

Such dramatic role-playing activities have several advantages. They permit students to use information in the light of the particular perceptions of the role being played. They make it possible to examine concepts and ideas from different viewpoints expressed in the role playing. They help promote understanding and deepen insights through the necessity of thinking as the character being portrayed. They can provide opportunity for greater understanding by having students act out roles and positions different from those they would tend to favor and approve. Such reversal of roles helps to deepen the awareness of the complex, controversial nature of much knowledge and of many issues.

Buzz Sessions and Group Work. Another broad category of student involvement includes strategies of buzz sessions, group work of a relatively short-term span, and committee work of longer duration. The buzz session can serve many useful purposes and functions as the name implies. It is an opportunity for students to meet together briefly in relatively small groups of four to seven to share with each other opinions, viewpoints, and reactions. These sessions rarely last more than fifteen to twenty minutes and require no advance formal preparation or lengthy follow-up.

A teacher can use the buzz session at the beginning of the school year to help students get to know each other. In such situations, the students can talk about themselves, their interests, hobbies, travel, and other matters of concern to young people. There need be no reporting back to the class from such a session, although a brief summary of the group activity might occasionally be desirable.

Buzz sessions can be used for informal discussion of certain aspects of the course content. In an English class, students can meet in small groups to discuss various short stories, essays, or books that they have read on an individual basis. In this way, they not only share reactions and opinions, but also become acquainted with a wide variety of literary material. Similarly, buzz sessions can be used to discuss comparisons of two or three literary works that have been studied by the entire class. In a foreign language class, buzz sessions can be used to give students practice in conversing and communicating in the specific language under study. The substance of the sessions will depend on the purposes desired and the content under study. The ideas and topics being discussed can range from opinions on certain films to discussions of travels at home and abroad, and critiques of literary works in the language being studied.

Buzz sessions in a social studies class could be used in such situations as the following:

1. After a study of a given problem or issue, students could share views as to the single most effective way of coping with the problem, whether it be pollution, transportation, or any similar matter of current importance.
2. Students can share their reading of newspapers and news magazines to provide exchange of views on current events.
3. Sessions can focus on hypothetical thinking: what would have happened if . . . ? or what would happen if . . . ?

Whatever the substantive nature of such discussions, these buzz sessions serve many other purposes. They provide an opportunity for all to participate in a way that is not possible in a total class situation. They help students learn the skills of listening as well as of talking. They can be used to let off steam when students seem restless, bored, or are in some way not responsive to the larger class session of the day. They help students learn to think in action while interacting with each other.

Committees and Small Groups. The use of small group work for a particular task requires longer involvement of perhaps two, three, or even more sessions. Sometimes these groups are considered committees and may function for a week or two or longer. Whatever the length of time, such group work is distinguished from the buzz group techniques by the specific task orientation, a planned involvement of all, and a more formal outcome in the form of an activity, project, or presentation.

Such group work can be used for (1) planning activities for various purposes, such as a party or field trip; (2) cooperative project work; (3) actual study of a specific unit of work.

The background experience of the students should guide the teacher in determination of the nature and extent of group work. With students who have had little or no experience in working together, it is wise to start with activities of interest that have an immediate or early visible result. For example, students might work in small groups on the planning of party or music activities. In classes where field trips are involved, whether to museums, theaters, civic centers, or historical monuments, the various aspects of planning can be handled by the students in small groups, each of which is responsible for one aspect of the trip.

Another early type of experience might involve discussion and decision making about matters of genuine interest to the class. For example, as students become more experienced in working together, they might engage in developing criteria for grading in their particular class situation or actually prepare evaluative instruments for various aspects of their course work.

With more experience, students can accept responsibility for projects that span a longer time period but still are of a direct nature and involve visible progress. In a science class, for example, small groups can be established for (1) the care of terrariums; (2) fish raising; (3) care and study of hamsters and mice; (4) care and study of various plants, among other possibilities. Students can take care of their respective projects, study various aspects of growth and development, observe, and make regular progress reports to the entire class. Similarly, students can work together in small groups on various ecology projects, or activities focused around study of nutrition vis-à-vis cost and advertising, or any number of consumer education projects. In such projects, there are usually clearly defined goals and clear-cut procedures for achieving them. The results of such study will have meaning for the entire class.

In English and social studies classes, group work can be used to help students acquire knowledge of the mass media—especially newspapers, radio and television —including the various kinds of writing and production involved and the roles of various personnel. Students could engage in the actual production of a class newspaper or magazine. In such an endeavor, the class could be so organized that certain pupils would be made responsible for editing, reporting, editorializing, writing columns, obtaining and writing advertisements, and similar duties. Students could specialize in reporting and writing about medicine, education, leisure activities, national and international affairs, or local and state issues.

A variation of this activity could be the production of a television news program or a documentary focusing on a specific issue of current interest. As with the class newspaper, students will gain rich insights into the processes of news gathering and reporting, as well as much knowledge about the substantive matters being reported.

As students gain more experience with group procedures and acquire more sophisticated skills, they can begin to handle more substantive aspects of course content through working together in genuine inquiry. More advanced skills of planning, hypothesizing, decision making, investigating, organizing, sharing, and reporting are involved. In addition to providing opportunities for inquiry and genuine interaction on important content areas, small group work makes possible the study of a wider variety of topics, issues, and problems than does a course conducted along more typical lines of total class attention to the same content.

Several examples of more substantive topics will help illustrate the value of such group involvement. In a study of transportation in a science class, groups might be formed according to the various means of transportation. One group studying the development of the automobile could investigate the internal combustion engine, the Wankel engine, and electric cars. A group investigating air travel could study the various types of lighter or heavier than air craft—balloons, prop and jet planes, and rockets. A study of sea travel could involve analysis of the use of wind, steam, diesel, atomic power, and various types of sea craft.

In a social studies class, groups organized along similar lines might focus on the historical development of the various means of transportation and their social and economic impact, with critical analysis of various issues related to transportation today. History teachers wishing to develop a sophisticated insight into the nature of revolution might set up several groups, each of which could concentrate on investigation of a specific revolution, American, Russian, French, Chinese, or Latin American. In the latter instance, students could develop broad guidelines in advance so that the separate groups will proceed in ways that will yield common bases for comparison at the conclusion of the group investigations. Thus, each group's investigation and report might be designed to include such considerations as long-term causes, immediate causes, class of people who instigated the revolt, method of revolt, and results.

Role of the Teacher

Whatever the activity or project, it is important to keep in mind the need to teach the skills of group functioning. The process of guiding student growth in participatory experiences is a major responsibility of the teacher. The teacher must come to know each student well, must be constantly aware that participatory skills must be learned, and must be perceptive in guiding group activities.

The teacher's role is significant at every stage of the process. It begins with a commitment to the value of and need for group instructional procedures. The attitude of teachers is important. The effective teacher knows that skills of group work must be taught, and so builds upon students' present levels of experience and skill. The effective teacher understands the difference between the kind of verbal noise that signifies purposeful group activity and the type of noisy interaction that suggests group disintegration. The effective teacher is aware of the many decisions involved in the use of group techniques and has the data and insights upon which to make such decisions.

For example, the teacher's first decision has to do with the appropriateness of a particular group procedure to the content under study and the purposes to be achieved. Subsequent decisions have to do with the readiness of students for group work, the size of the groups, the placement of students in particular groups, and the degree of help and guidance the teacher must provide. For students who have had little or no experience with group activities, the wise teacher begins with frequent buzz-group sessions of short duration to help students become familiar with verbal interaction among themselves. He can then move toward the establishment of groups or committees for relatively easy, direct, clearly defined tasks. As students gain experience and expertise, more sophisticated involvement can be expected of them.

The degree of direction and help supplied by the teacher will vary from student to student, from group to group, and situation to situation. Again, if group work is a relatively novel experience, the teacher may have to set specific guidelines at first, such as requiring the selection of a leader and recording secretary, and providing alternative suggestions regarding procedures and division of responsibility in the groups. It is helpful for the teacher to circulate from group to group, assuming whatever role seems appropriate at any given time—observer, resource, mediator, or participant—until students gain experience and confidence in handling group strategies. Of course, the teacher will have a variety of materials and resources available, as well as a fund of possibilities to suggest when asked.

An important responsibility of the teacher has to do with the placement of students in group situations. For group work to be most effective, a teacher should use a variety of approaches to such placement.

When buzz groups are set up, it is wise to use different techniques of student assignment so that over a period of time students will get to talk and work with all classmates. One might ask the five people in the corner to make up a buzz group on one occasion; on the next occasion, the five people in the row next to the board; or the next, every fifth pupil as we "count off" around the room.

Membership in groups or committees might be based on student choice of (1) classmates they would like to work with, or (2) the task, responsibility, or topic they would like to work on, as well as teacher assignments. If the teacher decides to make the assignment himself, he should always keep in mind student preferences, abilities, and inclinations.

Under most circumstances, the results of group work will be more productive if students can participate in groups of their own selection. However, there are times and reasons why a teacher may wish to assign students on the basis of one or another criterion. A student in his own selection over many months may not have experienced a certain kind of group process or project. To provide him with breadth of experience, the teacher may decide to assign him to a specific type of group. In other instances, the teacher may believe it wise to break up certain pairings or clustering of students to broaden their contacts with other pupils, to avoid or break down dependency relationships, or to find out more about a student's ability to function with different people.

Throughout the group work experience, the teacher has a valuable role to perform. It is helpful at the very beginning to circulate from one group to another to be available for questioning, to provide necessary guidance, or to get a "feel" for the interaction and progress within each group. After group plans are underway, individual students may need advice and guidance from the teacher relative to their particular responsibilities. Keeping in close touch also permits the teacher to detect any potential difficulties or trouble spots and makes possible wise decisions regarding occasional shifting of students from one group to another.

There are many skills involved in group procedures—planning skills, research skills, search for appropriate materials and references, note-taking and reporting techniques—for which the teacher is an ever-ready resource. Reporting techniques can be the kind of sharing with fellow group members that helps keep all abreast of progress, and the kind of sharing in which pupils report the result and products of their group endeavor to the entire class. For students who have had no experience in such group reporting, the teacher may have to suggest a number of possibilities or meet with the group frequently as students explore their own thinking.

For group work of relatively long duration, two weeks or more, the use of progress reports can be very helpful. Use them to help students become aware of their use of time, to assess the degree of accomplishment, to reappraise their plans, and to share with the rest of the class various problems encountered or bring helpful suggestions to the attention of other groups. The progress report can be oral or written and can vary in form in relation to the nature of the group work. A simple statement reporting how the group is getting along may be quite sufficient.

An important aspect of group work is the evaluative process that should accompany it at all stages, but especially at the conclusion of the endeavor. Not only results and accomplishments, but also the process engaged in throughout the group work, need assessment. In such appraisal sessions, students can identify areas of weakness and think through ways of improving group activities another time. The role of the teacher in helping students evaluate effectively and purposefully is crucial. During pupils' initial experience with group activities, the teacher will have to assume strong leadership in guiding evaluative sessions and procedures. As students gain experience in group work, they will be able to assume more and more responsibility for evaluation, as well as for all other aspects of group processes.

Some Caveats. It would be misleading to give the impression that once a decision has been made to use a particular discussion or group technique all will go well. Often that is not the case. As with all other learning activities, there will be successes and failures, progress and retrogression. It is during times of trouble that the role of the teacher becomes crucial.

Most problems arise as a result of unwarranted and exaggerated expectations of teachers relative to students' ability to handle group procedures and processes of inquiry. Teachers tend to overestimate the level of skill, degree of competence, and background of experience of the students. As a result, the teacher often does not provide for gradual involvement in such work, moving from the relatively easy to the more difficult. Frequently, the teacher does not provide sufficient help at the start of any such study, nor does he provide continuous guidance as the work proceeds.

It is important to recall that students in all likelihood will confront two types of problems, those associated with the processes of working together, and those involving the substantive aspects of an inquiry approach to learning. The first set of problems will require the teacher's help in guiding toward consensus and compromise, in helping to resolve personality differences, and in coping with overt behavior problems.

The second kind of problem requires constant attention to the many aspects of the discovery or inquiry approach—locating information, effective use of materials and resources, note-taking and organizational skills, and effective communication. The teacher should not assume that once the rudiments of these skills are taught little more needs to be done. Rather, as students confront different and more complex challenges in their discussion and group work, their prior learnings need to be reinforced and more sophisticated insights and skills need to be taught. Teaching, therefore, becomes a continuous, ongoing process.

A helpful procedure for the teacher to follow is to involve the students in direct discussion of such problems as often as seems appropriate and desirable. One of the objectives of participatory experiences is that of guiding students toward skill in analysis and evaluation of their own functioning and accomplishments. The more that students can analyze and assess the problems they face, the more likely they will be to arrive at sensible solutions. Such evaluation is part of the process of learning to work with others.

Another kind of problem likely to arise is that of individual students who in one way or another pose difficulties. There will be the reluctant student, the loner who prefers to work alone, who cannot or will not engage in group endeavors. There will be the aggressive, dominating type of student, ever eager to impose his will upon others. There will be the retiring, reserved student, content to do what is asked of him, but not likely to exhibit initiative or imagination. There will be the student whose abilities are of such a low order that much understanding, direction, and help will be required of his fellow group members and of the teacher.

There is, of course, no one way to cope with any of these problems. The teacher will have to be guided by his knowledge of the individual involved (as well as of the other students), by the nature of any given situation, by the past record of performance, by the objectives to be achieved, and by many other factors that will contribute to wise handling of problem cases.

Some Guidelines. In summary, some helpful guidelines for the teacher engaged in using group procedures include the following:

1. Start where the students are, assess their readiness for group activity, and plan accordingly.
2. Be alert throughout the process, and be ready to vary one's own involvement as the occasion requires, at times being a dominant figure, at other times a retiring one.
3. Assume a variety of roles—leader, resource, guide, mediator—as needed.
4. Have a multitude of materials and resources available and be ready to suggest others.
5. Provide a variety of opportunities throughout the year for student participation in discussion and group activities.
6. Keep helpful records of the nature of the group work used during the year and of each student's participation. Anecdotal records about individual students may also be helpful.
7. Encourage students to keep records, perhaps even a diary, of their experiences throughout the year in discussion and group work.
8. Be an active observer at all times, diagnosing, assessing, appraising, evaluating, and planning for improvement and progress.

Means and Ends

The uses of discussion techniques and group procedures can be viewed in terms of means and ends, for they serve both purposes. As means, they are processes and strategies used to achieve some specific instructional objective related to course content or substance. As ends, they are valuable learning experiences in themselves, providing their own rationale for use and analysis.

Means. As has been pointed out earlier, the use of various discussion techniques serves a number of purposes in the teacher's over-all instructional strategy. They can be an appropriate *means* of achieving specific content knowledge and comprehension. They can provide variety in learning activity and a needed change of pace. They can serve to reduce tension or resolve conflict. They can promote independent thinking and help to clarify beliefs and values. They provide opportunities for cooperative action as well as for independent study.

The teacher can view the use of the various techniques as a continuum that provides opportunities ranging from the relatively elementary to the highly sophisticated. For example, panels and buzz sessions can make possible the sharing of a wide range of opinions and views, and can provide a setting for the conveying of information, telling about, or exposition. Forums, debates, and round-table discussions are appropriate techniques for highlighting controversy and for expression of differing viewpoints. A science class could utilize them effectively in probing an issue, such as the ecology movement vis-a-vis traditional concepts of progress in technology and society.

Small groups and committees can operate at a more sophisticated level in exploring, probing, and examining complex issues, such as the morality of nuclear energy or nerve warfare, or various solutions to the energy crisis. As students acquire skills in group action, they can engage in problem-solving and research activities of an advanced nature through small group and committee planning and activity.

Ends. As *ends,* the process dimension of discussion and group work takes priority. The techniques and procedures can be viewed as ends in themselves, as learning experiences utilized to acquire skills of participation and cooperative action. Learning the ways of discussion is an important aspect of education. As such, the experiences help students acquire skills in expression, argumentation, exposition, planning, execution of·plans, and cooperation. Direct appraisal and evaluation are important in helping students gain insights relative to participant roles, their own functioning, their typical tendencies, strengths, and weaknesses. Skillful use of discussion and group work provides many opportunities for self-knowledge and self-actualization as an integral part of the participatory experience.

Analysis of Roles

An important part of discussion and group work as process to be studied is the need to understand the nature of the various roles assumed by participants. Already familiar are the formal roles of leader, whether as moderator, chairman, or designated leader of a small group endeavor, and the informal role of leadership assumed by various participants as discussion, planning, and sharing shifts from one student to another. Similarly, the role of cooperative participant or follower is a familiar one to all of us who find this often more comfortable than exerting leadership. Then, there is the frequent role designation of recording secretary for certain types of group sessions.

Even a cursory observation of group process reveals a multitude of other roles, reflected either subconsciously as an outgrowth of individual traits and characteristics, or assumed deliberately in an effort to facilitate or block group process. Several such roles can be readily identified. There is the facilitator, the group member whose contributions generally try to move forward the discussion or planning. There is the blocker, who tends to object, challenge, hold back, disrupt, or in other ways interfere with orderly progress. There is the mediator or compromiser, who attempts to help the group out of an impasse or controversy. There is the loner, who can be either a nonparticipant, or one who seeks to do his own thing and rarely engages in general cooperative action. There is the observer type who participates little but, at appropriate times, comments on the procedures of the group. The observer can help to clarify for the group its particular stage of development and progress, as well as the ways in which it has been functioning.

Many more roles could be identified, but several important points might well be made, whatever the number and types of roles delineated. If students are to be guided toward effective, cooperative activity, they need to be helped toward an understanding of these roles and of their own type of participation. They need to be encouraged to try different positive roles and need to be helped to change their more negative behavior. Especially to be noted are the dangers inherent in assuming dependency roles, whether the student becomes dependent on the teacher, on a specific classmate, on the leader, or on the entire group. One of the values of group techniques is the opportunity for growth in independent functioning. The teacher, therefore, must be a perceptive observer at all times in order to help students move in positive directions toward positive, effective, and productive roles.

Desirable Outcomes

Involvement in group work seems to result in greater participation when all students come together again in the total class situation. The participation in small groups seems to build confidence, develop verbal skills, and promote thinking and doing. As a result, these characteristics seem to carry over to behavior in large class situations.

Another promising aspect of the use of these processes is their contribution to growth in various affective realms. Group activities seem conducive to developing openness to ideas, acceptance of others, and sensitivity to people and beliefs, all qualities for which education claims to accept some responsibility.

A third desirable outcome is the generally more cooperative atmosphere in the classroom as a result of the more cooperative attitude of students. Genuine discussion and group work tends to promote a *we* feeling, a willingness to work together on common goals and projects. Such attitudes become a welcome substitute for the more usual competitive *I* versus *you* atmosphere of much of educational practice.

Some Concepts to Be Explored

It should be obvious that there is more to participatory activities than mere verbalization. In fact, there are many areas of inquiry devoted to rigorous study of key aspects of effective participation. Two that might be noted here are in the realm of group dynamics and in communication theory.

Group dynamics, or the study of behavior in groups, is a provocative area for investigation, and one which pays rich dividends for teachers and other educators. The teacher who wishes to become skillful in the use of discussion and group techniques could gain much help from the principles of group dynamics and the research that has been done in that area.

Similarly, an understanding of communication theory offers rich insights into the complexities of the act of communication. The current saying, "I know you think you heard what I said, but . . . ," illustrates the complex relationship between sender, message, and receiver. If discussion and group work are to reach their full potential in classroom practice, the teacher needs to bring to his work with students the insights and understandings to be gained from serious investigation of communication theory. Students need to be helped to acquire these same insights as they increasingly participate in an active way in the entire educational process.

ACTIVITIES

1. Identify several topics, issues, or problems in your subject fields suitable for genuine class discussion.

2. Identify the various groups to which you belong or in which you participate; also indicate all of the group experiences in which you have participated in the past week or two. Reflect on the kinds of skills needed to function effectively in them, and consider what you can learn from them that may be of value in your teaching.

3. Analyze your own participation in a recent group activity:
   a. What was the nature of your participation?
   b. What role did you perform?
   c. How effective was your participation?
   d. How might it have been more effective?

4. Investigate in some detail the distinctive characteristics of debate, forum, round-table discussion, and symposium. Suggest some appropriate uses for each, relative to specific content in your subject area.

5. Select three talk shows currently on television (or radio). Analyze and compare them in terms of the nature of the group interaction, the form of the discussion, the roles of participants, and other relevant characteristics.

6. Investigate the nature and use of the *sociogram.* Indicate ways in which you might use it vis-a-vis group work.

7. Investigate various ways by which teachers can discover students' (as a class and as individuals) readiness for discussion and group activities.

8. Develop three behavioral objectives for a specific instructional unit. Indicate which type of discussion techniques would be appropriate for the achievement of each objective.

9. If you are currently student teaching, keep a diary for a week of your use of group procedures. Indicate the purposes, nature of the technique, and an appraisal of success or effectiveness, along with identification of problems that arose.

10. As you pursue your study of this module, try to engage in various group activities with your college classmates. Assume various roles. Keep records of the involvement and interaction. Ask someone to serve as observer and help you analyze the process and its effectiveness.

SUGGESTED READING

Amidon, Edmund and Elizabeth Hunter. *Improving Teaching: The Analysis of Classroom Verbal Interaction.* New York: Holt, Rinehart & Winston, Inc., 1966.

Cartwright, Dorwin and Alvin Zander, eds. *Group Dynamics.* 3rd Ed. New York: Harper & Row, Publishers, 1968.

Clark, Leonard H. and Irving S. Starr. *Secondary School Teaching Methods,* 3rd ed. New York: Macmillan Publishing Co., Inc., 1975.

Clark, Leonard H. *Strategies and Tactics in Secondary School Teaching: A Book of Readings.* New York: Macmillan Publishing Co., Inc., 1968.

Harmin, Merrill, Howard Kirschenbaum, and Sidney B. Simon. *Clarifying Values Through Subject Matter.* Minneapolis: Winston Press, 1973.

Hock, Louise E. *Using Committees in the Classroom.* New York: Rinehart Pamphlet Series, Holt, Rinehart & Winston, Inc., 1959.

Hock, Louise E. and Thomas J. Hill. *The General Education Class in the Secondary School.* New York: Holt, Rinehart & Winston, Inc., 1960.

Keltner, John W. *Group Discussion Processes.* New York: Longmans, Green & Company, 1957.

Luft, Joseph. *Group Processes: An Introduction to Group Dynamics.* Palo Alto, Calif., National Press Books, 1970.

N.S.S.E. 59th Yearbook, Part II. *The Dynamics of Instructional Groups.* Chicago, 1960.

Raths, Louis E., Merrill Harmin, and Sidney B. Simon. *Values and Teaching.* Columbus, Ohio: Charles E. Merrill Publishers, 1966.

Thelen, Herbert. *Dynamics of Groups at Work.* Chicago: University of Chicago Press, 1954.

POST TEST

MULTIPLE CHOICE *Select the most appropriate response to each of the following:*

1. The major justification for helping students develop skills in discussion and group process is
   a. the inclusion of speech in the language arts curriculum.
   b. the failure of parents to accept responsibility for teaching these skills.
   c. the necessary respite that such activities provide from the more cognitive aspects of the instructional program.
   d. the prevalence of group activity and human interaction in everyday life and experience.

2. The use of small group or committee work techniques is most appropriate in relation to
   a. acquisition of specified information.
   b. development of psychomotor skills.
   c. promoting individual creative talents.
   d. an inquiry approach to learning.

3. All but *one* of the following are characteristic of total class sessions involving student interaction and an emphasis on inquiry:
   a. student involvement in decision making.
   b. teacher checking of lessons to determine right and wrong answers.
   c. probing analysis of concepts and issues.
   d. shifting leadership roles among the participants.

4. Fundamental to the importance of teaching group skills in the classroom is the view that the school
   a. exists solely for the transmission of knowledge.
   b. is intended to provide salable skills and career preparation.
   c. has a major responsibility to help socialize the individual.
   d. should concentrate on teaching students how to think.

5. The least formal of the following group discussion techniques is
   a. round-table discussion.
   b. symposium.
   c. debate.
   d. forum.

6. The greatest value in role-playing activities lies in
   a. enhancing the acting skills of talented students.
   b. permitting ego gratification on the part of some students.
   c. promoting the creative instincts of students.
   d. deepening insights and understandings relative to the issues and personalities involved.

7. To gain skill in spontaneous conversation in a foreign language, the most appropriate technique would be
   a. panels.
   b. debates.
   c. buzz groups.
   d. simulated TV programs.

8. The least important purpose of buzz sessions is
   a. acquisition of specific information.
   b. greater participation of all students.
   c. the opportunity for a change of pace and reduction of tension.
   d. sharing of many individual views and opinions.

9. Committee work differs from the buzz group technique largely on the basis of
   a. involvement of more students.
   b. greater focus on expressive skills.
   c. well-organized outcome relative to a specific task.
   d. more direct teacher involvement.

10. For students inexperienced in small group work, the best type of activity to start with would be
    a. production of a class magazine.
    b. planning of a field trip to a local museum.
    c. a survey of community consumer habits.
    d. committee study of several different revolutions.

11. In group work activities, it is important for the teacher to be an active observer at all times in order to
    a. assess and guide individual and group growth in participatory skills.
    b. prevent errors and misjudgment on the part of students.
    c. select appropriate leaders.
    d. direct student plans for class presentations.

12. The least likely outcome of small group and committee work is
    a. increased confidence on the part of individual students.
    b. increased competition among students.
    c. increased skill in self-direction.
    d. increased sensitivity to others.

Inquiry and Discovery Techniques

Leonard H. Clark

Jersey City State College

module 5

Discovery Teaching / Project / Case Study Method / Discussion and Discovery / Role Playing and Simulation / Inquiry and Formal Discussion

RATIONALE

In this module we shall examine a number of teaching strategies, all of which have elements of problem solving or discovery learning that we have combined under the heading of inquiry or discovery teaching methods. Although these two terms, *inquiry* and *discovery* do not have exactly the same meaning, they have much in common. Teaching methods that focus on inquiry feature learning by discovery, and methods that focus on discovery almost always involve some sort of inquiry by the pupils. The principal common factor in these teaching methods is that the pupils are expected to draw conclusions, concepts, and generalizations from either some form of induction, deduction, or application of principles to new situations. The premises behind these methods are that one learns to think by thinking, and that knowledge one figures out for himself is more meaningful, permanent, and transferable than concepts that teachers attempt to give to pupils ready-made.

SPECIFIC OBJECTIVES

In this module it is hoped that you will become familiar with the rationale for using inquiry and discovery strategies and tactics. It is also hoped you will be able to describe the procedures for teaching by each of the various inquiry and discovery techniques. Specifically, it is expected that at the completion of the unit you will be able to describe the following:

1. The advantages and disadvantages of using discovery and inquiry teaching methods as described in this module.

2. The advantages and disadvantages of using each of the methods listed, particularly as they relate to discovery and inquiry teaching.

3. General procedures common to teaching by any discovering, inquiring, and problem-solving technique.

4. The procedures for conducting each of the methods listed.

5. The procedures for conducting the study of controversial issues, as recommended in this module. The methods included in this module are discovery, problem-solving, project, research project, case study, socratic discussion, open-text recitation, use of thought questions, problem-solving discussion, value-clarifying discussion, role-playing, simulation, springboard, and formal discussion methods.

MODULE TEXT

The rationale for using the methods described in this module is the assumption that the pupil will actively seek out knowledge, rather than having it handed to him by some such expository teaching procedure as the lecture, demonstration, or textbook reading and reciting. Ordinarily, methods of the inquiry and discovery persuasion have several advantages over the expository methods. They offer good motivating activity. They give pupils opportunity to learn and practice the intellectual skills, to learn to think rationally, to see relationships and the disciplinary structure, to understand the intellectual processes, and to learn how to learn. They also result in more thorough learning, which is more meaningful, and they actively involve the pupils.

Inquiry and discovery methods also have several disadvantages. Usually they are costly in time and effort with no guarantee that the cost will pay off. Sometimes the truths that pupils discover for themselves are far removed from the truths the teachers have in mind. Slipshod thinking and investigating is difficult to eliminate and to correct. When pupils reach erroneous conclusions, reteaching may be more difficult than expository teaching would have been. Although teaching by inquiry and discovery when done well is usually more effective, it is not always more efficient. How much time one should take to rediscover well-known facts and principles is problematical, particularly in a time when there is so much to learn.

Discovery Teaching

The notion that pupil learning is more meaningful, more thorough, and therefore more usable when pupils seek out and discover knowledge, rather than just being receivers of knowledge, has been held by educational theorists for centuries. It is implicit in what we know of the teaching strategies of such master teachers as Socrates and Jesus of Nazareth, and in the theories of more modern thinkers such as Rousseau and Pestalozzi, not to mention twentieth-century educational philosophers such as John Dewey. Many practitioners today are convinced that these theories are true and they use discovery teaching as the heart of their teaching approach. Experience over the years indicates that, to an extent, they are right. If teachers will give pupils opportunities to draw conclusions from data that are provided or that they seek out for themselves, the pupils will benefit. Pupils also can learn from being shown, told, or conditioned. It is neither necessary nor wise for teachers to insist that pupils rediscover all the knowledge encompassed by the curriculum. Some of that knowledge can best be learned by expository methods. The effective teacher tries to use a mix of both discovery and inquiry strategies and expository strategies that seems most suitable to a particular teaching-learning situation.

The essential element in discovery learning is the pupils' drawing conclusions or generalizations or applying them to new situations. One method of doing this is to supply the pupils with information from which they draw conclusions. For instance, the teacher may show the pupils an experiment or a series of experiments which illustrate a generalization and then let the pupils infer the generalization by means of logical thinking. The thinking may be deductive or inductive (in this example, inductive, no doubt). Another approach would be that the pupils conduct an experiment and then draw the generalization from the results. This method differs from the cookbook laboratory method in that the pupil discovers the generalization rather than being told by the teacher or the laboratory manual what he is supposed to find and what the finding signifies. This type of discovery teaching is truly inquiry teaching, because the pupils do their own inquiring and research. It can also be problem solving if the pupils are allowed to go through the entire laboratory process themselves. Once the pupils understand the generalization or principle, either having discovered it or having been told it, they may discover how to use it in specific applications.

Actually much discovery teaching must be a combination of inductive and deductive teaching. If one understands the principles of map reading and the difficulty of pulling a wagon over steep mountains, map study will show a pupil why the pioneers took their Oregon Trail by South Pass and Bear Lake and through Idaho to Oregon rather than by the Lewis and Clark route. The basic model for conducting discovery learning consists of the following:

1. Select the generalization or generalizations.
2. Set up a problem situation.
3. Set up experiences that will bring out the essential elements during the problem solving, e.g. questions, demonstrations, and so on.
4. Set up experiences that will bring out contrasting elements.
5. Draw generalization or concept.
6. Apply the generalization or concept.[1]

Two of the best-known examples of the discovery approach are the Socratic and guided-discussion methods. However, it should be quite obvious that any inquiry method is a variety of the discovery approach.

Take a basic generalization in your field. What are some ways that a person could discover them?

A person builds notions or concepts by becoming familiar with things (ideas, beliefs, artifacts, or objects) that are examples of a class and those that are not. A child, for instance, by observation learns that certain characteristics signify an animal to be a dog and that other characteristics signify that an animal is not a dog by observing dogs and not dogs, or that certain characteristics signify being free and others signify being not free by seeing and hearing about instances when people or animals are free and not free. Pick a generalization or concept in your own major field. What experiences could you give a pupil so that he could discover from examples of positive and negative characteristics what the concept is and what it is not, and so define the concept or generalization in his own thinking?

Teacher's Role in Inquiry and Discovery. Since inquiry connotes seeking and discovering rather than learning from exposition, the teacher's role in inquiry teaching is to guide learning rather than to direct or dictate. In this role, he raises problems, issues, and questions that he hopes will catch the pupils' interest, start them thinking, and encourage them to investigate. While the pupils are investigating, the teacher guides their search. He tries to help them clarify their problems, map out their procedures, order their thinking, come to logical conclusions, and, finally, test and apply their conclusions. To keep inquiry learning on the road, a teacher should do the following:

---

[1] Leonard H. Clark and Irving S. Starr, *Secondary School Teaching Methods,* 3rd Ed. (New York: Macmillan Publishing Co., Inc., 1976), p. 231.

1. Be supportive and accepting.
2. Accentuate the positive.
3. Provide clues.
4. Encourage the exchange of ideas.
5. Accept legitimate hypotheses.
6. Warn and rescue pupils when they seem to lose their way.
7. Encourage pupils to make informed guesses.
8. Help pupils to analyze and evaluate their ideas, interpretations, and thinking.
9. Foster free debate and open discussion, and urge pupils to try to think things out with no threat of reprisals when their thinking does not conform to the expected or to the norm.

Obviously, these are tactics designed to encourage reflective and creative thinking. To stimulate independent, resourceful thinking a teacher can also do the following:

1. Check the pupils' data gathering techniques.
2. Ask thought questions.
3. Ask for interpretations, explanations, and hypotheses.
4. Question the interpretations, explanations, and hypotheses at which the pupil arrives.
5. Ask pupils what their data and information imply.
6. Ask pupils to check their thinking and their logic.
7. Confront pupils with problems, contradictions, fallacies, implications, value assumptions, value conflicts, and other factors that may call for a reassessment of their thinking and positions.[2]

In some types of discovery lessons, such as the controlled discussion, the free inquiry element of discovery teaching is likely to be minimal. In these lessons, the teacher is more often a director of learning than a guide.

Use of Thought Questions. All of the inquiry and discovery techniques rely on skillful use of thought questions. You should practice using them until their use becomes second nature. The following list should provide suggestions that will help you to develop proficiency in this type of questioning:

1. Use developmental questions emphasizing how and why rather than who, what, where, and when.
2. Follow up leads. Build on pupils' contributions. Give pupils a chance to comment on each other's answers; for example, "Do you agree with John on that, Mary?" or "Do you think this argument would hold in such and such case, John?"
3. Be sure the pupils have the facts before you ask thought questions about them. One way is to ask fact questions first and then follow up with thought questions. Another way is to lead in by means of good summary questions. Other ways are to incorporate the facts in the question itself or to give the

---

[2] Ibid., p. 225.

pupils fact sheets that they can consult as they try to think through suitable answers to the question. Similar results can be gained by putting the facts on the blackboard or on the overhead projector, by allowing pupils to refer to their texts, or by simply telling the pupils the facts before beginning the questioning.

4. Remember that the best thought questions usually do not have correct answers. In such cases, the thinking concerned is much more important than the answer derived. Be sure pupils back up their answers by valid, logical reasoning. Insist that they show their evidence and demonstrate why this evidence leads to their conclusion.

5. Encourage pupils to challenge each other's thinking and even that of their teacher. Good use of thought questions leads to true discussion rather than simple question-answer teaching.[3]

Problem Solving. Most inquiry is carried out by some variety of problem solving. The problem at hand may be exceedingly complex, requiring great skill and effort for its solution, or it may be so simple that solving it is almost automatic. But, in any case, the problem solving activity is one that requires thought and a search for a solution, which may be a generalization or a conclusion. Examples of problem-solving approaches include such diverse activities as writing term papers, attempting to identify an unknown chemical, preparing an oral report, composing a menu, balancing a budget, or repairing a gasoline engine. Essentially, any learning activity in which the learner has to hunt for or think out answers is a problem-solving activity. However, one should not dignify an activity with the name problem solving if he can find the answer by the process of simple recall.

The steps in problem solving have been described differently by different theorists, but essentially the process is as follows:

1. We become aware of a problem (it may be started by the occasion, by someone else, or by ourselves), isolate it, and decide to do something about it.

2. We look for clues for the solution of the problem.
   a. We think up possible solutions (hypotheses) or approaches to take in solving the problem.
   b. We test the tentative solution or approaches against criteria that will help us evaluate them adequately.

3. We reject the tentative solutions or approaches that do not meet our requirements and try new ones until we find one that is suitable, or we give up. In making our conclusions, we may accept the first solution or approach that appears adequate, or we may test all hypotheses to find the best one.[4]

This is essentially the process that John Dewey called a complete thought. In short, we must become aware of what the problem is; look for a solution; and check the solution to see if it is any good.

---

[3] Leonard H. Clark, *Teaching Social Studies in Secondary Schools: A Handbook* (New York: Macmillan Publishing Co., Inc., 1973), pp. 80–81.
[4] Ibid, p. 28.

The ability to solve problems, particularly academic problems, does not seem to come naturally to most people. Excellence in problem solving is a skill that must be learned, so must be taught. If teachers supervise pupils carefully at every stage of the problem-solving process, they may be able not only to help the pupils solve the problems, but also to help them improve their problem-solving techniques.

One of the perplexing truisms about problem solving is that often the reason no one solves a problem is because no one realizes exactly what the problem is. In 1729, young Benjamin Franklin conducted a now famous experiment to find out the relation of color to heat absorption and thermal conductivity. According to Crane,

> From a tailor's sample-card Franklin detached broadcloth squares of different colors and shades, laid them on snow in bright sunshine, and measured the relative depth to which they sank as the snow melted. It was a simple test; a schoolboy it has often been said, could have done it. But Franklin was the first to define the problem and to devise the experiment.[5]

Any schoolboy could have done it, but it took Franklin to think up the question, define it, and follow through. Pupils need help in finding questions to ask and investigate. A teacher can sometimes help them by suggesting problem areas or specific problems to them. This he can do directly or indirectly by setting the stage. In Module 1.4, you will remember, Mr. Jones set the stage by faking a temper tantrum and then capitalizing on the discussion that followed to awaken pupils to the problem areas they might explore.

The teacher also needs to see to it that the problems that pupils select are suitable for their purposes. Among the criteria that they can use to test the suitability of the problem are the following:

1. Is it pertinent to the course objectives?
2. Is it relevant to pupils' lives and to community life?
3. Is it feasible? Do we have the necessary resources? Can we complete it in the time available? Can the pupils handle it?
4. Is it worth the effort?

What would be interesting problem areas in your major field? Set up a list of eight or ten problems that pupils might investigate in the study of a topic in your major field. Why would each of these problems be good for pupils to investigate? Or why would it not be?

It is sometimes said that all secondary school learning must, or should be, problem-solving learning. Do you agree? Justify your position.

In selecting the problem, it is necessary to define it so as to set up the limits of the problem and to decide what must be done. Franklin's breakthrough in the study of heat absorption and thermal conductivity was caused because he was, evidently, the first person to define the problem. If one does not know exactly what the problem is, it is difficult to solve it. It is also difficult if the problem is too large and so impossible to focus on. Defining the problem by making it clear and

[5] Verner W. Crane, *Benjamin Franklin and a Rising People* (Boston: Little, Brown and Company, 1954), p. 42.

giving it clear limits makes the solving of a particular problem a more reasonable task than it would be if it were not defined.

Once the problem has been isolated and defined, we begin to search for ways to solve it. This process involves gathering the data we need to make tentative hypotheses concerning ways to solve the problem, and trying out or testing these proposed solutions.

The last step in the process is to accept or reject the proposed solution. If the first idea seems to be satisfactory, we may end our search right there; otherwise we may try out other hypotheses or resume our search for more data and ideas in hope of finding new hypotheses. It may even be necessary to redefine the problem. Finally we find a hypothesis that we do accept or we give up trying to solve the problem. These steps—getting the data we need, making hypotheses, and testing them—do not necessarily occur in a particularly orderly fashion although, of course, one has to think of a hypothetical solution before he tries it or rejects it. The hypothetical solution may come out of the data we have accumulated, or the data may be gathered as a way of testing or developing a hypothesis.

Project

In the context of education, the word *project* has become diluted in recent years to mean any unit of activity, individual or group, involving the investigation and solution of problems, planned and carried to a conclusion by a pupil or pupils under the guidance of the teacher. Originally, it was conceived as being of significant practical value and resulting in some tangible product of personnel value to the learner, such as the raising and marketing of a calf. To be worthy of the name, a project must be truly a problem-solving activity. In a true project the student plans, executes, and evaluates the entire undertaking. The teacher's role is simply to help, advise, and guide the learning.

Although ideally all projects should derive from pupils' interests, usually pupils have trouble finding and selecting suitable projects. Teachers can help them at this point in several ways; they can provide lists of suggestions or try to stimulate ideas by class discussion. Sometimes telling pupils what others have done in the past or having last year's pupils come to the class on a consulting basis to describe successful projects of the past work well. No matter how the pupils get the idea, when they finally pick out their projects, they should check them for suitability. The criteria that should be met are that the project should make a real contribution to a worthwhile learning objective; it should result in a worthwhile end project; and it should be reasonable insofar as time, effort, cost, and availability of resources are concerned.

To conduct a project requires a combination of restraint and guidance from the teacher. The pupils need to accept most of the responsibility for their projects, but they should not be allowed to flounder. The teacher must make himself available to assist the pupils when necessary and from time to time to check their progress without interfering. Taking the middle course between too much and too little requires both tact and good judgment.

Think up a half dozen projects in your subject field that would result in a project really valuable to the students who do them.

Research Projects. The research project is an interesting variety of the genre. In this type of project, the pupil, independently or as a member of a committee, investigates some matter and then reports on it. As a rule, this type of project is best done by the more academically talented pupils. Although pupils with little academic talent or interest usually do not do this type of activity well, they can accomplish appropriate projects reasonably well when the projects are interesting enough to them, when they have the necessary guidance, and when the roles given to them are not unreasonable for persons of their abilities. Often they can also make significant contributions to group research projects; however, less able pupils should not be forced to do research projects. They can usually gain more benefits from other types of activities.

The process used in a research project is that of any problem solving activity, as follows:

1. Decide exactly what it is that one is to try to find out.
2. Determine the problem so that it is manageable in the time available and with the materials and personnel available.
3. Decide on what tasks must be done to get the necessary data and who will do each job.
4. Gather the materials and equipment necessary.
5. Perform the data-gathering tasks.
6. Review and analyze the data gathered.
7. Draw conclusions and generalizations from the data gathered.
8. Report the findings and conclusions.[6]

Perhaps, as applied to research projects, these steps need some elucidation. Selecting a topic for research can be somewhat bothersome. Most students find it difficult to select a problem on which they can really focus. To be worthwhile, the research should be aimed at a specific problem. Large, diffuse, ill-defined topics seldom result in anything worthwhile. Teachers should help pupils select topics of manageable proportions. Gathering the information requires that the pupils have mastered certain skills and are cognizant of certain materials. Too many research projects are simply accounts cribbed from an encyclopedia. Teachers should help pupils develop skill in looking up and finding pertinent references. They also need help in developing research techniques. Few students take adequate notes unless teachers instruct them in the art of note-taking. Pupils also have great trouble with such research skills as use of scientific equipment, sampling, analyzing data, testing for fact, and interpreting statistics unless they receive special instruction and supervision. Research is not easy, and proficiency in the use of scholarly procedures and intellectual tools is difficult to attain unless students are carefully schooled and supervised in their use. Students also need help in seeing the significance of their data and in drawing valid conclusions and generalizations from their research. Special class sessions for teaching these intellectual skills are helpful and should be utilized, but most of the skill development in this area must be taught by supervising the individual efforts of student researchers.

Research projects usually are best conducted as individual or small group

---

[6] Clark and Starr, op. cit., p. 229.

activities. Very few of them are truly successful when conducted as whole class activities, although sometimes projects such as community surveys or the investigation and preparation of a report on a community problem can be very rewarding. The pupils in one New Jersey high school class, for instance, were concerned about racial prejudice in that school and community. As a class, they studied a number of references on the problem of prejudice, developed a questionnaire, gave the questionnaire to citizens in the community, analyzed the findings, and published the results. Some of the data and conclusions resulting from this study may be suspect in several ways. The study was the work of beginners, but the students found out much about race prejudice, about their community, and developed some familiarity with research techniques. Because the teacher carefully supervised the project and frequently criticized the pupils' efforts, errors were kept to a minimum, and the pupils learned through their mistakes as well as their successes.

Survey Questionnaires and Opinion Sampling. Surveys of the community or of the school population are among the most interesting types of research projects. If well planned and well conducted, they can teach the pupils much, but if poorly conceived and executed, they can lead to confusion, miseducation, and an upset community. Before one launches into a community survey, he should be sure that the pupils know well both the topic they are to investigate and the procedures they are to use. This can be achieved by direct teaching and practice in the class.

GATHERING THE INFORMATION. There are many ways to conduct the gathering of data: interviews, questionnaires, and observation, for instance. It is, of course, important to pick the right data-gathering technique and to aim it directly at the correct goal. To be sure that the technique is suitable and well aimed, the teacher and pupils must carefully examine the problem to see exactly what data is needed for its solution. Then they must design a strategy to obtain that information. If this strategy involves a questionnaire or opinion sampling this is the point at which one designs the instrument. Although the development of an instrument may not be so necessary if the strategy adopted involves interviewing or observation, probably the results will be more profitable and dependable if a data gathering instrument, such as a rating scale or check list is used. The pupils, of course, must be instructed and practiced in the use of these instruments so that they will not waste the time of the respondents and also so that the data gathered will be what was wanted. We shall discuss the construction and use of this sort of instrument later.

PROCESSING THE DATA. Once the data have been gathered, they must be interpreted. This part of the research can be somewhat tricky. Most persons are tempted to make generalizations and conclusions that are not justified by the data. Teachers should help pupils set up criteria by which to distinguish between significant and insignificant data. In some cases, to interpret the data, one may have to use simple statistics, but usually for class use careful inspection will suffice. The important point is to extrapolate cautiously. It is much safer to say that of the people we asked, 10 per cent said yes, 70 per cent said no, and 20 per cent did not answer, than to say that the people of the community reject the proposition. In this regard, pupils should be made aware of the difficulties of sampling and the need of an adequate sample as well as techniques for analyzing and interpreting their data. It is probably best to record and report the data in tabular form without comment.

For example: Question 1. Do you prefer Plan A or Plan B?
Total, 50 (100 per cent). A. 5 (10 per cent). B. 30 (60 per cent). No Answer, 15 (30 per cent).

PUBLISHING THE RESULTS. Publishing the results of a survey usually should be reserved for classroom use only. Only exceptionally good surveys rate publishing more widely and even they should not be published until cleared by school officials. There is no reason to publish anything that will not enhance the school's image or reputation as a scholarly institution.

BUILDING THE QUESTIONNAIRE OR OPINION SAMPLING. As many college and university graduate students have found out to their sorrow, to build an effective questionnaire or opinion sampling is not an easy task. The following suggestions may help pupils who attempt to use questionnaires or opinion samplings in research projects.

1. Be sure to include only those things that are needed in the questionnaire. If you can find the information in another way with reasonable ease, do so.
2. Be sure the questions are clear. Check them for ambiguities. To be sure that they are unambiguous, try them out on other pupils and teachers. You may find that you ought to rewrite many of them or explain the terms or references you are using.
3. Be sure the questions are easy to answer. Yes-no, one word check lists, or multiple choice questions are the easiest and quickest both to answer and to interpret. However, be sure to give the respondent a chance to comment. It is maddening to a respondent not to be able to say that the answer is "yes, but . . ." or "well, it depends on . . ." Forced choice items have no place in questionnaires written by public school pupils; they should be reserved for use by professionals or by graduate students.
4. Be sure to set up the questionnaire so that it will be easy to tally the answers. For instance, if the answers can be arranged so that they appear in a column on the right (or left) side of the sheet, it makes tabulating much easier. Additional remarks and comments cannot be made easy to tabulate, but space should be provided for them. Be sure to give the respondent room enough to write a reasonably long, but not too long, comment.

INTERVIEW FORMAT. To be sure that pupils conducting interviews ask the questions they should without taking up too much of the interviewee's time, or garbling the questions, or omitting necessary questions, the interview questions should be planned and written out before the interview. A written plan is necessary also because, if one hopes to get comparable data from the interviews, the pupils must ask all the respondents the same questions in the same way. Therefore, it is wise to develop a formal procedure, such as the following suggested by Popkewitz:

My name is _____. My class is doing a survey about student participation. I will be speaking to many students in your school and other schools. I would like to ask you a few questions.

A. Do you often discuss school issues with
   1. Friends?
   2. Class officers?
   3. School officials?

B. Have you ever attended a meeting (church, school board, union, etc.) in which school policy was discussed?

C. Have you ever taken an active part regarding school issues, such as writing a letter or presenting a petition?[7]

This format makes it easy for pupils to record answers to their questions. They should record the answers of the respondent immediately. If they try to depend on memory, they will get mixed up, forget, and, therefore, bring in incorrect data.

OBSERVATION TECHNIQUES. If research involving the use of observation techniques is to be successful, the pupils must be well prepared to observe carefully and profitably. The observation must be planned and the observers trained so that they see and report the data in the same way. For this purpose, the pupils should decide exactly what it is they must look for. In some instances, this means that they will have to decide upon the standards for establishing the presence or absence of the phenomenon, or for deciding the criteria for such categories as *much, some, little*. They will also need to devise some sort of instrument on which to record their observations. Frequently this instrument should be a check list in which the observers merely note the presence or absence of phenomena, as in the following:

1. Check the applicable item.
   a. Pupil selected a hot dish.
   b. Pupil selected a dessert.
   c. Pupil selected a coke.

Or the instrument may be a rating scale in which the pupil records his judgment of the amount or quality of the phenomenon present, as in the following:

The pupils' conduct in the cafeteria line was
      Very Orderly   Fairly Orderly   Disorderly
The pupils' conduct at their tables was
      Very Orderly   Fairly Orderly   Disorderly

In the constructing of these devices, teachers should try to help pupils concoct procedures that make observing, recording, and interpreting the data as simple and as easy as possible. When observing, recording or interpreting becomes unnecessarily complicated, the devices are usually accompanied by unnecessary errors.

Field Trip. One of the very best ways to make instruction real is to take the pupils out in the field to see and do things, such as to go to the theater to see a production of *Macbeth,* to go down to the swamp to gather specimens, to see ecological problems first hand, to go to the museum to see the works of great art, or to visit the site of a battle. Field trips, carefully planned and executed, can pay off in increased motivation and meaningful learning, but they require careful planning. In fact, of all the possible instructional activities, they probably require the most careful planning. Among the items one may need to consider in preparing for a particular field trip are the following:

[7] Thomas S. Popkewitz, *How To Study Political Participation,* How to Do It Series No. 27 (Washington, D.C.: National Council for the Social Studies, 1974), p. 5.

1. Talk over the trip with your principal and department head.

2. Take the trip yourself, if feasible, to see how to make it most productive and to see what arrangements should be made.

3. Arrange for details at the place to be visited. These arrangements include a schedule; the briefing of the host, or tour personnel, on what you want and what type of group you are; provisions for eating and rest rooms; and so on. Get clear information about fees.

4. Arrange for permissions from the school authorities and parents.

5. Arrange for schedule changes, excuses from other classes, and so on.

6. Arrange for transportation.

7. Arrange for the collection of funds, payments, and so on.

8. Arrange for the safety of pupils.

9. Arrange the itinerary, including all stops—rest stops, meals, and so on. Do not plan to rush. Allow plenty of time. Figure that someone will get lost, or be late, or something!

10. Establish rules of conduct.

11. Brief the pupils. Give them directions: what to do if lost or left behind, what to take along, what they are going to do, what they should look for, what notes they should take, what materials they should bring back. Give them a duplicated study guide.

12. Provide for follow-up activities. Taking along tape recorders and cameras will allow you to bring back a record of what you did and saw. Tape record interviews, talks, questions and answers, and take pictures of the people, places, and things seen as the basis of a class follow-up.

13. Take steps to see that no one is left out because of lack of money, race, religion, or ethnic background.

14. Arrange for other teachers and parents to help you.[8]

Figure 5-1 is a worksheet used for planning and reporting field trips at a New Jersey junior high school. Notice the meticulous detail that the board of education expects of teachers who conduct field trips. As you examine this form, ask yourself why the school board and school administrators have required each of the items they have listed.

Case Study Method

The case study is a special type of problem-solving method. It consists of a searching, detailed study of a particular situation, institution, decision, or issue from which pupils draw generalizations concerning the type. The case study can give pupils considerable understanding of difficult, complex matters.

Although the procedures for conducting case studies are quite simple, they are usually difficult to carry out. In general, they include the following procedures:

1. Select and define a topic or problem to investigate. The topic should be a specific case so typical of a larger area that studying it would throw light on to the entire area.

2. Identify, collect, and make ready the materials needed for studying the case in depth. Usually, most will be reading material, but do not forget that

[8] Leonard H. Clark, *Teaching Social Studies in Secondary Schools: A Handbook* (New York: Macmillan Publishing Co., Inc., 1973), p. 321.

Date _____

Teacher's Worksheet on Field Trip

This worksheet is intended both as a teacher's guide and a report. It should be handed in after the completion of the trip. Check applicable items as completed.

Trip to _____

Teacher _____ Subject _____ Date of trip _____

Group or section _____ Alternate date _____

Planning on Part of teacher

_____ Are the educational values of the proposed trip definite and clear? State them briefly:

_____ Figure the cost: Transportation $_____

                               Admissions $_____

                               Meals $_____

                               Total $_____

_____ Is the total cost figure sufficient, reasonable and within the reach of most of the group?

_____ Secure approval of the principal and turn in Permission for School Excursion (Form 132).

_____ Check school calendar with vice-principal and sign for date.

_____ Make arrangements with bus company, after securing at least two bids.

_____ Have the places you intend to visit been "scouted," either by you or someone you know?

_____ Chaperones to be secured: two adults per bus, one of whom must be a licensed teacher.

_____ If the trip takes two hours or more, is a bathroom stop available enroute?

_____ Have teachers made arrangements with the vice-principal for students left behind or for teachers' duties left "uncovered"?

Preparation of the Class

_____ Discuss purposes of trip with the class.

_____ Each child who is going must have Field Trip Permit signed by parents (Form 126).

_____ Discuss proper clothes to be worn by the students.

_____ Discuss conduct on bus, including:
         _____ No arms or heads to be out of windows.
         _____ Remain in seats except by permission.

Figure 5-1

_____ Trash to be placed in paper bags.

_____ Nothing to be thrown out of bus windows.

_____ Pupils remain in seats on bus at destination until teacher gets off first.

_____ Listen to teacher's directions for dismounting at destination.

_____ Discuss the method of control which is to be used during the trip:

_____ "Buddy System"—students are paired up and given numbers (1A-1B, 2A-2B, etc.) The pair must remain together. If they leave the main group, they must tell another pair where they are going. Students must immediately report the loss of a "buddy." Each chaperone will supervise so many sets of buddies.

_____ Or "Group system"—divide a busload into two or three squads, with a student leader *and* a chaperone in charge of each. Attendance to be taken by each group frequently.

_____ Or other system of control as planned by teacher and approved by principal.

_____ Eating arrangements to be explained to pupil. Need for staple foods, rather than a day of candy and soda, should be discussed.

_____ On day before trip, class should make a list of things to be looked for on trip.

On the Morning of the Trip

_____ Proper attendance taken in homeroom or classroom.

_____ Correct absentee cards sent to office.

_____ Correct list of those remaining behind turned in to office.

_____ Permission slips (Form 126) filed in main office.

_____ Students reinstructed on bus safety rules.

_____ Take first aid kit; also empty paper bags for car sickness.

_____ Check attendance *on the bus* immediately before leaving. Teacher in charge reports discrepancies to the attendance secretary in main office.

Follow-Up

_____ Has the trip been followed up by the class with evaluation—either written or oral—of ideas and facts learned?

_____ Write a brief evaluation of the trip: What were its values? Would you take a group on it next year? Other comments. Use space below.

_____

Signature of Teacher

Figure 5-1 *(Continued)*

sometimes films, pictures, or audio and video tapes may be better for your purpose. So may laboratory or field work.

3. Now that you have the things to work with, you are ready to begin the case study. Start with any good introduction. In the introduction, the pupils should get an understanding of the problem or issue before them, what they are attempting to find out, and the method of attack. This is the time when you sell the case study to the pupils so make your introduction persuasive. At this point, it may be wise to give out a study guide that the pupils can use as they investigate the case. The bulk of the study of the case can be done individually by pupils investigating individually with the study guide for a base. If one wishes, it is possible to proceed on a group or whole class basis through the use of discussions and the like. But the really important part of this phase of the case study approach is to study the particular case in depth, learn as much as one can about it, and draw conclusions.

4. Now the pupils share their findings and conclusions. They can do this in many ways; perhaps the most profitable is the free discussion. Role playing, panels, and symposia, may also prove very useful. In these discussions, the pupils should be encouraged to draw inferences from the case study, as he has been doing right along about the class of things the case study represents.

Discussion and Discovery

Socratic Method. Socratic questioning has been treated in an earlier module of this series. It is one of the very oldest of discovery methods of which we have any record. According to Plato, Socrates' method was to ask a series of questions by which he hoped to cause his pupil to examine his beliefs, upset his preconceptions, and then draw new conclusions. The secret of the method was in the use of questions that were both challenging and leading. This questioning requires a great amount of skill and a thorough knowledge, because the questioner must be ready to follow with a new appropriate question wherever the pupil may lead him. To make the system work well, the teacher should think out beforehand the type of questions he should ask. In fluid situations, it is impossible to anticipate what the answers will be and to be prepared for all contingencies. Probably that was why Socrates depended so much upon leading questions, such as, All people want to be happy, don't they? Handled by an expert, such as Socrates was, the Socratic method can be a superb instrument for examining and discovering ideas.

Controlled or Guided Discussion. The controlled or guided discussion is an attempt to adapt the Socratic method to the exigencies of large classes found in most schools. Basically it consists of the following three steps:

1. Select certain generalizations to be learned.
2. Furnish the pupils with information by means of lectures, reading, film, or other expository devices or techniques.
3. Utilize probing questions to guide the pupils as they draw principles and generalizations from the information they have been given or have found in

their reading or study. This method is not a true discussion or a true in-quiry. As usually conducted, it is very teacher-centered and seldom open-ended. In carrying it out, the teacher continually asks pupils challenging, thought-provoking questions, designed to arouse their thinking in an attempt to persuade them to arrive at the conclusions or generalizations he has set up as his goals.

For an example of how one might use a guided discussion to develop a gen-eralization, let us revert to the Oregon Trail example to which we referred earlier. Let us suppose that we wished to have the pupils realize that the terrain has con-siderable impact on the location of routes. We could then initiate a lesson in map study and perhaps a reading, describing travel along the trail. Then, in discussion, we could ask questions such as (1) What seems to be the most direct route from Missouri to Oregon? (2) What are the disadvantages of this route? (3) In setting out to select a route to Oregon, what factors would you, as a pioneer, look for?

As a result of this type of questioning, it is hoped that the teacher will be able to draw the conclusion that, in setting out a route, one must consider such elements as slope, water, and attitudes of the natives. To reinforce these ideas, one might compare the route selected for the Oregon Trail with the routes selected for super tankers bringing oil from the Arabian oil fields to the East Coast of the United States.

Open-Text Recitation. In the controlled discussion, there is no reason that the pupils should not have before them the information to be used in drawing their conclusions. Controlled discussions should not be exercises in remembering, but in discovering. In the lesson we have just seen, the maps and written information provided are resources that can make the lesson more meaningful and productive if the pupils can refer to them during the class. This sort of class is often called an open-textbook recitation. It has already been discussed in Module 3. The point in this type of lesson is to develop a discussion in which pupils can defend their ideas, justify their contributions, and check on proposals while the class is in progress. Such discussions may or may not be open-ended. Although the open-textbook recitation is ordinarily conducted as a controlled discussion, there is absolutely no reason why textbooks and references should not be used in true discussions. Probably it would be preferable in many instances if many open-textbook recitations were conducted as true discussions rather than as controlled discussions.

Controlled
Discussion

True (open)
Discussion

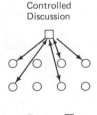
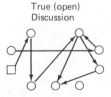

Teacher □

Pupil ○

Figure 5-2 *Flow of Conversation in Discussions.*

Problem-Solving Discussion. Discussion can be used both as a means of inquiry and intellectual discovery if the problem under discussion is important to the discussants and if conducted so that it is free and permissive, yet also disciplined and orderly. Rap sessions or bull sessions will not suffice, but well-conducted dicussions are excellent for solving problems, because they bring out so many ideas from so many different people. Group members usually have many differing values, biases, insights, standards, conclusions, and beliefs. Open discussion reveals these differences and frees group members to examine, or at least to defend, their own values and beliefs and consider the values and beliefs of others. Because it is difficult to maintain narrow stereotypic thinking in such circumstances, the discussion tends to open group members to new ideas, to stimulate new thinking and, perhaps, to create answers to the problems to be solved.

The procedures for conducting a discussion that is aimed at solving a problem are just about the same as those for carrying on any other type of discussion. Although they, or other discussions, seldom hue strictly to the line prescribed by the most logical development, they should follow the general patterns of the problem-solving process. As adapted for discussion groups by Burton and Wing, these procedures include the following points:

1. The group becomes aware of a problem that it believes can be solved by talking it out.
2. The group defines the problem. This defining process may be quite difficult and time-consuming.
3. The group analyzes and explores the problem so that all will understand it. The process includes (a) determining what the facts are; (b) becoming acquainted with the values, backgrounds, and levels of maturity of the various group members; and (c) discovering the hidden objectives, if any, of individual group members.
4. The group thinks the problem through together. This process will undoubtedly be slow and orderly. Errors will be made and time consumed, but the procedure is necessary.
5. The group brings resources to help explore the problem. A pooling of ignorance solves no problems, so the group seeks out the information it needs from whatever sources promise to be most fruitful.
6. The group develops the "machinery and organization" necessary for co-operative thinking as it goes along. These are not set up in advance.
7. The group continually summarizes, casts straw votes, and projects tentative solutions as the discussion goes along, so as to delay making premature final conclusions and to bring about the consensus of all its members.
8. The group continually evaluates its progress, both as to process and to substance.
9. The group comes to a tentative conclusion which it tries out in actual situation.[9]

You recognize, of course, that these are the procedures used by all successful committees, society meetings, town meetings, and the like to solve problems brought before them.

[9] Adapted from William H. Burton, Roland B. Kimball, and Richard L. Wing, *Education for Effective Thinking* (New York: Appleton-Century-Crofts, Inc., 1960), p. 328.

As a group discussion leader, how does your role in a controlled discussion differ from that in a problem-solving discussion?

Value-Clarifying Discussions. Discussions of the inquiry type can also be useful for helping pupils discover and understand values. As in problem-solving discussions, the teacher should encourage pupils to think freely. To create and maintain a supportive class climate that will stimulate thought, the teacher should avoid the use of leading questions, preaching, informing pupils that their opinions are wrong, and other tactics that cut off thinking, or force pupils into giving lip service to positions that they may not believe in, or that impede the consideration of alternative positions. Value clarifying discussions must be open ended, so, as Raths, Harmin and Simon point out, the teacher who hopes to use the discussion for developing clear values (1) helps them to examine alternatives and consequences in issues; (2) does not tell them, directly or indirectly, what is "right" for all persons and for all times; (3) is candid about his own values, but insists that they not be blindly adopted by others; (4) sometimes limits behavior that he considers ill advised but never limits the right to believe or the right to behave differently in other circumstances; and (5) points to the importance of the individual making his own choices and considering the implications for his own life.[10] As a rule, value-clarifying discussions are kept short. One can launch them by any of the springboard techniques already described in this module.

Role Playing and Simulation

Role Playing and Problem Solving. Role playing and simulation can be used effectively in inquiry and discovery teaching. By attempting to simulate a real problem, students may get real insight into the nature of a problem situation. Role playing may be used to clarify attitudes and concepts; demonstrate attitudes and concepts; deepen understandings of social situations; prepare for real situations (such as practicing the interview procedures to be used in a survey); plan and try out strategies for attacking problems; test out hypothetical solutions to problems; and practice leadership and other skills. Role playing has a number of drawbacks, however. Role playing is slow; is often not realistic enough so that false concepts result; and is serious business, but it is a temptation to think of it as entertainment.

As you already know, role playing is an unrehearsed dramatization, in which the players try to clarify a situation by acting out the roles of the participants in the situation. To carry out a role-playing session, the following procedures are recommended:

1. Pick a simple situation, not a complicated one, to role play. Two to four characters usually are quite enough.
2. Select a cast who will do the job. Use volunteers, if feasible, but only if the volunteers are equal to the task. It is preferable to sacrifice self-selection for effectiveness. Sometimes it is helpful to select several casts and run through the role playing several times, each time with a different cast. Dif-

---

[10] Louis E. Raths, Merrill Harmin, Sidney B. Simon, *Values and Teaching* (Columbus, Ohio: Charles E. Merrill Publishers, 1966), p. 115.

ferent interpretations of the parts should give the audience more data from which to draw their inferences and make their discoveries.

3. Be sure that the characters in the cast understand the situation, the purpose of the role playing, and their roles. To this end, brief the players well and then discuss their roles with them. Sometimes it is helpful to outline the general line they should follow and to rehearse the first few lines. However, too much direction and too much warmup can ruin the role playing by stereotyping the interpretations.

4. Brief the audience. Be sure everyone understands what the players are supposed to be trying to do.

5. Stage the role playing. Let the role players interpret freely. However, if they get hopelessly lost, it may be necessary for you to stop the role playing and reorient the players.

6. If it seems desirable, repeat the role playing with reversed roles or with different role players.

7. Follow up the role playing with a discussion about what happened in the role playing and its significance. At this point, the teacher should encourage pupils to come to some conclusions and make some generalizations (although it may be more satisfactory to leave the discussion open-ended). Sometimes the discussion may reveal new or different interpretations and concepts that warrant a replaying of the roles and further discussion and analysis.

Simulation. In this age of computers and space exploration, everyone must be familiar with simulation, simulators, and simulations. Basically a simulation is an enactment of a make-believe episode as much like the real thing as possible, but with some of the dangerous and complicating factors removed. The embryonic truck driver does not suffer dire results from his mistake if he pulls in front of a speeding bus when he is driving his driver education simulator; the beginning aviator crashes with impunity when the plane she stalls is simulated; and the soldier who mishandles his new weapon in a dry run without live ammunition kills no one. Simulations of this sort, although in our examples largely aimed at developing skills, can be useful for helping pupils to gain insights into difficult matters. The young, aspiring lawyer who tries a case in a simulated courtroom not only gains skill in legal practice, but also gains insight into the law of the case being tried. In the social studies classroom, the pupils simulating the management of a business are learning what happens when they overbuy, overprice and make strategic errors.

In these simulations, the student has gone through the process in what he was learning in a real way. That is the value of simulation. By taking roles in the simulated activity, the pupils, it is hoped, will come to understand the real situation and how to act in it.

Simulations differ from role playing in that their scenarios must be carefully drafted. In these scenarios (1) the pupils are assigned definite roles that require that they take specific action in a well-defined situation, and (2) the pupils are confronted by simulated, real-life situations that require them to take actions just as they would have to in real life (or at least as close to real life as feasible). These actions may lead to new predicaments that require new actions. In taking action, the player is not free but stays in character and keeps his actions within the limits prescribed by the role he has assumed and by the realities of the simulated situation.

If you are to produce a simulation, the following procedure may prove to be useful:

1. Prepare the material, equipment, and props that will be needed.
2. Introduce the plan to the pupils. Explain what the purpose of the simulation is. Give the directions for playing it.
3. Assign roles. Probably it is best to pick the players yourself. Accepting volunteers or selecting pupils by chance may result in disastrous miscasting.
4. Brief the pupils in their roles. Be sure they understand them.
5. Conduct the simulation. Follow the scenario to the letter.
6. Follow up with a critique in which pupils have a chance to discuss what they have done and to draw generalizations.

Inquiry and Formal Discussion

The methods we shall now discuss briefly are not so much inquiry and discovery methods as they are methods for reporting and clarifying what has already been inquired into and discovered. Still, they do provide for thinking, for reexamination, for applying, and for discovering new insights. They also have the advantage of combining free discussion, pupil participation, and large class audience activities. These methods are the round table, the panel, the forum, the symposium, the formal debate, the British debate, and the jury trial. In general, all of these methods follow a similar pattern. The common procedure of this general pattern in formal discussion is that first, several participants present positions, arguments, points of view, or reports, and then the other members and the audience ask questions and discuss the matter. In large groups, this discussion is usually only a question-and-answer period, but in smaller groups, it may be a true free discussion.

Formal discussions have many uses. Among them are the following:

1. To report the findings of committees, research, and investigation. This is perhaps the most common use of formal discussions. Panels may consist of representatives of several committees or a single committee.
2. To present the findings of individual investigations.
3. To add a measure of pupil participation to large group instruction.
4. To vary the pace of the class.
5. To furnish springboards for beginning a discussion or class investigation.
6. To get differing viewpoints and information before the class. Formal discussions are excellent when they are used as a strategy for making pupils aware of the many sides of an issue, or for presenting the different points of view, beliefs, or opinions on matters of all sorts. They are very useful for presenting a fair picture of the various positions concerning a controversial matter.
7. As a culminating activity which reviews and ties together what has been learned in a unit or course.

Panels, Symposia, Round Tables, and Forums. In the following paragraphs we shall present some suggestions for conducting panels, symposia, round tables, and forums. The distinguishing characteristics of these techniques have been delienated as follows:

Round Table—a quite informal group, usually five or fewer participants, who sit around a table and converse among themselves and with the audience.

Panel—a fairly informal setting in which four to six participants with a chairman discuss a topic among themselves, followed by a give-and-take with the class. Each participant makes an opening statement, but there are no speeches.

Forum—a type of panel approach in which a panel gives and takes with the audience.

Symposium—a more formal setting in which the participants present speeches, representing different positions and then respond to questions from the audience.

Debate—a very formal approach, consisting of set speeches by participants of two opposing teams and a rebuttal by each participant.[11]

The procedure for preparing and conducting panels takes the following pattern:

1. Pupils and teacher select the topic, problem, or issue to be discussed.
2. The pupils do whatever background investigation is necessary. This may be in the form of individual or committee research projects. If so, they are, of course, carried out in the same manner as any other research project.
3. The pupils and teacher decide on the format of the presentation—panel, symposium, round table, or forum.
4. The pupils prepare their presentations.
5. The teacher and pupils clarify exactly what the procedure will be so that there is no confusion about who is to do what and when he is supposed to do it. These details can be worked out by the panel acting as a planning committee.
6. The pupils carry out the formal presentation and discussion. In order to encourage audience participation, it may be wise to require pupils to take notes; ask pupils to summarize, either orally or in writing, the major points of different positions; give quizzes on the formal presentation and discussion; and ask pupils to evaluate the logic and accuracy of the presentation.
7. The formal discussion is followed by a general open discussion or a question-and-answer period.

CHAIRING THE PANEL. The chairing of the panel can be a crucial element in its success or failure. Ideally, it is best that the chairman be a pupil. This is not always feasible, however, because few pupils can handle this responsibility well without being instructed. Therefore, the teacher should probably chair the first panels until the pupils learn the job. Among the duties of the chairman are the following:

1. To introduce the panel, explain its purpose, outline the procedure, tell the audience what to expect, set the mood, and fill in any necessary background.
2. To conduct the panel by introducing the participants at the proper moment,

[11] Clark and Starr, op. cit., p. 206.

stopping them when their time is up, moderating their give and take, and summing up and tying together when necessary.

3. To moderate the free discussion or question-and-answer period that follows the formal discussion. In moderating, the chairman encourages questions, elicits comments, refers questions to panelists, and, in general, stimulates and directs the discussion and questioning.
4. Finally, to close the discussion by summarizing, pointing out important considerations, and thanking the panelists and other participants.

Now let us look at procedures for carrying out some of the various other types of formal discussion.

Formal Debate. The most formal of all discussion techniques is the debate. It is so formal that many teachers doubt its effectiveness in ordinary classrooms. Other teachers advocate it, because debate (1) provides depth study of a controversial matter; (2) gives two sides of an issue; (3) can be very interesting; and (4) clarifies the controversy at issue. On the other hand, these advantages are offset by its formality, its emphasis on black and white thinking, its involvement of only a few pupils, and its tendency to focus on skill in debating rather than on discovering the truth.

To consider a debate, it is necessary to have a proposition, such as Resolved: that the entire cost of public schools in every school district should be borne by the state; two teams of debaters, one arguing for the proposition and one arguing against it; and a formal procedure in which each team member makes a formal presentation for a set number of minutes and later a rebuttal to the arguments of the other team. The order of presentation and rebuttal is first speaker for; first speaker against; second speaker for; second speaker against; first rebuttal for; first rebuttal against; second rebuttal for; second rebuttal against. After the final rebuttal, there is usually a general discussion. This discussion is conducted by a moderator who also introduces the topic of the debate, introduces the speakers, and closes the meeting. Because most formal debates outside the classroom are held as contests between debating teams, it may be advantageous to have the class or a panel of judges decide which team presented the better case. Many teachers, however, feel that this competition detracts from the classroom atmosphere and therefore do not recommend it.

British Style Debate. Some of the disadvantages of the formal debate are avoided in the British style debate. This type of debate is patterned after procedures made famous by the British Parliament. Briefly, it consists of principal spokesmen on each side to present the arguments pro and con and then to invite comments and questions pro and con alternately. When you use this technique, we recommend that you do the following:

1. Select question or proposition to be debated.
2. Divide the class into two teams, one for the proposition, the other against it.
3. Select two principal speakers for each item.
4. Direct the principal speaker of each team to present his argument in a five-minute talk.

5. Direct the second speaker for each team to present his argument in a three-minute talk.
6. Throw the question open to comments, questions, and answers from the other team members. In order to keep things fair, alternate between members of the pro and con teams.
7. Let one member of each team summarize its case. Often this is done by the first speaker, but if a third principal speaker does the summarizing, it makes for better class participation.
8. Follow up with general discussion.[12]

Jury Trial Technique. Another formal discussion technique that mitigates some of the disadvantages of the formal debate is the jury trial. This is, of course, a type of role playing or simulation in which the players try the merits of a proposition as though in a court of law. The procedure can be made as complicated or as simple as one wishes. The procedure we recommend for this type of formal discussion is as follows:

1. Select an issue or problem to debate. It adds interest if one of the pupils can act as a defendant.
2. Select lawyers, researchers, and witnesses for both sides. These groups can be as large as you wish, but if too large they become cumbersome. The teacher can act as judge, or, better yet, some responsible pupil can be named for that responsibility. Another pupil should be selected to be court stenographer or recorder to keep a record of what transpires. All members of the class who are not lawyers, researchers, witnesses, or court officials, are the jury.
3. All pupils research the problem. The lawyers and witnesses should get the facts from their own research and from that of other class members.
4. Conduct the trial.
   a. The lawyers open up with their arguments.
   b. Witnesses present their evidence.
   c. Lawyers question and cross examine.
   d. Lawyers from each side sum up. Each should point out how the evidence favors his side, of course.
   e. The judge sums up, points out errors in the arguments, fallacies, misstatements of fact, and gives the charge to the jury.
   f. The class, acting as the jury, votes on which side won the argument.[13]

SUGGESTED READING

Aronstein, Laurence W., and Edward G. Olsen. *Action Learning: Student Community Service Project*. Washington, D.C.: Association for Supervision and Curriculum Development, 1974.

[12] Ibid.
[13] Ibid.

Gorman, Alfred H. *Teachers and Learners,* 2nd ed. Boston: Allyn & Bacon, Inc., 1974.

Hill, William Fawcett. *Learning Through Discussion: Guide for Leaders and Members of Discussion Groups.* Beverly Hills, Calif.: Sage Publications, Inc., 1969.

Leonard, Joan M., John J. Fallon, and Harold von Arx. *General Methods of Effective Teaching: A Practical Approach.* New York: Thomas Y. Crowell Company, 1972.

Livingstone, Samuel, and Clarice S. Stoll. *Simulation Games.* New York: The Free Press, 1972.

Massialas, Byron G., and Jack Zevin. *Creative Encounters in the Classroom.* New York: John Wiley & Sons, Inc., 1967.

Murphy, Gardner. *Freeing Intelligence Through Teaching.* New York: Harper and Row, Publishers, 1961.

Plato. *Meno.*

Raths, Louis E., et. al. *Teaching for Thinking.* Columbus, Ohio: Charles E. Merrill Publishers, 1967.

Raths, Louis E., Merrill Harmin, and Sidney B. Simon. *Values and Teaching.* Columbus, Ohio: Charles E. Merrill Publishers, 1966.

Samalonis, Bernice L. *Methods and Materials for Today's High Schools.* New York: Van Nostrand Reinhold Company, 1970.

Schmuck, Richard A., Mark Chester, and Ronald Lippitt. *Problem Solving to Improve Classroom Learning.* Chicago: Science Research Associates, Inc., 1966.

Shaftel, Fannie R., and George D. Shaftel. *Role Playing for Social Values: Decision Making in the Social Studies.* Englewood Cliffs, N.J.: Prentice-Hall, Inc., 1967.

Shulman, Lee S., and Evan R. Keeslar, eds. *Learning By Discovery.* Chicago: Rand McNally & Co., 1966.

POST TEST

1. Give two advantages of inquiry over expository methods.

_____

_____

2. Give two disadvantages of inquiry over expository methods.

_____

_____

3. Should pupils be free to challenge each other's thinking?

_____

4. Should pupils be allowed to challenge the book?

_____

5. Describe the steps in problem solving.

_____

_____

_____

6. Name two criteria that can be used to test the suitability of a problem, according to this module.

_____

_____

7. Pupils have difficulty finding projects to do. Give at least two suggestions for helping them find them.

_____

_____

8. Is it ordinarily good policy to publish class survey results outside the school?

_____

9. What devices can one use to objectify the recording of observations?

_____

_____

_____

10. What techniques are recommended in order to standardize interviews?

_____

_____

11. Tell how to conduct a case study.

_____

_____

_____

_____

_____

12. Tell how to conduct a Socratic dialogue.

_____

_____

_____

_____

13. What is the difference between a controlled discussion and a true discussion?

_____

_____

_____

14. How does conducting a value-clarifying discussion differ from conducting a controlled discussion?

_____

_____

_____

_____

_____

15. Outline the procedure for conducting role playing.

_____

_____

16. Why use simulations?

_____

_____

17. Describe how to conduct a British debate.

_____

_____

_____

_____

_____

18. What are two of the ways suggested for enlisting audience participation during panel presentation?

_____

_____

19. What procedures would you use for launching and carrying out student research projects in your classes?

_____

_____

_____

_____

_____

20. Describe what the distinguishing characteristic of discovery teaching is.

_____

_____

Reading and Study Skills

Leo Auerbach

Jersey City State College

module 6

What Kind of Reader Are You? / Every Teacher Is a Reading Teacher / The Reading Process / Building Vocabulary / Improving Comprehension / Teaching How to Study / Developing Flexibility in Reading / Helping Problem Readers

RATIONALE

Why bother reading? This challenge from our media-oriented students makes us reexamine the need and importance of reading. Part of the answer is that reading is one key to educational success. Aside from strictly physical activities, virtually every aspect of learning uses reading as a major component. Even when demonstration and imitation are necessary, the written word is turned to for explanation and elaboration. So far, no other medium equals books as the repository of culture, the storehouse of information and ideas, the source of enlightenment and pleasure. They can be used repeatedly and without restriction of time. Properly used, books can propel us to new levels of understanding and mastery, both of ourselves and of the world. They enrich our personalities, expand our horizons, provide us with varied experiences, help organize our thoughts and feelings, and stimulate our creativity. As a result, reading contributes to our social and vocational effectiveness. Moreover, full, democratic participation in this complex and rapidly changing world demands even higher levels of literacy. To help every student become an effective reader is clearly a major responsibility of the schools. As we are convinced of this, we, in turn, can convince our students.

Furthermore, we know that when reading skills are inadequate or minimal, time is wasted, frustration can become overwhelming, and the loss of interest may start the cycle which blocks further learning. Mastery of reading is a significant problem in today's schools. Research indicates that from one quarter to one third of secondary school students cannot read their textbooks. Data on school dropouts reveal that more than three times as many poor readers as good readers drop out of high school before graduation. The public is rightly concerned, since stories about reading scores and comparisons of results make front page stories in our largest newspapers. Families know that reading achievement is used as a predictor of success in academic work, on college-admission examinations, on civil-service tests, and in career placement and upgrading. The ongoing Right to Read program is based on the recognized gap between student needs and student accomplishment. As educators, we must accept this challenge to help all our students develop functionally adequate reading skills. At the same time, recognizing the value of reading, we work to increase every student's performance to the highest possible level. We are continuing them on a lifelong process, making a major contribution to their growth and development, and to the richness of their lives.

SPECIFIC OBJECTIVES

Following a list of objectives and an unusual test of your own reading habits, this module will discuss the reading process, will elaborate on techniques and activities to improve reading, and will provide a post test on the entire module. As a result of working through this module, you should be able to do the following:

1. Identify the major features of the reading process.
2. Define the subject matter teacher's responsibility for teaching reading.
3. List activities for building vocabulary.
4. Describe the major aspects of reading comprehension.
5. Characterize good homework assignments.
6. Describe procedures for the use of textbooks and study guides.
7. Identify the features of good questions to accompany reading.
8. Describe the steps in effective study.
9. Explain scanning and skimming and list their uses.
10. Distinguish between recreational reading, critical reading, and imaginative reading.
11. List the features of critical reading and problem solving.
12. Identify the special features of reading maps, charts, graphs, and diagrams.
13. Distinguish among various types of problem readers.
14. Plan activities to include directed reading, supervised study, and diagnosis of reading difficulties.

MODULE TEXT

What Kind of Reader Are You?

In an important sense, you already know a good deal about reading. Yet, before you undertake to help others, it should be useful to examine your reading habits as well as your general ideas about reading. What kind of reader are you? Slow and plodding or rapid and superficial, word-for-word or idea-to-idea, absorbed or impatient, easily distracted or off in another world? You have been reading for many years. Within each day you may read a considerable variety, notes, signs, letters, information on boxes, a newspaper or two, a magazine, part of a book. Because you take reading for granted, you may never have stopped to evaluate yourself as a reader. This preliminary test will not measure your reading ability, but will help you explore your habits, experiences, knowledge, and ideas before you read the rest of the module. Before you are ready to commit yourself to a mental answer, reread the set of questions. Stop at each numbered set and let your thoughts wander in many directions before continuing with the next set.

1. When you first picked up this book, did you look through the table of contents? Did you see how the entire book was organized? Did you read the module headings? Were you curious about any special features?
2. Did you open the book at random or choose a section in which you were interested? Did you sample any of the module's content? How quickly did you read it? How carefully and how critically? On the basis of your first impressions, did you decide how much you would get out of this book? Do you always rely on your own judgment or sampling, or do you usually consider someone else's opinion, a friend's, a teacher's, a librarian's?
3. Do you read everything at the same speed or with the same attention to individual words? Have you ever tried to speed up your reading? What

were the results? Have you tried to read mainly for ideas, rather than for specific facts to remember?

4. What happens when you come across words of which you may not be too sure? Do you skip them and expect to figure out the gist of what you are reading from the parts that you do know? Do you look up unfamiliar words in a glossary or dictionary? Do you try to fit the meaning in the passage?

5. When you finish reading a new selection, passage, or chapter, do you think over what you have read or do you just go on to the next reading? If you stop to think it over, do you jot down notes on what you have read or discuss it with other people?

6. Are you satisfied with the way you have done homework? Are you efficient or are you slow and impatient with yourself? Do you have good study habits or would you like to improve them? How would you try to achieve higher stages of self-discipline?

7. When you encounter statistics, graphs, or charts, do you skip them or do you spend time studying them? What is their real value to you? What was the author's purpose in using them?

8. Do you continue serious reading mainly in the area of your school major? Are you satisfied with your present reading interests?

9. How well do you read instructions on tests, in books, on recipes, on hobby materials, or similar sets of directions?

10. Have you enjoyed reading fiction, poetry, plays, and other forms of imaginative writing? Have any books had an effect in the way you think or feel about life, other people, yourself, the world, or the future?

11. How quickly do you find numbers in a directory, dates and events of a person's life, specific facts in newspapers, reference books, or textbooks?

12. Are you easily distracted when you read, or do you concentrate enough to forget the place or time or your other responsibilities? What factors can make the difference?

13. Where do you look for the main ideas in books, newspapers, and magazine articles? What makes it possible to remember more content more readily?

14. Do you review for tests by reading over the entire material for which you are responsible? Does reviewing make you nervous or pressured, or are you reassured by refreshing your memory?

15. Have you read material with which you disagreed? Were you bothered by the facts, the author's opinions, his bias, his tone, his language, his attitudes, values, and beliefs? How did it affect your reading? Did you take any action? Did you work out your own viewpoint, using evidence collected through research? Have you ever changed your mind as a result of reading?

16. How would you sum up your own purposes in reading? Should teachers read in special ways, for themselves, for preparing their teaching materials, and procedures for anticipating their students' reactions?

Since there are no right or wrong answers on this test, there is no score. However, the areas touched on and the problems raised in this survey will give you insight into the discussion and procedures which follow. The way you explored your own habits, experience, and knowledge will help you apply your answers to the problems of reading and study techniques. It should be clear from the items included that all of us can continue to improve our reading for the rest of our lives.

Every Teacher Is a Reading Teacher

Consciously or unconsciously, every teacher is a reading teacher. No reading takes place without content, and the content that teachers must use is their own subject matter area. Although severe problems require the help of a reading specialist, the subject matter teacher is the expert in his or her field. The teacher knows the concepts and specialized vocabulary to be mastered, the materials and activities to be used, the sequence of growth and maturity, and the kinds of learning to be measured and evaluated. Different content requires different reading styles and approaches, a fact which becomes especially apparent when the student leaves the elementary grades. Within a single school day, the student may confront equations, diagrams, and problems of mathematics, the technical vocabulary, detailed data, and causal explanations of science, the chronological or thematic presentation of events and the interpretations of social studies, the imaginative or expository literature of English, and a host of other specialized reading materials. No one teacher handles them all, but all teachers must be prepared to help each student. By examining the reading process as a whole and then proceeding to its specific elements, the subject matter teacher can better understand his or her own contribution.

The Reading Process

Reading is an active process; it does not happen to the student and it is not done for him. Since it requires attention or a favorable attitude or set, it is not mechanical. An aroused interest or a felt need starts it and keeps it going. The reader's feeling of purpose is the motivating and effective, sustaining force. Most basically, reading is a thinking process, since its central aspect is extracting meaning from print. The essential unit of meaning is the idea, the concept, the thought, the image, the statement. Meaning does not emerge from an arbitrary string of words, but from words in relationship. The sum total of these relationships makes up the context of the reading material, and only within a context do words (or other symbols) have meaning. Understanding and enlarging contexts is the reader's major goal. Finally, reading is a developmental process, changing with the ideas, concepts, or operations which increase with the reader's life experience. Guided by this general framework, the teacher can understand and utilize the major subdivisions of reading skills and activities: building vocabulary, improving comprehension, and developing flexibility.

Building Vocabulary

Provide Many Direct and Indirect Experiences. Direct and indirect experiences are major sources of new words or new meanings of familiar words. In prereading and postreading discussions, the teacher draws upon teen-age students' expanding, outside experiences, and supplements these with trips, interviews, talks by visitors, illustrations, models, films, film strips, television, and recordings. All these concrete presentations or associations are strong contributors to growth in word power.

Encourage Wide Reading. "The most important means of vocabulary development is wide reading. This is at once the most painless and the most rewarding way of building one's vocabulary. In wide reading the student not only meets many new words in different fields but also becomes familiar with their different meanings in a variety of contexts."[1] With increments of contact or meaning at repeated encounters, the student gradually incorporates the words into his vocabulary. The competent reader who practices this on his own can be encouraged or praised by the teacher for his acquisition of unfamiliar words. The reluctant reader needs the teacher's help in finding books or magazines that deal with his interests. Sanford Patlak, a physical education instructor and coach, succeeds in involving students in reading all kinds of books on sports. He learns the student's reading levels and discusses their individual interests. From his large, carefully acquired and readily available supply, he recommends books appropriate in content and reading ease. When students return books, he manages to chat informally, a practice they carry over to their own interaction. His encouragement, guidance, and enthusiasm make reading continuous and habit-forming for some otherwise reluctant readers.[2]

Teach Vocabulary Directly. Direct attention to vocabulary through planned, systematic instruction must supplement incidental learning. Such devices include the following:

1. Provide appropriate context. "Words take their exact meanings from the context in which they are used. The dictionary defines only certain limits within which a word may range. The situation in which the word is used, the other words used with it, and the ends in view all affect its meaning."[3] Any vocabulary exercise or practice which a teacher plans must include a context, in the form of one or more sentences. "Context is *the* major tool in vocabulary expansion."[4] Recall the experience of deriving meanings of unfamiliar words from suitable contexts. Then contrast this with the problem of selecting one meaning from the variety listed in the dictionary.

2. Teach key words. Key words or "stopper" words to be encountered by students in new assignments or units should be taught by the teacher prior to the assignment. These may be precisely the words with multiple meanings, so that the specific meaning in the new material must be demonstrated, obviously in context.

3. Utilize word attack devices. To develop understanding of word meanings, various word attack devices can be used. If there are roots, prefixes, and suffixes which can be pinpointed, these can be separated and analyzed. Long words can be divided into easy-to-manage syllables. Sounding out the words, placing the

---

[1] Ruth Strang, Constance M. McCullough, and Arthur E. Traxler, *The Improvement of Reading,* 4th ed. (New York: McGraw-Hill Book Company, 1967), p. 241.

[2] H. Alan Robinson and Ellen Lamar Thomas, eds., *Fusing Reading Skills and Content* (Newark, Del.: International Reading Association, 1969), pp. 81–88, and Ellen Lamar Thomas and H. Alan Robinson, *Improving Reading in Every Class,* abridged ed. (Boston: Allyn & Bacon, Inc., 1972), pp. 301–307.

[3] Strang, McCullough, and Traxler, op. cit., p. 240.

[4] Thomas and Robinson, op. cit., p. 20.

proper stress, hearing and recognizing the auditory components, are other valuable parts of word attack.

4. Encourage and teach use of the dictionary. "When a student learns to make appropriate and frequent use of the dictionary, he is strengthening his power to keep his vocabulary growing for life."[5] Perhaps the key word is "appropriate." The dictionary is a resource with which students need help. Among the necessary dictionary-use skills for vocabulary growth are the following:

 a. Using guide words.
 b. Selecting the best fitting meaning.
 c. Recognizing differences in meaning.
 d. Figuring out pronunciation by proper use of the key.
 e. Syllabication, stresses, and blending.
 f. Relating the meaning to word derivation.
 g. Using information about nuances of meaning among synonyms.

The teacher who provides experience with any or all of these skills, to a whole class, to small groups, or to individual students, contrasts sharply with the one who merely says, "Look it up in the dictionary."

5. Utilize word slips or vocabulary notebooks. Recording words on a word slip or in a vocabulary notebook, if the practice is connected with the other four activities, may be the task which sets the student on the road to independent vocabulary growth. On small slips of paper or in a notepad, he records the word and the sentence in which it was used. When convenient, he looks it up and lists the meaning that fits the context. The pronunciation should be recorded if it presents a problem, and the derivation may be helpful in remembering the meaning. Some find 3 x 5 index cards useful, while others use bookmarks to write down the word, which they later transfer with the sentence to a notebook for full treatment.

Improving Comprehension

We read in order to understand, regardless of what we read and whether we read for information or for pleasure. Some writers distinguish three levels of comprehension: (1) reading the lines, (2) reading between the lines, and (3) reading beyond the lines.[6] This is a useful analysis which we shall follow in this module.

Reading the Lines. Reading the lines refers to the literal meaning of the material, clearly the most basic level, without which no other is possible. When we note that about one third of secondary school students cannot read their textbooks, we mean that they do not comprehend the material, even on this literal level. Whether the words, sentence structure, concepts, or any combination of these create the problem of comprehension, or whether the student's training, ability, or background is involved, must be determined by the teacher. Through

[5] Ibid., p. 33.
[6] Strang, McCullough, and Traxler, op. cit., pp. 11–12.

direct and indirect questions, the teacher informally diagnoses pupils' problems and checks his diagnosis by experimenting and observing responses. Then, he can use alternate texts, varied reading assignments, and different guide questions to assist students with this level. Prereading and postreading discussions are essential to provide stimulus and reassurance. Reading the lines is usually tested by questions such as, What is the author telling us? What evidence is he giving for his statements? What does the sentence (paragraph, selection, chapter, book) mean?

Reading Between the Lines. The second level, reading between the lines, is one in which the reader "recognizes the author's intent and purpose, interprets the thought, passes judgment on his statements, searches for and interprets clues. . . , distinguishes between fact and opinion, and separates his own ideas from the author's."[7] The reader also judges the merit of the author's evidence or sources. This is obviously a mature level of reading, requiring thinking and experience. Reading between the lines involves answering such questions as, Why do you think the author wrote this? What does this mean to you? Do you agree or disagree with it? Why? Can you separate the author's facts from his opinions? Do the opinions seem to follow logically from the facts? Are you convinced by his facts, evidence, and judgments, or do you have opinions which are different? In what ways are your sources of evidence different from the author's?

Reading Beyond the Lines. Reading beyond the lines "involves deriving implications, speculating about consequences, and drawing generalizations not stated by the author."[8] The process of analysis also leads to a new synthesis by the reader, when his initiative and originality lead him to new insights and to reflection on the significance of the ideas. This goal is perhaps the highest and most difficult to attain; yet, some aspects of it are within reach of the more mature pupils. As teachers, we can offer such questions as, If what the author says is true, what additional conclusions, which he does not mention, can we draw? What other reactions can we or other people have to the same material, and why? If things had been different from ways mentioned by the author, how would this have changed our viewpoint? What changes can be expected to occur if things continue as the author predicts? What changes would you like to see, and why? How would they become possible? Why are these alternatives important? To whom? What new directions of thinking has this reading started for you? (Reading imaginative literature, especially drama and poetry, commonly involves reading beyond the lines.)

Devices that will help students improve comprehension include the following:

1. Provide background experience. The same kinds of experience listed under Building Vocabulary apply here with great force. The nonreading experiences—trips, talks, films, records, and television—may help supply a background of concepts, of familiar information, of prior learning, which makes new learning easier and more enjoyable. "To achieve full comprehension, the reader must know not only the semantic and structural meaning, but he must have had some experience related to the author's ideas."[9] In practical classroom terms, this quotation signi-

---

[7] Ibid., p. 12.
[8] Ibid.
[9] Ibid., p. 11.

fies that the teacher must investigate the students' backgrounds—in life experience as well as in reading—before assigning new reading. Besides specific vocabulary, the students need a preview of the basic concepts to be encountered and assistance in recognizing the value and relevance of the new material. What themes they will meet and what importance they may have in their lives—as students, as adolescents, as citizens, as human beings—are a natural introduction. Questioning to elicit background and to establish direction and purpose is part of the teacher's contribution to the students' success in reading.[10]

2. Give fully developed homework assignments. You may remember assignments of the type, "For tomorrow, read Chapter 14 and answer questions 1–4 at the end of the chapter." Whether the assignment was on the board or was dictated by the teacher, it was assumed that all or most students would read the material, write full answers to the questions, and be adequately prepared to participte in the next lesson. The teacher may have been relying exclusively on these assumptions for the next day's activities. In the light of our knowledge of the reading process and of student needs and abilities, let us evaluate this kind of assignment.

No reason is given for doing the assignment. Presumably, the teacher knows the sequence, or this may be the next chapter in the text. Since no subject or topic is mentioned, no frame or reference is suggested. No stimulus to thinking, especially the problem-solving variety, no arousal of curiosity, no attention-grabbing or interest-generating activity appears. The only student experience tapped by this assignment is the knowledge that the routine requires simple obedience. If the material were interesting in itself, students might be self-motivated. Yet, only a few minutes of class time and some imagination are all that is needed to develop a dramatic, challenging, provocative, or stimulating start to the homework assignment. For a long-term assignment, such interest-stimulating motivation is indispensable. Similarly, assistance with major concepts, varied sources of material, and suitable problems for projects should be included when needed as integral parts of assignments and assignment making. Assignments should also anticipate problems in reading and provide for them in matters such as student interest, background or experience, new concepts, vocabulary, structure, and tone. Differentiated assignments can individualize learning. By imaginatively adopting the student's point of view and building assignments creatively from there, the teacher can really reach the learner.

3. Teach pupils how to use their textbooks. In the subject matter areas, some schools still use a single textbook for all students on the same grade level, although in recent years more schools have begun to vary the books according to ability levels of students. Whether or not your school uses one or many textbooks, though, most of the time the books you must use have been selected by others. Having inherited these hand-me-downs, the teacher is obliged to determine how well they will serve his classes. Is the material organized in a way best suited to inform or satisfy his students? Is the presentation readable, comprehensible, and adequate? We can say one textbook is better than another only when we apply these questions to specific classes and students. Hence, some teachers use different textbooks for different groups within the same class. So long as areas of common learning are included, there is a basis for whole-class discussion. There may be

---

[10] David L. Shepherd, "Reading in the Subject Areas," in *Reading For All,* ed. by Robert Karlin (Newark, Del.: International Reading Association, 1973), pp. 173–179.

other advantages. If different groups or individuals have undertaken supplementary work, different sources are essential.

Spending time on cooperative examination of textbooks pays dividends to the teacher and to the class. A review of the textbook prior to any assignment can include the following:

a. The table of contents, both for over-all scope of treatment, organization, and for detail.
b. The preface, foreword, and introduction for statements of purpose and use as well as acknowledgment of assistance.
c. The major parts, chapter headings, introductions and summaries.
d. Problems for solution or study.
e. Special aids, such as illustrations, diagrams, footnotes, and reference materials.
f. Appendices, glossaries, and indexes.

Because these features are underutilized by most students, the teacher should plan to teach the parts of a book, making use of available textbooks. The skills needed for mastering this material appears later in this module in the discussion of flexibility. Planning a session on problems of the organization and features of textbooks is both natural and rewarding.

4. Utilize study guides and questions. A valuable device for the detailed reading of chapters is the study guide. In some respects, a study guide is an elaboration of the assignments, with questions as the core and suggested readings as aids to finding answers. Organized according to content—thematic, chronological, conceptual, logical—the guide should include both easy and difficult reading, basic and enriched materials. The questions set one or more of the following tasks for the student: (a) following directions; (b) grasping details or facts; (c) finding the main thought; (d) recognizing the sequence of ideas, events, or steps in a process; (e) recognizing relationships of time, place, cause and effect, motives and reactions; (f) drawing inferences or extracting implied meanings; (g) anticipating outcomes; (h) recognizing tone, mood, and intent; (i) drawing comparisons and contrasts; (j) making generalizations; and (k) evaluating or judging according to acceptable criteria.

As in all questioning, whether oral or written, used in class or in connection with outside reading, the teacher must make sure that

a. Questions are definite and clear.
b. Questions aim at recognizable, meaningful, and attainable goals.
c. Questions are challenging and thought provoking.
d. Questions are adapted to the background, abilities, needs, and interests of the students.

Formulating good questions is worth all the time and effort a teacher can give. Eventually, the student learns to develop his own questions, the stage at which purpose and direction reflect the concerns close to him. For further discussion, see Module 3 which treats questioning. It is the study guide, with its major questions, allowance for a selection of specific subdivisions, and provision for varied resources, including multiple readings, which is an ideal vehicle for individualizing education.

5. Use directed reading lessons. Sometimes, textbook material is difficult because of the nature of the topic, the age and relative inexperience of the students, the vocabulary and concepts, or some combination of these factors. The teacher may plan a directed reading lesson in which the techniques discussed in the Building Vocabulary and Improving Comprehension sections of this module are combined with the experience of reading the selection in class. In the directed reading lesson, new words and meanings, new concepts and problems are introduced, and old material and experiences are reviewed for clarifying the connection between the old and the new. The selection is skimmed, and teacher and students formulate questions to guide a more careful reading. Following this reading, a discussion based on the questions, as well as any new ones that have arisen, rounds out the experience and prepares the way for independent study.

Teaching How to Study

Writers who for many years have observed and experimented with students' study habits have generally agreed on the main features of efficient study skills. These skills are embodied in the procedure called *PQ4R*. As Thomas and Robinson indicate, "PQ4R is a package of techniques that should be effective in improving the reading of chapter-length materials when the student's purpose is thorough understanding of the content. . . . The steps in the procedure are Preview, Question, Read, Reflect, Recite, and Review.[11] Studies have shown that even top honors students benefit from studying and using these techniques. Since study skills are usually the haphazard result of trial and error, all students need help. Expository, informational materials in any subject area can be the basis for "how to study" sessions, with steps being worked on separately before the total approach is attempted. Let us examine each of the steps more closely.

Preview. This step provides for an overview or survey of the material. "How does an author help you learn in just minutes what a chapter will contain? How can you make the best use of these clues? What are the advantages in making an advance survey?" Brief practice under teacher guidance can help make this step automatic. Experience with the parts of a textbook can serve as a useful preliminary. Headlines, subtitles, introductory paragraphs, and summaries are invaluable for a picture of over-all content. Questions which the student prepares on his own, mentally at least, may touch on his own background, his expectations, the type of material, its relative difficulty, the sequence and structure of presentation, and the author's purpose and main ideas. Since different subject areas have special features, some flexibility is needed, but all study materials should be treated with this overview, survey approach. The five minutes spent on an easy chapter or the fifteen minutes spent on a difficult one are well spent. They provide the student with "an accurate map of the rugged terrain."

[11] Thomas and Robinson, op. cit., p. 70. The authors acknowledge their debt to Francis P. Robinson, Donald E. P. Smith, and Thomas F. Stanton.

Question. As in all reading comprehension, this is the crucial step. Ways of helping students acquire this skill include turning headlines into questions, formulating main ideas as questions, searching for deeper, more probing questions than the surface ones, and pretending to be the teacher and asking questions which might be used in class or on examinations. Anticipating possible answers is frequently helpful in both the actual reading and in leading to more and deeper questions.

Read and Reflect. If the student starts with questions, he must read to find answers. This involves looking for meaning with full attention and at a speed adapted to the difficulty of the passage, sometimes pausing completely. The tasks enumerated in the section on textbooks cover the kind of reading vital to effective study. All aspects of reading the lines, reading between the lines, and reading beyond the lines are important. Reflecting is not a separate step but an essential component of the reading step. Since study is more than memorization, more than preparing for a class discussion or a test, this emphasis makes information "the *foundation* for higher-level thought."[12] Recognizing how important and useful the knowledge is, the student becomes a "studier," a thinker rather than a repository of facts.

Recite. This step is really a self-reciting operation. No matter how many times a student rereads a difficult chapter or passage, he does not understand until he can answer in his own words: What have I read here? Some experts advise looking away from the printed material or covering it, at least half the time. One suggestion to students from Thomas and Robinson: "See it! Say it! Hear it! Draw or write it!" is a four-way reinforcement. The variety itself helps you recall. The change of pace—eyes, voice, ears, pencil—keeps you alert and increases absorption."[13] Through this technique, instead of a semi-passive memorization, the student turns half-learned to fully-learned material. He selects because he understands what is important. Only as an aid does he make notes, choosing one or more of the marking and note-making techniques: marginal lines, underlining, see-through coloring, marginal mininotes, numerals, asterisks, question marks, check marks, capsule summaries, quick outlines in his own shorthand, notebook jottings, and others. Whatever keeps the student mentally active, not copying absentmindedly or semi-automatically, may be helpful. If to his note making he adds the processes of his own reflections, interpretations, and evaluations, his own brainstorming, he is making full and meaningful use of the self-reciting step. Since developing good habits in this area requires work and students may have acquired such ineffective methods as repeated rereading and excessive underlining, the teacher must teach this step directly and provide sufficient practice.

Review. Think of your own experiences with forgetting, or perhaps consult a psychology textbook with material on short-term memory, long-term memory, retention, and recall. Whatever shape the curve of forgetting takes, we all personally experience the decay of learning. To counteract some of this, we reread both immediately after completing a chapter and after a period of time. Review

---

[12] Ibid., p. 79.
[13] Ibid., p. 94.

helps us regain a broad, over-all view of the chapter and helps check on important details. Spacing review over a day or a longer period dramatically increases retention, yet requires shorter times for each successive rereading. Only this arrangement makes "quick review" an effective, meaningful exercise.

Supervising Study. Since studying is individual, some teachers neglect to plan for it in class, the library, laboratory, or resource center. Yet that is the only way to supervise it. On the basis of observation of students' habits, the teacher recognizes their individual needs, provides appropriate materials and assignments, offers help with questions and procedures, checks on understanding, and evaluates progress. The time spent on this kind of individualized, supervised study is a major contribution to students' reading skills and their learning.

Developing Flexibility in Reading

Look through a typical page of a textbook in social studies, science, mathematics, English, business education, music, and a foreign language. You can recognize the need for building vocabulary and improving comprehension. Consider the student moving from one classroom to another or undertaking his homework assignments. Besides adjusting to diverse content, he must also shift gears in his rate and style of reading. In these, the teacher must help by both direct teaching and providing varied practice. Obviously, textbooks cannot be read as though they were light fiction; yet, some people are taken in by the national obsession with record-breaking reading speeds. Since speed reading is definitely not for most school work, our question should be: In what ways and for what purposes should reading speeds be varied?

Scanning. Scanning is the most rapid reading method. It is used for locating specific items of information: a name, an address, a date, a phrase. Used with directories, dictionaries, indexes, tables, maps, and columns, this form of search involves having an image or word clearly in mind, so that an entire body of material can be scanned or reviewed quickly, without the reader having to understand or to perceive all the words. Sometimes the single words or facts for which one is looking seem to pop out of the context. Exercises in any subject matter area can be easily devised by the teacher. Use the simple experience involving class examination of a textbook. Since students must consult many resources quite rapidly, this skill is essential.

Skimming. Skimming, another rapid form of reading, is used for surveying the content of a book, chapter, or article, for such purposes as getting the heart or gist of the material, its general structure or plan, or the points of view or facts bearing on a particular problem. The eyes seem to float down the page, lighting on main ideas or significant phrases or key words. Besides its usefulness as a rather close sampling during initial reading, skimming is also useful for quick review. The preview step in the study skills procedure lends itself to skimming. Teacher-created exercises for finding answers to questions about main points are a typical use of this technique.

Recreational or Light Reading. Recreational or light reading is the fairly rapid form of reading one uses when the material is easy or fast-moving and the main purpose is entertainment or passing the time pleasantly. Readers have no problem recognizing the type of material or situation for which this technique is appropriate. Most frequently, this category includes the reading of narrative, biographical, or journalistic material. The humorous and the sentimental also fall within its range.

Close Reading of Imaginative Literature. Close reading of imaginative literature is sometimes confused with recreational or light reading, both traditionally lumped together as Reading or Literature and assigned by the English or language teacher. While enjoyment remains the major aim, the more artistic or more complex material requires mature response, depending on "imaginative entry"[14] into fiction, drama, or poetry. Among other tasks, close reading develops perception of meaning, interpretation of character motivation and interaction, and evaluating structure and effect. Learning to read better is a lifelong activity, since the fusion of emotional and intellectual responses, and the cultivation of sensitivity and insight remain a challenge to even the most highly skilled readers. Its special problems are perhaps best handled by English and language teachers. Ideally, the abilities involved should become the property of all students.

Studying. Study reading has been dealt with in the Improving Comprehension section of this module.

Critical Reading. Critical reading is another example of the slow, careful reading that requires mature cognitive processes. Since its main purpose is developing independent thinking and skills in analysis and judgment, the process has numerous components. The reader first has to recognize what the author is saying. Then the reader weighs the evidence for reliability, accuracy, and representativeness, tries to separate opinion from fact, and identifies the viewpoints and biases of the writer. In analyzing the material, the reader checks the author's assumptions and logic, and traces the relationship between the evidence, assumptions, and conclusions. The critical reader detects fallacies and recognizes the way the author intends him to draw inferences. He is alert to propaganda devices or emotional appeals. Sensitive to tone, style, and diction, the reader is critical in the most alert and positive way. Through reading experiences in the subject matter areas, the student meets the challenge of the open marketplace of ideas and grows in intellectual maturity.

Some Special Aspects of Reading. RESEARCH. No new reading skills or rates are needed for research, but it does require an effective use of scanning, skimming, study, and critical reading.

PROBLEM SOLVING. This involves a combination of skills and rates similar to reference work. It may be required in almost any subject matter area. In science, mathematics, and social studies it may be especially necessary to focus on a problem, separate the relevant from the irrelevant, make the problem

---

[14] Dwight L. Burton, "Teaching Students to Read Imaginative Literature," in *Teaching English in Today's High Schools,* ed. by Dwight L. Burton and John S. Simmons (New York: Holt, Rinehart & Winston, Inc., 1970), pp. 90–105.

manageable, attack it with appropriate resources and processes, work out the pattern of explanation, and present the solution. Most careful reading and re-reading are essential at every stage.

READING MAPS, GRAPHS, CHARTS, TABLES, DIAGRAMS, AND ILLUSTRATIONS. When reading such graphic aids, one should first preview the materials. Previewing materials reveals their general nature and relevance to other material. The headings set the context of the data, and special terms or symbols are explained in the key or code. Scanning can be used to spot specific facts or details, but complete reading is required for careful study. For clarification and enrichment, moving back and forth between the text and this type of material may have to be repeated. Besides the author's interpretation or analysis, the reader must determine how the information, concepts, or conclusions fit his own critical framework. The reader must use his independent judgment.

Helping Problem Readers

All teachers should know about the different kinds of problem readers, to recognize those who can be helped in regular classes, and those who need special treatment. Readers have numerous individual differences, but almost all can be helped to improve. Therefore, subject matter teachers along with reading specialists and English teachers share the responsibility for helping problem readers.

1. Slow readers may be slow learners who, because of a below-average rate of maturation, need relatively easy materials with which they can cope. These materials should contain the basic or common learnings agreed upon as essential to the subject. Instruction should feature spaced repetition and adequate explanation. Work should be planned for small groups or individuals who need encouragement. Slow pupils respond to teachers who show patience and understanding. Pupils can overcome the social or emotional problems acquired as a result, perhaps, of unfavorable comments by previous teachers or of their recognition that other students work on more difficult material.

2. Able retarded readers work below their capacity for some reason. Building interests is fundamental and can be done by connecting reading with activities in which they are successful. Within the subject matter area, practice in skills that are inadequately developed can move them from present levels to higher levels of performance. Variety of materials (textbooks, supplementary resources, homework assignments, and individualized projects) plus encouragement can help build their confidence and achievement. Such readers can recognize their problems, set their own purposes, and increase their voluntary reading.

3. Culturally different, economically impoverished, or educationally disadvantaged readers may have difficulty because of language or language variety differences, home or environmental conditions, or previous educational experiences. Since most school materials are sources of difficulty to these students, special programs offer the best remedy. To be sure, building vocabulary, improving comprehension, and developing flexibility are the same reading objectives as for all readers, but special knowledge, training, and expertise are needed for effective teaching of these students. The subject matter teacher should work with the reading specialist in order to outline the concepts, which should be handled sequentially, and to identify materials that will stimulate progress by these students.

4. Although bright or gifted students may not be thought of as problem readers, many have poor reading and study habits. Frequently, they need help overcoming boredom or distraction by being offered materials that are varied, absorbing, intellectually challenging, and rewarding. The rapid readers can benefit from instruction in study skills, from critical and imaginative reading which require interpretation and evaluation, and from creative reading. Encouraging them to plan a balanced program with reading, social experiences, outdoor and recreational activities, and unscheduled time helps them place their reading progress in a reasonable perspective and enables them to reach a higher level of achievement.

5. Retarded students with emotional, visual, auditory, and neurological problems require individual diagnosis and treatment. Teachers should be alert to the need to identify such students and to guide them to those specialists who can provide help.

Summary

In this summary we will briefly touch on the main points of the preceding text. As you read try to fill in the details of the various points that are raised.

This module attempts to show you how to improve your own reading skills, but primarily how to help pupils learn to read and study more effectively. After all, it points out, everyone who teaches must be a teacher of reading.

Reading is an active process in which people attempt to extract ideas, concepts, thoughts, or images from the pattern of words set forth on the printed page. The reader's major goal is always to understand and enlarge contexts. It is to this end that he directs all reading skills and activities. To help him become proficient, you as the teacher must be able to help him with each of the major subdivisions of reading skills and activities: building vocabulary, improving comprehension, and developing flexibility.

To build pupils' vocabulary it is recommended that you (1) provide pupils with many experiences, (2) encourage wide reading, and (3) teach vocabulary directly. Direct teaching of vocabulary requires you to (1) provide appropriate contexts, (2) teach the key or "stopper" words, (3) utilize word attack devices, (4) encourage and teach the use of the dictionary, and (5) utilize word slips or vocabulary notebooks.

There seem to be three levels of comprehension: reading the lines, reading between the lines, and reading beyond the lines. To help pupils learn to read at the highest level, you should (1) provide background experience, (2) give fully developed homework assignments, (3) teach pupils how to use their textbooks, (4) utilize study guides and questions, (5) use directed reading lessons, and (6) teach pupils how to study by the PQ4R method (Preview, Question, Read, Reflect, Recite, and Review) or some similar technique.

To develop flexibility in their reading, you should teach pupils to adjust their speed and style of reading to their reading objectives and the type of material to be read. Some reading should be scanned, some skimmed, some read lightly, some read closely, some studied, and some read critically. Frequently, a combination of methods is desirable or necessary.

You will find that problem readers in your classes will include slow learners; able retarded readers; culturally, economically, or educationally disadvantaged pupils; bright pupils who do not read as well as they should; and pupils with physical or emotional problems. Each of these should be treated in a special way in order to give them optimum help.

SUGGESTED READING

Burton, Dwight L. "Teaching Students to Read Imaginative Literature," in *Teaching English in Today's High Schools*. 2nd ed., ed. by Dwight L. Burton and John S. Simmons. New York: Holt Rinehart & Winston, Inc., 1970.

Herber, Harold L. *Teaching Reading in Content Areas*. Englewood Cliffs, N.J.: Prentice-Hall, Inc., 1970.

Karlin, Robert. *Teaching Reading in High Schools*. 2nd ed. Indianapolis: The Bobbs-Merrill Co., Inc., 1972.

Karlin, Robert, ed. *Reading For All*. Newark, Del.: International Reading Association, 1973.

Loban, Walter, Margaret Ryan, and James R. Squire. *Teaching Language and Literature: Grades Seven–Twelve*. 2nd ed. New York: Harcourt Brace Jovanovich, Inc., 1969.

Robinson, H. Alan, and Ellen Lamar Thomas, eds. *Fusing Reading Skills and Content*. Newark, Del.: International Reading Association, 1969.

Spache, George D., and Paul C. Berg. *The Art of Efficient Reading*. 2nd ed. New York: Macmillan Publishing Co., Inc., 1966.

Stauffer, Russell G. *The Language Experiences Approach to the Teaching of Reading*. New York: Harper and Row, Publishers, 1970.

Strang, Ruth, Constance M. McCullough, and Arthur E. Traxler. *The Improvement of Reading*. 4th ed. New York: McGraw-Hill Book Company, 1967.

Thomas, Ellen Lamar, and H. Alan Robinson. *Improving Reading in Every Class*. Abridged ed. Boston: Allyn & Bacon, Inc., 1972.

POST TEST

In the following test, select from each group of four statements the one which is most accurate. State the reasons why you believe your choice is best. Then explain the shortcomings or inadequacies of the other statements.

1. **a.** Reading is most important for impressing people socially.
   b. Reading is essential to success in every subject matter area, except strictly physical activities.
   c. Reading is valuable because it may help in getting better jobs in later life.
   d. Reading is the major means for controlling the environment.

   _____
   _____
   _____
   _____
   _____
   _____

2. a. Reading is the responsibility of the English teacher.
   b. Reading can only be developed by reading specialists.
   c. All subject matter teachers are responsible for reading improvement.
   d. Reading skills cannot be taught because they depend mainly on the native ability of students.

_____

_____

_____

_____

_____

_____

3. a. Repeated drill on graded word lists is the best way to learn new vocabulary.
   b. Acquiring vocabulary depends mainly on understanding the contexts in which words appear.
   c. Key words should first of all be looked up in a dictionary.
   d. The meaning of words is more clearly explained by roots, prefixes, and suffixes than by their use in sentences.

_____

_____

_____

_____

_____

_____

4. a. Unlike other reading, textbook mastery mainly involves "reading the lines" and memorizing them.
   b. All textbooks are equally satisfactory for learning study skills.
   c. When a school uses a single textbook for each grade, all students should be expected to learn the same content.
   d. A variety of textbooks should be used to allow for individual differences among students.

_____

_____

_____

_____

_____

_____

5. a. If a teacher wants to discuss a subject in class the next day, every student has to do the same homework assignment.
 b. Homework assignments should be varied according to the abilities of students.
 c. Long homework assignments are a good way to make students read rapidly.
 d. Good homework assignments do not have to involve student interests.

_____

_____

_____

_____

_____

6. a. Reading with numerous questions in mind is the best way to check on comprehension.
 b. Questions to guarantee comprehension should keep close to the literal meaning of the reading material.
 c. The most helpful questions are those which appear at the end of each chapter in a book.
 d. Questions in study guides are needed mainly by the slowest students.

_____

_____

_____

_____

_____

7. a. Almost all students need help in developing effective study skills.
 b. As long as students pass tests, we can assume that they know how to study.
 c. Study skills develop naturally over a period of time as a student matures.
 d. All the steps in studying can be mastered with one good explanation by the teacher.

_____

_____

_____

_____

8. **a.** Scanning means reading very carefully to seek out each important word.
   b. Scanning is reading quickly with the mind set on finding specific information, such as a date, a formula, or any important fact.
   c. Scanning is very quick reading which helps the reader decide whether to reread the material more carefully.
   d. Scanning is done by sweeping the eyes back and forth over the words to test speed or eye movements.

   _____

   _____

   _____

   _____

   _____

9. **a.** Skimming involves looking for phrases to underline or to memorize.
   b. Skimming means reading very quickly to pick out a word or idea here and there.
   c. Skimming allows for reading every other sentence.
   d. Skimming uses "floating down" the page to find main ideas and key phrases.

   _____

   _____

   _____

   _____

   _____

10. **a.** Critical reading means judging how much fact and how much opinion an author has included, how much bias and how much fairness he shows.
    b. Critical reading involves deciding whether an author's style is appropriate to his material.
    c. Critical reading refers to judging whether one writer or one book is better than another.
    d. Critical reading means using personal taste to decide what the student would like to read and report on.

   _____

   _____

   _____

   _____

   _____

11. **a.** Maps, charts, graphs, tables, and illustrations are included to help people who cannot read the text.

   b. Maps and other graphic aids are used to decorate pages so that they do not have only straight text.

   c. Maps and other graphic aids usually include material that is not in the text.

   d. Maps and other graphic aids are usually important additions to the visual and conceptual content of a text.

   _____

   _____

   _____

   _____

   _____

12. **a.** Except for a few special cases, most people read as well as they are able.

   b. Every reader can learn to become a better reader by applying interest and effort.

   c. Because we do a great deal of reading to succeed in school or to get along in life, we automatically learn to become better readers.

   d. By continuing to increase our reading rate and the variety of reading material we become better readers.

   _____

   _____

   _____

   _____

   _____

Providing for Individual Differences

Leonard H. Clark

Jersey City State College

module 7

Necessity in Providing for Differences in Pupils / Knowing the Pupil / Administrative Provisions / Differentiating Assignments / Units, Contracts, and Learning Activity Packets / Special Assignments for Special Pupils / Individualizing Instruction / Special Help / Continuous Progress Plan / Use of Self-Instructional Devices / Using Small Groups and Committees for Individualizing Instruction / Independent Study / Acceleration / Projects / Making Time for Individual Instruction / Accepting Different Evidence of Accomplishment / Need for a Variety of Materials / Teaching Homogeneously Grouped Classes

RATIONALE

No one is exactly like anyone else. Even identical twins are not identical. In spite of the similarity in their genetic background, environmental factors beginning even before birth shape each twin in his own peculiar way. And for other people, the differences in genetic structure make the chances of anyone's being an exact duplicate of anyone else completely nil. Brothers and sisters may have family resemblances; tenth graders may have some traits in common, as do members of honors sections, secondary education majors, and college professors; yet each one is an individual and looks and behaves differently from everyone else.

The ways in which individuals differ are manifold. Not only are there differences in physical appearance, but each person has his own personality traits. Some of your pupils will be quick, some slow; some academically intelligent, some stupid; some socially skillful, some socially inept; some eager, some phlegmatic; some interested in your subject, some not; some male, some female; some friendly, some hostile. Some of these differences may be of no importance as far as school is concerned. Whether a girl's eyes are blue, grey, or brown does not really matter (except perhaps to certain boys and even then the boys' reaction is only incidental to a combination of other, more powerful influences). Others are extremely important for teaching, because what is good education for one person may not be good for another. Therefore, in this module we shall try to present to you some of the differences in pupils that you should consider in your teaching; some ways of finding out important characteristics of individual pupils; some of the curricular and organizational schemes that have been invented by school administrators to provide for differences in pupils; and strategies and tactics that you can use in your own classes, not only to cope with the problems of individual differences, but also to use these differences to enhance your effectiveness as a teacher.

SPECIFIC OBJECTIVES

Specifically, at the completion of this unit you should be able to do the following:

1. Describe resources and devices teachers can use to know more about pupils so that they can adjust their teaching to individuals. Specifically, you should be able to tell how to use the cumulative record, observation, pupil conferences, parent conferences, pupil assignments, questionnaires, test results, and sociometric devices described in Module 2.
2. Describe ways in which administrators attempt to provide for individuals. Among the plans you should be able to describe are (a) curriculum tracks; (b) tracks, streams, and homogeneous groups; (c) promotion schemes including continuous promotion, minicourses, half-yearly and term promotion, and nongraded plans; (d) curriculum provisions including electives,

minicourses, and extracurriculum; and (e) the use of teaching aides, learning centers, and modular schedules. You should also be able to summarize the arguments for and against the use of plans featuring the principle of homogeneous groups.

3. Describe how to conduct such strategies and tactics as differentiating the assignment; using homogeneous groups within the classroom; conducting the class as a laboratory; units; contracts; learning activity packets; special assignments; individualizing instruction; special help; laboratory classes.

    Also, continuous progress plans; self-instructional devices; study guides; self-correcting material; machines for teaching; correspondence and television courses; use of small groups and committees; independent study; accelerating brilliant pupils; and projects.

4. Describe methods by which one can make time for individual instruction.

5. Describe approaches for teaching certain homogeneous groups, such as (a) academically talented pupils; (b) academically incompetent pupils; and (c) children of poverty. You will be asked to demonstrate that you can meet these requirements by answering test questions, based on the text material presented in this unit.

MODULE TEXT

Necessity in Providing for Differences in Pupils

As we have already observed, pupils differ in many ways: physical characteristics, interests, intellectual ability, motor ability, social ability, aptitudes of various kinds, background, experience, ideals, attitudes, needs, ambitions, dreams, and hopes. Furthermore, each person learns in his own way and at his own rate. His interests, his prior background, his innate and acquired abilities, and a myriad of other personal and environmental influences shape how and what he learns. That is why no two pupils ever learn exactly the same thing from any particular learning experience.

That these statements represent a basic condition of humanity carries with it at least one profound implication for teaching: *It is ridiculous to believe that any teaching strategy or school organization that treats pupils as though they were all alike can succeed.* The fact of individual differences in pupils requires that teachers find teaching strategies and tactics that accommodate individual differences. Therefore, you ought to develop skill in techniques that will allow you to capitalize on pupils' differences so that your teaching may become more thorough, efficient, and effective.

Keuscher comments on the need for individualized instruction, as follows:

I. Philosophically, it is consistent with the principles upon which our form of government, which spawned our educational system, is based.

II. The very nature of our democratic system and the way it functions demands knowledgeable, thinking participants.

III. Assembly-line methods are tending to produce mass-produced, standardized citizens at the expense of individuality.

IV. As society grows increasingly complex, there is a greater demand for a diversity of talents and skills.

V. It is probably the most efficient way to educate if one focuses on the product rather than just the process.[1]

Unfortunately, in practice most schemes for individualizing instruction do not approach the ideal. Most of the techniques now used to provide for individual differences in pupils are simply techniques by which teachers manipulate course content so that it is easier for some pupils and more difficult for others; give some pupils more work than they give others; allow some pupils to progress more or less rapidly than others do; or combine these techniques.

True individualization of instruction would require a quite different approach. Its emphasis is on the development of the individual to his fullest potential.

The accent is not so much on the differences as it is on the development. Therefore, individualized teaching goals and subject matter vary from individual to individual, according to his needs, activities, and aspirations. Difficulty and speed are also considerations, but the principal thrust should be on providing each individual with the curriculum best suited for him.[2]

Knowing the Pupil

In order to provide for individual differences adequately, it is really necessary to know something about your pupils' strengths and weaknesses, their interests, goals, backgrounds, and attitudes. You cannot expect to provide for differences you know nothing about. To find out the information you need to know about pupils, you have a great number of tools available. Among them are the cumulative record folder; observation; conferences; and questionnaires such as interest finder, autobiographical questionnaire, test results, and sociometric devices. These are all described in Module 2. If you are not conversant with them, review Module 2.

Administrative Provisions

For years, school administrators have been trying to provide for the differences in pupils administratively. In the earliest times, they provided different types of schools for persons with different goals. For example, in medieval times, the clerk-to-be was educated in a monastery or church school, but the would-be knight was apprenticed as a page to an influential knighted lord, who trained the aspirant to knighthood. In seventeenth-century Massachusetts, the minister-to-be went to Harvard for his academic training, but the tradesman was schooled in his trade in a private venture school, or as an apprentice.

Curriculum Tracks. Today, the practice of providing different routes for pupils with different vocational and academic aims continues. Some school systems still

---

[1] Robert E. Keuscher, "Why Individualize Instruction," in Virgil Howes, *Individualizing of Instruction* (New York: Macmillan Publishing Co., Inc., 1970), p. 7.

[2] Leonard H. Clark and Irving S. Starr, *Secondary School Teaching Methods,* 3rd ed. (New York: Macmillan Publishing Co., Inc., 1976), Chap. 8.

provide different schools for youths planning for different vocations, but in most school systems, at the high school level, these differences are accommodated by offering a variety of curricula in comprehensive high schools. By a judicious selection of courses or curricula, pupils can prepare themselves for college entrance, or for a specific vocation, or, if they wish neither college nor vocational preparation, they can select a general program. The offering of a choice of curricula is probably the most common administrative or organizational method of providing for individual differences at the high school level. It is not used so frequently at lower grade levels, however.

Homogeneous Groupings. TRACKS OR STREAMS. Some school systems are set up on the basis of pupil ability. For instance, one sequence might be for honors groups, a second sequence for college preparatory students, a third sequence for general students, and a fourth sequence for slow learners. These different sequences —sometimes called tracks or streams—may differ from each other in difficulty and complexity of content, rate of pupil progress, and methods of teaching. Thus, the pupils in a mathematics honors group move through to the study of calculus in the twelfth grade, but a slow group might never go beyond the development of basic computational skills.

HOMOGENEOUS GROUPS. Tracks or streams are, in effect, a type of homogeneous groupings. Homogeneous groups are formed by dividing the pupils into class sections, according to some criterion or combination of criteria. Usually the criterion is ability. However, it might be sex (boys' physical education), or educational-vocational (Business English or college preparatory English), or even interest. In any case, the reason for forming homogeneous groups is to provide for the differences in pupils and make teaching easier. Theoretically, when classes are grouped homogeneously, it is easier to select content and methods that will be suitable for all pupils in that group.

To a degree, homogeneous grouping works. When all the pupils in an advanced mathematics class are bright and interested, teaching them is easier. There is no doubt of that. It is easier to find content and methods suitable for everyone if the group is homogeneous. Nevertheless, homogeneous grouping is not necessarily the answer to the problem of individual differences in pupils.

In the first place, homogeneous groups are not truly homogeneous. They are merely attempts to make groups similar, according to one or two criteria. Girls' physical education classes are homogeneous in that they are limited to girls, but the girls are not all alike, physically, mentally, emotionally, or socially. Even if one were to have a section of girls' physical education in which all the girls were interested in sports, there would still be great differences in the characteristics and capabilities of the girls. *The pupils in homogeneously grouped classes are not homogeneous. All homogeneous grouping does is to reduce the heterogeneity of classes; it makes the problem of providing for individual differences in pupils a little more manageable.*

It is most important that you remember this point. Many teachers act as though they thought their classes really were homogeneous. Do not let this happen to you. Always keep in mind that a homogeneous class is one in which your school administrators have tried to reduce the spread of one or more pupil characteristics. The other characteristics run the full gamut just as in the heterogeneous classes. In classes grouped according to ability, although the range of academic ability may be reduced, the range of interest, ambitions, motivations, and goals is probably just as wide as in any other class. Even though the range of ability in a high ability class may be quite large—ranging from a little better than average to genius or near genius—a thirty-point range in I.Q. in such a class would be quite normal. Similarly, a slow class may consist of pupils who cannot learn, presumably because of lack of innate ability, pupils who cannot learn because of gaps in their background or poor preparation in earlier classes, and pupils who could learn easily if they ever tried. No matter how much one attempts to homogenize classes and no matter what plan of grouping is used, you as the teacher will always face the problem of providing for differences in individuals. Homogeneous grouping can reduce the problem, but it cannot eliminate it.

Homogeneous grouping brings with it several built-in problems of its own. One of these is the danger that, in ability grouping schemes, the less talented pupils may be shortchanged. Teachers who teach slow classes often feel frustrated. Many of them seem to feel that being asked to teach classes of slow learners is somehow demeaning. After all, they are subject matter specialists and, they believe, to spend their talents on the less-than-bright is to waste those talents. Such teacher attitudes defeat the purpose of ability grouping. If you feel this way, perhaps you should not go into teaching. Anyone who wishes to teach should be willing to adapt his teaching to the talents of the pupils with whom he must work.

Another danger is that the content and methods used will not be those best suited for the pupils being taught. Frequently, classes of bright pupils are hurried through their courses without any real mind-stretching experiences. Of course, bright pupils learn more quickly, but just learning more of the same is hardly the way to develop their talent to the full. Perhaps even more dangerous is the common practice of watering down academic courses for slow pupils. The result is dull, drab, boring teaching day after day. If you teach homogeneously grouped classes, you should adjust your content and your teaching strategies and tactics to the pupils so that the classes will be productive experiences that result in expanding pupils' minds and their mastering skills and concepts worthwhile to them now and in the future.

In practice, the less academically inclined pupils are more often shortchanged than are other pupils. Because so often their courses are merely watered down versions of academic courses, their classes may not only be a waste of time, but actually harmful to them. The courses are seldom structured so that pupils can capitalize on the strengths they have. Instead, the assumption is that these pupils cannot learn. Since little is expected of them, they do little. There is little fun, or success, or relevancy to anything important to them to motivate them. In the classes in which pupils most need challenging and motivating, there is no challenge and little motivation. In addition, these pupils do not have a chance to learn from the help and the example of their more talented peers. Pupils learn a great deal from each other. Consequently, slow youths do benefit from associating with talented pupils, and bright youths can learn from slow pupils. It is unfortunate that in so many instances the classes for slow pupils have become educational ghettos. There is no boy or girl in a public school who cannot learn if given the proper opportunity and encouragement.

Review the material on homogeneous grouping and recall your own school experiences. Do you favor homogeneous grouping? Many people claim homogeneous grouping to be undemocratic. Do you think it is? Can you think of any reasons why bright pupils should be required to sit in the same classes as slow pupils? Is it fair to them to be in such classes?

Promotion Schemes. The old-fashioned techniques of "skipping grades" and "keeping pupils back" are also administrative devices used to provide for differences in pupil ability. Years ago, in order that the period skipped or repeated might not be too long, city systems instituted half-year courses. Under this sort of plan, pupils were promoted every half year. Nowadays, many systems schedule half-year and quarterly courses and even short minicourses. One of the most promising developments is the movement toward continuous promotion schemes in ungraded schools.

CONTINUOUS PROMOTION. Continuous promotion plans consist principally of dividing the course work of the curriculum into short modules. As each pupil completes one module, he is ready to go on to another. Usually, the pupils are issued learning activity packets, which contain the instructions and materials for studying the module so that each pupil can work through the modules on his own, at his own time, and at his own speed. Theoretically, at least, continuous progress plans are an excellent means of providing for individual differences. Pupils who find that they are not ready to move on when the class moves on are not forced to do so, and pupils who finish the unit quickly are not forced to wait for others to catch up. Furthermore, it may not be necessary for all pupils to follow the same order of units. Not only may one be able to change the order of the module, but one can, in effect, build his own sequence or course by electing to skip certain modules, or to select additional or different modules from those laid out for the other pupils. Although it seldom happens in practice, in theory, the pupils, by their choice of modules, can have courses and curricula specially tailored to meet their own needs in continuous progress programs.

NONGRADED SCHOOLS. In another type of nongraded program, courses are offered at various levels. Pupils are not placed in courses because they are in the tenth or eleventh grade, but because they have reached a certain level of academic proficiency. In such a program, quite possibly a course would not be a tenth-grade course, but, rather, the class might consist of pupils from all of the secondary school grades.

Curriculum Provisions for Individual Differences. Curriculum builders try to introduce provisions for individual differences into their curriculum design. We have already cited the various curricula, tracks, or streams that one finds in the ordinary high school. In addition, curriculum builders try to provide for differences in interest and goals by providing a diversity of courses, extending from the humanities through the fine arts, and the practical arts to the vocational subjects and into the extracurriculum. To give pupils an adequate opportunity to study in areas that appeal to them, the curriculum builders provided electives in the program. A good selection of electives allows pupils to pursue special interests and to explore special bents. They allow pupils to add both breadth and depth to their course selection. Even further variety is offered by the extracurriculum, which allows pupils to elect activities for the fun of it.

A promising new movement is bringing still more variety to the school curriculum. Many schools are introducing minicourses, short courses that may extend from a few weeks to a full term, depending upon the school. These courses may offer credit or they may not. Some of them are offered as a result of pupil requests. Pupils may or may not cooperate in the planning and carrying out of the courses. Minicourses may vary from the depth study of an academic problem to the discussion of youthful problems, to the development of hobbies, or to the serious study of contemporary trends in music. When the courses are concerned with viable content and provide a large enough choice of attractive alternatives, minicourses can be really valuable tools for individualizing instruction.

Use of Teacher Aides. Three other recent innovations provided by the administrations of some schools may make it easier for teachers to provide for individual differences. They are the introduction of teacher aides, the establishment of learning centers in the schools, and the adoption of flexible modular daily schedules.

Teacher aides can make it easier for teachers to provide independent and individualized study. By using aides to do the time-consuming chores, teachers have more time to work with individuals and small groups. Among the things that aides can do to help individualize instruction are the following:

1. To help pupils as they practice.
2. To help pupils as they work at their desks.
3. To help follow up.
4. To tutor.
5. To supervise and help small groups.[3]

Learning Centers. Learning centers are places where pupils can go to study under supervision. When these centers are provided with adequate facilities, pupils can do much independent study away from the lock step of the traditional classroom. Flexible modular schedules give pupils time in which to engage in independent work. In such schedules, pupils meet with their teachers in regular classrooms at specified times. At these times, the pupils receive their assignments, which they do independently in the learning center under the supervision of a teacher assistant. Frequently, the independent study is outlined in a learning packet, a contract, or a study guide. At other times, the pupils' time is not structured so that they can be free to get to the learning centers to do their independent study. For example, study the following schedule of seventh graders at the Hightstown intermediate school in Hightstown, New Jersey.

Monday	Mods 1–3	Unstructured or unassigned time. The student has the option of reporting to any of the six learning centers. In addition, the library is available, as well as the student center.
	Mods 4–6	Social Studies Middle Group
	Mods 7–9	Spanish
	Mods 10–12	Science Large Group
	Mods 13–15	Math Middle Group
	Mods 16–19	Unstructured (lunch included here)

[3] Gertrude Noar, *Individualized Instruction* (New York: John Wiley & Sons, Inc., 1972), pp. 66–67.

Mods 20–22   Language Arts Large Group
Mods 23–26   Clubs and Activities

Tuesday   Mods 1–3   Science Middle Group
    Mods 4–6   Unstructured
    Mods 7–9   Spanish
    Mods 10–12   Phys. Ed.
    Mods 13–14   Math Small Group
    Mods 15–18   Unstructured (includes lunch)
    Mods 19–21   Language Arts Middle Group
    Mod 22   Unstructured
    Mods 23–26   Clubs and Activities

Wednesday   Mods 1–2   Social Studies Small Group
    Mods 6–9   Unified Arts
    Mods 10–12   Music
    Mods 13–15   Math Middle Group
    Mods 16–18   Unstructured (includes lunch)
    Mods 19–20   Language Arts Small Group
    Mods 21–22   Unstructured
    Mods 23–26   Clubs and Activities

Thursday   Mods 1–3   Unstructured
    Mods 4–6   Social Studies Large Group
    Mods 7–9   Spanish
    Mod 12   Unstructured
    Mods 13–15   Science Middle Group
    Mods 16–18   Unstructured (includes lunch)
    Mods 19–20   Language Arts Small Group
    Mods 21–22   Unstructured
    Mods 23–26   Clubs and Activities

Friday   Mods 1–3   Phys. Ed.
    Mods 4–6   Music
    Mods 7–9   Science Middle Group
    Mods 10–12   Math Middle Group
    Mods 13–19   Unstructured (includes lunch)
    Mods 20–22   Language Arts Middle Group
    Mods 23–26   Clubs and Activities[4]

Differentiating Assignments

In the ordinary lesson, even though the lesson objectives may be the same for everyone, there is usually no reason why everyone should have to do exactly the same activities. Consequently, one can provide for differences in ability and interest by differentiating the assignment, such as specifying different learning activities for different pupils or groups of pupils. Pupils who do not read well may be asked to read in works that are less difficult than those required of the better readers. Or pupils more able in mathematics might be assigned the difficult prob-

[4] Fred S. Wien, "Flexible Modular Scheduling," *New Jersey Association of Teacher Educators Journal,* **17**:11–12 (Spring 1974).

lems while the less able do the easier problems. Or the bright and quick pupils might be given longer, more demanding assignments.

Differentiating Length and Difficulty. One way to carry out the differentiating of assignments according to length or difficulty of the work is to divide the class into groups or committees. You might, for instance, divide your class into three groups. One group might be assigned readings in a rather difficult text. It might also be asked to solve or react to some quite difficult problems. The second group might read selections that are somewhat less demanding and work on easier problems. The third group's reading assignment might be extremely easy with no real problems to confront them at all. In this case, all are studying the same thing, but at different levels of difficulty.

Differentiating Type of Work. You can differentiate your assignments by allowing pupils to do different types of work to achieve the learning objectives. Capitalize on the different interests and abilities of the pupils. Perhaps some pupils might learn best through art, some through reading, and others through acting things out. There is no reason why everyone should do the same thing. What is important is that pupils achieve the understandings, skills, and attitudes that are the learning objectives.

For example, not everyone needs to express his understanding of the ante-bellum South by writing essays and answering questions about it. Many other media are available. Talented youngsters might produce illustrations of life in the South; a boy interested in mechanical drawing might draw a layout of a plantation; a girl interested in homemaking might investigate the menus of the era, or run up a costume appropriate to the period; a young engineer might construct a cotton gin; a young choreographer might score and dance a ballet in the *Gone with the Wind* motif; a poet might contribute some lyric poetry, perhaps an ode or two.[5]

Although differentiating assignments by giving different assignments to small groups and committees is a relatively easy way to do it, there is no reason why differentiation cannot be done on a more individualized basis. For instance,

in the study of Ancient Man, pupils with low reading ability might read such easy reading material as the Abramowitz pamphlet, *World History Study Lessons,* while others read such difficult and esoteric material as the final chapter of Von Koenigswald's *The Evolution of Man.* Others might be reading in such varied works as Chapters 2 and 3 of Van Loon's *The Story of Mankind,* Ashley Montagu's *Man: His First Million Years,* a *National Geographic* Magazine article (e.g., Cynthia Irwin, Henry Irwin, and George Agogino, "Ice Age Man vs. Mammoth," June 1962, **121:**828–836, or Thomas R. Henry, "Ice Age Man, the First American," December 1955, *Life* Magazine articles on Ancient Man, or the Dell Visual paperback *Prehistory*). Or they might be reading the first unit "Days before History" in Hartmann and Saunders text, *Builders of the Old World,* or Chapter 1 of Black's textbook, *Our World History.*[6]

Usually, the procedure to follow is to give pupils a number of options from which each selects his own activities. You will probably find it best to offer these options in a study guide that you issue to the pupils before they start their work.

---

[5] Clark and Starr, op. cit., 3rd ed., p. 159.
[6] Ibid., p. 268.

You can also differentiate single lessons. For example, in a mathematics lesson, you might assign certain pupils examples 1, 4, 5, and 8, while others do 2, 3, 6, 7, 9, and 10. Usually, however, you will find that, in order to differentiate your classes in any meaningful way, you need a longer period of time. Ordinarily, the differentiated assignment should be a long assignment covering a period of several weeks.

Homogeneous Groups Within the Classroom. Another way to differentiate work in a class is to set up homogeneous groups within the classroom. This practice is very common in the elementary schools. There is no reason why it should not be very common in secondary schools, except that, as a rule, secondary school teachers are less well trained than elementary school teachers to do this. Grouping can be accomplished in several ways, as follows:

1. Divide the class into groups on the basis of scholastic ability or ability in the subject.
2. Divide the class in accordance with pupil interest.
3. Divide the class according to goal. Pupils who are interested in the same or similar goals can work together.
4. Divide class according to needs; for instance, pupils requiring remedial work will work together.

Methods for differentiating class assignments so as to meet the needs of the various groups have already been discussed.

Plan an assignment for the class with three homogeneous ability groups.

To conduct several groups in one class is hard work, but it is not impossible. Rural schools for many years have conducted multigrade classes with good results. The essentials are (1) to be sure that everyone has something worthwhile to do; (2) to encourage pupils to participate both in planning and in implementing plans for group work; (3) to supervise the group carefully, always being sure to see that every group gets its share of attention, guidance, and help. The use of written assignment sheets and study guides may help the groups keep to their tasks.

Conducting the Class as a Laboratory. Another way to differentiate the work in the class is to conduct the class as a laboratory. This type of approach is best served by long-term assignments, as in the unit plan. In the laboratory, pupils work in small groups or as individuals under the guidance of the teacher. No one is necessarily working on the same project at any particular time. Rather, one group may be working on a group report; another group may be setting up a demonstration; some individuals may be doing research for their projects; and others may be studying required or optional readings. The laboratory period is a work period.

When you conduct a laboratory, you should use a procedure somewhat like the following. There is no set procedure for teaching by the laboratory method, however.

Give out a general study guide, unit of work, or learning packet that outlines what is to be done in the unit. The activities may be required or optional. Let the pupils select the activities they plan to do from the study guide or suggest activities themselves.

Let the pupils execute their plans. They may look things up in the pamphlets, books, and magazines. They may play the tapes and records or look at the films, film strips, or slides. They may do these activities as individuals or as committees and usually in any order they choose. They may confer with each other and help each other.

Help, guide, and supervise the pupils as they work.

a. Observe pupils to diagnose poor study habits.
b. Show pupils where to find information.
c. Show pupils how to use the tools of learning.
d. Clarify assignments.
e. Show the pupils how to get the meat out of their studying.
f. Help pupils form goals for study.
g. Help pupils summarize.

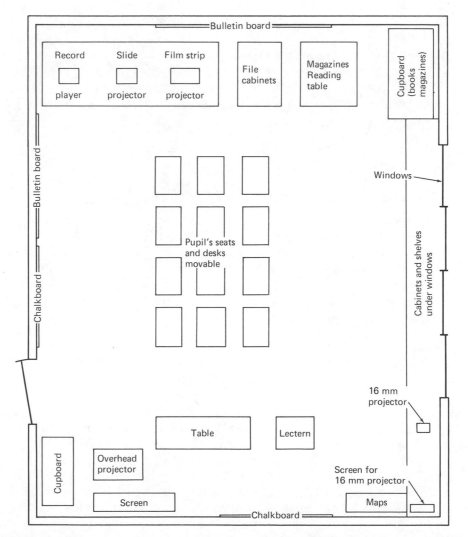

Figure 7-1 *A Classroom Laboratory.* [*Source:* Leonard H. Clark, *Teaching Social Studies in Secondary Schools: A Handbook* (New York: Macmillan Publishing Co., Inc., 1973), p. 126.]

h. Point out errors and incorrect procedures.
i. Suggest methods for attacking problems.[7]

As a means of providing for individual differences, laboratory classes have many merits. When properly done, they allow the pupils to work on a learning sequence that is his alone. The loose structure of the laboratory allows pupils to work at different speeds. The swift, or more able, can move as quickly as they wish without waiting for the slow, and the slow do not have to push themselves unreasonably to keep up with their swifter colleagues. There is no need for all pupils to do the same things in a laboratory setup. The pupils, under guidance, can select the activities that they feel will be most useful. It is quite permissible for pupils to learn in different ways. However, unless the laboratory method is given form, as in the unit, contract, or modular approach, the laboratory can become chaotic and the learning experiences of the pupils, meaningless.

For the laboratory method to work best, the classroom should be set up as a laboratory. The better equipped the room, the better. The pupils should have easily available a classroom library of pertinent books and other reading matter, audio-visual materials, and plenty of work space and material with which to work. Most of this material should be kept in the classroom permanently. Overhead projectors, film strip projectors, tape recorders, for instance, should either be assigned as permanent equipment or, if that is not feasible, on long-term loan. Books can be borrowed from the main library for the duration of the course or unit. All of this material and equipment should be set up so that it is readily available to pupils when they need it. Figure 7-1 shows an example of a classroom laboratory in a suburban New Jersey high school.

Units, Contracts, and Learning Activity Packets

Units, contracts, and learning activity packets are specialized versions of long-term differentiated assignments. They differ from each other only in detail. In spite of the surface differences, they are all versions that have been in use by educators for more than a half century.

Unit Teaching. In many schools, a unit is simply a topic about which a number of lessons are grouped. For instance, a teacher of English, who was teaching lyric poetry for a couple of weeks, might say that she was teaching a unit on lyric poetry, even though her teaching consisted of nothing more than a series of nonrelated lessons having to do with lyric poetry. More sophisticated teachers would not consider a series of lessons on a topic as a real unit. Rather, they believe the unit to be a "method of organizing subject matter, teaching techniques, and teaching devices so as to facilitate individualization of instruction, motivation, pupil planning, pupil responsibility for their own learning, and teaching emphasis on the higher levels of psychomotor, cognitive, and affective learning."[8] This type of unit has

[7] Leonard H. Clark, *Teaching Social Studies in Secondary Schools: A Handbook* (New York: Macmillan Publishing Co., Inc., 1973), p. 125.

[8] Clark and Starr, op. cit., pp. 113–14.

been described in Module 1.4. Combined with laboratory work, it is one of the most useful ways to provide for individual differences.

Learning Activity Packets. Learning activity packets (also called instructional learning packets, learning modules, instructional modules, or learning packets) are developed in much the same way as are units. They are really an adaption of the unit idea to meet the demands for individualized instruction, independent study, pupil acceptance of the responsibility for much of their own learning, and continuous progress promotion plans. They differ from units in that they place more emphasis on the individualized aspects. The procedures for building learning activity packets are included in Module 1.

The learning activity packets are best used in continuous progress plans in which pupils proceed at their own speeds and in their own direction under teacher guidance. Learning activity packets may also be given to pupils for independent study in traditional courses. They then would be handled just as any other independent study assignment or project. The implementation of a continuous progress plan will be explained in a later section of this module.

The Contract Plan. Both units and learning modules can be set up as contract. In a contract, the pupil agrees to do a certain amount of work of a certain quality during a certain period of time. In return, the teacher agrees to award him with a certain mark. Teachers frequently forget to specify that the pupil must meet both the requirements of *quality* and *quantity*. Quality control is sometimes quite difficult when teaching with the contract plan.

The procedure for setting up and using the contract plan is explained in Module 1.4.

Special Assignments for Special Pupils

Another way to differentiate the assignment is to give special assignments to special pupils. These special assignments may be done as part of the regular classwork, in addition to the regular classwork, or instead of regular classwork. For example, in one English class, it became evident that one of the pupils, although quite bright, was having a great deal of trouble with the ordinary classwork because he had not learned basic writing skills. So the teacher found special materials that were aimed at correcting his problem, wrote out a special study guide for him to follow, and put him to work on correcting his problem on a part-time basis. In that same class, a truly brilliant pupil obviously found the work too easy. The teacher took him off the ordinary course work and substituted a series of assignments from the syllabus of a literature course, given by a nearby liberal arts college. The boy did very well at this college-level work that took the place of the ordinary high school work for an entire term. Pupils should be expected to work on such special assignments both during class time and out of class as homework. You can work with these pupils during the class period if you conduct the class as a laboratory or have small group and individual study sessions. You can also work with them during free periods and during the hours before and after school.

Individualizing Instruction

The ideal way to provide for individual differences would be to provide each pupil with a curriculum and lessons tailor-made for him. Since every pupil is different, then every pupil should have a different curriculum and different learning experiences planned for him. At present, this is beyond our means. The differentiated assignments, units, and modules that we have described so far provide only partial differentiation for individuals or small groups, although modules may offer a good approach to the ultimate goal. In this section, let us consider some techniques that allow the teachers to concentrate on individual instruction.

Review the uses of such techniques as the unit, the laboratory class, the learning activity packet, the module, the contract, and special assignments. In what ways could you truly individualize instruction when using these techniques? Do any of the administrative devices available really individualize instruction?

Special Help

Undoubtedly, the most usual way to individualize instruction is to teach pupils on a one-to-one basis through the special help that most teachers give to pupils who need assistance for one reason or another. Teachers have always given special help to those who seem to need it and probably always will continue to do so, no matter how sophisticated teaching methods become. Pupils who are having difficulties and pupils who are doing well both need special help. At times, just inspecting a pupil's work and giving him a pat on the back, or encouraging him to continue, or suggesting a new line of attack may be all that is needed. Often, to be of any real benefit, the special help will entail tutoring, or devising special instruction aimed specifically at correcting a pupil's faulty learning, or helping a pupil with some task that he finds difficult. Perhaps the most interesting type of tutoring is when you help a pupil work on a difficult, advanced, independent project. To really help the pupil who is having academic difficulty and the pupil who need special guidance as he forges ahead independently requires that teachers giv pupils individualized assistance. In such cases, the teacher, either as a tutor or a guide, must teach pupils individually.

Continuous Progress Plan

The continuous progress plan combines the use of learning activity packets or learning modules with a laboratory approach. Even if a school is not set up according to the continuous progress plan, you can arrange your own courses according to the plan. The procedure recommended for a continuous progress plan has been presented in Module 3.

Use of Self-Instructional Devices

Learning activity packets are self-instructional devices. They consist of the materials to use, instructions on how to use them, and self-correcting exercises and tests so that the pupils can instruct themselves. Self-administering and self-correcting materials of this sort make it much easier to individualize instruction. The fact that each pupil has directions, materials, and self-correcting tests and exercises frees him and the teacher from the necessity of lock-step education. A teacher need not spend so much time telling what to do, how to do it, or giving and correcting exercises and tests. The time saved can be given over to individual instruction, tutoring, or special help. Homemade self-administering, self-correcting materials can be gleaned from a teacher's own experience and from old workbooks, textbooks, and tests. Although a teacher would not want to use an outdated text, its exercises might be easily adapted for self-correcting exercises.

Study Guides. Study guides are useful for individualizing instruction whether or not they are part of a module, unit, or contract. Special study guides that show pupils how to carry out individual assignments or special projects can be very effective. Keep them on file. When a pupil wants to start a project or assignment, he can go to the file, draw out the study guide, and go to work. A good special study guide may tell the pupil what to do, how to do it, present questions and problems to get him to think, and point out things he should look for. Exactly what it should contain, of course, depends upon the activity for which it is designed. Special study guides are discussed more fully in Module 11.

More general study guides have been described in discussion of the unit. In the study of philosophy, for instance, perhaps the study guide might consist of a series of questions for the pupil to consider; in science, it might point out selections to read, experiments to conduct and how to conduct them, what to observe, exercises to be done, and ideas to be considered.

Self-Correcting Materials. Self-correcting materials, exercises, and tests can relieve a teacher of much busy work. Use them for diagnosis and practice. Do not use them for casting up term marks or for deciding whether a pupil has passed a unit or module. Mastery tests and similar teacher-administered and corrected, evaluative instruments should be used for that purpose. If self-administered, self-correcting materials are used for marking, it places too much responsibility on the pupils and tempts them to be dishonest.

In making self-administering, self-correcting exercises and tests, put the answers on a separate sheet of paper, or print them upside down on the test, or place them in the teacher's file. Even when it makes no difference, few people have enough willpower to resist the temptation to peek when the answers are easily available. Whatever arrangement you decide on, be sure that the pupils write their answers on separate sheets. Do not let them write on the test or exercise paper; then you can use the exercises or tests for other pupils and other classes. Some teachers feel that the best procedure is to keep all test and exercise papers on file so that pupils can obtain them whenever they need them; others pass them out with the study guide.

Machines for Teaching. Many of the new media devices are useful as self-instructional devices. The language laboratory, for instance, which is little more than a tape recorder or combination of tape recorders, is used for practice of pronunciation and pattern drills in a foreign language. There is no reason why this machine cannot be used for practice in oral English, dictation in business courses, and similar exercises. Some of these machines can play a number of tapes at once so that different pupils can practice different exercises at the same time or exercises in different languages.

But such sophisticated equipment is not really necessary. If every pupil had a tape of his own, he could record at any time that he and the tape recorder were free. Tape recorders can be used for any number of other individualized lessons. Pupils can listen to different tapes, just as they read different books and articles. Exercises and lessons can also be put on tape for individual consumption. Teachers can dictate lessons and instructions to the tape recorder. The resultant tape can be played by individual pupils in class or during free or unscheduled periods. The tape will tell the pupil what to do, ask him questions, and give him information. If he finds the assignment difficult, he can repeat the playing of the tape or portions of the tape until he is satisfied. In order that the recorders are not too noisy, insist that pupils wear earphones while listening to them.

The eight-millimeter, self-loading, individual viewing, motion picture projector can be used in the same way except that, ordinarily, the film to be used must be purchased rather than homemade. Homemade lessons can be prepared for the 35-mm. slide projector, however. Prepare a sequence of slides that tells your story. Unless you are willing to go to the trouble of making captioned slides or taping a commentary to go with the slides, you can ditto a commentary that the pupils can read as they look at the slides. Individual viewing of slides can be arranged easily by placing a screen of white cardboard close to the projector. With a little experimenting, you will be able to project a small but clear image that makes for very fine individual viewing. If possible, use a machine that allows you to preload your slides in trays for automatic or semi-automatic viewing. Be sure the slides are numbered so that the pupils will not get them mixed up. Also mark the slides at the top right corner so that pupils will load them into the machine right side up.

Filmstrip and motion picture projectors can be used in the same way, but you will probably have to use commercial materials rather than your own tailor-made lessons. Procedures for individualizing the use of these devices are described in Module 10.

Teaching Machines. The most sophisticated self-instructional devices are teaching machines that use automated teaching programs. These devices, particularly in their most sophisticated version as computer-assisted instruction, have tremendous potential for individualizing instruction. Because they are "autoinstructional," they make it possible for pupils to proceed at different speeds and in different directions. With a good computer-based program, there seems no reason why instruction could not be almost entirely individualized. Machine teaching, however, got off to a poor start because of poor programming, and computer time is both expensive and difficult to provide to the ordinary classroom. If you have these devices available to you, use them as you would other self-instructional devices.

Correspondence and Television Courses. Perhaps the best tested of all self-instructional devices is the correspondence course. It has been used with great success for many years. Television and radio courses are also available. Many of these are excellent. Correspondence and television courses can be used to offer individual pupils instruction that otherwise would not be available to them. Pupils with special needs should be encouraged to make use of these kinds of courses. Use them just as you would any other learning activity packet.

Using Small Groups and Committees for Individualizing Instruction

To individualize instruction, a teacher may divide the class into groups or committees according to ability, interest, need, or task to be completed. The groups may or may not all study the same topic. Perhaps it is better if they do not.

Teach the groups just as you would any other small groups or committees. You should follow those steps which apply to the situation. Not all of the steps will apply to all small group and committee work. Feel free to adapt them as necessary. The following steps provide an outline well suited for most committee work:

1. Pick a leader and a secretary.
2. Define the task.
3. Set the objectives.
4. Set up a plan.
   a. What tasks must be done?
   b. What material and/or equipment must be secured?
   c. How will information be shared among the committee members?
   d. What records or notes need be kept?
   e. Who will do each of the various tasks? When will the tasks be done?
   f. What are the time limits?
5. Implement the plan.
6. Share the results with each other.
7. Plan how to report the findings.
8. Make the report.[9]

Independent Study

One of the goals of education is to help pupils to learn to work independently; consequently, pupils should have practice in working independently. Independent study is one way to teach pupils to become self-sufficient, self-directing, responsible scholars. When the independent study concerns things that are important and interesting to the pupil, as it always should in secondary schools, it has an excellent motivating effect. To conduct independent study well, however, is quite difficult. One has to steer a course between too much guidance and consequent hampering of the pupils' independence, and not enough guidance and consequent chaos.

In conducting independent study, you should take the following precautions:

1. Be sure that the independent study to be taken is appropriate. Pupils tend to bite off too much, or to wander off into irrelevant areas. Sometimes they wish to do things for which the school does not have the proper facilities, equipment, or material. Try not to let pupils elect to do studies that they are going to have to give up before they finish. Study guides and learning activity packets eliminate much of this danger, but they also confine pupils to preplanned topics that sometimes may not be appropriate for the needs of individual pupils.

---

[9] Clark, op. cit., p. 96.

2. In the beginning, have the pupil map out quite definitely what he hopes to accomplish and how he hopes to accomplish it; at this point, it may be wise for him to prepare a written agenda or plan for your approval. If the independent study plan follows a study guide or learning activity packet, much of this problem can be alleviated, although it may still be wise for the student to decide on a time schedule or agenda.

3. Keep a running check on each pupil's progress. All of us know how easy it is to put off term papers and other independent study. By checking, you can also catch potential difficulties, correct errors, and help misguided pupils to get back on the track before it is too late. Schedule conferences with the pupils so that you will be sure that you check on everyone sufficiently and do not neglect anyone. Also take pains to be available to pupils and to let pupils know you welcome their requests for advice and guidance.

Acceleration

Some individuals can move more rapidly through courses than other pupils. This is possible if a teacher prepares units or learning packets in advance. It is also possible to allow pupils to accelerate in traditional classes by giving them special assignments or, more frequently, by letting pupils move through the ordinary assignments more rapidly. If you do not have the year's work entirely mapped out, there is probably no reason why the pupil should not follow last year's course work. If you do have a syllabus or curriculum guide, then the planning for accelerating the exceptional student is relatively easy. Another easy way is to let pupils work through the readings and exercises of a good textbook or workbook, plus supplementary work. Or you might draw upon items and exercises from other textbooks or workbooks. Test banks can be very helpful in this situation.

Evaluating accelerated pupils' work may be something of a problem. Use the exercises and problems in the textbook and workbook. To save building extra tests, you might have pupils demonstrate what they have learned by writing summaries of the topic.

Projects

The project is a form of independent study in which an individual or a small group attempts to produce something—a map, a model, a booklet, a paper, or a report. To qualify as a real project, the product should be something of tangible value to the pupil such as a vase, or a lamp, or some article made for one's own pleasure and use, or as a present.

Pupils should do projects because they want to and because the product to be completed seems valuable to them. Therefore, they should decide whether to do a project, what project to do, and how to do it. You, as a teacher, should limit yourself to advising and guiding the pupil so that his project will be successful. Projects laid out by teachers are not really projects; they are assignments.

When you use projects in your teaching, the following procedure is recommended:

1. Stimulate ideas by providing lists of things pupils might do, asking former pupils to tell about past projects, suggest readings that might give pupils ideas for projects, or use class discussion to explore possible projects.
2. Let pupils select a project or not. Pupils who do not wish to do a project should be allowed to do something else.
3. Let the pupil plan the procedure he will follow. Help him with his planning.
4. Guide the pupil as he proceeds with his plan. Help him as necessary.
5. Evaluate the pupil's work.

Making Time for Individual Instruction

Individual instruction is an extremely time-consuming way of teaching. Unless one is willing to relinquish the center of the stage and allow pupils to accept much of the responsibility for their own learning, it is an impossible task. To help pupils to make the right decisions, you will have to provide them with self-instructional materials, study guides, learning packets, and self-administering and self-correcting tests and exercises. With these materials, the pupils can move ahead without waiting for you. Without them, you will never find time to do all the work that needs to be done with each individual.

In addition, arrange for pupils to help each other. Young people often learn better from their peers. Bright pupils can help the slower pupils, but more effective perhaps is to let the average or slow pupil, who has mastered a concept or skill, help pupils who have not yet done so. Be careful that you do not exploit your successful students, however.

If you keep your classes informal, as in the laboratory approach, you will find that you have much more time to do important things than if you keep to formal classes. Still, no matter what approach you use, you will be busy.

Accepting Different Evidence of Accomplishment

If, in order to provide for individual differences, we allow pupils to learn in different ways, we must also allow for different evidences of pupil progress. Of course, everyone should attain the essential learnings. However, if we allow some pupils to learn through the dance, and some to learn by making models, then we should consider the special learnings that are concomitant with these learning activities in estimating pupil achievement.

Need for a Variety of Materials

To provide for individual differences one must have things to do with. The single textbook course will no longer suffice. We need material to suit a variety of interests and different ability levels. Not only do we need a variety of materials, but also we need them to be where the pupil can get them when he needs them. The classroom suitable for truly individualized instruction must be full of attractive, usable materials, readily available for pupil use. Such a classroom would in itself be a resource center—truly a laboratory for learning.

Teaching Homogeneously Grouped Classes

In many schools, pupils are grouped homogeneously, either by a deliberate plan of homogeneous or ability grouping, or by selection as the more academically talented pupils tend to select the more academically rigorous courses, or by a combination of both these influences. In these circumstances, varying your course content and methods of teaching according to the type of class will make your teaching much more effective.

The Academically Talented. You can use all of the secondary school teaching methods in classes for the academically talented, because most of them were first invented with academically talented pupils in mind. The important thing is to make the work interesting and challenging and to give the pupils plenty of opportunity to use their talents. The following suggestions may help you:

1. Encourage the talented to think. Use problem solving, inquiry, and open-ended assignments. Insist that pupils dig into the subject. Hold them to a high level of analysis and critical thinking.
2. See to it that the talented keep to high academic standards. Do not accept sloppy thinking or sloppy work. Force them to discipline themselves and their thinking.
3. Don't hold them back. Give them a chance to move on to the new, the interesting, and the challenging. Don't make them repeat what they already know.
4. Be sure they become well grounded in the academic skills.
5. Give them lots of responsibility for their own work. Let them plan and evaluate. Encourage independent study and research.
6. Use high-level materials: original sources, college textbooks, and adult materials.
7. Use the seminar discussion strategy in which pupils present and criticize original papers or reports and discuss topics in depth. Be sure that their discussions hew to a high level of criticism and thinking.

Teaching the Academically Incompetent. The slow sections cause teachers problems because the pupils, as a rule, find most school work difficult and un-appetizing. Because it seems difficult for them and they often fail, most academically incompetent pupils develop an aversion to school work. Your job, when you have a section of these pupils, is to try to make the work interesting to them, to build up their skills so that they can perform reasonably well, and to make the school situation less distasteful to them.

Among the things you can do are the following:

1. Try to make the work seem important and relevant to their own lives. Use subject matter that has meaning and significance to them personally. Show them how their learning will pay off in personal benefits.
2. Diagnose. Find out what their difficulties are and help them overcome them. If they have the necessary skills or background, try to find a way of remedying any difficult situation.

3. Emphasize the development rather than the remedial aspects. Review and summarize frequently. As much as possible, apply new learning to practical situations.

4. Avoid infantile materials. If a pupil has not learned something in five years, going over it in the same way once again will not correct the deficiency. Try to use lively new approaches. Keep the material to be learned adult even if it must be simple. Keep problems and activities short and easy.

5. Take your time. Avoid rushing the pupils. Present new work slowly. Move forward in short steps. Don't take short cuts. Teach the details. Be sure pupils have the basics before you move on. Be sure your explanations are simple, clear, and thorough.

6. Encourage, praise, and help. Build up the pupils' confidence and self-esteem as much as you can.

7. Use concrete subject matter. Keep abstractions at a minimum. Let pupils work with things rather than with words.

8. Give plenty of individual attention. Help pupils with their study skills and with subject matter. Be patient, understanding, and helpful, but not bossy.

9. Use lots of audio-visual materials. They should be simple and clear, but of high-interest level.

10. Give them plenty of practice in thinking. They need to learn how to think logically just as much as the bright pupils do. Use the same discussion techniques as you would with bright pupils except that with the slow learners you will probably have to provide the basic data.

11. Let pupils learn from each other. They may gain much, both intellectually and socially, from helping each other. Besides, it makes the learning process less threatening.

12. Give such pupils plenty of opportunity to do their assignments in class. Do not count on their getting much accomplished as homework. In supervised study sessions, you can help them and they can help each other.

Children of the Poor. The children of the poor are bright, slow, and average, just as other pupils are. The bright ones should be treated just as any other bright pupils, and the slow ones as any other slow pupils. However, because of the concomitants of poverty and life experiences, there are some special considerations that you should keep in mind even though they may not apply to specific pupils.

Poor youths are likely to be disaffected and suspicious of school. Much of the school work they have had has seemed irrelevant to their lives. They may feel that in the school situation the cards are stacked against them. Sometimes, at least, they are probably right. Their past schooling may have been inadequate. Consequently, they may be academically incompetent even though they may be potentially brilliant. Their customs and life styles may be considerably different from those espoused by the school. Often, the language that is native to them is not the standard English that the school believes to be requisite for scholastic success. (Do not mistake, as many have done, language differences for an inability to express oneself. The children of poor parents are usually fluent in a rich but nonstandard English dialect.) The language may be deficient in words by which to express abstractions, however.

The characteristics we have just pointed out tend to be dysfunctional in the ordinary secondary school class. To some extent, then, one makes adjustments in curriculum and methods when teaching poor youth. Still, on the whole, the same tactics and strategies should be used for both poor and affluent youth, due allowance being made for the differences in each particular situation. Courses for poor youth should not be watered down. Neither should course requirements. Poor youth have the same potentials as rich youth. To water down the courses and requirements is to demean them and to deprive them of the benefits of a good education. Intensive remedial work should be provided whenever needed, and every effort should be made to make the course work relevant to the lives of the pupils.

Following are twelve suggestions that may help you when teaching the children of the poor.

1. Respect the pupils as people. If their culture is different learn their taboos and mores; respect their culture just as you hope they will learn to respect yours.
2. Pay great attention to motivation. Fight anti-intellectualism by showing pupils that the subject matter is worthwhile. Point out its practical value. Pick topics to study that have obvious importance.
3. Be sure the course content has meaning to the pupils and relates to their lives and interests. Be sure the content helps the pupils to understand themselves and their role so that they can learn how to function in society. Do not put this at a low how-to-do-it level, but at a high enough level so that they can understand what is really involved. Give them real work. Do not feed them pap. If the pupils cannot do the work required of them, substitute work they can do, but make it something respectable.
4. Give pupils opportunities to succeed. Praise them when they do well, but avoid gushiness. Make it evident that you expect them to learn just like everyone else, that you see no reason why they cannot, and that you intend to see to it that they really get their money's worth out of the course.
5. Be firm, strict, and definite, but not harsh. Harsh measures may seem to work on the surface but, as a rule, they make it more difficult to carry out any meaningful communication or real learning.
6. Use laboratory techniques, individual instruction, and individual help on basic skills. Adjust the subject content to the needs of the pupils. Because many of the pupils are physically oriented, they enjoy working on concrete projects. Begin at the pupils' level and then move toward the more abstract and academic.
7. Use simple language in the classroom. Worry less about the words pupils use and the way they express themselves and more about the ideas they are expressing. Let them use their own idioms without carping on grammar, syntax, and the like.
8. Use unstructured discussions of real problems. Unstructured discussions may help you understand the pupils and help them learn how to express themselves. In selecting problems to study,
   a. Be sure the problems seem real to the pupils.
   b. Be sure to pick problems they will accept.
   Sometimes they do not recognize problems as problems. Sometimes they do not want to. In such cases you may get them to see the truth by challenging their thinking. The Socratic method is useful for this purpose. Use it to pursue the faulty thinking of individual pupils. However, in doing so, be careful to let each pupil keep his self-respect. On the other hand, do not force pupils into discussions they would rather avoid. There is no point in discussing what they already know too much about.
9. Use inductive approaches. Pupils seem to respond better to open-ended questioning than they do to memorizing, for instance.

10. Sometimes pupils greatly enjoy and profit from role playing and dramatization. Simulations like *City I, Consumer,* and *Poor People's Choice* seem to go very well.
11. If pupils have not learned basic skills because of failures in the elementary school grades, help them learn those skills.
12. Use a variety of reading materials. Use multiple readings in laboratory fashion rather than the single textbook. Use adult material of low reading level. Use materials other than reading matter for pupils who cannot read: tapes, recordings, video, films, and pictures. Where no suitable reading matter is available, prepare your own.[10]

A Final Comment. The individualization of instruction requires that you provide opportunities for pupils to work toward different goals, to study different content, and to work in different ways. Just to vary the rate or amount of work the pupils do is not enough. A list of fifteen techniques and methods you might use follows. Each of these methods or techniques has been described somewhere in this module. As you go through the list, see if you can describe how to carry out each of the techniques.

1. Vary your tactics and techniques in classes according to the abilities and personality characteristics of your pupils.
2. Run your class as a classroom laboratory.
3. Utilize the facilities of the social studies laboratory or resource center.
4. Utilize small-group instruction.
5. Differentiate your classwork and homework assignments.
6. Give special assignments to individual pupils or small groups.
7. Use individual or group projects.
8. Encourage independent study.
9. Use the unit method and unit assignments.
10. Use self-instructional materials such as self-correcting assignments, learning packets, programmed materials, teaching machines, computer-assisted instruction, materials, and correspondence and television courses.
11. Give pupils special help.
12. Use the contract plan.
13. Use a continuous progress scheme. (You can run your course on a continuous progress plan even if the plan has not been adopted schoolwide.)
14. Use minicourses.
15. Use a variety of textbooks, readings, and other materials.[11]

SUGGESTED READING

Alexander, William, and Vynce Hines. *Independent Study in Secondary Schools.* New York: Holt, Rinehart & Winston, Inc., 1970.

Bergeson, John B., and George S. Miller. *Learning Activities for Disadvantaged Children.* New York: Macmillan Publishing Co., Inc., 1971.

Bottom, R. *The Education of Disadvantaged Children.* Englewood Cliffs, N.J.: Prentice-Hall, Inc., 1970.

[10] Clark, op. cit., pp. 133–134.
[11] Ibid., pp. 124–125.

Dell, Helen Davis. *Individualizing Instruction*. Chicago: Science Research Associates, Inc., 1972.

Duane, James E. *Individualized Instruction Programs and Materials*. Englewood Cliffs, N.J.: Educational Technology Publications, 1973.

Howes, Virgil M. *Individualization of Instruction: A Teaching Strategy*. New York: Macmillan Publishing Co., Inc., 1970.

Karlin, Muriel, and Regina Berger. *Successful Methods for Teaching the Slow Learner*. Englewood Cliffs, N.J.: Prentice-Hall, Inc., 1969.

Noar, Gertrude. *Individualized Instruction: Every Child a Winner*. New York: John Wiley & Sons, Inc., 1972.

Ornstein, Alan C., and Philip D. Vairo, eds. *How to Teach Disadvantaged Youth*. New York: David McKay Co., Inc., 1969.

Otto, Wayne. *Remedial Teaching*. Boston: Houghton Mifflin Company, 1969.

Shelton, B. *Teaching and Guiding the Slow Learner*. Englewood Cliffs, N.J.: Prentice-Hall, Inc., 1971.

Shiman, David A., Carmen M. Culver, and Ann Lieberman, eds. *Teachers on Individualization: The Way We Did It*. New York: McGraw-Hill Book Company, 1974.

POST TEST

1. What does true individualization of instruction entail?

_____

_____

_____

2. Give a theoretical justification for homogeneous grouping.

_____

_____

3. Explain "homogeneously grouped classes are not homogeneous."

_____

_____

_____

_____

4. Sometimes homogeneous grouping shortchanges the less academically inclined pupils. How and why?

_____

_____

_____

5. What are the supposed merits of continuous promotion?

_____

_____

_____

6. What is the principal reason for introducing minicourses?

_____

7. What is the advantage of having a learning center?

_____

_____

8. Name at least two ways in which one can differentiate an assignment.

_____

_____

9. What is meant by the term classroom laboratory?

_____

_____

_____

_____

10. Why is the unit approach a good method for providing for individual differences?

_____

_____

_____

11. Why is the learning activity package a good instrument for individualizing instruction?

_____

_____

_____

12. What is the essential difference between a learning contract and a learning activity packet or unit?

_____

13. Why are study guides useful in individualizing instruction?

_____

_____

_____

14. For what would you use self-correcting materials?

_____

15. How can you adapt a slide projector for individual viewing?

_____

_____

16. How can you adapt a motion picture projector for individual viewing?

_____

_____

_____

17. How can you make time for working with individuals?

_____

_____

18. What difference in teaching style does homogeneous grouping require of you?

_____

_____

_____

_____

Measurement and Evaluation

Isobel L. Pfeiffer

University of Akron

module 8

Teaching Model / Evaluation and Measurement / Criterion-Referenced and Norm-Referenced Tests / Types of Tests / What Makes a Good Test?

RATIONALE

Evaluation is an integral part of the educational scene. Curricula, buildings, materials, specific courses, teachers, supervisors, administrators, equipment—all must be appraised in relation to student learning, the ultimate goal of the school. When gaps between anticipated results and achievement exist, attempts are made to eliminate those factors that seem to be limiting the educational output, or otherwise to improve the situation. Thus, educational progress occurs.

Since effective learning requires that the learner know how he is doing, the teacher must provide opportunities and instruments for checking progress. This student need for feedback in learning is similar to the teacher's need. A teacher, to be effective, must build on student skills, knowledge and attitudes, so data on what the student knows, feels, and can do is necessary. To plan appropriate learning activities requires continuous student feedback to the teacher to indicate progress and problems. Then the teacher can recycle, provide alternate activities if progress is slow, or bypass unnecessary practice when concepts are mastered. The importance of continuous evaluation in teaching mandates that the teacher knows about testing. He must develop skills in constructing and using tests.

SPECIFIC OBJECTIVES

In this module, we shall define the general terms related to evaluation. We will consider what makes a good test and relate the criteria to standardized and teacher-made tests. Procedures to assist the teacher in producing a test will be suggested. Advantages and disadvantages of different types of test items will be examined.

At the conclusion of your study of this module, it is expected that you will be able to do the following:

1. Define evaluation and measurement, indicating two specific differences between the terms.
2. Explain the distinction between a norm-referenced test and a criterion-referenced test, and give an example of the appropriate use of each.
3. List five criteria for selecting a test and cite a purpose for each criteria.
4. Set up a table of specifications for a unit test and classify five items in correct cells in the table.
5. Cite five different uses of test results.
6. Give four different types of objective questions, and indicate one advantage and one disadvantage of each type.
7. Specify four guidelines for a teacher preparing an essay test.
8. Define percentile, stanine, and grade equivalence, and explain a use of each.

9. Select correct answers on a twenty-five item post test with no more than five errors.
10. Diagram a teaching model, and indicate where evaluation is utilized.

MODULE TEXT

Teaching Model

When Bob Kelly begins his daily trip to his job, his usual route is Lincoln to Main, Main to College and College to the parking lot beside Central High School. Since construction has started on the new highway, Bob sometimes has to change his route. If the Lincoln-Main intersection is blocked, he goes on Washington to Lake Street, and then over to Main. In the fall, when the family is still staying at the cottage, his drive to work takes him in a southeasterly direction instead of the northwest route he takes from home. Then, occasionally, he has an errand, mailing a package or returning a book to the library. Again his trip is adjusted to the situation. How are such revised routes planned? Often with little conscious effort, since the driver is familiar with the area, knows where he is going, where he is, and what must be accomplished enroute.

If Bob Kelly is driving in a city unfamiliar to him, he plans his route more carefully, using a map or specific directions provided by someone who is acquainted with the area. In such a situation, he may recognize another question. Without a street number, sign, or other recognizable clue, he may not know when he reaches his destination. So the final target, which is obvious in a familiar situation (going to work), may not be so easily determined in a strange or unfamiliar setting.

The teacher's plans for the educational journeys of the students in a class require answers to the same basic questions: Where are we going?; Where are we now?; How do we get where we are going?; and How do we know when we get there?

These are questions that must be considered in educational evaluation. The answers provide the teacher with the basis for working with individuals and with groups. Since, in the never-static educational setting, the answers are ever-changing, the teacher continuously assesses and adjusts flexible plans to the new situation.

The basic question of goals, or where are we going, is in a broad sense determined by society. State requirements and limitations, school board policies, curricula, and courses of study usually evolve with input from all segments of the community. Major factors considered include society, the students, the school, and the future. The purpose and philosophy of the school provide broad objectives for the teacher; guidelines in the course of study provide a framework within which the teacher makes selections of content and strategies (what and how). For those individuals who feel that process is a crucial goal of education, the strategies relate to objectives. If one objective is that the student will be able to demonstrate a rational method of attacking a new problem, then surely a problem-solving approach must be implemented in the classroom. The teacher, in selecting specific objectives and activities appropriate for the situation, exerts considerable influence on the learning environment and helps determine where we are going.

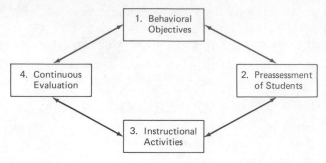

Figure 8-1 *Learning Cycle.*

"Start where the student is" is a cliché to teachers. Nevertheless, the statement emphasizes the need to know where we are before reasonable plans for progress can be made. A student who reads at the third-grade level is not going to be able to cope successfully with a social studies text written on the seventh-grade reading level. A student who does not comprehend percentage is not ready for interest problems. Diagnostic tests are one tool for determining where we are. Other evaluation procedures can also provide information about skills and understanding, such as reading a paragraph and giving an oral summary to indicate comprehension, driving a golf ball to demonstrate the skill, and writing a description of a picture to reveal how well the student can write a paragraph. Students are frustrated and do not progress educationally when they are bored by tasks that they have already mastered, as well as by tasks that require skills or knowledge which they do not have. Information about a student's achievement provides a basis for appropriate planning to stimulate further development.

Information about where we are going (objectives) and where we start (achievement and attitude of students) enables the teacher to propose several plans for reaching the goals. Selection and implementation of a plan and of appropriate learning activities require continuing evaluation to check on progress and to adapt strategies to promote the desired student behavior. Students may work as individuals or in groups on common goals or on specific individualized objectives. When student feedback indicates satisfactory attainment of objectives, the teacher moves to a new unit, problem, or content area, and develops another learning cycle.

In the learning cycle (Figure 8-1), evaluation is critical. It establishes the starting point, provides data on progress, and indicates arrival at the destination. A teacher then must recognize the need for good evaluation and measurement, and must develop skill in preparing effective instruments.

Evaluation and Measurement

The terms *evaluation* and *measurement* are related. Measurement refers to quantifiable data and relates to specific behavior. Tests and the statistical procedures used to analyze the results are the emphases in measurement. Evaluation includes measurement data plus other types of information, such as anecdotal records, and written and oral performance ratings. Evaluation also involves a value judgment factor. A teacher may share the information that May Grisso received the top score in East High School on the College Entrance Examination Board Scholastic Aptitude Test (SAT); this statement refers to measurement. However, when the teacher adds that May has not been an outstanding student in the English program at East, evaluation has occurred. Measurement is descriptive and objective, whereas evaluation involves information from varied sources including subjective value input.

Assessment and *appraisal* are two other terms often used. Both of these suggest going beyond the quantifiable information to a personal interpretation or evaluation. The National Assessment of Educational Progress is dealing with measurement in specific content areas for ages 9, 13, 17, and for adults. Since this testing covers the United States and is expected to provide data to improve the curriculum, the use of assessment as a synonym for evaluation seems appropriate.

Criterion-Referenced and Norm-Referenced Tests

The distinction between criterion-referenced and norm-referenced tests is important to the teacher. *Criterion-referenced tests,* sometimes called mastery tests, are designed to check whether or not the basic objectives of a learning segment have been met. The student is expected to answer all questions correctly. Unless the learner can meet the established level of performance, he is given more opportunity to work with the concepts. Programmed materials rely on these tests. Readiness for the next package or step of a program requires satisfactory completion of the preceding one. The *norm-referenced test,* on the other hand, is designed to indicate comparison with others who have taken the test to determine an individual's standing in a group. The purposes of the tests differ. The criterion-referenced test deals with essentials in the learning unit and is designed so that students can answer all items correctly. The norm-referenced test, instead, is designed to discriminate and is poorly constructed if students answer all items correctly. Probably both kinds of tests have a place in the high school today. The teacher, recognizing the differences in purpose and use, must select or construct the appropriate type.

The teacher may use a norm-referenced test to determine a student's reading level. The individual's score in relation to the group may be expressed in various ways. Percentile rank is commonly used. If George Howe's reading score is at the 35th percentile for tenth graders, then 35 of 100 tenth graders who took the test scored below George. Another frequently used system for representing relative performance is stanines. This standard, nine-point scale was developed during World War II as a simple and usable norm. A single digit from a low of 1 to a high of 9 indicates where the individual score falls in relation to the group. See Table 8-1. George Howe's reading score at the 35th percentile rank can also be described as in stanine 4.

Grade equivalents are sometimes used to represent the relative performance of

Table 8-1 Comparison of Percentiles and Stanines

Stanine	1	2	3	4	5	6	7	8	9
Percentile	1—4	5—11	12—23	24—40	41—60	61—77	78—89	90—96	97—100

students on a test. This method is expressed in two numbers; for example, 9.4 shows the arithmetic average (mean) of students in the fourth month of the ninth grade. The calendar year is divided into ten parts, nine representing the school year and one for summer vacation. George Howe's grade equivalent of 8.2 indicates that, according to the test, he as a tenth grader reads as well as the average student in the second month of the eighth grade.

These three methods of expressing scores are used to indicate how an individual score compares to the group. Percentile and grade equivalent are perhaps more easily understood by parents and teachers. The stanine and other standard scores are more useful because the difference between steps remains the same.

Types of Tests

Achievement tests are designed to measure the student's level of accomplishment: how much a student has learned about a subject area or a segment of that subject. *Teacher-made tests* are usually achievement tests prepared by the teacher to measure student learning in a specific area. A *pretest* is given prior to planned instructional activities. The pretest should provide information about student background pertinent to the content and should help the teacher plan more efficiently. Prerequisite skills and concepts that have not been acquired can be incorporated in the plan. Unnecessary duplication can be eliminated. Students with expertise in the area can be utilized in the instructional program. A *post test* is given at the end of instruction to indicate student achievement at that point. The difference between pretest and post test scores gives an indication of student growth.

A *standardized test* is one prepared with careful research by testing experts so that the instrument represents desirable test characteristics. A test manual that is usually available provides information about administering the test, scoring it, and interpreting results. Norms also are provided as a basis for comparison to a large group or population. The best source of information about standardized tests is *The Mental Measurement Yearbook*[1] in which tests are listed with descriptive information, including the sources and critical reviews.

An *objective test* is one that can be scored consistently; the answers are either right or wrong. This type of test is probably most frequently used in schools. True-false, multiple choice, and matching are examples of types of questions used on objective tests.

Essay tests require original student responses to a question, and are considered subjective measures. The answers cannot be considered right or wrong, but involve such value judgment as "more logical," "better evidence," or "more important point."

Speed tests include time as a factor in the test. This should be applied only when the time involved in the performance is critical. Typing tests are commonly timed.

Power tests are those that allow the student sufficient time to respond to the items. A teacher should provide time for 90 per cent of the students to complete a test in which time should not be considered as a part of the test.

---

[1] O. K. Buros, *Mental Measurement Yearbook* (Highland Park, N.J.: Gryphon Press, various noncumulative editions.)

A *diagnostic test* is specifically designed to determine the students' deficiencies. A *readiness test* is constructed to find out whether the student has the understanding, skills, and, sometimes, motivation to go to the next level.

A *performance test* is designed to indicate the level at which the student can accomplish a specific skill, usually psychomotor in emphasis. The physical education programs utilize these tests, such as in shooting baskets or in executing a tennis serve. Vocational education uses performance tests frequently, also.

The purpose of this section is not an exhaustive study of types of tests, but an examination of terms commonly used by classroom teachers. Many other designations of types of tests can be found.

What Makes a Good Test?

The teacher who is constructing a test or selecting a test for use must be concerned about some basic characteristics: validity, reliability, objectivity, usability, and discrimination. Validity, the most important, refers· to whether the test measures what it is supposed to measure. The key questions concerning validity are the following:

1. Does the test adequately sample the content area?
2. Does the test involve the cognitive, affective, and psychomotor skills that are important to the unit?
3. Does the test relate to all the behavioral objectives for the unit?

Standardized tests involve more complex analysis of validity when results are used for prediction.

Reliability refers to the consistency of results (e.g., a scale is reliable if it always records ninety pounds when one weighs a ninety-pound object on it). Test results may not be consistent because of test conditions, poorly designed or worded questions, errors in scoring, and a number of other chance variables. Human errors, such as errors in grading or errors in reading questions, are inevitable. However, instrument-centered errors as well as pupil-centered errors are taken into consideration by some of the statistical treatments. The teacher who is selecting a standardized test or producing different forms of a test to administer to several sections of a class may wish to investigate this concept further.

Objectivity refers to freedom from subjective judgments for both the teacher and student. This characteristic implies careful attention in the construction of items and in the selection of the form of items for the test.

Usability refers to the practical aspects of time and resources required for the test, compared to the value of information obtained. An essay test, for instance, may be easily prepared by the teacher, but the time involved in grading the test for twenty-eight students may make such a test impractical. Although the preparation of an objective test requires more time initially, the grading is relatively quick and easy. Sometimes grading tests involves rather strict time limits because reports on students are due at a specified time, such as at the end of a semester. Cost or equipment required may eliminate the consideration of certain standardized tests.

Discrimination refers to the ability of a test to separate pupils on the basis of how well they perform on the test. Discriminating power is not a factor in a criterion-referenced test. However, in tests given to determine the individual's position in a group, the differentiation ability of the test is crucial. The teacher should make an item analysis of tests to determine the difficulty and discriminatory power of each item as a basis for revising the test. The use of computers in many schools facilitates item analysis, but since the procedure involves only counting and dividing, the teacher untrained in statistics can handle it. Quite specific guidelines for the difficulty and discriminating power of the items in a well-constructed test are available.[2]

Validity. Very specific suggestions can be made to help the teacher construct a test to measure what is supposed to be measured. A table of specifications should be constructed. This two-way grid indicates behavior in one dimension and content in the other (see Table 8-2). In this grid, behavior relates to the three domains: cognitive, affective, and psychomotor. Cognitive domain, involving mental processes, is divided, according to Bloom's taxonomy, into six categories: (1) simple memory or knowledge; (2) comprehension; (3) application; (4) analysis; (5) synthesis (usually involves an original product in oral, written, or artistic form); and (6) evaluation. See Module 1.2 for a fuller explanation of this domain.

The teacher examining objectives for the unit should decide what emphasis should be given to the behavior and to the content. For instance, if vocabulary development is a concern for this class, then probably 20 per cent of the test on vocabulary may be appropriate, but 50 per cent would be unsuitable. This planning enables the teacher to design the test to fit the situation, rather than a haphazard test that does not correspond to the objectives either in content or behavior emphasis. Since knowledge questions are easy to write, tests often fail to go beyond that level even though the objectives state that the student will analyze and evaluate. The sample Table of Specification for a unit in World Literature on Understanding Others (Table 8-2) indicates a distribution of questions on a test. Since this test is an objective test, no items test synthesis, affective, or psychomotor behaviors. If these categories are included in the unit objectives, some other additional evaluative devices must be used to test learning in these categories. The teacher could also show the objectives tested, as indicated within parentheses in Table 8-2. Then a check on inclusion of all objectives is easy.

Objectivity. To make tests more objective, test builders have invented several types of so-called objective test items which, when properly used, tend to reduce the amount of subjectivity and human error, particularly in the scoring. The following paragraphs give examples of a number of different types of objective test items, with some suggestions that should help you in constructing such items.

SUPPLY (SHORT OR COMPLETION) ITEMS. Supply test items, such as *short answer* or *completion items,* require the student to recall the correct answer. They differ from recognition list items, such as true-false or multiple-choice items, in that the pupil must actually supply the answer rather than select one from a set of alternatives.

---

[2] J. Stanley Ahmann and Marvin D. Glock, *Evaluating Pupil Growth,* 4th ed. (Boston: Allyn & Bacon, Inc., 1971), p. 191.

Table 8-2 Table of Specifications

CONTENT	BEHAVIORS								TOTAL
World Literature	Cognitive						Affective	Psychomotor	
Understanding Others	Knowledge	Comprehension	Application	Analysis	Synthesis	Evaluation			
I. Vocabulary Development		3 (1, 2)	2 (2)						5
II. Individual Selections			1 (8)	2 (7)		2 (7)			5
III. Literary Forms and Style	1 (3)		1 (3)	1 (6)		2 (6)			5
IV. Comparison of Culture	2 (4, 5)			3 (4)					5
V. Comparison of Values	3 (5)			1 (5)		1 (8)			5
TOTAL	6	3	4	7		5			25

Example: *Short answer item:*
Give the name of the author of the short story, "The Beggar."
Completion item:
The name of the author of "The Beggar" is _____.
(Anton Chekov)

The advantages of these items include the reduction of student guessing and ease of construction. Dangers include emphasis on recall of a specific word or factual detail which is not essential; subjectivity in grading when unanticipated responses, legibility, and spelling are involved; neglect of higher cognitive behaviors; and focus on rote memory.

Suggestions for writing short answer items include the following:

1. Design the items so that there is sufficient information to indicate clearly one correct response.
2. Avoid copying statements directly from textbooks.
3. For completion items, put the blank at the end or near the end of the statement.
4. Try to develop items which require the student to go beyond the knowledge level.
5. Avoid ambiguous statements.
6. Provide sufficient space for writing the answer.

TRUE-FALSE ITEMS. *True-False items* are declarative sentences which the student marks as true or false statements.

Example: A right triangle is necessarily a scalene triangle. (False)

One advantage of true-false items is the wide sampling of content possible in a short time. The choice between alternate answers is a realistic task for the student since he often must make such decisions in the real world. The items are relatively simple and time-saving to construct. Grading is easy. On the other hand, the fact that guessing is encouraged by the 50–50 chance of success is a disadvantage. Another disadvantage is that there is danger of overemphasis on details and on the lowest level of the cognitive domain when writing true-false items. Further, brief statements that are completely true or false are hard to phrase. Although these items are not suitable for controversial content, they can be useful for stimulative or instructional tests.

Some suggestions for constructing these test items include the following:

1. Use statements related to significant objectives.
2. Write statement clearly and precisely, avoiding ambiguities.
3. Use positive statements; avoid negative statements since they tend to confuse students.
4. Avoid specific determiners, such as never, all, often, or usually, which frequently identify a statement containing them as true or false.
5. Try to develop items that require more than knowledge for responses.
6. Do not use statements directly from the text.
7. Make true and false items similar in length.
8. Do not overload test with either true or false statements.
9. Arrange a random pattern of correct responses.
10. Provide a simple method for indicating response, so grading is accurate.

MATCHING ITEMS. *Matching items* consist of two sets of terms to be matched to show some indicated relationship. Literary titles may be matched with authors; definitions, with words; geographic names, with locations; dates, with events; statements or examples, with principles; people, with identification; symbols, with terms; causes, with effects; parts, with units to which they belong; short questions, with answers.

Example: In the blank provided, indicate the correct solution for the equation by marking the letter of the answer. Use a letter only once.

_____ 1.	$2x + 3 = 7$.	A. $x = 9$.
_____ 2.	$4x = x + 9$.	B. $x = 7$.
_____ 3.	$6x - 7 = x - 2$.	C. $x = 5$.
_____ 4.	$9 - 4x = 2 - 3x$.	D. $x = 4$.
_____ 5.	$\frac{2}{3}x = 6$.	E. $x = 3$.
		F. $x = 2$.
		G. $x = 1$.
		H. $x =$ Correct answer is not listed.

[Correct answers are 1-F; 2-E; 3-G; 4-B; 5-A.]

Another format for matching items is providing a list of terms or phrases which are then applied to a series of items.

Example: Each of the following statements is a sentence. Decide whether the sentence is simple, compound, complex, or compound-complex. Then put the letter corresponding to the correct choice in the blank at the left.
A. Simple.
B. Compound.

C. Complex.
D. Compound-Complex.

_____1. During the summer, many families plan vacation trips, and the national parks are crowded.
_____2. If you want a cabin in Yosemite during July, your reservation must be made months in advance.
_____3. Camping is a popular and economical way of traveling.
_____4. A family that camps must plan carefully for a pleasant trip.
_____5. Preparing your own meals is an important economy.
[Correct answers are 1-B; 2-C; 3-A; 4-C; 5-A.]

The matching of items is a means of checking student recognition of relationships and associations. Many items can be handled in a short period of time. However, the emphasis is usually on knowledge. A teacher may have difficulty finding content that is appropriate and providing plausible incorrect responses.

Suggestions for constructing matching test items include the following:

1. Limit alternatives in a set to ten or twelve; more can be very confusing and time-consuming for students.
2. Each set should be homogeneous.
3. Include two or three extra choices from which responses can be chosen. This practice decreases the possibilities of guessing.
4. Arrange choices in a sequential order, such as alphabetically, or in time sequence.
5. Put all of both sets on the same page so the student does not have to turn from page to page.
6. Make directions clear and specific. Explain how matching is to be done and whether responses are used more than once.
7. Keep the response items short. Otherwise, student time is used in searching through responses.

MULTIPLE-CHOICE ITEMS. *Multiple-choice items* provide a statement or question and a number of possible responses. The student selects the correct or best response. There is a possibility of measuring not only knowledge, but comprehension, application, analysis, and evaluation with multiple-choice items. Guessing is substantially reduced with careful construction of responses so that the undesired ones seem plausible. The time required for preparing and taking multiple-choice items may discourage students who dread a long test.

Example:

_____1. An individual is most likely to receive a severe sunburn in the middle of the day because
  a. we are slightly closer to the sun at noon than at any other time.
  b. when the sun's rays fall directly on a surface, more energy is transmitted than when the rays fall obliquely on the surface.
  c. when the sun is directly overhead, the rays pass through less filtering atmosphere than when the sun is lower in the sky.
  d. the air is warmer at noon than at other times of day.
[Correct answer is *b*.]

Suggestions for constructing multiple-choice items include the following:

1. Arrange the possible responses in a vertical list to help the student see his choices.
2. Provide four or five choices.
3. Be sure all responses would seem plausible to students who do not know the correct response.
4. Be sure every choice has grammatical consistency with the question or incomplete statement.
5. Make the correct answers about the same length and vocabulary level as the others.
6. State the problem or question clearly in the introduction so the choices are as brief as possible.

SITUATION ITEMS. Situations followed by statements to be checked or classified can be set up to measure various cognitive levels.

Example: Bill Collins planned a large garden to help cut down food expenses for his family. He purchased a quantity of ladybugs and placed them in the garden area. Check statements that are good reasons for his action.

_____1. Ladybugs are colorful insects.
_____2. The ladybug improves the fertilization of tomatoes and squash.
_____3. Ladybugs encourage cross-pollination of sweet corn.
_____4. The ladybug is a natural enemy of aphids.
_____5. Many gardeners want ladybugs in their gardens.
_____6. The garden yield may be increased when ladybugs are in the area.
_____7. Ladybugs help control certain insect pests.
[Correct answers are 4, 6, 7.]

Items of this type are difficult to build. These situations are often difficult to present briefly, and providing appropriate ways for the student to respond may challenge the ingenuity of the teacher.

Correcting Objective Tests. Objective tests can be designed so that pupils answer the items directly on the test or on answer sheets. In some schools, teachers may have facilities for checking tests by machine. Then, of course, the tests should be set up to use answer sheets. If you do not have machine scoring available, you may still wish to use answer sheets to save time and effort when marking tests. If answer sheets are used, they should be arranged so that the student can move easily from the test to the answer sheet. One way to do this is to make the column on the answer sheet correspond with the pages of the test.

For many teachers, marking on the test paper is an advantage because the test can be returned to the student and used for teaching those areas not mastered. To simplify marking, teachers should have all answers arranged at the left side of the page. Keys can be prepared either to fit over this section with cutouts for the student's answers or to place beside the student's responses. Keys that indicate correct responses should be accurately prepared and written in colored ink so the key is easily identified. All possible answers should be included in the key. Use of a colored pencil to mark incorrect responses speeds the counting of errors. In Module 9, ways of assigning grades to tests will be discussed.

Essay Tests. Since objective questions do not provide the student an opportunity to organize ideas or show his creativity, they limit his freedom of response. Essay questions are so named because the student responds in an essay form that varies from a sentence or two to many pages in length. Essay questions are suitable for assessing learning at the higher cognitive and affective levels. To reduce the element of student guessing, the questions must be clear and specific. Because writing responses to essay questions is time consuming, the number of essay questions one can use in a test is severely limited. This fact makes it difficult to cover all the objectives.

Although the essay test takes less time to construct than the objective test because it involves fewer questions, the scoring of essay tests is time consuming, and consistency of scoring is hard to maintain.

You should prepare your students to take essay tests. In your preparation, you should (1) discuss the meaning of such terms as compare, contrast, and illustrate; (2) develop suitable responses to sample questions; (3) stress the importance of the careful reading of questions; (4) stress the planning of responses; (5) conduct activities in which the students practice how to attack essay questions; and (6) consider such bothersome elements as padding answers, proofreading, and legibility.

Examples of essay questions:

1. Discuss the essay test as a measure of achievement.
2. Compare essay and objective tests in relation to the following factors: (a) validity; (b) reliability; (c) usability; (d) discrimination; and (e) objectivity.
Exercise: Why is the second question an improvement over the first?

Suggestions for constructing essay questions include the following:

1. Expected student answers should relate to significant content and behavior, as indicated in the table of specifications and objectives.
2. Phrase the items clearly and specifically so the students know what is expected of them.
3. The number and complexity of the questions should be reasonable for the time limits so the students can demonstrate their achievement.
4. The questions should pose an interesting and challenging problem for the student.
5. If spelling, grammar, and writing style are to be scored, students should be informed about how much these factors will influence the scoring.
6. All students should write on the questions given. This increases reliability.
7. The point value of the questions should be indicated.

SCORING ESSAY QUESTIONS. Scoring essay questions is difficult since it requires much time and involves subjectivity. You can make your handling of this task more effective by following certain procedures.

Write out a model answer when you construct the item. Sometimes, as you attempt to respond to your own questions, you will see some of the ambiguities and can improve the question.

Assign points to the various subparts of the response. In doing so, consider how many points will make an answer excellent, acceptable, or unacceptable.

Score each test anonymously so that the identity of the student is not a factor.

Score the same test question at the same time for all the students; for example, read and score all answers for question 1 before you start reading the responses to question 2.

Consider the use of a two-step scoring procedure. In this procedure, reading the answers and rating the responses into three categories (excellent, acceptable, poor) is the first step. Rereading and scoring points is the second step. Some teachers prefer to assign points on the first reading. However, sorting followed by scoring gives one a chance to add unpredicted responses to the point array before the actual scoring.

Read each set of answers through without interruption when possible. Fluctuations in the feelings and attitudes of the reader are lessened when no external interference occurs.

Try to disregard irrelevant factors. If neatness is not a criterion, then it should not influence scores. When handwriting is not a part of the objective measured, then handwriting should not be a factor.

Finally, if essay tests are used, teachers are obligated to score the tests with as much reliability and objectivity as possible. The questions that are carefully designed can provide information about students' achievements which helps the teacher plan for students' growth and evaluate his own instructional activities. Good questions can also stimulate the student to find relationships, synthesize ideas, apply concepts, and evaluate a variety of materials.

Item Analysis. Item analysis involves examining each test question to determine its strengths and weaknesses. Usually such analysis is concerned with the level of difficulty and with discriminating power. Level of difficulty is determined by the percentage of pupils who have answered the item correctly. Discriminating power refers to how effectively the item differentiates between the students who did well and those who did poorly on the test.

ITEM DIFFICULTY. Difficulty of a test item is easily calculated. First, tabulate the number of students who correctly answered the question and divide by the number of students who tried to answer. Then, multiply by 100 to change the quotient to a per cent.

Example:
There were 19 students who correctly answered a question of 25 who responded to the question.

$$\text{Item Difficulty} = \frac{19}{25} \times 100 = 76.$$

For norm-based tests, the items answered correctly or incorrectly by all or most of the students contribute little to determining the norms. In fact, the level of difficulty should be near 50 per cent. One recommendation is that only items in the 40 to 70 per cent range should be included in a test.

ITEM DISCRIMINATION. The index of discrimination may be calculated on different bases. One procedure is to use the upper and lower 27 per cent of the scores. Perfect discrimination of an item would mean that all the students in the upper group answered correctly and all in the lower group answered incorrectly. Such precise differentiation between groups seldom occurs. The difference between the number of students in the upper group who answer the test item correctly and the number of students in the lower group who answer the item correctly is divided by the number of pupils in both groups.

Example:
Of 100 scores, the top 27 include 20 correct responses on item A; the low 27 include 8 correct responses on the same item.

$$\text{Index of Discrimination} = \frac{20 - 8}{54} = \frac{12}{54} = .22+$$

The index varies from $+1.00$ to -1.00. Positive one indicates complete differentiation in the desired direction. Any negative value indicates the item discriminates in the wrong direction and is therefore unsatisfactory. Any discriminatory values above $+0.40$ are considered good. The range $+0.40$ to $+0.20$ is called satisfactory. Teacher-made tests that are norm-referenced should have more than half of the items with an index discrimination of $+0.40$ or above, and forty per cent of the items with a satisfactory index. No items should have a negative index.

General Suggestions. FILE OF TEST ITEMS. Tests should be analyzed and revised by the teachers. Reusing the same tests encourages cheating. But using the good questions of a test, eliminating or improving the poor items, and adding new items produces a better test than writing all new items.

Keep a file of your good questions as a convenient way of improving tests. To construct a test item file, put the question on one side of a file card and information about the item on the reverse side. File the question by unit, problem, or other convenient classification. These cards can then be pulled, sorted, and used as a basis for a new test. Since frequent short tests may be important for feedback to both teacher and student, you can use them to develop the test item file rapidly. Then questions for a unit test or semester examination will be readily available. Objective questions and essay questions from your test file may be combined in the same test.

WHEN SHOULD TESTS BE GIVEN? Since tests can fulfill different purposes, when a test should be given depends on the purpose. Before making realistic plans for instructional activities, a teacher must know the level of student achievement. This information can be obtained through testing. To work with individual students effectively, a teacher needs a diagnosis of the deficiencies of the student. Testing can provide this information. Effective learning requires feedback to the student that testing can provide. Grades or reports on progress of students ordinarily include some test results as a part of the evaluation. Students want information about their capabilities and talents to help them make vocational and educational choices. Testing can provide some data for these decisions. In the appraisal of materials, teaching strategies, and programs, test results are one source of data. Each of the purposes mentioned suggests when the test results can be used. Continuous evaluation means tests are given as the data from the testing is needed.

CHEATING. You can discourage cheating by clarifying what the behavioral objectives are and how the objectives will be evaluated. A teacher should give the students information about time allowance for the test, the type of test, its purpose, and general content. Use other means of evaluation to provide more opportunities for students who do not perform well under the pressure of a test situation. Keep alert while the test is given, discourage student communication, and circulate to see how the students are progressing. Such awareness on the part of the teacher tends to hamper some of the tactics often used in cheating. With the emphasis on measurement so the teacher and students can plan together for a better teaching-learning situation, cheating loses its appeal for students.

If several sections of a class are to take the test, the teacher should vary some of the questions. Perhaps, the multiple-choice sections could be the same, but the true-false and essay questions could be varied. Three different forms of the test could be prepared. Sometimes each class could use a different form; other times, one third of each class might use one form. A variety of approaches in different tests will show students that the teacher wants to be fair. In individualized instruction, group tests are eliminated; personal growth becomes a motivation and eliminates the purposes of cheating.

Cheating is a persistent problem whenever group testing is done. The teacher minimizes the problem by using tests as a part of the instructional program and including other sources of information in grading. Cheating is discouraged by teacher circulation and sensitivity to the problem.

Summary

This module has indicated that testing is an integral part of a teaching model. Criterion referenced and norm referenced tests both have a place in the school. Validity, reliability, usability, discrimination and objectivity are discussed as they relate to teacher made tests. Advantages and disadvantages of types of objective items (supply, true-false, matching and multiple choice) are presented. There are suggestions for writing good items of each type. How to construct and score essay questions is also considered. To insure that the objectives are adequately covered both from the content and behavior dimensions, a table of specifications is recommended. Since tests are such an important part of the teaching-learning situation, as well as the general educational scene, the teacher must purposefully work to develop skills in test construction and utilization. Accountability requires that the responsible teacher collect data on the effectiveness of teaching. Test results are an important part of these data.

SUGGESTED READING

Ahmann, J. Stanley, and Marvin D. Glock. *Evaluating Pupil Growth,* 4th ed. Boston: Allyn & Bacon, Inc., 1971.

Beatly, Walcott H., ed. *Improving Educational Assessment and an Inventory of Measures of Affective Behavior.* Association for Supervision and Curriculum Development. NEA, Washington, D.C.: 1969.

Bloom, Benjamin S., ed. *Taxonomy of Educational Objectives Handbook I: Cognitive Domain.* New York: David McKay Co., Inc., 1956.

Brown, Donald J. *Appraisal Procedures in the Secondary Schools,* Englewood Cliffs, N.J.: Prentice-Hall, Inc., 1970.

Gorow, Frank F. *The Learning Game: Strategies for Secondary Teachers.* Columbus, Ohio: Charles E. Merrill Publishers, 1972.

Harrow, Anita J. *A Taxonomy of the Psychomotor Domain*. David McKay Co., Inc., New York: 1972.

Krathwohl, David R., Benjamin S. Bloom, and Bertram B. Masia. *Taxonomy of Educational Objective. Handbook II: Affective Domain*. David McKay Co., Inc. New York: 1964.

Mager, Robert F. *Measuring Instructional Intent*. Belmont, Calif.: Fearon Publishers, Inc., 1973.

Newman, Isadore, Bill J. Frye, and Carole Newman. *An Introduction to the Basic Concepts of Measurement and Evaluation*. College of Education, The University of Akron, Akron, Ohio: 1973.

Noll, Victor H., and Dale P. Seannell. *Introduction to Educational Measurement*. 3rd ed. Boston: Houghton Mifflin Company, 1972.

Sanders, Norris M. *Classroom Question. What Kinds?* Harper and Row, Publishers, New York: 1966.

Schoer, Lowell A. *Test Construction: A Programmed Guide*. Allyn & Bacon, Inc., Boston: 1970.

POST TEST

MULTIPLE CHOICE *Insert the correct answer in the space provided.*

_____ **1.** A criterion-referenced test is constructed so that
   a. each student will attain a perfect score if he has mastered the objectives.
   b. the student will be compared to other students and his position in the group determined.
   c. the test measures what it is supposed to test or meets the criterion established.
   d. the deficiencies of a student are located in a specific area of behavior.

_____ **2.** Evaluation and measurement are defined so that
   a. the terms are synonymous.
   b. evaluation includes measurement.
   c. measurement includes evaluation.
   d. measurement and evaluation are not directly related.

_____ **3.** The items on a true-false test are *least* likely to
   a. measure complex cognitive behavior.
   b. encourage guessing.
   c. cover a quantity of material in a short time.
   d. take a reasonable amount of teacher time for constructing and checking.

_____ **4.** Supply (completion or short answer) items should be constructed
   a. with the blank at the beginning for easy grading.
   b. with hints such as the first letter of the term to limit responses.
   c. with several blanks so the student has several chances to respond correctly.
   d. with emphasis on important content so item is worthwhile.

_____ 5. Which teacher comment about scoring essay tests will improve the reliability of the test?
   a. "I like to read all the student's answers at one time to get an overview of what he knows."
   b. "I can do a better job of scoring when I don't know whose paper I'm reading."
   c. "The time it takes to separate test papers item by item is time I could use more profitably for other purposes."
   d. "I can tell how much a student knows by scanning his paper."

_____ 6. In a model of teaching, testing is essential in
   a. the writing of objectives.
   b. preassessment of students.
   c. implementation of instructional plans.
   d. evaluation of learning.
   e. a and b.
   f. b and d.

_____ 7. Multiple-choice items are superior to matching and to true-false items for some purposes because they
   a. save teacher time in construction and grading.
   b. decrease the number of questions the student can answer in a specified time.
   c. measure cognitive processes beyond memory.
   d. increase student choices in the test situation.

_____ 8. Student scores on standardized tests can be expressed in terms of
   a. percentile rank.   c. grade equivalent.
   b. stanine.   d. all of these.

9–13. *If the following Table of Specifications is set up for a unit in short stories in ninth-grade English, indicate the appropriate placement of the tally for each question listed. Put the letter(s) of the correct cell in the blank. Use the highest cognitive level involved.*

CONTENT   COGNITIVE BEHAVIOR

	Knowledge	Comprehension	Application	Analysis	Synthesis	Evaluation
Vocabulary	A	D	G	J	M	P
Literary Style	B	E	H	K	N	Q
Elements of the Short Story (Plot, Characters, Setting, Theme)	C	F	I	L	O	R

_____ 9. Ten items listing synonyms to be matched with ten of thirteen words given.

_____ 10. What effect on the reader is expected when the author tells the story in the first person?

    a. The reader is an observer of the action.

    b. The reader identifies with the author.

    c. The reader gets a broad insight into the motivation of all characters.

    d. The reader quickly perceives the theme of the story.

_____**11.** Compare the "Tell Tale Heart" with "The Fugitive" in regard to

    a. point of view.   **b.** setting.   **c.** plot.

_____**12.** At the end of "Split Cherry Tree," Pa feels that Professor Herbert is a "fine man" because

    a. Professor Herbert had a good education.

    b. Professor Herbert respected the gun Pa carried.

    c. Professor Herbert treated Pa as a worthy individual.

    d. Professor Herbert displayed his intelligence to Pa.

_____**13.** Select the best story you read and defend your selection, using four criteria for a good short story.

    14–20. *Check the purposes for which teacher-made tests can be appropriately constructed*

_____**14.** Diagnosing student instructional needs.

_____**15.** Indicating level of student achievement.

_____**16.** Predicting vocational success.

_____**17.** Indicating psychological problems.

_____**18.** Determining effectiveness of teaching.

_____**19.** Showing whether instructional objectives have been attained.

_____**20.** Measuring the effectiveness of an experimental program.

    21–25. *Match the correct test characteristic with the question asked about the test. Use a term only once.*

_____**21.** Does the test measure what is supposed to be measured?

_____**22.** Can the test be constructed, administered, and scored conveniently?

_____**23.** Are the results consistent?

_____**24.** Do the test results show the different achievement levels of the students?

_____**25.** Are results affected by the student or the scorer?

a. Comprehensiveness.
b. Correlation.
c. Discrimination.
d. Efficiency.
e. Objectivity.
f. Reliability.
g. Usability.
h. Validity.

Marks and Marking

Isobel L. Pfeiffer

University of Akron

module 9

Grading and Evaluation / Assigning Marks to Tests / Observation Techniques / Grading Themes / Evaluation of Individualized Instruction / Self-Evaluation / Grading and Reporting / Grading Systems / General Suggestions

RATIONALE

Grading is time consuming and frustrating for most teachers. What should be graded? Should marks represent student growth, level of achievement in a group, effort, attitude, general behavior, or a combination of these factors? What should determine grades—tests, homework, projects, class participation, group work, or all of these? How can individualized instruction be graded? These are just a few of the questions that plague the teacher when decisions about grades must be made.

The report card may be one of the few communications between the school and the student's home. Unless the teacher and the school have clearly determined what grades represent, the report card may create misunderstanding and dissatisfaction on the part of parents and students. The grading system then, instead of informing the parents, may separate the home and the school which have a common concern—the best development of the student.

The development of the student includes the cognitive, affective, and psychomotor domains. Consequently, paper and pencil tests provide only a portion of the data needed to indicate student progress. Different methods of evaluation must be utilized to determine how the student works and what he can produce. The teacher needs a repertoire of means of assessing learner behavior and products.

Although grades have been a part of the secondary school for only 100 years, they have become entrenched. Both parents and students have come to expect evaluations. Some critics suggest that the emphasis in school is on getting a high grade rather than on learning.

There have been complaints about subjectivity and unfair practices. As a result, a variety of systems for evaluation has evolved. If the teacher is aware of some alternative grading systems, he may be able to develop a grading process that is fair and effective for his situation.

SPECIFIC OBJECTIVES

This module will consider some of the purposes of grading. The differences between criterion-referenced and norm-referenced grading will be examined. Some practices in evaluating tests, themes, and other student products and student procedures will be suggested. Self-evaluation will be discussed along with pros and cons of peer evaluation. We will scrutinize some of the problems involved in grading in such situations as individualized instruction or contract teaching. Practices in grading will be discussed.

Upon completing the study of this module, you should be able to perform all the following:

1. Indicate purposes accomplished by norm-referenced grading and by criterion-referenced grading.
2. Set up a frequency distribution for a set of test scores and estimate the stanines.

3. Explain three criteria for an effective grading system.
4. Discuss grading in relation to the normal curve, individualized instruction, themes, homework, and class discussion.
5. List and describe four instruments for evaluating the behavior and products of secondary students.
6. Indicate specific reasons for helping secondary students develop self-evaluation skills.
7. Construct a rating scale for some activity or product appropriate to content area, such as cookies in food class, laboratory procedures in a chemistry class, group discussion in social studies.
8. Explain three means of evaluating affective objectives.
9. Demonstrate how a teacher might set up a point system for grading a class at the end of six weeks.
10. Select appropriate answers to the post test with no more than three errors.

MODULE TEXT

Grading and Evaluation

Grading is an unpleasant task that teachers dread. The aversive reaction of teachers results from a number of factors including (1) lack of clarity about what grades represent; (2) inability to communicate student behavior—content mastery in the cognitive domain, study skills, affective response—with a symbol; (3) parent and student confusion about the communication; (4) guilt about subjectivity in determining grades; and (5) concern that grades may adversely influence student behavior, vocational or employment opportunities, and further educational goals.

Evaluation is a requisite in effective learning. Unless a learner knows how he is progressing, he cannot make the modifications necessary to achieve the goal. He may be practicing incorrect procedures; for example, in spelling, he may be learning incorrectly a word that he miscopied. Feedback to keep the learner on target is necessary. When the student is performing well, the positive reinforcement facilitates learning.

Evaluation and grading are not synonymous. Evaluation implies the collection of information from many sources, including measurement techniques and observation. These data are then the basis for value judgment for such purposes as diagnosing learning problems, recommending vocational alternatives, and grading. Grades are only one aspect of evaluation, and are intended to communicate educational progress to both parents and students. Some questions that must be considered by individual teachers and schools are the following:

1. What should be the criteria for marking—comparison with a group, self-development, or both?
2. What kinds of experiences are involved—academic achievement, attitudes, study patterns, personal habits, or social behavior?
3. What consideration should be given to the psychological effect of grades on students? A student who is consistently unsuccessful may be convinced that he is worthless or inadequate. A student who is academically talented may, with little effort, receive high grades and be satisfied with mediocrity.

4. What form of marking is best for communicating—a percentage plan, a letter system (A, B, C, D, F or a modification of this plan), pass/fail, a written description, several grades (one for achievement, one for social skills, and one for study habits), or a combination of these?

The school system or the individual school in which you will teach has, undoubtedly, its own procedure for grades. This procedure is the one that the new teacher interprets and uses for his own teaching assignment. However, there are always means of adapting a system; for example, student conferences can always be used by a teacher to supplement any grades, parent conferences by phone or in person can be individually scheduled, or descriptions of student work and progress can be written as letters to parents to explain grades.

Probably the greatest benefit of any grading system is the fact that teachers must establish criteria and priorities. Someone must decide just what student behavior is important in the teaching-learning situation and what the criteria for effective performance are to be. The decisions may be made by the teacher, by students, or through a cooperative effort. All students should know exactly what the decisions are, and the decisions should be definitely reflected in the learning activities and evaluation. Behavioral objectives must be carefully selected and clearly stated as a basis for effective learning.

Criterion-Referenced and Norm-Referenced Grading. There are two basic approaches to grading. One is similar to norm-referenced measurement. Just as in norm-referenced measurement, the emphasis may be to establish the relative position of an individual in a group, so that in grading, the communication may be designed to show how the individual compares to the group. This type of grading is termed *norm-referenced grading*. The other approach is *criterion-referenced grading*. In continuous progress curriculum or other individualized programs, the criteria-referenced concern is with the individual's progress. Grading then emphasizes individual development, often including both achievement and work skills.

The philosophy of these two approaches is different. The norm-referenced grading reflects a competitive social structure. The grade is assigned to indicate how a student compares with other students. The top grade, usually A, generally means that the students receiving that grade have learned the content better than most other students in the class. The lowest grade, F or U in many scales, shows that the student has done poorly and has achieved less than others in the class. In general, the teacher assumes that the group of students approximates a normal distribution or bell-shaped curve. Such a distribution of marks follows a pattern of a similar number of A's and F's and of B's and D's. In the curve, shown in Figure 9-1, A's and F's each represent 7 per cent of the students; B's and D's each represent 24 per cent, and 38 per cent of the students receive C's. In other situations, the allocation may be 5 per cent for A's and F's, 15 per cent for B's and D's, and 60 per cent for C's. Many other allocations of grades on the normal curve have been used by teachers to fit certain groups. In the example given, the teacher is arbitrarily saying the class or classes represent the total population of this age group. Because of such factors as the location of secondary schools, alienated students, special classes, and tracking programs, the assumption that a class has a normal distribution is unrealistic. Consequently, the teacher must adapt any such

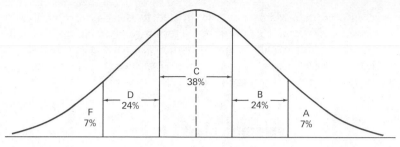

Figure 9-1 *Possible Distribution of Marks.*

plan to his particular situation. The teacher intuitively places a group of students on the normal curve. The practice of using a normal curve is considered objective by many teachers. Yet, the arbitrary selection of segments for letter grades, as well as the placement of the class or classes on the curve, involves teacher subjectivity.

One frequent problem in norm-referenced grading is what to do with students in the high academic track. Should all receive A's and B's? If a wider grading scale is used for them, does it represent the students' achievement accurately for college entrance? For example, does C in an advanced English class mean the same level achieved by a student getting C in an average class? Probably the achievement in the advanced class represents more complex content and more sophisticated activities by students. To counteract the grade effect of a more difficult curriculum, some schools have special procedures for indicating advanced work on transcripts that are sent to colleges or to prospective employers. The same kinds of difficulties may arise with students from other academic tracks. Employers may interpret grades so that expectations for performance are unrealistic. Then, of course, the school is blamed. Grades often have an effect extending beyond the school.

Criterion-referenced grading is based on whether or not a student achieves the specified objectives for the course. The objectives must be clearly stated to represent important student outcomes. This approach implies that effective teaching and learning result in high grades (A's) for most students. In fact, when a mastery concept is used, the student must accomplish the objectives before he can handle the next learning task. The philosophy of teachers who favor criterion-referenced procedures recognizes individual potential. They accept the challenge of finding teaching strategies to help a student develop from where he is to the designated level. Instead of wondering how Sam compares with Ted, the comparison is between what Ted could do yesterday and what he can do today.

Most grading is either norm-referenced or criterion-referenced. In beginning typing classes, for example, a certain basic speed and accuracy are established as criteria. Perhaps only the upper third of the advanced typing class is to be recommended for advanced secretarial courses. The grading for the beginning class might appropriately be criterion-based, but grading for an advanced class might better be norm-referenced. Sometimes both kinds of information are needed. A report card for a junior high student in his eighth year of schooling might indicate how he is meeting certain criteria, such as an A grade for addition of fractions. Another entry might show that this mastery is expected at sixth-grade level. Both criterion and norm-referenced data may be communicated to the parent and students. Appropriate procedures should be used: a criterion-referenced approach to show whether or not the student can accomplish the task, and a norm-referenced approach to show how well he performs compared to others. Sometimes, one or the other is needed; other times, both are required.

Assigning Marks to Tests

When a test has been given and checked, it can be used as an instructional tool. Students can see their errors and correct them. However, more than a raw score or number correct is needed for meaningful interpretation. In a criterion-based test, if the acceptable level of performance is achieved, the student moves to the next task. If the acceptable level is not met, the student is recycled to study the material again. The norm-referenced test needs further study. A frequency distribution is made by listing the scores from high to low and by showing the number of students with each score, as shown in Table 9-1.

This organization of information enables the teacher to make some descriptive statements about the entire class and to compare individuals within the group. The teacher may choose to assign grades by inspection. Natural breaks in scores are noted and used in determining letter grades.

Standard scores can be used for grading also. One of these, stanines, can be estimated simply. The middle score is the starting point and can be established by dividing the number of pupils by 2 and counting from either the top or bottom of the distribution. This score of the middle individual is called the median. In Table 9-1 there are 25 students. So the thirteenth score is the median—that is, 20. This point can then be used to estimate stanines, a standard nine-point scale frequently used today. Table 9-2 shows the percentage of scores in each stanine subgroup.

Table 9-1 Distribution of Scores on English Test

Score	Frequency
25	1
24	3
22	4
20	5
19	2
18	3
15	1
14	2
13	2
10	1
9	1
	N = 25

Table 9-2 Approximation of Scores in Each Stanine

	Lowest	Lower	Low	Low Average	Average	High Average	High	Higher	Highest
Stanine	1	2	3	4	5	6	7	8	9
Percentage of Scores	4	7	12	17	20	17	12	7	4

Table 9-3 Allocation of Grades to Stanine Subgroups.

Distribution Score Frequency	Progress Grade	Explanation
25 — 1 - - Stanine 8	A	20% of 25 = 5, 5 scores should be in Stanine 5.
	B or	
24 — 3 - - Stanine 7	B	Score 20, the median, has a frequency of 5.
22 — 4 - - Stanine 6		17% of 25 = 4.25, 4 scores should be in Stanines 4 and 6.
20 5 Stanine 5	C	Score 22 has a frequency of 4 but we must combine 18 and 19 for a frequency of 5.
19 — 2		
18 — 3 - - Stanine 4		12% of 25 = 3, 3 scores should be in Stanines 3 and 7.
15 — 1		Score 24 is no problem, but scores 14 and 15 must be combined.
14 — 2 - - Stanine 3		
	D	7% of 25 = 1.75, 2 scores should be in Stanines 2 and 8.
13 — 2 - - Stanine 2		Only 1 score remains for Stanine 8.
10 — 1		4% of 25 = 1, 1 score should be in Stanines 1 and 9.
9 — 1 - - Stanine 1	F	Since 2 low scores remain, they would fall in Stanine 1.

Table 9-4 A Stanine Exercise

RAW SCORE	FREQUENCY	STANINE*	MEDIAN =
35	1		Stanine 5 = __% of 32 =
34	1		
32	2		Stanines 4 and 6 = __% of 32 =
31	3		
30	5		Stanines 3 and 7 = __% of 32 =
28	1		
27	1		Stanines 2 and 8 = __% of 32 =
26	4		
25	3		Stanines 1 and 9 = __% of 32 =
24	3		
21	2		
20	2		
19	1		
18	2		
10	1		
N = 32			

* Indicate stanines with numbers and brackets in the column provided.

To use this approximation to establish stanines for the scores recorded in Table 9-1, apply the following procedure: Use the middle score as the starting point (in this distribution the middle score is 20). Then find the number of scores to be allocated to each of the stanines according to the per cents noted in Table 9-3. (Remember that all of the same scores must be in the same stanine.) Finally, if you wish, allocate letter grades to the stanine subgroups, as in Table 9-3.

This standard score is relatively easy to establish with the table of approximate percentages and can be used to equalize the value of different tests. When raw scores are used, a test with 100 items is weighted more heavily than one of thirty items. Also, the difficulty or variability of the test is not considered in raw scores. Standard scores take both of these factors (difficulty and variability) into account. The single-digit stanine is adaptable to a point system for grading as well as to letter grading. The teacher can easily justify C grades for stanines 4, 5, and 6 and match the other stanines to letter grades. The stanine, for norm-referenced tests, assumes normal distribution.

Observation Techniques

The learner progresses most efficiently when he knows what his goals are, how he is progressing toward those goals, and what behavior changes are needed for their achievement. Continuous evaluation, then, is needed for this process to occur. Tests, if well constructed and appropriately used, provide some of the measurement data. But student performance, in addition to paper and pencil testing, is another source of information about student learning. For example, skill in shooting fouls can be appraised only by an actual demonstration on the gym floor. Threading the sewing machine, preparing a lunch, and making a speech are other competencies which can only be appraised by student activities in real or simulated situations. Sometimes the final result or product is the focal point; at other times the procedure is important. The preparation of the soup, the sandwich, and the dessert for a lunch may each be appraised. But, at some point, there must be co-ordination of the procedures so that the hot soup and sandwich are ready to serve together, and the dessert is available at the appropriate time. The evaluation of products and procedures is an integral part of the teaching-learning situation. Means for such evaluation must be planned and utilized to help the student learn.

Observation techniques are used in evaluating procedures and products. Problems arise in determining the major factors in the appraisal, the distinction of quality levels and establishing, quantifying, or marking steps. When students are presenting speeches to enlist support for some specific cause, should the basis for evaluation be the logic of the appeal, the speaker's poise and posture, the number of listeners who changed their point of view, the organization of the speech, or all of these? What is to be evaluated depends on the situation and corresponds to the objectives involved. These criteria for evaluation should be established by the teacher, students, or both before the students plan their speeches.

Various methods of summarizing observations include rating scales, check lists, and anecdotal records. If, for instance, an oral report is prepared for social studies, the following items might be included in the rating scale:

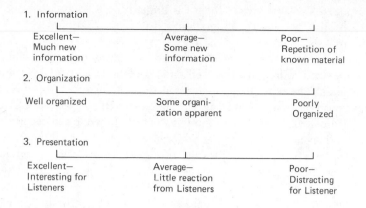

1. Information

Excellent—	Average—	Poor—
Much new	Some new	Repetition of
information	information	known material

2. Organization

Well organized	Some organi-	Poorly
	zation apparent	Organized

3. Presentation

Excellent—	Average—	Poor—
Interesting for	Little reaction	Distracting
Listeners	from Listeners	for Listener

The rating scale might be prepared either by students, as they select the major criteria for good reports, or by the teacher. Preparing such an evaluation instrument can be a learning situation in which students analyze behavior and specify desirable aspects of the behavior. The scale might be used by the teacher, by the student presenting the report, or by the class.

Self-evaluation skills should be developed by students. Using the rating scale and comparing results with the teacher rating or with the class rating (average) could be a step in developing skills of self-analysis for the student. He also might do a self-evaluation after his presentation to the group, and compare it with one done later after hearing an audio-tape of his talk. For instructional purposes, the rating provides feedback to the student to help him improve his performance. The evaluation may also be used by the teacher as input for the grading of the student.

The check list is another method for use in observing student behavior. The sequence of activities may be important, but characteristics of student behavior and skills needing further development may also be listed. If the students are working in small groups, such items as the following might be included:

Behavior	Yes	No	Uncertain
1. Begins work promptly			
2. Explains his point of view			
3. Listens to others			
4. Is a leader sometimes			
5. Is a follower sometimes			
6. Keeps group working on the task			
7. Is pleasant to others in the group			
8. Makes worthwhile contributions			

The check list not only is a useful device for the teacher in observing behavior, but also reminds students about their own activities.

Anecdotal records are simply brief, written statements of what has been observed. The anecdotal record should provide objective evidence about the procedure or product. Each anecdotal record is limited to recording a single situation. It can be useful to a teacher in understanding an individual student and planning for his learning.

When an anecdotal record is used, the teacher indicates that the characteristics of the procedure or product are not well enough defined to organize into a check list or rating scale. The teacher who uses anecdotal records for evaluation is compiling information instead of relying on memory. By regularly collecting and recording this information, he is guarding against the tendency to recall only recent data and critical incidents that might otherwise make his evaluation unfair and biased. Sometimes, anecdotal records may not present data on all students. Unless the teacher consciously plans to write for different students and include all of them, the anecdotes will usually deal with the excellent or poor students.

A log differs from an anecdotal record in that a log is a daily record. Using a log lends itself to ensuring that one is getting observations of all students. The log also might tend to show development patterns since it is an ongoing record.

Teachers need to experiment with different ways of collecting information about student learning. When a variety of procedures is used, the teacher and students will be able to develop devices appropriate to specific situations.

Anecdotal records and logs are useful for evaluations of an informal nature. Tests, reports, projects, and products are formally evaluated. Questions asked during or outside of class, explanations to peers, listening, and unassigned contributions to the class (bringing a new book to class or a clipping for the bulletin board) are activities which are informally evaluated. These behaviors can be interpreted as approach (favorable) responses in the affective domain.

Learning in the affective domain is particularly difficult to measure. Whenever a teacher communicates an attempt to evaluate such behavior, students can easily fake the responses. The teacher, however, must be aware of what influence his teaching has on the attitudes of students. Unless students retain or improve their attitudes toward the subject and toward school, the teacher is failing to do an effective job. Some of the student responses that should cause a teacher to examine his objectives and learning activities include pain, fear, anxiety, frustration, embarrassment, boredom, and discomfort.[1] The teacher does not try to develop a system of grading these informal areas. Nevertheless, the teacher should evaluate the influence of his teaching in this area of feelings. Unsigned questionnaires provide considerable useful information. Course-related student behaviors that are indicators include the incidence of dropping class, absence, tardiness, submitting unrequired papers and projects, evidence of careful work on assignments, and volunteering for special activities.[2]

The interest in value education today forces each teacher to evaluate the affective behavior of the students with whom he works. Ingenuity is needed in developing and using various techniques for collecting data about student reactions. Observations can provide a considerable amount of this information. When adverse reactions of students appear to result from his teaching, careful analysis of the total teaching-learning environment is necessary.

---

[1] Robert F. Mager, *Developing Attitude Toward Learning* (Palo Alto, Calif.: Fearon Publishers, Inc., 1968), pp. 49–57.
[2] Ibid., pp. 79–81.

Grading Themes

English teachers perhaps more frequently than any other group are concerned with the evaluating of student writing. Social studies, health, science, and even mathematics assignments also involve the writing of reports or essays. Probably all teachers at some time evaluate written compositions of students. Many factors are involved in such evaluation and should be specified in accordance with the objectives.

These factors fall into two general categories, content and mechanics. Content encompasses ideas, organization, style, wording, and similar areas. Mechanics deal with grammar, punctuation, spelling, and neatness. Since to some students the two areas seem totally unrelated, teachers may choose to give an evaluation for each category. The symbol A/C on a theme graded by one English teacher indicates the paper to be excellent as far as ideas and style are concerned, but mediocre mechanically; the grade preceding the slash represents content, and the grade following the slash represents mechanics. Some teachers give specific value of mechanical errors to encourage the student to proofread carefully. In an English class, frequent mistakes might be classified, and penalties established. An example of such a system follows:

Major errors—run-on or fragmentary sentence; muddled sentence.
  (One such error reduces mechanics grade a letter.)
Serious error—nonagreement of subject and verb; nonagreement of pronoun with antecedent; lack of antecedent; incorrect word.
  (Three of these reduce grade a letter.)
Minor errors—misspelling, errors in capitalization, punctuation mistakes.
  (Five of these reduce grade a letter.)

These classifications change as students develop more skill in mechanics. The classifications or penalty may change each semester or each grading period.

When objectives are improved proofreading and sensitivity to mechanical errors, the teacher may use the themes in proofreading activities before final evaluation of the themes. For example, a group of students may exchange themes and read them to catch any spelling errors, then exchange again and read for capitalization and punctuation accuracy. These activities not only provide student opportunities for learning, but assist the teacher in correcting errors.

Since grading content and style is much more subjective than checking mechanical errors, the teacher should frequently provide models of well-organized and interesting writing. The selection of student writing for use as models is useful to the teacher and is a reward system for students. Student judgment of style and content can be cultivated through use of models and through peer grading of themes (without names, of course). If students read several themes and rank them as to content, important aspects of writing style can be emphasized and illustrated. Teachers of all content areas can use these same approaches to improve student writing: models, discussion, peer sharing, and evaluating of written work.

Teachers may not evaluate all student themes with the same emphasis. On some occasions, a paragraph may be written for a specific purpose—perhaps to explain how to do a task. Mechanics may not be graded at all. The teacher should indicate to the class what objectives are involved in the student writing and in the evaluation. Teacher time, student interest, and needs are several factors to be considered. Grading themes is time consuming. A teacher must determine whether the time required in such effort pays off in student progress. Unless the student gets feedback on his writing within a reasonable time and learns from the teacher evaluation, for instance, the teacher may have spent his time inefficiently. Sometimes, it is wise to set up a system for correcting themes. One system that seems to be advantageous is to ask students to write on alternate lines and then to insert corrections on the blank lines. This arrangement facilitates checking; when a student is required to rewrite the entire theme, the teacher must reread the entire theme, and often finds new errors in the process. Giving a second grade for the correction of mechanical errors may be desirable.

Occasionally, it may be useful to evaluate themes as you circulate around the classroom while the students are writing. By reading as students are producing the composition, the teacher may be able to offer suggestions and correct some errors on the spot. Such a strategy provides variety and utilizes teacher time for individual problems. Help in organizing themes while writing may result in important learning for the student.

Evaluation of Individualized Instruction

Individualized instruction requires individual evaluation and grading. Teachers have found no one way to deal effectively with the variety of starting levels, speed of learning, motivation, distractions, projects, and activities. In a continuous progress curriculum, when diagnostic tests are given and assignments are developed to provide the learning experiences the student needs to progress in the subject area, he may be doing lessons that are different from those of all other students in the group. How should his progress be evaluated?

Sometimes the student and teacher can together establish goals for the individual. These goals may be the basis for a progress grade. The report might also include the norm level of this work. Marvin may be working in general mathematics on basic multiplication facts. Since he is accomplishing the objectives for his learning tasks, his progress is good. However, the task is one that an average fourth-grader masters. Marvin's evaluation should probably include both his learning and the level of the task. The evaluation of a student who works quite slowly should show his growth and give some indication of his work pattern. Can such information be most satisfactorily communicated to students, parents, other schools, and employers by letter grades, written comments, or some other system? This is another unanswered question in grading. The school provides a procedure which the teacher must utilize as best he can to fit his situation.

Contracts are another individualized approach that teachers evaluate. Contracts may be set up for the class with basic requirements for a passing grade, and options for higher grades. A six-week contract in U.S. history might include such options as the following:

D
  Read text assignments.
  Attend class.
  Get at least 50 per cent on three tests given.

C {
In addition to the previous requirements, participate in class discussion. Report to class on one current event related to each of three content sections.

B {
In addition to the previous requirements, read a book from the list provided, and participate in a panel discussion to share ideas from the book with the class.

A {
In addition to the previous requirements, plan and carry out an individual project, such as study of a community agency or investigation of a specific problem. This project must be approved by the teacher.

Each student makes his selection and writes his contract. The teacher must be aware of quality in this arrangement. Each contract should include time limits and criteria for satisfactory work. The choice by students, as well as timing and quality level provide for individual differences.

Other uses of contracts may involve more student planning. Groups of students may prepare learning packages that include objectives, resources, activities, and tests. Then, individual contracts may be written regarding the use of these learning packages, their evaluation, or the production of additional packages. Some teachers prefer to use contracts for independent study. The student then will be planning his own objectives, activities, resources, and evaluation. Teacher assistance is important in the contracts that are more student-centered. Guidance in setting reasonable objectives and in selecting appropriate activities helps the student recognize his own strengths and limitations. Students also recognize some of the opportunities and limitations of their environment. Providing for specific evaluation in the contract is important because when the bases for grading are established, misunderstandings are less likely to arise. Usually both self-evaluation and teacher-evaluation should be included in the grading plan for contracts.

Self-Evaluation

Self-evaluation is an important goal of the secondary school as well as one aspect of the evaluation process. An effective person, according to perceptual psychologists, must have a positive self-concept. He must think well of himself, recognizing his capabilities and accepting his limitations. To achieve such self-understanding requires not only having experienced success, but guidance in self-analysis. To meet these needs, the teacher should provide opportunities for each student to seriously consider what he has learned, how much he has progressed, and what learning style he has developed. One procedure is the use of rating scales or check lists. These instruments emphasize the criteria for evaluation. They give the student a means of expressing his feelings to the teacher, and give the teacher another input of data to use in evaluation. A follow-up conference, in which teacher- and self-ratings are compared and explained, can be mutually beneficial. Probably a joint evaluation should be the final result of such a conference.

Any of the devices developed for evaluating student products and procedures can be utilized for self-evaluation. In addition one can construct specific instruments to encourage self-evaluation. The student may compare responses he made early in the school year with those he made near the end of the school year. Such comparison may provide the student with information that he has not recognized about his own growth. Items similar to the following may be used:

I. Check appropriate responses. If other terms should be added, write them in the blanks.
1. My assignments are turned in
    a. promptly.
    b. late.
    c. on time.
    d. occasionally.
    e. never.
    f. _____.
2. My classmates in general consider me
    a. a friend.
    b. a nobody.
    c. a person to ridicule.
    d. an enemy.
    e. _____.
3. I consider myself to be
    a. intelligent.
    b. one who has difficulty learning.
    c. average in intelligence.
    d. the smartest in the class.
    e. the slowest student in the class.
    f. _____.
4. My work in school represents
    a. the best I can do.
    b. enough to get by.
    c. my preferences; I do what I enjoy.
    d. as little effort as possible.
    e. whatever will keep the teacher satisfied.
    f. whatever keeps my parents satisfied.
    g. _____.

Open-ended questions may also provide information to students and teachers. Examples: What have you learned in class this week that you can use outside of school? What have you learned about yourself during this unit?

Some students prefer to let the teacher do the evaluating. The teacher, however, has a responsibility to encourage self-evaluation. Only when an individual recognizes his strengths can he utilize his potential. As a human being, he has limitations which must be considered realistically as he sets his own personal goals. The teacher contributes to the development of adolescents when he accepts a student as an individual whose unique capabilities must be encouraged. With this acceptance and with successful experiences, the student has a basis for developing and maintaining self-respect and a feeling of worth. Such a positive self-concept is not only an educational goal in itself, but is a prerequisite for maximum learning. Self-evaluation is an essential of the secondary school program and should be implemented by each teacher.

Grading and Reporting

The first step in grading for report cards is to formulate an evaluation plan. This plan should spell out exactly what will be evaluated and what the relative importance of each factor will be. It should be established prior to the teaching so that both the teacher and the students understand the importance of the various activities. A teacher may, for example, in considering plans for six weeks in biology, decide that important activities are (1) class participation; (2) homework assignments; (3) tests (three in number); (4) laboratory performance; and (5) special projects. The importance of these may be established by points, weights, or percentages. The teacher may arbitrarily select a number of points or the appropriate weights as in the following example:

	Points	Weight	Percentage
1. Class participation	150	3	30
2. Homework assignments	50	1	10
3. Tests	150	3	30
4. Laboratory performance	100	2	20
5. Special projects	50	1	10
	500		100

This decision indicates that tests and class participation will receive equal emphasis; laboratory work is one fifth of the grade; homework and special projects together are considered as important as laboratory work.

Then the teacher must plan the appraisal in each area. Evaluation of class participation cannot be done fairly at the end of six weeks without periodic information. The teacher should sample the class participation throughout the grading period. For example, the discussion on Tuesday of the first week might be evaluated in classes A and B, on Wednesday in classes C and D, and on Thursday in classes E and F. The schedule could be rotated so that the appraisal of discussion would provide a good sample of student behavior. Students who were absent or did not contribute might be deliberately involved in the next evaluation. The teacher should use a system of evaluation that considers the quality as well as the frequency of participation. Marking should be done as soon after class as possible so that the situation is recalled.

Teachers evaluate homework in different ways. Some simply check to see whether the assignment was done. Others spot check assigned work. Perhaps question 2 is used as the basis for grading one assignment, and then questions 1 and 6 may be used next time. Sometimes teachers have students check their own work. Since the purpose of discussing assigned work in class is to increase learning, the correcting of papers before they are turned in may have merit. Procedures probably should be varied. However, one should always keep in mind the fact that homework may be the effort of a student, a group of students, a parent, or some other person. Some teachers encourage cooperative study and prefer short, frequent quizzes for the appraisal of daily work.

Evaluating, laboratory performance, and special projects would involve such evaluation instruments and procedures as ratings, check lists, or logs. Points from these evaluations would necessarily be totaled for each student. Then a frequency distribution could be made and grades assigned by inspection, or by some other procedure, such as using stanines. The teacher should consider the time involved in the procedures and attempt to simplify his work.

Let us consider an example from a biology class. The teacher has elected to use a five-point scale. He finds that one of his students, Sue Myers, has the following weighted evaluations:

		Evaluation		Weight		
1.	Class participation	5	×	3	=	15
2.	Homework	4	×	1	=	4
3.	Tests	3	×	3	=	9
4.	Laboratory performance	5	×	2	=	10
5.	Special projects	2	×	1	=	2
			Total		=	40

The frequency distribution for the class follows:

Total Frequency Scores	The median is 34
47–1	
45–2	
42–3	
41–1	
40–5	
36–3	
35–1	
34–4	
29–2	
27–2	
25–3	
18–1	
17–1	
15–2	
13–2	
N = 33	

The teacher now applies the grading system of his school to this distribution. There is no accepted way to decide how grades should be allocated. Considering the total situation, the teacher makes the choices that seem most reasonable. The process of grading is a time-consuming, subjective endeavor.

Indicate how you would assign grades A, B, C, D, and F to the given distribution in the example just cited. Then compare with some ideas of experienced teachers (mentioned at the end of this module).

Grading Systems

What are the possible ways of grading? The most familiar are the five-point letter scale and the percentage systems. Other systems include the written evaluation plan, the pass-fail system, or a combination of other systems.

At present, the most popular grading system is the use of letter grades in a five-point scale: A, B, C, D, F or U. Some schools use numbers 1, 2, 3, 4, and 5 rather than letters. Often descriptive phrases are used to explain the letter marks, such as A = outstanding achievement or D = minimum achievement. Sometimes letter grades are combined with the percentage system. Then, percentage cutoffs are used for the letter grades, as A 95–100 or D 70–76. In some schools, the five-point scale is modified adding plus (+) or minus (−) to the letters to indicate the upper area or lower area of the letter grade's range. This modification, in effect, changes the five-point scale to a thirteen-point scale.

Percentage grading systems, which were formerly popular, are used less frequently today. The trend has seemed to be toward a marking system that provides broad areas to indicate general information about individual achievement in comparison to the pattern of the group. However, more schools seem to be trying to develop grading procedures that show the progress of individual students.

An alternative calls for written evaluations instead of letter or numerical grades. As utilized by the Parkway Program in Philadelphia, this plan makes it possible to report the achievement of the student, his strengths and areas needing improvement, social skills, and study habits. Such evaluation is more meaningful to parents and students. It also requires careful consideration by the teacher of the individual as a person. However, writing such reports is time consuming for the teachers, so it may become a vague statement with trite phrases, especially if the teacher tries to write many of these reports at one sitting.

Some schools are using pass-fail grading; they report only if the pupil's work is passing or failing, satisfactory or unsatisfactory. The rationale to support such a system is that it creates a better learning atmosphere. Fewer anxieties and less competition reduce cheating and yet students work to meet the objectives. Disadvantages include the lack of stimulation for certain students, the possibility that the evaluation will be neglected, and the fact that excellence goes unrecognized or unrewarded. Because of these disadvantages, some school systems have introduced a three-category system: Honors/Pass/Fail. In an attempt to gain the advantages of both systems, some school systems use both grading systems. In such a plan, for instance, the required courses might be graded with the usual letter grades, but the student might have an option to request pass-fail grading for an elective course.

In addition to subject grades, report cards often include information regarding attitude and habits. A conduct grade to represent social and personal behavior in the school environment has generally been discontinued. Each teacher evaluates the student in regard to his personal and social traits. Frequently, these are reported with coded numbers. The numbers may represent specific behaviors such as (1) study habits are good; (2) assignments are incomplete or unsatisfactory; or (3) improvement in work is evident.

Another way of including evaluation in social and study skills is a five-point scale, ranging from 1—Student initiates opportunities to learn, and displays excellent study habits, to 5—Student is apathetic, uncooperative, and disturbs others. When separate symbols are used to separate achievement from other student behaviors, communication between the teacher, the student, and home is facilitated.

Whatever grading system is used, certain essential elements that should be included in the evaluation process are the following:

1. Learning objectives should be clearly understood in advance, with criteria for measurement and levels of performance.
2. The teacher should communicate meaningfully, either in written or oral form to the student, in discussing with the student his strengths, weaknesses, and suggestions for improvement with respect to the objectives of the course.
3. The student should be involved in self-evaluation of strengths and weaknesses, and should plan improvement in meeting the course objectives as well as his own learning goals.

4. Time is needed for the teacher and student to share perceptions and engage in a discussion of each other's evaluation.[3]

School report systems usually include periodic grading (six or nine weeks), semester grades, and averages for the year. These stipulated marking times necessitate that the planning and use of evaluation procedures be continuous. Interim reports to parents should be used whenever a student seems to change his general behavior. Improved performance, as well as less favorable trends, should be reported to the student and to the home. The school can encourage students greatly by commendations for progress. In some communities, contacts between the home and school always involve problems. Positive reinforcement can help students and also amicable school-community relations.

General Suggestions

Since evaluation is an integral factor in the teaching-learning process, you must do the following:

1. Provide a variety of instruments to appraise the behavior of students and to focus on the development of the individual.
2. Use appraisal procedures continuously so as to contribute to the positive development of the individual student. Such an emphasis requires that the evaluation be important to the student and related to what he considers important. Effective evaluation is helping the student know his competencies and achievement. It encourages further learning and the selection of appropriate tasks.
3. Adapt the marking system of the school to your situation.
4. Avoid using grades as a threat or overstressing them for motivational purposes.
5. Consider your grading procedures carefully, preplan them carefully, and explain your policies to the students.
6. Involve the students, whenever feasible, in setting up criteria and establishing the relative importance of activities. Such cooperative planning is a learning experience for students and encourages self-evaluation.
7. Incorporate continuous evaluation in your learning activities to be sure that students are aware of their progress.
8. Strive for objective and impartial appraisal as you put your evaluation plan into operation.
9. Try to minimize arguments about grades, cheating, and teacher subjectivity by involving students in the planning, reinforcing individual student development, and providing an accepting, stimulating learning environment.

Activity Answer Sheet

Answers for stanine exercise:
    Median = 26
    Stanine 5 = 20% of 32 = 6.4 or 6

[3] Glenys G. Unruh and William M. Alexander, *Innovations in Secondary Education,* 2nd ed. (New York: Holt, Rinehart & Winston, Inc., 1974), p. 49.

Stanines 4 and 6 = 17% of 32 = 5.44 or 5
Stanines 3 and 7 = 12% of 32 = 3.84 or 4
Stanines 2 and 8 = 7% of 32 = 2.24 or 2
Stanines 1 and 9 = 4% of 32 = 1.28 or 1

Because approximations must be made and one score must be in a single stanine, the following are possible. Always start with stanine 5.

	Possible Scores	*Possible Scores*
Stanine 1	10	10
Stanine 2	18–19	18
Stanine 3	21–22	19, 20, 23
Stanine 4	24–25	21, 24
Stanine 5	26	25, 26, 27
Stanine 6	27–30	28, 30
Stanine 7	31	31
Stanine 8	32	32
Stanine 9	34–35	34, 35

Possible grades for the biology class:

Scores Frequency

```
47–1 ⎫
     ⎬ A
45–2 ⎭
42–3 ⎫
41–1 ⎬ B
40–5 ⎭
36–3 ⎫
35–1 ⎪
34–4 ⎬ C
29–2 ⎪
27–2 ⎪
25–3 ⎭
18–1 ⎫
17–1 ⎬ D
15–2 ⎭
13–2   F
─────
N = 33
```

If biology is a course for select students,
40–47 = A
25–36 = B
13–18 = C

If stanines are estimated,
45–47 = A
41–42 = B
25–40 = C
15–18 = D
13 = F

SUGGESTED READING

Ahmann, J. Stanley and Marvin D. Glock. "Determining and Reporting Growth," *Evaluating Pupil Growth,* 4th ed. Boston: Allyn & Bacon, Inc., 1971.

Brown, Donald J. "Assigning Grades: The Paradoxes, the Inequities and the Plain Tomfooleries," *Appraisal Procedures in the Secondary Schools.* Englewood Cliffs, N.J.: Prentice-Hall, Inc., 1970.

Kirschenbaum, Howard, Sidney B. Simon, and Rodney W. Napier. *Wad-Ja-Get? The Grading Game in American Education,* New York: Hart Publishing Company, Inc., 1971.

Mager, Robert F. *Developing Attitude Toward Learning*. Palo Alto, Calif.: Fearon Publishers, 1968.

Newman, Isadore, Bill J. Frye, and Carole Newman. *An Introduction to Basic Concepts of Measurement and Evaluation*. Akron, Ohio: College of Education, The University of Akron, 1973.

Oliva, Peter F. *The Secondary School Today*, 2nd ed. Scranton, Pa.: Intext, Inc., 1972.

Renner, John W., Robert F. Bibens, and Gene D. Shepherd. "Using Evaluation," *Guiding Learning in the Secondary School*. New York: Harper and Row, Publishers, 1972.

Schoer, Lowell A. "Assigning Marks," *Test Construction: A Programmed Guide*. Boston: Allyn & Bacon, Inc., 1970.

Unruh, Glenys G. and William M. Alexander. *Innovations in Secondary Education* 2nd ed. New York: Holt, Rinehart & Winston, Inc., 1974.

Wilhelms, Fred J., Ed. *Evaluation as Feedback and Guide*. Washington, D.C.: Association for Supervision and Curriculum Development, NEA, 1967.

POST TEST

Select the best answer to complete the statement and put the correct letter in the blank at the left.

_____ **1.** In setting up a frequency distribution the teacher begins by
   a. listing all scores.
   b. arranging scores from low to high.
   c. finding the middle score.
   d. tabulating scores.

_____ **2.** Use of the normal curve in grading implies that the teacher
   a. has an average class.
   b. will know how many A, B, C, D, and F grades to give.
   c. will make judgments about assigning grades.
   d. is using a fair and impartial system.

_____ **3.** If a teacher wants three tests to have equal weight,
   a. the raw scores must be changed to standard scores.
   b. the raw scores are simply added for a total score.
   c. each test score is assigned a letter grade which is translated to points and the points are totaled.
   d. each test score should be expressed as percentage correct and the three should be added.

_____ **4.** An advanced class received the following scores on a science test: 29, 16, 20, 23, 28, 25, 11, 15, 26, 17, 20, 23, 27, 25, 23, and 19. What is the median?
   a. 26
   b. 15
   c. 23
   d. 21

_____ **5.** An effective grading system is *least* likely to
  a. be limited to academic achievement.
  b. include evaluation of a variety of student behaviors.
  c. be able to provide criterion and norm-referenced grades.
  d. provide information about the achievement of objectives.

_____ **6.** Student products and processes are evaluated by
  a. one of the following devices: a rating scale, check list, anecdotal record, log.
  b. teacher, student, and peers.
  c. the criterion established in the behavioral objective.
  d. the procedure and individuals appropriate to the intent of the objective.

_____ **7.** Homework is an important phase of learning activities in many classes and consequently should be
  a. carefully graded by the teacher.
  b. utilized for learning.
  c. occasionally collected and spot checked.
  d. considered as a major.

_____ **8.** When contracts are used in a class, the major purpose of evaluation is to
  a. grade the students.
  b. consider whether the student accomplished the amount of work he selected.
  c. determine the quality of student achievement.
  d. increase self-analysis and development through individual goals and criteria.

_____ **9.** Class participation can be graded easily and fairly
  a. at the end of the grading period.
  b. by a plan of daily grading.
  c. by a planned schedule of grading each class.
  d. by keeping anecdotal records.

_____**10.** Students learn best when they are
  a. reminded of their shortcomings so that they are more realistic in setting goals.
  b. accepted as worthy individuals and are encouraged to undertake challenging tasks.
  c. homogeneously grouped and are encouraged to work together on similar tasks.
  d. heterogeneously grouped and are encouraged to work together on similar tasks.

11–15. *A group from the Student Council of Walton High School studied grading systems. Its report to the Advisory Committee included a statement of purpose for grading. Read the following statements and check those which provide valid reasons for grades.*

_____**11.** Teachers can control student behavior with grades.

_____**12.** Colleges and employers can get information about students.

_____**13.** Grades give a student information about his progress.

_____**14.** Grades replace learning as a motivation for students.

_____**15.** Grades encourage continuous evaluation of student learning.

16–19. *Miss Taylor decided to use a weight system for six week grades. The four items selected were class participation; tests; group project; and assignments. She decided that the most important phase of the learning activities was class participation which should be half of the grade. The group project and tests were of equal value, but the assignments were half as important as the tests. Set up a system of weights for Miss Taylor to use. Put the appropriate number at the left.*

_____**16.** Class participation.

_____**17.** Tests.

_____**18.** Group Projects.

_____**19.** Assignments.

20–25. *Indicate in the blank provided which of the following situations require*
        a. *criterion-referenced grades.*
        b. *norm-referenced grades.*
        c. *both kinds of evaluation.*
        d. *neither type of evaluation.*

_____**20.** To select students for continuing the study of French from French II classes.

_____**21.** To find students to do special projects in their special interests for biology.

_____**22.** To assign a transfer student to the appropriate English class in a three-track English program (slow, average, advanced).

_____**23.** To choose students for competition in the state science tests.

_____**24.** To select an appropriate learning package for individualized instruction in geometry.

_____**25.** To decide whether a student should go to the next level of instruction in a continuous progress general science curriculum.

Teaching Tools

Leonard H. Clark

Jersey City State College

module 10

Audio-visual Aids / Projection and Projectors / Moving Pictures As a Teaching Tool / Television / Tape Recorders and Record Players / Multimedia

RATIONALE

Once upon a time, when mankind was young and reading and writing had not yet been invented, men and women taught their children by means of very simple tools. Telling children what they should know must have been an important teaching technique in early times. But there were other teaching and learning methods, too. Boys learned to hunt by practicing with spears, by throwing sticks, and by simulated hunts of simulated animals. Parents taught geography by maps drawn in the sand. Religion was taught by pictures drawn on the walls of caves. History, customs, and lore of a group were portrayed by dance and drama. From the very earliest times, teachers have depended on teaching tools to make their teaching effective and interesting.

Today, teachers still depend on teaching tools to make their teaching effective and interesting. In some respects, our modern teaching tools are more sophisticated than those of old. Yet, we use our new tools for the same purposes and in much the same ways that our forefathers did: to make things clear, to make instruction real, to spice up the teaching-learning process, and to make it possible for pupils to teach themselves. It is impossible to teach without some tools.

This module will try to show you how to use effectively the type of teaching tool called audio-visual aids. The aim will not be to teach you how to run the machines and gadgets that make up modern pedagogical technology, but to develop a philosophy for using them and to develop strategies for incorporating these gadgets and other technologies into your teaching. *Technology* is a word with wide meaning. So is the word *medium*. Technology includes machines and techniques. A technique for individualizing instruction is as much a part of educational technology as a teaching machine. Medium refers to any intermediate agency, means, instrument, or channel. A lecture, a movie, a television show, a newspaper, and a picture all are media by which persons can transmit ideas to other people. We should be careful not to confuse technology with gadgetry and medium with the mass media. Each word has wider meaning. Further, we should be careful to remember that *medium* is singular and *media* plural. There is no such thing as *a media,* only a *medium.*

SPECIFIC OBJECTIVES

The principal purpose of this module is to acquaint you with the technological devices and materials that teachers speak of as audio-visual aids. It is hoped that by the end of your study of the unit you will have command of a general strategy for the use of audio-visual aids, and will know, in general, something about the various types of audio-visual aids available to you, and how to use them.

Specifically you will be expected to be able to do the following:

1. Describe the basic procedures for preparation, guiding instruction, and follow-up as they apply to the use of audio-visual materials.

2. Explain a half dozen ways in which opaque projection, overhead projection, moving picture projection, and slide projection each can be used to enhance instruction.
3. Explain at least three methods for making overhead transparencies.
4. Describe how to prepare and use overhead transparency flip-ons or overlays.
5. Describe how to use masks for overhead transparencies.
6. Describe how to prepare a slide program step by step.
7. Describe step by step the general procedures one should follow when showing instructional films.
8. Describe step by step a procedure for using 16-mm. projection for individual or small group instruction.
9. Give arguments for use of silent and sound moving pictures, and show for what each may be used.
10. Name one source of information about free films available for instruction.
11. Name at least three uses that can be made of the commercial cinema for classroom instruction.
12. Describe how to make use of commercial television.
13. Explain step by step how to conduct instructional television classes to include (a) duties of the television teacher; (b) role of the classroom teacher in preparation, guiding learning, and follow-up; and (c) preparing the classroom for television instruction.
14. Describe the role of educational television.
15. Describe how educational television may be used to enhance classroom instruction.
16. Describe how commercial television may be used to enhance classroom instruction.
17. Describe step by step Haney and Ullman's recommended principles for using taped recordings and records.
18. Describe at least three ways to mix audio-visual media.
19. Explain the advantages of mixing instructional media.

You will be required to demonstrate that you can perform the requirements of the objectives in a post test.

MODULE TEXT

Audio-visual Aids

Certain teaching tools fall into the category we commonly call audio-visual aids. In this category, we can include such teaching tools as films, charts, overhead projectors, filmstrips, models, microscopes, pictures, slides, graphs, phonograph records, maps, mock-ups, audio tapes, globes, terrain boards, radio, opaque projectors, chalkboards, television, and flannelboards.

Try to identify each of the teaching tools listed as audio-visual aids. Show in what way each can be used to aid instruction.

These teaching tools are just what their common name suggests: audio-visual aids to teaching. It is important to remember that their role is to aid you in your teaching. They do not do the teaching. Rather, it is you, as teacher, who selects the objectives, orchestrates the teaching plan, evaluates the results, and follows up. If you think of these tools as aids, your teaching will benefit.

Uses of Audio-visual Aids. You can use audio-visual aids in many ways to make your teaching more effective. Use them to make clear the concepts that you wish your pupils to learn. Seeing a picture of an escarpment may give pupils a clearer idea than hearing a thousand words on the topic. Use audio-visual aids to eliminate verbalism. Altogether too much of our schooling consists merely of words which we parrot but do not really understand. We all mouth platitudes, and can reel off definitions for words of which we have only the vaguest comprehension. By portraying things and giving pupils real or simulated experiences, audio-visual devices can give pupils real meanings for their words. Actually seeing the power of the atmosphere crush a vacuumized can makes real the concept of air pressure. Using a model to present the forces that cause a volcano to erupt also makes that concept real.

Audio-visual materials and devices can add interest and variety to your classes. Skillful use of audio-visual material can be a great motivator and can add life and color to the classroom. Furthermore, the use of audio-visual aids tends to reinforce learning. Use them to put your points across. Well-used audio-visual aids add to the impact of the presentation. The cliché that one picture is worth a thousand words is true. The more important truth is that the skillfully used audio-visual aid reinforces the presentation so that you have both the picture and the thousand words working for you.

Sometimes, teachers feel that the use of audio-visual aids sugar-coats learning and so is undesirable. Don't be misled. Remember that your job is to teach so that pupils learn something well enough to remember it. Any device that will help you achieve that end is good. The teaching device that will get the idea across is the one you want to use, even though its use may not appear academically rigorous. The use of audio-visual aids is an essential for making teaching effective.

List the ways in which one can use audio-visual aids to make his teaching more effective.

General Audio-visual Teaching Procedures. Few teachers use audio-visual aids as efficiently and as effectively as they should, partly because the techniques for using them seem to be so easy that they never bother to become really expert in them, partly because of mistaken ideas about instruction and learning, and partly because of inertia. To use audio-visual aids well requires considerable effort. Too many teachers are unwilling to pay this price to become more effective teachers. Many others fail to realize that the techniques they are using are not really effective but that a little more effort and a different approach might raise their level of teaching effectiveness and efficiency. The use of audio-visual materials involves four steps: (1) selecting the proper audio-visual aid; (2) preparing the audio-visual aid; (3) using the audio-visual aid; and (4) following up the audio-visual aid.

SELECTING THE PROPER AID. It would be difficult to think of anything more important in teaching than to select the proper tool. Using the wrong tool not only will not add to your teaching effectiveness, but may actually cause a potentially effective class to become ineffective. To be sure that aids you select are effective, you should consider their suitability, visibility, clearness, level of understanding, ease of presentation, and availability.

Suitability is, of course, the most important consideration in selecting the aid. In making your choice, consider such questions as Will using this aid really help you achieve your objective? Will this film really help you get across the concept at which you are shooting? Will this picture give an accurate understanding of the facts in the case? Will this bring out the points you have in mind or would some other device be more effective? Which would be the better or best of the aids available, for instance, the working model of the machine or the animated film, or would it be possible to use both?

In choosing an audio-visual aid, always remember also that the visual aid the pupils cannot see, the aid that is too complex for them to understand, and the aid that you cannot get when you need it are not very helpful.

To be sure that the aid is effective, if it is at all possible, you ought to look it over and try it out before you use it in class. This advice is particularly important for films, filmstrips, slides, video tapes, and records. Many of these seem to have little resemblance to their catalog descriptions. They may turn out to be a sheer waste of time, so the wise teacher checks them out as well as he can before the class begins.

PREPARING FOR USE OF THE AUDIO-VISUAL AID. To use audio-visual aids well usually requires advance preparation, both psychological preparation, in which you prepare the pupils to get the most out of the audio-visual aid, and physical preparation, in which you prepare the physical conditions for use of the aid. Sometimes, as with the use of the chalkboard, the preparation needed is minimal. All you need do is to identify the aid and tell what you intend to do with it. For much chalkboard work, not even that is necessary. At other times, you will need to prepare extensively and in detail. When introducing films, film strips, recordings, and pictures, usually you ought to spend considerable time setting the scene. In your introduction, you will probably need to make clear the purpose of the activity, suggest points to look for in the presentation, present problems to solve, and, in general, take whatever steps you deem necessary so that pupils will get the most from the use of the aid.

The physical aspects of the preparation for use of your audio-visual may be crucial. In using audio-visual materials and devices, attention to details may make the difference between success and fiasco. If you have no chalk, if there is no extension cord, if the pupils cannot see, if the machine will not run, your audio-visual aid will be less than effective. Consequently, you should check carefully before the class begins. Will everyone be able to see and hear? Are the pictures, slides, or transparencies all present and in order? Is the machine in running order? Is it properly adjusted? It may be wise to try things out under conditions as similar as possible to those you expect in the class when you teach.

GUIDING THE AUDIO-VISUAL ACTIVITY. The purpose of audio-visual teaching tools is not to replace teaching, but to make teaching more effective. Therefore, you cannot expect the teaching tool to do all the work. You have to make it work for you. Perhaps you will have to explain certain points, show the relationships, and point out the concepts being demonstrated. Perhaps you will need to give the pupils a study guide or list of questions. You may think it necessary to repeat the audio-visual presentation, or stop for a full-fledged discussion of the points being raised by the picture, poster, or film.

FOLLOWING UP AUDIO-VISUAL ACTIVITIES. You should follow up all your audio-visual presentations. Check questions may suffice. In the case of films, records, and similar activities, the follow-up should usually be more extensive. The follow-up should make clear to the pupils any points that remain fuzzy and clarify any misunderstandings which the audio-visual presentation may have left. Quizzes, review, practice, and discussion all can be used to tie together loose ends, to point out and drive home the major concepts, skills, and attitudes to be learned, and to emphasize that watching or listening to audio-visual materials is not a purely recreational activity.

Projection and Projectors

Projection machines make it possible to bring into the classroom experiences that otherwise would be impossible. For example, a film of Egypt can show pupils aspects of life in a distant land that they may see in no other way. Or the projection of the image, of an artifact, of a picture, or of a book page on the screen can show all the pupils at once what you want them to see without interrupting the flow of the class by having the pupils pass the object around the room. Among the most common and most useful kinds of projectors are the opaque projector, slide projector, filmstrip projector, overhead projector, and, of course, the motion picture projector. Modern technology has improved these machines so that their operation is almost automatic. No longer need anyone be afraid to operate these projectors.

Operating Projectors. This module is not the place to tell you how to run the various machines used as audio-visual aids. Each has its own idiosyncracies peculiar to its own make and model. However, there are a few general principles that you ought to learn and to remember about projectors. Almost every one of them is simple to operate, so no one should be afraid to attempt to run a projector. The day is gone when it was necessary for teachers to turn their responsibilities for machine operation over to fifth graders. You ought to become familiar with all of the machines you may have to use some day. Practice on the various machines until you have mastered them. It may save your having to figure out a strange machine in a stressful situation.

First read the directions. The more difficult machines usually have the directions printed somewhere on the machine. These directions will show how the machine's operations differ from others of its ilk although the general principles are always more or less the same.

Projectors all have to be focused. Focusing is done by adjusting the distance from the light source to the lens and/or the lens to the screen. In a slide projector or a movie projector, the light source is in back and the lens in front. In an overhead projector, the light source is on the bottom and the lens on top. The light passes from the light source through a slide or transparency (frame) and through the lens to the screen. What you have to do is to move the lens back and forth (or up and down in the case of the overhead) until you get a clear picture. Usually the best technique is to move from a blur through a sharp focus until the image starts to blur again and then turn back to the point of sharpest focus. The image can also be brought into focus by moving the projector toward or away from the screen. This fact is important to remember when you find that you cannot move the lens far enough to focus the image sharply.

The point of all this is that no matter what machine you have to deal with you focus by establishing the proper distance between lens and light source, and lens and screen. So whatever machine you have you look for something by which to adjust the distance.

Now for a little review. If you are faced with a new overhead projector you have never seen before, how would you go about focusing it, once you have found out how to turn it on? If the projector was a filmstrip projector rather than an overhead projector, what difference in focusing would you expect? Appropriate answers to these exercises follow:

1. Look for some method of moving the lens of the overhead projector up and down.

2. For the filmstrip projector, look for some way to move the lens back and forth. Once you have located the method of adjusting the lens, you load a transparency or filmstrip on the machine and adjust the lens. If you cannot move the lens far enough up or down (or back and forth) to get a sharp focus, move the machine or the screen to adjust the distance between lens and screen.

The Opaque Projector. The opaque projector is in some ways more difficult to learn to operate successfully. It usually requires a dark room and may be hard to focus and awkward to use, but once you have the hang of it, you will find it to be one of the most useful of classroom tools. With it you can project on to a screen, a white wall, or even a chalkboard the image of pictures, printed matter, tests, and three-dimensional objects. Use it for the following purposes:

1. Project pictures and other opaque materials that are too small for pupils to see easily from their seats. This practice eliminates the necessity for passing such material around the class. It also allows everyone a chance to see the material at once, and gives you a chance to point out details and clear up questions while everyone can see.

2. Enlarge maps and project them on a suitable surface to trace the boundaries, rivers, and other features represented.

3. Project pupils' work so all pupils can see it as you discuss it. This is an excellent device to show pupils good practice, or to allow pupils to react to each other's work.

4. Project illustrative material in pupil reports. Often, shy pupils do well at reporting when they can use projection as a support.

5. Project work on the chalkboard for evaluation and correction.

6. Project illustrative material for lectures and teacher or pupil talks.

The great advantage of the opaque projector is that it projects the image of the real thing. It is not necessary to prepare a slide or a transparency. All that one needs to do is to place the material to be projected on the bed of the projector, turn the projector on, and focus it. Focusing objects such as the pages of a book which will not lie flat may be something of a problem, but usually with patience you will obtain clear images on a screen.

Let us suppose you have never used an opaque projector before. You have loaded a picture on the tray, turned the projector on, and removed the lens cover. You have an image on the screen, but it is not in focus. How do you focus it? (The answer, of course, is to find some way to move the lens back and forth. Assuming that the axis of the machine is horizontal, you adjust the lens back and forth until the focus is as sharp as can be.)

Overhead Projection. One of the most versatile of teaching tools is the overhead projector. Every classroom should have one just as every classroom should have a chalkboard. It can be used in full daylight. It allows the teacher to point things out or to make notations from the front of the room without turning his back to the class or standing in front of the material he wants the pupils to see. It allows one to prepare material ahead of time and save it for use again and again. With the help of flip-ons, it makes it easy to show development and changes and to compare and contrast. It can be used to record the progress of a discussion. The overhead projector can both make your teaching more effective and reduce the amount of time that you must spend on tiresome chores such as copying material on the chalkboard.

A few ways in which the overhead projector may be used follow.

1. Write on it as on a chalkboard while the class proceeds. When the time comes to move on, just roll up the acetate or take a new blank sheet. In this way, you do not have to erase and so can come back to reconsider, if necessary.
2. Use it to emphasize points by projecting them as they come up in class.
   a. Write points on the transparency as you go along.
   b. Flip on preprinted materials at propitious moments.
   c. Uncover blocked out preprinted material as the points come up. To keep preprinted material out of sight, simply cover it with opaque material until the proper moment.
3. Present pictures, drawings, diagrams, outlines, printed matter, and maps.
4. Project an outline form. Fill it in as you go along.
5. Project an outline. Cover it. As you proceed, uncover the points as they are made.
6. Reproduce or enlarge maps.
7. Project grids for graphing.
8. Project silhouettes.
9. Project tests and quizzes.
10. Correct tests, quizzes, and papers. Project the correct answers by writing on the transparency. Transparencies made on spirit duplicators are excellent for this purpose because one can also make duplicate copies. It is possible for the teacher to go over something projected on the screen or board while the pupils follow along on their own copies.

Preparing Transparencies. Overhead projectors project images in the same way that motion picture projectors and slide projectors do by shining light through a transparent film or glass. They will not project opaque substances except to make silhouettes. Transparencies may be bought ready-made. Many excellent ones are for sale by the various supply houses; however, they are extremely easy to make.

Even though the transparencies you make may not be as finished as the commercially made, you will probably find that your own homemade transparencies are more effective for your purposes than those commercially available. After all, when you make your own, you can tailor them to your own needs, something a stranger cannot do, no matter how expert he may be. You can make satisfactory transparencies for overhead projection by the following methods:

1. By using a Polaroid camera. Polaroid sells a special film for this purpose.
2. By drawing or writing directly on acetate. Usually a frosted acetate, frosted side up, seems to work better for this purpose than smooth, clear acetate. Use India ink, drawing ink, transparent color pencils, felt tipped pens, or grease pencils (china marking pencils) for writing directly on acetate. If you wish to project in color, remember to select an ink or pencil that is translucent. Opaque inks and pencils project only in black, or in silhouette. Grease pencils (china marking pencils) work very well, but the pencils sold by supply houses specifically for making transparencies may be better. If you use felt tipped pens, check to see whether the ink and the acetate are compatible. Sometimes the ink of the felt tipped pens will not stick to the acetate.

   Impromptu transparencies can be made by simply writing or drawing while the transparency is on the machine. One can make up a transparency as the class progresses, for instance, by recording on a transparency the important points made in a discussion. For more finished transparencies, the following procedure is recommended:
   a. Sketch the transparency on a sheet of paper.
   b. Cover the paper with the acetate transparency sheet.
   c. Trace the sketch. Use drawing ink.
   d. Add color if you wish. Use translucent colored inks, felt tipped pens, or transparent color pencils.
   e. Spray with a clear plastic to give permanence.
   f. Mount the transparencies, if you wish.
3. One can also make transparencies on spirit master duplicating machines. If you wish, the machine will make color transparencies. The technique for making such transparencies includes the following:
   a. Make a spirit master as you would for any other duplicating. Use color if you wish to project in color.
   b. Place the spirit master on the duplicating machine and run through two or three sheets of paper to be sure it is working properly.
   c. Take a sheet of frosted acetate, frosted side up, and hand feed it through the duplicator.
   d. Spray the resulting transparency with a clear plastic.
   e. Mount the transparency if you wish. A clear sheet of plastic placed over the transparency face when mounting will give it additional protection.
4. Transparencies may be made on several types of copying machines. With these machines, one can make transparencies from books or from single sheets of printed or typed material. The capabilities of the machines differ according to their design and the copying process used. Consequently, one should become familiar with a machine's capabilities and the technique for operating it before attempting to make transparencies.

5. By lifting pictures from magazines and similar sources if the paper of the magazine is clay-coated. Probably the easiest of several ways to lift a picture is the following method which uses clear Contact paper:

   a. Test the paper to see if it is clay-coated. To do this, wet your finger and rub it along the border of the picture. If greyish white substance rubs off on your finger, the paper is clay-coated.

   b. Cut a piece of Contact paper to fit the picture. Contact can be purchased in any home-center, wallpaper or hardware store, variety or five-and-ten-cent store.

   c. Place the picture face up on a flat surface.

   d. Remove the protective covering from the Contact and place the Contact on the picture, sticky side down.

   e. Bind the Contact to the picture. Rub from top to bottom and left to right. Use a straight edge or a rolling pin. Be sure you get a good bond all over; you should have no air bubbles or creases when you get through.

   f. Place the Contact with the picture bonded to it in a pan of water.

   g. Add a teaspoon of detergent and let soak for at least half an hour.

   h. Remove the picture and Contact from the water. Slowly and easily pull the paper (picture) from the Contact. *Do not rush this step. Be sure to leave the picture and Contact in the water long enough before you try to separate the picture from the paper. If the picture does not come clean, the transparency will be worthless.*

   i. Wipe off any residue of paper or clay with a soft wet rag or a piece of cotton.

   j. Blot off any excess moisture with a paper towel.

   k. Let dry.

   m. Spray with clear plastic.

   n. Mount, if you wish.

MOUNTING TRANSPARENCIES. If you wish, you can mount your transparencies. Mounting transparencies has certain advantages when it comes to preserving and storing them, although, in some cases, the added length and width makes them difficult to transport and file. Mounts are necessary if one intends to attach flip-ons to the transparency. Otherwise, except for certain machine-made transparencies that are very thin, mounting is not an absolute necessity.

MAKING A TRANSPARENCY OVERLAY. A transparency overlay is one that you can flip on to another so as to change the detail being presented. Thus, if the basic

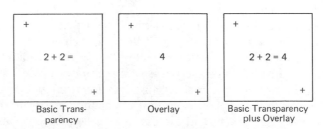

Basic Trans-   Overlay   Basic Transparency
parency   plus Overlay

Figure 10-1 *Transparency with Overlay.*

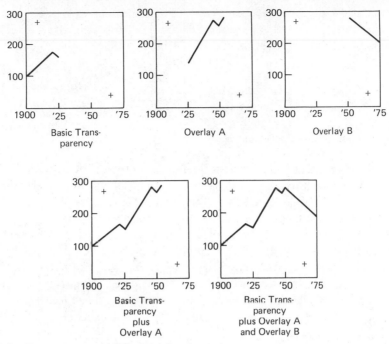

Figure 10-2 *Transparency with Several Overlays.*

transparency was an outline map of Europe, for example, one flip-on might show the national boundaries prior to 1914, another the boundaries in 1921, another in 1940, and another in 1974. Or the basic transparency might show the formula: $2 + 2 =$ and the overlay shows the answer: 4. By adding the overlay to the basic transparency one can show the complete formula: $2 + 2 = 4$. This is illustrated in Figure 10-1.

Or if we wish to show the variation of a phenomenon during the first quarters, we could combine overlays of a graph as in Figure 10-2.

You make overlays or flip-ons for transparencies in exactly the same way that you make the transparencies. You can just lay them on top of the basic overlay, if you wish, but usually it is better to hinge them to the base transparency's mount. Separate overlays tend to get mixed up and to mix you up. Hinges can be purchased or made out of a piece of tape (Figure 10-3).

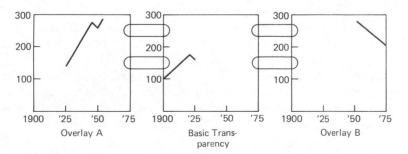

Figure 10-3 *Graph Presented with Hinged Overlays.*

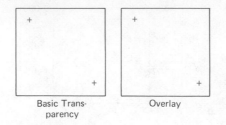

Basic Trans-   Overlay
parency

Figure 10-4 *Overlay Line Up Technique.*

Use reference marks (+) at the top left and bottom right corners of the basic transparency and each overlay so that you can match them up properly and easily, as shown in Figure 10-4. When the + marks on the overlay fit exactly over the + marks on the basic transparency, the two are properly aligned.

Masks are opaque overlays that block out a portion of the transparency so it will not be projected. You can make a mask by laying a piece of paper over the area not to be shown, or you can hinge a piece of light cardboard or plastic so that it will cover the area you wish to block off. The latter procedure is advantageous when one wishes to use the transparency again and again. Masks are useful for heightening the dramatic impact of the information to be shown by the transparency during the class.

Suppose you want to present an outline of a lecture point by point as you proceed through the lecture. How could you do it with the overhead projector? In your answer you would mention (1) writing the points out on the transparency as you lecture, or (2) preparing the transparency beforehand, covering it with a mask, and uncovering the points one by one as you lecture.

How would you go about making an impromptu transparency? (One method is to write or draw on the acetate with a grease pencil or similar pencil.)

What type of pencil must you use in making a transparency if you wish to project in color? (A translucent pencil.)

Slides and Filmstrips. Slides and filmstrips are variations of the same medium. Most of what one says about one of them also applies to the other. As a matter of fact, many filmstrips projectors are also slide projectors and vice versa. In this section, we shall treat them as different media, but remember that they are close relatives.

Using the Slide Projector. Thirty-five millimeter slides are available in great abundance. Commercially produced slides can be purchased through school supply houses and photography and other stores. Others can be obtained from pupils, friends, neighbors, and relatives. It is quite possible to make your own slides. With a little practice, you can learn to copy pictures, book pages, documents, and maps with a 35-mm. camera. Pictures you take of scenes and events may be excellent teaching aids. You may even find use for your vacation pictures. Information concerning techniques for use in copying documents and taking other pictures can be found in photographic manuals and works on audio-visual aids and educational technology.[1]

---

[1] *Copying,* Eastman Kodak Publication M1 (Rochester, N.Y.: Eastman Kodak Co., 1969); *How to Make Good Pictures,* Eastman Kodak Publication AW1 (Rochester, N.Y.: Eastman Kodak Co.); *Producing Film Strips and Slides,* Eastman Kodak Publication S-8 (Rochester,

Slides may be used in a number of ways. A most effective technique is to use single slides to illustrate important points or concepts. Another technique is to arrange a series of slides into a slide program, as in a filmstrip. If you wish, you can prerecord your own commentary and sound effects, and synchronize them with the slides, although for most class purposes this really is not necessary. Slide projection can also be adapted for individual or small group use. For individual or small group viewing, the image can be thrown onto a sheet of cardboard no larger than the projector itself. Many teachers place white paper in a cardboard box and project into it. This procedure has the advantage both of shielding the image from outside light and of keeping it from distracting other pupils. Slide projection is excellent for illustrating, clarifying, motivating, summing up, and for introducing study, discussion, or research. Use slides as springboards. Encourage pupils to build slide programs and illustrated reports as individual projects. Projecting two or more pictures at once makes it possible to show comparisons and contrast. This technique is an excellent way to make concepts and facts clear and to stimulate thinking.

PREPARING A SLIDE PROGRAM. Slide programs are quite easy to prepare. Pupils can and do make excellent programs. Basically the procedure is to do the following:

1. Decide on your objectives.
2. Decide on the points you want to make.
3. Select slides that will make your points. Use slides that are good technically if you can. However, sometimes it may be necessary to use a slide that is photographically less than good to make your point.
4. Arrange these points into an outline or scenario.
5. Arrange the slides in sequence according to the scenario.
6. Make title and commentary slides, and/or prepare an oral or written commentary.
7. Place the slides in the projector tray. Be sure they are in proper sequence. If you will be using a single shot projector, place the slides in order and number them.
8. If you plan a written commentary, run off the commentary so all may see it. This type of commentary is good for small group and individual work. If you plan an oral commentary, you or someone else may read or give the commentary extemporaneously as the slides are shown. This procedure is most common. However, if you wish, you can tape record your comments. If you do, be sure to introduce some sort of signal into the tape so that the operator will know when to go to the next slide. If you have the proper equipment, it is quite easy to produce a taped program in which the slides are changed automatically by an electronic signal, but such sophistication is not really necessary.

Practice building a lesson around one or two illustrative pictures or diagrams. What are the advantages of using this tactic?

N.Y.: Eastman Kodak Co., 1969); Jerold E. Kemp, *Planning and Producing Audiovisual Materials,* 2nd ed. (San Francisco: Chandler Publishing Co., 1968); and Leslie W. Nelson, *Instructional Aids* (Dubuque, Iowa: William C. Brown Company, Publishers, 1958).

If you were to make up a slide show, what criteria would you use for selecting the pictures? Would you ordinarily prefer to have it accompanied by an audio-taped commentary, or to supply the commentary yourself as the slides are presented? What are the advantages and disadvantages of both approaches? Compare your comments with those in the following section.

USE OF FILMSTRIPS. Filmstrips are, in effect, a series of slides strung together on a roll of film. They may be used in much the same way as slide programs. In fact, sometimes it may make for more effective teaching if you treat frames as individual slides. Studying an individual frame alone even for an entire period has much to recommend it. Although presumably filmstrips have the advantage of having been put together by an expert in a ready-made sequence, many filmstrips on the market are deadly. Studying single frames or short sequences may be more interesting and effective. Nowadays many filmstrips come with recorded commentary and sound effects. These may be extremely impressive. On the other hand, perhaps you would rather provide your own commentary as the filmstrip progresses. In any case, when using the silent filmstrip, you should try to involve the pupils as much as possible. In slow classes, often, pupils love to be asked to read the captions of silent filmstrips. Stop to discuss the implications of the pictures as you show them. If you let one of the pupils run the projector, it relieves you of this chore and makes at least one pupil interested. Usually, to run through an entire filmstrip without stopping for give-and-take and the sharing of ideas makes the class monotonous. For this reason, one should be very careful when selecting sound filmstrips. Unless they are unusually well done, they may be boring.

Filmstrips are excellent for small group and individual work. Use individual screens or screens in boxes. You may, or may not, want to give pupils study guides to use as they view the filmstrips individually. If they do have such study guides, it makes it possible to study completely on their own. With some filmstrips and slide programs, study guides are not really necessary because directions, problems, and other instructional matter that one would expect in the study guide appear on the filmstrip itself.

MAKING A FILMSTRIP. It is possible to make filmstrips, but to do so requires special equipment or special skills. Ordinarily, what one must do, in effect, is to make a slide program and then have an audio-visual person turn it into a filmstrip with his special equipment. If one has good slide projection equipment, making filmstrips hardly seems worthwhile. The slide program will do almost everything the filmstrip can do. If you wish to make filmstrips, however, you can find detailed instructions in such texts as Jerold E. Kemp's *Planning and Producing Audiovisual Materials,* 2nd ed. (San Francisco: Chandler Publishing Company, 1968), or technical manuals such as *Producing Slides and Filmstrips,* Publication S-8 (Rochester, N.Y.: Eastman Kodak Co., 1969).

How could one adapt a filmstrip projection for individual and small group work? (By setting up a projector with small screen or box, using earphones for sound, or perhaps using a written commentary or study guide.)

Cite several reasons why it might be better to use only parts of a filmstrip than the whole thing. (Many filmstrips are largely irrelevant and likely to be boring.)

Moving Pictures As a Teaching Tool

Moving pictures can be one of the most useful of all the teaching tools currently available. They can be used to arouse interest, to change pupils' attitudes, to clarify pupils' concepts, to stimulate thinking, to summarize, to reinforce learning, to demonstrate, and to bring into the classroom vividly much that could otherwise only be talked about. They make wonderful springboards for further learning. In this section, we will discuss both instructional movies made for use in the classroom, and general purpose or entertainment films.

We have not cited any disadvantages to the use of movies. Can you think of any? There are several. Among the disadvantages you might list are that some movies are irrelevant; many are incorrect and give pupils incorrect notions; pupils treat movies as entertainment rather than as learning features; movies may emphasize elements that you do not want emphasized in your course; movies are not very adaptable because it is difficult to excerpt what you want; movies are difficult to get and to show when you need them; and movies require special provisions for projection.

Procedures for Showing Instructional Films. As you already know, instructional films are those that are designed for classroom use for instructional purposes. They range from presentations of literary masterpieces to short sequences on how to use a certain piece of equipment. Since they are instructional tools, it is usually important that you select films that are pertinent to your teaching objectives, and use the film when these objectives are the basis of the content to be shown. If you cannot get the film you want when you want it, it is usually better either to adjust your teaching calendar so that you are teaching the proper content when you can get the film, or to skip it altogether. However, in some courses some films are of general enough interest so that they can be used at almost any time during the year. Once selected, the film, if possible, should be previewed. It is important also to order films early.

At the time of the film showing, once the projector has been set up and threaded, it is wise to try it to see that everything is working. Moving picture projectors are quite rugged, as a rule, but in the school situation they usually get a maximum of use and a minimum of maintenance. Checking the equipment, therefore, is essential.

You would be very wise to learn to troubleshoot the minor difficulties liable to occur in the different machines you have in your school. Many of the common difficulties can be corrected easily and quickly if one is familiar with the equipment. You ought to be able to change the fuses, lamps, and exciter lamps and to determine when a machine is not threaded properly. In older machines, it is important to understand the type of loops and tension required in threading, but in newer machines such matters are not so critical.

Once you are ready to start, introduce the film. Be sure that the pupils know what it is they are supposed to be doing. Unless you make a point of this, they may think of the movie simply as entertainment. Let them know what they should look for and what questions to think about. In some cases, you may want to give them a study guide to follow. Then as soon as everyone is ready, start the movie and keep quiet. Do not make comments while the movie is running. If you must interrupt for some purpose, stop the machine, say what has to be said, and restart it. To talk while the movie is in progress is silly. All you do is interrupt the film. Besides, no one can hear you anyhow. Usually the need for comment can be anticipated and taken care of by your introduction to the film. On the other hand, do not be afraid to stop the film for class discussion or explication if it seems advisable. By so doing, you may make instructional films much clearer. Movies that present a story, however, probably should not be interrupted, because interruptions may destroy the film's impact.

Upon completing the movie, follow it up. Discussion of what was presented is always in order. Written work, tests, problems, or reading on the topic, and practice of a skill demonstrated in the film are also useful. The point is to make sure that the pupils profit from the showing. If there is no adequate follow-up, films will become just recreation. Sometimes the follow-up will show the necessity for showing the movie again. This is often true when teaching skills. Then you may want to stop the film, have the pupil practice, and then show the film again.

Introducing, setting up, and following up films, if done well, are likely to be time consuming. Consequently, you should be careful to allow yourself plenty of time for the introduction, showing, follow-up, and any emergencies that may occur. If a film breaks, wind the film around the takeup reel several times, mark the break with a slip of paper, and continue with the showing. This procedure will allow you to continue with the presentation and yet notify the audio-visual or film library people of just where the break was. Do not try to repair the break yourself. Amateur, extemporaneous, hasty splicing, or attempts to pin, paper clip, or tape broken film together only make it more difficult for the next user of the film.

SILENT FILM. In this age of sound, one tends to forget how valuable silent films can be. The visual impact may be all that is needed. Sometimes it is better to be able to provide your own commentary. There are times when one would do well to turn off the sound on sound films and use your own or pupil commentary. Furthermore, silent films lend themselves to techniques in which teachers emphasize and clarify by stopping the film and repeating vital sequences as they explain and amplify the film presentation.

Can you think of any instance when it might be wise to shut off the sound and use your own commentary?

INDIVIDUALIZING INSTRUCTION. Films can be used for small group and independent study, as was pointed out in Module 7. Single concept films and 8-mm. cartridge projectors are excellent for this purpose. Single concept films are excellent because they concentrate on the single concept. The 8-mm. cartridge machines are ideal for individual work, because they are so easy to use, as illustrated in Figure 10-5. Any pupil can insert the cartridge and operate the machine. Because the screen is part of the machine, there is no problem of devising a screen for individual projection. This is shown in Figure 10-6.

Standard 16-mm. equipment can also be used for small group and individual work. To prepare a 16-mm. machine for small group work, connect earphones to a junction box plugged into the speaker output. Use a sheet of white paper or a cardboard box for a screen. If you put the group viewing the film in a corner of

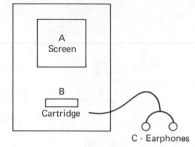

Figure 10-5 *8mm Cartridge Projector Suitable for Individual Viewing.*

the classroom and the pupils use earphones, they can watch movies to their hearts' content without disturbing anyone.

A similar technique can be used to prepare a 16-mm. projector for independent study:

1. Load the film and thread the projector.
2. Plug earphones into the speaker outlet.
3. Arrange a sheet of paper, or use a box for a screen.
4. Give pupils directions in a written guide. Instruct them about how to turn on the machine, run it through, and stop it at the end of the film. (A good technique is to have the pupils stop the film before it is completely run out and then back it up to the starting point so that the projector will be ready for the next user before the machine is turned off. This technique may not be necessary if the machine is self-threading. However, using it may save some confusion.)[2]

Using General Purpose Commercial Films. The commercial cinema can be a considerable instructional aid, especially in English, foreign language, and social studies courses. Films playing in local theatres can be used as a basis for oral and written reports. Films that all can see, such as those shown in school or at theater parties, make excellent bases for discussion and other exercises and reports.

To be aware of new films that you might use in connection with your teaching, you ought to scan the notices of coming attractions and read the reviews in newspapers and magazines. Pupils can do much of this type of work for you. Let them tell the class about appropriate films that they have seen or seen reviewed. Theater managers will usually be glad to cooperate with you. They can tell you when they expect to show recommended films. Sometimes, if they have reason to expect a good house, they can arrange for a showing of film classics and other requested films, and for special showings of regularly scheduled films. Film classics are also available in 16-mm. for use in schools. These 16-mm. films may be either feature length or short subject. Showing feature-length films may create something of a schedule problem. This problem can be avoided by scheduling the movie after hours or in episodes. Scheduling movies is not a great problem in schools that have truly flexible schedules. Don't forget to make use of the movies on television.

[2] Reprinted by permission from Leonard H. Clark, *Social Studies in Secondary Schools: A Handbook* (New York: Macmillan Publishing Co., Inc., 1973), p. 315.

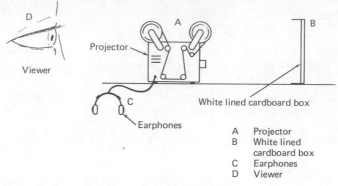

Viewer

Projector

Earphones

White lined cardboard box

A   Projector
B   White lined
      cardboard box
C   Earphones
D   Viewer

Figure 10-6   *16mm Projector Set Up for Individual Viewing.*

Sometimes they are excellent. You can find out about them as you would about any other television programs. Many excellent films, fit for classroom use, are available from the governmental agencies and from Chambers of Commerce, industry, and travel services. Often these movies are better for your purposes than the usual instructional films. You can find out about them by writing to the agencies concerned. For information about films available, see such references as *Educator's Guide to Free Films.*[3]

Among the tactics and strategies teachers use in order to utilize commercial films are the following:

1. Announce films that are coming to town or on television, and discuss how they might contribute to the course.
2. List films as optional activities. Have on the chalkboard or bulletin board a list of films in local theaters or TV that would be useful for optional activities such as oral or written reports.
3. Arrange theater parties for exceptional movies.
4. Discuss films that all pupils have had a chance to see.
5. Assign exercises and reports, such as the following, based on *The Bridge Over the River Kwai,* a classic movie that reappears on television from time to time. Map out a route for the railroad from Bangkok to Rangoon, using a large-scale map. Draw a series of map overlays, showing the positions of the various armies in Southeast Asia during the period from the fall of Burma on. Make a terrain map, showing the terrain, vegetation, and principal obstacles. Where did the Japanese actually put their railroad? Would you select the route they did?[4]
6. Utilize such activities as the following:
   a. Terrain study.
   b. Climate and weather study.
   c. Study of strategy and tactics.
   d. Study of people of the area—religion, economy, social customs.
   e. Map study of campaigns.

[3] Randolph, Wis.: Educator's Progress Service.
[4] Adapted from Leonard H. Clark, "Social Studies and The Bridge Over the River Kwai," *School Paperback Journal,* **2:**18–20 (Oct. 1965).

f. Study of important individuals.

g. Placing of the event into the context of history. Of what importance was it? What led up to it? What resulted from it? What if it had never come off?

h. Checking the movies against other sources to see if they present the event, period, or characters accurately. For instance, *Becket* presents Thomas Becket as the leader of the Anglo-Saxon cause. Was he really?

i. Dramatic criticism.

j. Comparison of the picture with the book.

k. Study of architecture, art, or customs as shown in the movie.

l. Study of characterization. Old movies can be used in history courses to illustrate a period because they are history itself. Even formula Westerns can be used. For example,

(1) Read the statement by Gary Cooper in which he says

the public has been fed a false concept of the West. . . . The fact is that the real West was actually populated by pioneers with guts—many of them with brains too—and the gunmen were parasites.

Youngsters growing up today have no real concept of American history from 1850–1900. . . . What's happened now is that movies and TV have made a uniform out of the cowboy's colorful character and put him in a background of Chicago and New York gangsterism. Only the costumes are western.[5]

Watch several Westerns to see how they falsify history. What elements of the TV story are right? Which wrong?

(2) What period of history can be included in the Wild West? What brought on this period? What caused it to close? What geographic area is represented by the cattle country of the period? What was the mining area? What was the purpose of the cattle drives? Where did they take the cattle? Do the scenes in the pictures properly represent the type of grazing land that was used during this time? Why, or why not? How can one find out?

Television

Everyone in the United States knows that television is a powerful medium. Yet very few teachers and school systems have made optimum use of its potentialities. Its use presents scheduling, curriculum, and physical problems that most school systems have not been willing to face up to.

For purposes of professional discussion, television programs can be divided into three categories: instructional television, educational television, and general commercial television. Instructional television refers to programs specifically designed as classroom instruction; educational television, to programs of public broadcasting designed to educate in general, but not aimed at classroom instruction; general commercial television programs include the entertainment and public service programs of the television networks and local stations.

[5] William D. Boutwell, *Using Mass Media in the Schools* (New York: Appleton-Century-Crofts, 1962), p. 28.

Instructional Television. As we have just noted, television is seldom used well in schools. Probably in Utopian circumstances, television should not be used for classroom instruction, but rather should be reserved for supplementing ordinary curricula and instruction. Nevertheless, sometimes instructional television that takes on the role of classroom instruction is necessary in circumstances in which courses cannot be successfully mounted, because they are beyond the capabilities of the local resources, staff, and facilities. By using television well, schools can offer pupils courses that otherwise would be impossible. In other school systems, because of a desire for economy or in an attempt to bring the pupils in touch with master teachers and the very best teaching, instructional television courses have been introduced as substitutes for the regular courses.

Where instructional television courses have been introduced, the fact that the television class is taught by a master television teacher does not relieve the classroom teacher of his teaching responsibilities. He must plan, select, introduce, guide, and follow up, as in any other course. Otherwise, the television teaching will leave the pupils with learning gaps and misunderstandings. In spite of the marvels of television and other machines, pupils still need the personal guidance of all teachers. To use instructional television properly, you should follow a procedure similar to the following:

1. Prepare yourself for the telecast. Preview it if possible. Study the guides and any other advance material available.
2. Prepare the setting.
   a. Arrange the classroom and warm up the set.
   b. Prepare and distribute any materials and supplies needed.
   c. Discuss the lesson to be viewed with the pupils. Teach any background vocabulary necessary for understanding the instruction telecast. ·
   d. Guide the pupils' learning.
      (1) In work-type lessons, circulate to help your pupils.
      (2) Take notes of pupil reactions and evidences of lack of understanding or misunderstanding.
   e. Follow up.
      (1) Question and discuss.
      (2) Reteach and clarify as necessary.
      (3) Provide additional experiences—particularly ones that will allow pupil participation, creativity, problem solving, and critical and creative thinking.[6]

This same procedure also holds for supplementary programs that are used to fill out, deepen, and enrich the day-by-day instruction.

General and Educational Television Programs. In addition to instructional television programs, there are general and educational programs that you can utilize in your teaching: regular commercial programs, special events, and general cultural, educational, informational, and enrichment programs of the Public Broadcasting System and independent educational television stations. Both public broadcasting stations and commercial stations offer a multitude of programs that can be used to supplement and enrich your teaching. Probably the foremost examples include news programs, news specials, and interview programs such as

[6] Clark, *Teaching Social Studies in Secondary Schools: A Handbook,* op. cit., p. 317.

"Meet the Press" and "Face the Nation." Such programs can be excellent sources of material for use in all sorts of courses, not only, as you might surmise, for courses in the social studies. For example, every day the weather map and the radar patterns shown on the weather report portion of the news give one ammunition for the study of highs, lows, air currents, and the reading of weather maps. Science editors report on new developments in science almost every day and bring to our attention important science knowledge in their science news specials. Stock market reports are basic to the study of business and economics courses.

Ordinary commercial programs may turn out to be the best sources of all. All radio dramas occur in time and place and are subject to dramatic and literary criticism. They can be used to establish historical and literary concepts. We have already seen how movies can be used for such purposes. What would make a better subject for the study of plot or characterization (or lack of it) than many of our television dramas? Music is omnipresent. Even "commercial messages" can be used. They give almost unlimited opportunities for the study of logic, propaganda, and rhetoric.

Educational television courses, such as those given by the public broadcasting stations or by colleges on commercial stations ("Sunrise Semester"), often include lectures, demonstrations, and background information usable for high school courses. Although these courses may be aimed at adults taking the courses for college credit, they are usually not too difficult for many high school pupils.

Look at the television news and commentaries. Can you find anything that you might find useful as supplementary material for a course in science, business, mathematics, foreign language, art, or music?

FINDING USEFUL PROGRAMS. To find what programs that you might use will be telecast locally, you can consult such references as your local newspaper, news and television magazines, your local television guide, professional journals such as *Today's Education,* and television station and network publicity releases. Sometimes you can obtain helpful information about future programs suitable for school use by writing to the stations or networks.

USING TELEVISION PROGRAMS. Unfortunately, perhaps, television studios do not ordinarily adapt their schedules to those of the secondary schools. This problem may be met in several ways. One solution is to tape the programs for replaying during the class period. Recent advances in video-tape technology have made it possible to record programs relatively easily. Attention should be paid, however, to copyright laws, although presumably video-taping single programs for classroom use but not for rebroadcasting should be interpreted as falling under the fair use clause. In spite of the desirability of video-taping programs, audio-taping of talk programs such as "Meet the Press" or "Face the Nation," or a press conference, should be adequate for most classroom use. Another solution is to ask the pupils to view the telecast at home. This solution is fraught with problems because not everyone will be able to watch the television program. Some may not have television sets available (they may not own one, or it may be preempted at that hour. If Father plans to watch the Monday night football game, he may not take kindly to an assignment of ballet viewing in the middle of the second period), and others may not have the time available. Consequently, it may be that you should make such assignments selectively to certain individuals or committees who will report what they have seen and heard. Sometimes, when a major event is to be telecast on several channels, you might do well to ask different pupils to watch different channels so that they can compare the coverage. The difference in opinions of various commentators on a Presidential message might be quite revealing, for instance. In any case, the assignments made to the pupils must be clear and followed up. Some teachers find it helpful to list the assignments, questions, and projects on the bulletin board.

PHYSICAL ARRANGEMENTS FOR TELEVISION CLASSES. When using television in the classroom, one should, of course, try to be sure that everyone can see and hear sufficiently well. The following are guidelines for the physical arrangement of the classroom that should make the use of television most effective:

1. Use 21- to 24-inch screen television sets with front directional speakers.
2. Place the sets so that each pupil has an unobstructed line of sight.
3. The screen should not be more than thirty feet from any pupil.
4. The set should be about five and one half feet from the floor (that is, about the same height as the teacher's face).
5. The vertical angle of sight from any pupil to the set should never be more than 30°; the horizontal angle, never more than 45°.
6. The room should be kept lighted so that pupils can see to take notes.
7. No glare should reflect from the screen. To reduce glare one can
   a. Move the set away from the windows.
   b. Tilt the set downward.
   c. Provide the set with cardboard blinders.
8. The sound should come from front directional speakers. If several sets are in use in one room, it may be better to use the sound from only one set than to have it come from several sources. In large rooms for large-class instruction it may be more satisfactory to run the sound from one set through a public address system.
9. Pupils should have adequate surface space for writing.
10. To allow for quick, easy transition from the telecast, television classrooms should be fitted out with adequate audio-visual equipment, display space, filing and storage space.[7]

Tape Recorders and Record Players

You will find that audio-tape recordings and records are excellent media for many purposes. In addition to bringing music, speeches, plays, and other dramatic devices to the class, they can be used to support other media. (What would movies and television do without the background of the sound track?) Audio-tape can also be used to record one's own performance so that one can criticize his own work. Such recording is essential in the study of language and speech.

In using audial activities in your classes you would do well to follow the suggestions made by Haney and Ullmer.

1. Develop a utilization plan. Preview audio materials, listening to them carefully and critically, and identify the learning outcomes for which they are appropriate. Identify the important terms and concepts contained in the program and make plans to

[7] Reprinted by permission from Leonard H. Clark and Irving S. Starr, *Secondary School Teaching Methods,* 3rd ed. (New York: Macmillan Publishing Co., Inc., 1976), p. 315.

ensure that prerequisite concepts are understood by the pupils. Decide on a presentation technique. You may wish to play the audio materials once and then have a follow-up activity; to play them in segments with activity interspersed; to play them through once and then again with frequent stopping for discussion or practice; or to provide some kind of handout that guides pupil participation. Also, an important part of developing a utilization plan is to decide on test items that will be used to measure learning that results from the listening experience.

2. Prepare the children for listening. Try to stimulate interest in the program by making introductory comments. Explain the program and the reason for using it. You might list key words or concepts on the chalkboard or employ a handout to guide pupil participation. The important thing is that they be given a good idea of what will be expected of them in terms of learning from the listening experience.

3. Play the program. Encourage pupils to listen quietly and carefully. Some method of evoking their participation should be employed, whether the participation is to be overt or implicit. Overt participation might be in the form of taking notes, recording observations, completing statements, or answering questions. Implicit or overt participation can be improved by encouraging the children to concentrate on what they are hearing, to analyze what is being said, to arrange facts or concepts in their minds, to react to different points of view, or to devise solutions to problems presented.

4. Engage in follow-up activity. After most media presentations, it is a good idea to have some type of activity to ensure that learning has taken place, to fill in the gaps where the presentation fell short of expectations, to clarify misunderstandings, or to extend the learning to new but related areas. The discussion is a popular form of follow-up, but there are other activities, such as pupil projects, reports, panel discussions, a game or simulation, or a field trip. The presentation and the follow-up activity together should constitute an integrated and total learning experience.

5. Evaluate learning from the listening experience. Evaluation of the outcomes of a media event is really no different than evaluating outcomes of conventional events. The important thing is to confirm that desired learning has taken place and that the teacher's utilization strategy has been effective.[8]

These suggestions are similar to those we have made for other media. Used as recommended, these principles should make your use of audio media much more effective.

Multimedia

You should use different media to reinforce each other. You will do so naturally some of the time, such as when you write on the chalkboard to illustrate a problem you are discussing. But you ought to make an effort to combine media in ways that will make your teaching more effective and exciting. You can do so by using different media in sequence or by using them simultaneously. The essential ingredient is that the media support each other and the objectives of your lessons. For instance, you might want to show a picture of a scene, then a map of the area, and then a taped narrative describing what travel was like. Or you might present all three simultaneously; as the taped narrative plays, you could point out features referred to by the narrative on both the map and the picture. In teaching the westward movement, for instance, one might project a map of the

[8] John B. Haney and Eldon J. Ullmer, *Educational Media and the Teacher* (Dubuque, Iowa: William C. Brown Co., Publishers, 1970), p. 50.

West on the chalkboard, and then with colored chalk trace routes west on the board as you project pictures of the terrain and other features on an adjacent screen. Techniques using two or more screens can be very interesting and informative. For instance, while you hold a picture on one screen, you can flash a series of close-ups on another. Or you could put up two pictures side by side and compare and contrast them. Or you could present a schematic on one screen and a picture of the real thing on another, or a picture on one screen and pictures about it on another. Similarly, such presentations could be combined with the use of models, realia, or sound tracks. There is no limit to what you can do if you are ingenious and venturesome. Almost anything will serve as long as the media used support each other and the objectives of instruction. If the media are not compatible and do not complement each other, they may confuse rather than clarify, however.

SUGGESTED READING

Refer to Module 11 for a list of suggested readings on teaching tools.

POST TEST

1. How can audio-visual aids help to reduce verbalism?

_____

_____

_____

2. In selecting an audio-visual device what should you consider?

_____

_____

3. What is the basic principle about focusing that has to be taken into account when focusing a projector?

_____

_____

4. If you had a series of small prints that you wanted pupils to look at and study, what is probably the most efficient method of presenting them to the pupils?

_____

_____

5. What would be an advantage of running off a transparency and a ditto sheet of an exercise on a spirit master?

_____

_____

6. Can it be done?

_____

7. What is the essential, practical difference between an opaque projector and an overhead projector?

_____

_____

_____

8. A supervisor was heard to say that the overhead projector was the teacher's best friend. What is so good about this kind of projector?

_____

_____

_____

9. How would you go about making a hand-drawn colored transparency?

_____

_____

_____

_____

_____

10. How is a transparency overlay or flip-on used?

_____

_____

11. What is the purpose of a mask when used with an overhead projector?

_____

_____

12. How can you adapt a slide projector for individual or small group viewing?

_____

_____

13. How does one prepare a slide program?

_____

_____

14. What should you do if a motion picture film breaks?

_____

_____

_____

15. What can you do to make pupils understand that films are instruction, not entertainment?

_____

_____

_____

16. Many people seem to think that movies are the audio-visual aid par excellence, but they have many disadvantages. What are three of them?

_____

_____

_____

_____

_____

_____

17. Once the film is completed and the machine turned off, what should you, the teacher, do?

_____

18. How might you utilize commercial films showing at local theaters or on television in your instruction?

_____

_____

_____

19. How do Haney and Ullman recommend that one prepares the pupils for listening to taped or recorded audio materials?

_____

_____

_____

20. Give at least one example of a multimedia presentation.

_____

_____

_____

Materials of Instruction

Leonard H. Clark

Jersey City State College

module 11

Textbooks / Other Materials in Print / Display and Display-type Devices and Materials / Teaching by Machine / Sources of Teaching Materials / Obtaining Free and Inexpensive Materials

RATIONALE

This module continues our study of teaching tools. We shall look at some materials of instruction and teaching tools not considered to be audio-visual aids. Whether they are or not, we shall leave it to you to decide.

SPECIFIC OBJECTIVES

Specifically, it is expected that you will be able to do the following:

1. Explain the pros and cons of textbook use.
2. Describe recommended procedures for using textbooks.
3. Describe how to teach with multiple readings.
4. Describe criteria to consider when selecting textbooks.
5. Describe how other printed matter and duplicated materials, such as paperbacks, workbooks, study guides, newspapers, periodicals, and springboard materials may be used in your teaching.
6. Explain how to use display devices including the chalkboard, bulletin board, flannel board, and flip chart.
7. Explain how to use pictures, illustrations, charts, graphs, and posters.
8. Explain how the teaching machine teaches.
9. Tell what procedures a teacher should use in teaching by machine.
10. Describe several sources of procuring free art, inexpensive teaching materials, and references for finding what materials are available.

MODULE TEXT

Textbooks

Of all the materials of instruction, the textbook has had the most influence on teaching content and method. For many teachers, it has been the "be all and end all" of their instructional life. This is unfortunate because, properly used, the textbook is merely one of many teaching tools. Do not let it dominate you. You, not the textbook, are supposed to be the master.

Although textbooks are only teaching tools, they can be of great value, particularly to beginning teachers. You will find them very helpful in your planning, because they (1) provide an organization or structure for the course; (2) provide selection of subject matter that can be used as a basis for determining course content and determining emphases; (3) provide a certain number of activities and suggestions for teaching strategies and tactics; and (4) provide information about other readings, sources of information, audio-visual and other aids, and other teaching materials and teaching tools.

You will also find that a textbook can make an excellent base for building interesting, high-order, learning activities (discussion, inquiry, research activities) that call forth critical thinking and other higher mental processes. On the other hand, textbooks are far from being the ideal tool some teachers take them to be. They have many faults. They tend to usurp too large a place in the teaching and curriculum. In addition, their construction is usually too rigid to allow them to fit in easily in an enlightened modern classroom situation: they are frequently dull, they discourage the reading and studying of more profitable materials, they are often superficial, and they do not allow for differences in pupils' talents, interests, and goals.

To get the most out of your textbooks and to avoid their weaknesses, it is recommended that you do the following:

1. Become really familiar with the textbook before you use it.
2. Use the textbook in your planning as a source of structure if it seems desirable to do so, but do not let yourself become chained to the book.
3. Use the text as only one of many materials and activities. Use other readings, simulation, role playing, discussion, films, and pictures.
4. Use problem-solving approaches in which the text is but one source of data.
5. Use only those parts of the book that seem good to you; skip the other parts; rearrange the order of topics if you think it desirable. In other words, adapt the text to your pupils and their needs.
6. Use additional or substitute readings to allow for differences in pupils.
7. Provide help for pupils who do not read well.
8. Teach pupils how to study the text and to use the parts of the text, such as table of contents, index, headings, charts, graphs, and illustrations.
9. Use the illustrations, charts, graphs, and other aids included in the textbook in your teaching. Build lessons around them; study them.
10. Encourage critical reading. Compare the text to source materials and other texts. Test it for logic and bias.
11. Teach vocabulary.
12. Incorporate as you work in a multiple-text teaching strategy.

Introducing the Text. Because pupils seldom know how to use their texts efficiently and effectively, Cartwright has suggested that on the first day before they begin to read, you introduce the pupils to the textbook in a lesson in which you and they discuss the following:

1. The title page.
   What information does it give?
   When was the book written? Has it been revised?
   Who is the publisher? Where was it published? Do these indicate any likelihood of bias?
2. The preface.
   What does the author claim he intended to do?
   What was his purpose?
3. Table of contents.
   How much weight is given to various topics? How can we use the information contained in the table of contents to help us study the text?

4. The list of maps, charts, and illustrations.
   What is the importance of these devices? How can one use them to aid his study? Choose examples of each—maps, charts, tables, graphs, illustrations—and have pupils find essential information in them.
5. Appendix.
   What does appendix mean? What is it for?
6. Index.
   Use drill exercises to give pupils practice in using the index. These can be made into games or contests.
7. Glossary.
   What is a glossary? Why is it included? Utilize exercises that call for looking up words and then using them in sentences.
8. Study the aids at the ends of chapters.
   How can study questions be used? Which are thought questions? Which are fact questions?
9. Chapter headings, section headings, paragraph leads, introductory overviews, preliminary questions, and summaries.
   What are the purposes of each of these? Use exercises that call for getting meaning from aids such as these without reading the entire text.[1]

Selecting the Textbook. Because textbooks play such a large part in most classes, they should be selected carefully. In many schools, textbook selection is made by a committee of teachers. In some, teachers select their own texts. No matter what selection process is used, the text should be tested for such criteria as the following:

1. What is the date of the copyright? Is the information and interpretation presented up to date?
2. Who is the author? Is he competent in the field? Does he write clearly and well?
3. Is the book suitable for the objectives of your course? Does it cover the proper topics with the proper emphases?
4. Are the topics arranged in a desirable sequence? If not, can the sequence be altered or portions omitted without disrupting the usefulness of the book?
5. Is the content accurate and accurately presented? Is the book free from bias?
6. Are the concepts presented clearly? Are they adequately developed with sufficient detail or is there a tendency to attempt to jam in too many ideas too compactly?
7. Are the vocabulary and language appropriate for the pupils of the class?
8. Does it presume background knowledge and experiences that the pupils do not yet have?
9. Does the author make good use of headings, summaries, and similar devices? Does he give opportunity for the readers to visualize, generalize, apply, and evaluate the content?
10. Are the table of contents, preface, index, appendices, and glossary adequate?
11. Does the book provide suggestions for use of supplementary materials?
12. Does it provide a variety of suggestions for stimulating thought-provoking instructional activities?
13. Are these suggestions sufficiently varied both as to level and to kind?
14. Does the author document his sources adequately?
15. Is the book well illustrated? Are the illustrations accurate, purposeful, and properly captioned? Are they placed near the text they are designed to illustrate?

[1] William H. Cartwright, *How to Use a Textbook,* How to Do It Series, No. 2, rev. ed. (Washington, D.C.: National Council for the Social Studies, 1966).

16. Does the book have suitable maps, charts, and tables? Are they clear and carefully done? Does the author refrain from trying to cram too much data onto his maps and charts?
17. Is the book well made? Does it seem to be strong and durable?
18. Does the book look good? Is the type clear and readable? Do the pages make a pleasant appearance with enough white space?[2]

Item seven of this list of criteria refers to the reading level of the textbook. Sometimes this information is supplied by the textbook publishers. If it is not, you can derive an index of the reading level by applying a formula, such as the Lorge formula or the Dale and Chall formula.[3]

A simple method for discovering whether a textbook is too difficult for the pupils is to ask them to read selections from it aloud. If they can read it without stumbling over many of the words and can tell you the gist of what the selections said, you can be quite sure the selections are not too difficult.

Multitext Approaches. More and more modern teachers are no longer satisfied by the single textbook approach to teaching. Some of them have substituted a strategy in which they use one set of books for one topic and another set for another. This strategy does provide some flexibility, but it is really simply a series of single texts. Others, usually more knowledgeable and more proficient teachers, utilize a strategy which incorporates the use of many readings for the same topic at the same time. This multiple-reading strategy gives the pupils a certain amount of choice in what they read. The various readings allow for differences in reading ability and interest level. By using a study guide, all the pupils can be directed toward specific concepts and information, but they do not have to all read the same selections.

To carry out this type of multiple-reading approach, do the following:

1. Select your instructional objectives.
2. Select a number of readings that will throw light on these objectives. Be sure that there are several readings for each goal. Try to provide for variations in pupils' reading level and interests when you make your selections.
3. Build a study guide that will direct the pupils toward the goals and suggest readings appropriate to the goals.
4. Let the pupils select the readings that they will pursue to carry out the provisions of the guide.

Other Materials in Print

The number and amount of printed materials suitable for instruction is almost infinite. Besides textbooks, there are other books, periodicals, pamphlets, and

---

[2] Reprinted by permission from Leonard H. Clark and Irving S. Starr, *Secondary School Teaching Methods,* 3rd ed. (New York: Macmillan Publishing Co., Inc., 1976), p. 266.

[3] Typical readability formulas are described in the following references: Edgar Dale and Jeanne S. Chall, "A Formula for Predicting Readability," *Educational Research Bulletin,* **27**:11–20, 37–54 (Jan.–Feb. 1949). Irving Lorge, "Predicting Readability," *Teachers College Record,* **45**:404–419 (March 1944). Use these formulas with caution. They are only rough indices

brochures. Many of these are available without cost or for only a small fee. Newspapers and magazines are excellent sources of reading matter for every one of the subject fields. They are also excellent sources of materials for bulletin boards. You should start making a collection of things you might use now, if you have not already done so. Once you have begun teaching, pupils and pupil committees can be utilized to do the gathering.

Paperbacks. The paperback revolution of a decade or two ago opened up a great reservoir of fairly inexpensive reading matter for use in our classes. Paperbacks make the multiple-reading approach practicable. They also "make it possible to read primary sources rather than snippits, and both extensively and intensively rather than being exposed only to a single textbook account. With inexpensive paperbacks it is much easier to provide pupils with opportunities to analyze and compare works, a practice which is almost impossible if one uses only the ordinary textbook or anthology."[4]

Workbooks. Many schools use workbooks in their classes. Although many educators scoff at the use of workbooks, they can be very useful tools. As a matter of fact, the Learning Activity Packets that are so highly recommended by modern theorists are really a variation of the workbook. So are the duplication exercises that are so often prepared by teachers.

We offer a few comments about using workbooks:

1. Try to find workbooks that emphasize thinking and problem solving rather than simple rote learning.
2. Use workbooks as a springboard for higher learning.
3. Follow up the workbook assignments. Correct them. Use their exercises as bases for next steps.
4. Let pupils work on different exercises or different workbooks. There is no advantage in everyone's doing the same workbook exercises at the same time. However, if pupils are using workbooks not designed to accompany your text or syllabus, it may be necessary to cut and edit the workbook exercises so that they will match your course.

Mimeographed and Ditto Material. All that has been said about workbooks also applies to mimeographed and ditto exercises prepared by the teacher. When using these materials you should consider also the advisability of using answer sheets so that you can save the duplicated material and it can be used again. Sometimes teachers require pupils to retain their exercises and answers in a notebook. The result is a sort of combination workbook and review book.

Prepare a number of exercises with answer sheet that require a high level of thinking rather than rote memory learning. Don't be fooled. This is not an assignment. Do your exercises really call for high-level, mental activity?

Duplicated Springboard Materials. As you have probably already learned, in pedagogical circles, we have given the name of springboard to materials or activities that, it is hoped, will be jumping-off places for pupil inquiry, investigation, or

---

[4] Clark and Starr, op. cit., p. 274.

discussion. Among the materials used for springboard are films, film clips, and video-tapes. Many consist of duplicated or printed reading matter, sometimes purchased from commercial sources, but more often homemade. Among the types of homemade springboard material you can make are descriptions of real or imagined situations that should arouse the curiosity of the pupils, case studies, historical accounts, news items, stories, and anecdotes. When you select material to be duplicated as a springboard, try to be sure that it will arouse the pupils' interest and stir up open-ended questions. Springboards are discussed in Module 5.

Study Guides. Among the most common uses of duplicated materials for instruction is the study guide (previously discussed in Module 1.4). Study guides are especially useful for pupils who are working alone or in small groups in individualized, laboratory-type classes, for students involved in special assignments, independent study, research activities, or supplementary assignments, and for such special activities as field trips, and movie or TV watching. Their purpose is to provide the pupils with directions and suggestions for carrying out the activity and for getting the most from it, and questions and problems designed to guide their study and to stimulate their thinking. Among the things that may be found in a study guide are purpose, directions to follow, questions to answer, problems to solve, things to do, answer sheets, suggested reading, and suggested follow-up activities. An example of a special study guide follows.

Specimen Activity Guide or Job Breakdown
Job Breakdown
Project: Screwdriver—Wooden handle
Part: Handle—Hard maple
Size 1¼″ sq. × 4″
 1. Layout diagonals both ends.
 2. Drill center holes.
 3. Drill one end $\frac{31}{64}$ diameter × $1\frac{11}{16}$ deep.
 4. Assemble ferrule and wood.
 5. Turn $1\frac{1}{16}$ diameter entire length.
 6. Turn ¼-inch radius knurled end.
 7. Mill six grooves equidistant .050 deep.
 8. Turn ½-inch radius.
 9. Sandpaper wooden surfaces only.
10. Get instructor's approval.

Other more general study guides can be found in Module 1.4.

Display and Display-type Devices and Materials

There are ever so many ways of displaying information and materials for pupils to see. We have already discussed projectional techniques in a previous module. We shall now present some more prosaic devices and materials. In using all of them, the following general rather obvious principles apply: They should be clearly visible, be attractive, catch the eye, be simple, be clear, make a point, have a center of interest, and avoid clutter and confusion.[5]

[5] Leonard H. Clark, *Teaching Social Studies in Secondary Schools: A Handbook* (New York: Macmillan Publishing Co., Inc., 1973), pp. 303–304.

Chalkboards. Chalkboards are so ubiquitous that we tend to forget them when we speak of teaching tools. That is probably one reason why so many of us fail to get the most out of them. Yet, chalkboards are about the most useful and versatile of the visual aids that we have available to us. They are useful for presenting subject matter, for reinforcing oral explanations and presentations, for clarifying difficult concepts, for illustrating, for pupil presentations of their work, and for practice activities. They are very flexible instruments; just a swipe of the eraser and you are ready for something new. This flexibility is also a cause of one of its disadvantages. Chalkboard work is impermanent and transitory. The swipe of the eraser that makes it ready for something new also destroys the old material. One cannot save material placed on a chalkboard without rendering the chalkboard useless for anything else. In this respect, the flannel board and overhead transparencies are much more useful.

Because the chalkboard is potentially a powerful instrument and is so often used thoughtlessly, it is not inappropriate to suggest to you a few pointers that may make your use of it more efficient and effective, such as the following:

1. The material on the chalkboard must be visible and legible if it is to do any good. When you are using the chalkboard, be sure that the pupils can see easily. Stand out of the way. Use a pointer or a yardstick. The old expression about a better door than a window applies to teachers, too.
2. A clean, neat, orderly board improves the impact of the presentation. Use the eraser. Take off material you no longer need as soon as you are finished with it. Cluttered boards not only detract from the appearance of the room, but they also tend to become confusing.
3. If the board work is simple and tasteful, it will be more effective. Leave plenty of "white space" so that the material you want to emphasize shows up.
4. Judicious use of color, underlining and boxes will make important points stand out. Diagrams, rough drawings, and stickmen are also useful for emphasizing and clarifying.
5. When possible, boardwork that is to be used later should be covered until you are ready to use it. One way to do this is to pull a map or screen down over it. Another way is to cover it with wrapping paper taped to the board, although this technique may be difficult in the rush of ordinary classes.

Flannel Boards. Flannel boards and their close relatives, felt boards, hook and loop boards, and magnetic boards have many of the advantages and uses of chalkboards. They are best used for immediate presentations rather than for displays over a long period of time. In some ways, they are not as flexible or useful as chalkboards; in others they are more so. They do have several advantages over them.

1. One can prepare the material to be presented in advance.
2. The material to be presented can be saved to be used again.
3. They can be used very dramatically. Just slap the material up for all to see at the propitious moment and drive home your point. It is probably this feature that makes its advocates claim that flannel boards are 50 per cent more effective than chalkboards.

4. They are especially useful for showing change and development, because it is so easy to add or to subtract from the display without the disturbance that erasing creates. This also makes them excellent for reinforcing points. Just put up or take off the appropriate word, caption, or picture to make your point.

MAKING A FLANNEL BOARD

1. Cut a piece of plywood or similar board to the desired proportions.
2. Cover the plywood with felt, suede or long napped flannel, nap side out. Stretch it tight, and tack or staple it to the board. The result should give you a smooth, tight, nappy surface to which light sandpaper-backed paper figures and the like will adhere.

MAKING FLANNEL BOARD MATERIALS. To make these display materials use any of the following procedures:

1. Cut out pictures, figures, or what you will from magazines, books, paper, lightweight cardboard, flannel cloth, or similar materials.
2. a. Glue, not paste, pieces of sandpaper, sand side out, to the back of the picture or figure. It is not necessary to cover the entire back. Sandpaper at the corners, or strips crossed on the center of the back will usually do, but don't be too stingy.
   b. Cover the back of the material with rubber cement. Sprinkle sand on the rubber cement while it is still wet. Let dry.
   c. Using a brush and long strokes, cover the back of the material with water glass (sodium silicate). Sprinkle with sand while still wet.
   d. If the letters or figures are made from felt, flannel, roughened construction paper, oilcloth, blotting paper, or light sponge, they do not need any sandpaper backing. Just press them on the flannel board as is. Or,
   e. Paint the back of the letter or figure with oil-based paint. Spray or sprinkle with flocking.
3. Use strips of yarn for decoration, to show relationships, or to make letters. It will stick to the flannel board without backing.[6]

Felt Board and Hook and Loop Boards. Felt boards are simply flannel boards made with felt rather than flannel. Stiff felt-backed dining room table pads make excellent felt boards. Hook and loop boards are the commercially prepared boards used by speakers, salespersons, and television studios. They are made of the type of materials used for Velcro fasteners. They are somewhat more dependable than homemade flannel boards. They are used in exactly the same manner as flannel boards.

Magnetic Boards. Magnetic boards are also used in the same manner as flannel boards. These boards are made of thin sheets of iron or steel-based metal to which materials are attached by means of small magnets. To make a magnetic board, one simply cuts the sheet of metal to the desired size, paints it with automobile enamel or blackboard paint, and either nails it to a wooden frame or tapes the sharp edges so that they will not cut the fingers. Galvanized iron screening, stapled or tacked to a wooden frame, also makes a satisfactory magnetic board. Materials for displaying on magnetic board can be made simply by gluing materials to small magnets with heavy-duty glue or mending cement. If the magnetic board is enameled,

[6] Clark, Ibid., pp. 306–307.

you can write on it with a grease pencil; if painted with chalkboard paint, with chalk.

Make a flannel board or a magnetic board. What size would be best for your purpose, do you think?

List and compare the advantages and disadvantages of the chalkboard, flannel board, and overhead projector.

Bulletin Boards. Bulletin boards are, or should be, instructional tools. You should treat them as such, not as classroom decorations. They can be used to motivate, interpret, supplement, and reinforce. To be useful teaching tools, they must be kept up to date and aimed at the objectives of the unit being taught. Following are a number of suggestions for effective use of bulletin boards:

1. Bulletin boards should be carefully planned. In planning the board, select one of the instructional aims of the unit and gather material suitable for that aim. Cull out the most desirable materials until you have only what seems to be the best of the lot. Resist the temptation to use too much material. Then sketch out a plan for presenting the material you have selected. In your plan try to do the following:
    a. Make the display tell a story.
    b. Have a center of interest. (Only one central idea or theme to a board.)
    c. Use lines or arrows to draw the viewer to the center of interest.
    d. Be sure it is visible and eye-catching. Be sure captions and pictures are large enough to strike the eye. Keep captions brief and clear.
    e. Utilize questions, action, and drama to attract attention.
    f. Provide for plenty of white space. There should be no solid blocks of material and no clutter. Again, resist the temptation to use too much. A few well-selected things will have more impact than a large hodge-podge.
    g. Consider using unusual materials, such as three-dimensional objects, combining the bulletin board with a table display, or other devices for giving the bulletin board zip. Color variety and humor add spice. To build a mood, coordinate the colors to the ideas or atmosphere you wish to present.
2. Turn the planning and preparation of the bulletin boards over to a pupil committee. You might have a competition to see who prepares the best board.
3. Be sure the materials are secured firmly and neatly. Consider the use of invisible fastening, such as bulletin board wax or adhesive plastic, or loops of masking tapes with the adhesive side out. Fasten one side of the loop to the material and the other to the wall. Or, double-faced adhesive tape, or tape tack units. These are a thumbtack stuck through a piece of adhesive tape with the adhesive side out. Fasten the tape to the material and fasten it to the bulletin board. Sometimes, fastening with brightly colored thumbtacks makes the display more interesting.
4. To be sure that the bulletin board stays up to date, keep a calendar or schedule for changing it.
5. Start a collection of bulletin board materials. Encourage pupils to bring in materials for your collection.

Charts. Charts can be used for displays just as bulletin boards are, but, as a rule, they are better suited for explaining, illustrating, clarifying, and reinforcing points in specific lessons. Among the many types of useful charts are lists, graphs, organizational charts, flow charts, pictorial charts, diagrammatic presentations of cause and effect and other relationships, multicolumned lists showing contrast or comparison, and time charts and time lines. In general, the principles previously mentioned concerning the use of chalkboards and bulletin boards also apply to the use of charts. Clarity, simplicity, and dramatics are essential considerations. At the risk of a certain amount of repetition, we list the following suggestions:

1. Most of the charts used in classrooms should be the work of pupils who have found out the information, planned how to represent it, and executed the plan themselves.
2. Charts should be planned ahead. Sketch out the chart on a piece of paper before beginning the chart itself. Pencil in the details of the chart lightly before inking them in.
3. Make the chart simple. One major point is quite enough for a chart.
4. Make the chart clear. Avoid confusing detail. Do not crowd it. Use symbols one can understand.
5. Make charts eye-catching. Use colors and pictures.
6. Make charts forceful. Emphasize a central idea.
7. Be sure charts are visible. Make letters and symbols large enough. Leave plenty of white space so the message stands out.
8. Keep everything in proportion. Be careful of spacing.
9. Avoid too much printing and writing. Let the chart tell its own story. To avoid too much printing on the chart, use a legend and keyed symbols.

Tips on Graphs. Since graphs are a specialized type of chart, the suggestions for making and using graphs follow those for constructing and using charts. In addition the following tips may prove valuable:

1. Keep the graph in proportion. This is particularly important.
2. Don't try to show too much on the same graph. If you wish to show several phenomena, use several graphs.
3. Be sure to select units that fit your idea and your paper. In making pie graphs (circle graphs), note that one percent $= 3.6°$ ($100\% = 360°$).
4. Be sure there is a common base line for all phenomena represented. Have the base line start at zero.
5. Be sure the total to which individual items are compared is shown.
6. Use color coding to show contrast, comparisons, or growth. Be sure the key tells exactly what each symbol represents.
7. Be sure to credit your sources.
8. Be sure the title is brief but clear.

Flip Charts. Flip charts are used frequently in elementary schools, sales meetings, and television studios. They are really series of charts, set on a tripod, to illustrate points in the lesson. Certain map sets and series of biological charts are examples of commercially prepared flip charts. Homemade flip charts can be made on large pads such as those artists use for sketching. All one does is to prepare a series of charts on the pages of the pad so that you can flip the pages over as you need them. They should be used more in secondary schools.

The simplicity of the flip chart's design makes it possible to move back and forth easily from chart to chart as one desires. Separate charts, arranged in order on top of each other and mounted on an easel or even stood on a chalk tray, can be used in exactly the same way although they are usually a little more difficult to manage physically.

Pictures and Posters. A picture is worth a thousand words, it is said, so let's use them effectively and save ourselves some breath. They make excellent tools for clarifying and illustrating what one wishes to teach. They make good springboards for inquiry. They can be used for sparking interest in the topic. Sometimes an entire lesson can be built around a single picture.

In using pictures, there are no special techniques necessary. As in any other teaching, the teacher should try to guide the pupils. One of the best ways to do so is to ask questions that will guide pupils into interpreting. Another is to point out what pupils should look for and to explain its significance. The teacher must also be careful to use only pictures that are pertinent and useful. One must avoid showing pupils pictures just for the sake of showing them. Also, avoid passing pictures around the room while the class is in progress. When the pupils are looking at the pictures, they are no longer paying attention to the class instruction. It is better practice to use the opaque projector.

Finally, don't forget that most pictures in textbooks were put there because the author thought they shed light on the content being studied. Detailed study of the pictures in the texts, using controlled discussion, or open-ended questioning techniques may prove to be very rewarding.

When selecting a picture to show to the class, keep in mind the following criteria:

A picture should be suitable for the purpose, make an important contribution to the lesson, be accurate as to authenticity, be easy to understand, be interesting, and should be easily visible to the entire class.

Find a picture, poster, or other illustration. Build a lesson plan around it.

Posters have somewhat of an advantage over other pictures for display and instructional purposes. They are usually large and striking. Commercially printed or preprepared posters can be used in the same manner as other pictures. Making posters can be an interesting, worthwhile pupil activity. If you wish to use poster-making as one of your activities, do the following:

1. Discuss the possibilities with pupils.
2. Discuss the criteria of good poster-making.
   a. Aim at getting one idea across.
   b. Use as few words as possible.
   c. Make key words stand out. Use contrast, size, or color for this purpose.
   d. Keep the design simple.
   e. Leave plenty of white space.
3. Have pupils block out their designs on a sheet of paper, and get teacher approval of the design.
4. Let the pupils execute their own designs.

Teaching by Machine

The teaching machine acts as a sort of mechanical tutor that meets pupils in a one-to-one relationship. The machine does not teach, but rather presents a teaching program to the pupil. It is the teaching program that really does the teaching. The machine is just the delivery system, whether it is a high-powered computer or a simple programmed book.

The teaching program, which really does the teaching, is made up of the subject matter content arranged into a system so that it can be presented in a manner that will, supposedly, best utilize the principles of behavioristic psychology. Basically, there are two types of programs: *linear programs* and *branching* (or *extrinsic*) *programs.*

The difference between these types of programs is that the linear program

1. If you have not read the article, "Interaction Analysis in the Classroom," do so now before you continue.	1. When you have completed your reading, go to the next question.

2. The Flanders system of interaction analysis assumes that
  a. the verbal behavior of an individual is an adequate sample of his total behavior.
  b. nonverbal behavior is the only important index of classroom interaction.
 	
  a. ☐   b. ☐
	2. "a" is correct.

3. In this system, all teacher statements are classified as either _____ or _____	3. restrictive or encouraging
4. Restrictive or encouraging behavior indicates the amount of _____ the teacher gives the student.	4. freedom
5. The teacher has a _____ regarding behavior.	5. choice
6. If the teacher is restrictive, he _____ the freedom of the student to respond.	6. minimizes or limits
7. If the teacher is encouraging, he _____ the freedom of the student to respond.	7. maximizes

8. All of the statements which occur in the classroom are categorized in one of three major sections. These sections are:
 	
  1. _____
 	
  2. _____
 	
  3. _____
	8. teacher talk, student talk, and silence or confusion

Figure 11-1 *An Excerpt from a Linear Program.* [*Source:* Miles C. Olson. *Learning Interaction Analysis:* A Programmed Approach (Englewood, Colo.: Educational Consulting Associates, Inc., 1970).]

consists of a series of very easy frames or steps—steps so easy that the pupil progresses through the program without ever making a mistake. In the linear program, every pupil goes through exactly the same process. The branching program is made up of much larger and more difficult steps. If a pupil completes a frame successfully, he moves on to the next one. If he does not, then the program or machine reteaches him until he can answer the same or similar question or problem again. In effect, the pupil with the machine's aid builds himself an individual program as he goes along. In a sophisticated branching program, it is quite possible that no two pupils will complete exactly the same sequence of frames.

The procedures in both types of program have much in common:

1. The machine presents the pupil with some content and then asks him a question or puts a problem to him.
2. The pupil answers the question or solves the problem.
3. The machine corrects the pupil's answer and then tells him what to do next.
4. In the case of the linear program, the pupil always moves on to the next step. In the case of the branching or extrinsic program, if the pupil response is incorrect, the machine reteaches him and then either returns to the original question (or problem), or moves on to a different question calling for the same knowledge.

As a teaching strategy, programs have several real advantages. They have clearly defined objectives; they follow a carefully planned learning procedure; they keep the pupil actively involved in his own learning; they give the responsibility for learning and the rate of learning to the pupil, and they give the pupil immediate feedback concerning his progress.

Because they are flexible tutoring devices, teaching machines are ideally suited to individualizing instruction, and they relieve the teacher of some of the more tedious and mechanical teaching chores so that he can spend more time working at high-level activities. For instance, while some pupils are drilling on essential skills or learning basic content on the machine, teachers can work with other pupils individually or in small groups, or teachers can delegate the teaching of information to the machine so that he can concentrate on teaching the higher cognitive and thinking skills and processes that are apt to be neglected in ordinary classes.

Use teaching programs and teaching machines (including computer-assisted instruction) to individualize instruction, to teach basic skills and information, to provide pupils with the background necessary for discussion, inquiry, and problem-solving activities, and to free yourself for giving pupils individual attention and teaching them at the higher levels. When teaching with machines, it will be necessary for you to do the following:

1. Guide and supervise the pupils.
2. Continually check the pupils' progress.
3. Select suitable programs for individual pupils and see to it that the pupils go through these programs correctly.
4. Provide follow-up activities. (Programmed activities make good springboards, but teachers must provide the follow-up).

5. Provide other types of instruction. (Programmed teaching should not be overused. Some pupils find it boring.)
6. Evaluate pupil progress. (Programmed material is learning and practice material. It is not a test. It should never be graded. Teachers must provide other criteria—tests, papers, class discussion—to use as a basis for evaluation and reporting.)

Other kinds of self-administered, self-correcting materials are discussed in Module 7.

Sources of Teaching Materials

Ingenious teachers can find almost limitless supplies of teaching materials available from a host of sources. Much of this material is free for the asking, and other material is available for a small fee. To find out what is available, turn to your local curriculum guides and resources units and to those of other schools and communities. You will also find other publications, such as the bulletins of your state department of education and professional organizations, very helpful. Many educational periodicals list and review new materials. In addition, there are a number of reference works that specialize in listing instructional materials. Among the reference works that you might find useful are the following:

An Annotated Bibliography of Audiovisual Materials Related to Understanding and Teaching the Culturally Disadvantaged. Washington, D.C.: National Education Association.

Annual Paperbound Book Guide for High Schools. New York: R. R. Bowker Co.

Bibliography of Free and Inexpensive Materials for Economic Education. New York: Joint Council on Education.

Educational Film Guide. New York: H. W. Wilson Co.

Educator's Guide to Free Films. Randolph, Wis.: Educators Progress Service.

Educators' Guide to Free Film-Strips. Randolph, Wis.: Educators Progress Service.

Educators' Guide to Free and Inexpensive Teaching Materials. Randolph, Wis.: Educators' Progress Service.

Educators' Guide to Free Social Studies Materials. Randolph, Wis.: Educators Progress Service.

Film Guide for Music Educators. Washington, D.C.: Music Educators National Conference.

Free and Inexpensive Learning Materials. Nashville, Tenn.: Division of Surveys and Field Services, George Peabody College for Teachers.

Freedom, Florence B., and Esther L. Berg. *Classroom Teachers' Guide to Audio-Visual Material.* Philadelphia: Chilton Book Co., 1971.

Index to Multi-Ethnic Teaching Materials and Teaching Resources. Washington, D.C.: National Education Association.

Lembacher, James L. *Feature Films on 8mm and 16mm,* 3rd ed. New York: R. R. Bowker Co., 1971.

List of Free Materials Available to Secondary School Instructors. New York: The Educational Services of Dow Jones and Company, Inc.

Materials List for Use by Teachers of Modern Foreign Languages. New York: Modern Foreign Language Association.

Mathies, Lorraine. *Information Sources and Services in Education*. Bloomington, Ind.: The Phi Delta Kappa Educational Foundation, 1973.

Miller, Bruce. *Sources of Free and Inexpensive Pictures for the Classroom*. Riverside, Calif.: The Bruce Miller Publications.

————. *Sources of Free Travel Posters*. Riverside, Calif.: The Bruce Miller Publications.

————. *So You Want to Start a Picture File*. Riverside, Calif.: The Bruce Miller Publications.

National Tape Recording Catalog. Washington, D.C.: National Education Association.

Some Sources of 2x2-inch Color Slides. Rochester, N.Y.: Eastman Kodak Co.

Sources of Free and Inexpensive Pictures for the Classroom. Randolph, Wis.: Educators' Progress Services.

Sources of Slides and Filmstrips (S-9). Rochester, N.Y.: Eastman Kodak Co.

Free Materials in the Classroom. Washington, D.C.: Association for Supervision and Curriculum Development.

U.S. Government Films for Public Education Use, Superintendent of Documents. Washington, D.C.: Government Printing Office.

U.S. Government Printing Office. Thousands of publications and catalogs available.

Zuckerman, David W., and Robert E. Horn. *The Guide to Simulation/Games for Education and Training*. Lexington, Mass.: Information Resources, Inc., 1973.

The following periodicals are a sampling of those that carry information about instructional materials and how to procure them:

Audio-Visual Instruction
A V Communication Review
Educational Screen and Audio-Visual Guide
The English Journal
Journal of Business Education
Journal of Health Education, Physical Education and Recreation
Journal of Home Economics
Music Educators' Journal
The Mathematics Teacher
School Arts
The Science Teacher
Social Education
Social Studies

Browse through the list of materials included in some of the sources listed. Select free or inexpensive material that would be suitable for your courses. Write for it. Prepare a list of more expensive materials that seem to you highly promising.

Community As a Resource. The community itself may be the best of all the resources available to you. It can provide places and things to see first-hand in the field, and it can provide speakers and materials of instruction for use in the classroom. To take advantage of the many community resources available, every school needs a community resource file. If your school does not have one, you should collect information about resources yourself and record it on 5x8 cards. A central file would be more efficient, but a file of your own is usually well worth the effort. In it there should be such information as the following:

1. Possible field trips.
    a. What is there?
    b. How is location reached?
    c. Who handles arrangements?
    d. Expense involved?
    e. Time required?
    f. Other comments?
2. Resource people.
    a. Who are they?
    b. How they can help?
    c. Addresses?
3. Resource material and instructional materials obtainable locally.
    a. What is it?
    b. How is it procured?
    c. Expense involved?
4. Community groups.
    a. Names and addresses?
    b. Function and purpose?
    c. Type of thing with which they can help?
5. Local businesses, industries, and agencies.
    a. Name?
    b. Address?
    c. Key personnel?

Making One's Own Materials. Many teachers enjoy making their own teaching materials. Besides the duplicated materials so common in elementary and secondary school classes, teachers make slides, transparencies, tapes, and all sorts of audio and visual teaching aids. Doing so can be a great deal of fun and satisfaction. It also has the advantage of giving you the material you want, not what some professor or publisher thinks you want. Suggestions for making some of these aids are presented elsewhere in this volume, and in a number of references.

Obtaining Free and Inexpensive Materials

As we have pointed out, much material is available without cost. Pictures are available in a multitude of magazines. Commercial houses and government agencies have reams of printed material they would like to give you, and sometimes also samples, filmstrips, and other audio-visual materials. All that is required to obtain these materials is a letter of request. In your letter, state who you are, what you are asking for, and why you want it. Write your letter on official school stationery. Sometimes, it is useful to have pupils write the letter. If you have pupils do this, be sure to check over the letters to see that they meet the standards of good letter writing, and countersign it so that the recipients will know the request is valid.

Once you get the material, you must examine it carefully before using it with pupils. Some of the things will turn out to be useless and others so overladen with bias or sales pitch that they are impossible to use. In evaluating materials, use such criteria as the following:

1. Will the material really further educational objectives?
2. Is it free from objectionable advertising, propaganda, and so on?
3. Is it accurate, honest, free from bias (except when one wishes to illustrate dishonesty and bias, of course)?
4. Is it interesting, colorful, exciting?
5. Does it lend itself to school use?
6. Is it well made?

SUGGESTED READING

Alcorn, Marvin D., James S. Kinder, and Jim R. Schunert. *Better Teaching in Secondary Schools,* 3rd ed. New York: Holt, Rinehart & Winston, Inc., 1970. Chaps. 9–11.

Brown, James W., Richard B. Lewis, and Fred R. Harcleroad. *AV Instruction: Technology, Media, and Methods.* New York: McGraw-Hill Book Company, 1972.

Deterline, William A. *An Introduction to Programed Instruction.* Englewood Cliffs, N.J.: Prentice-Hall, Inc., 1962.

Eboch, Sidney C., and George W. Cochern. *Operating Audio-Visual Equipment,* 2nd ed. San Francisco: Chandler Publishing Co., 1970.

Ely, Donald, and Vernon S. Gerlach. *Teaching and Media.* Englewood Cliffs, N.J.: Prentice-Hall, Inc., 1971.

Erickson, Carlton W. H., and David H. Carl. *Fundamentals of Teaching with Audiovisual Technology,* 2nd ed. New York: Macmillan Publishing Co., Inc., 1972.

Grambs, Jean D., John C. Carr, and Robert M. Fitch. *Modern Methods in Secondary Education,* 3rd ed. New York: Holt, Rinehart & Winston, Inc., 1970. Chap. 6.

Haney, John B., and Eldon J. Ullmer. *Educational Media and the Teacher.* Dubuque, Iowa: William C. Brown Co., Publishers, 1970.

Hoover, Kenneth H. *The Professional Teacher's Handbook.* Boston: Allyn & Bacon, Inc., 1973. Chap. 16.

National Society for the Study of Education, *Media and Symbols: The Forms of Expression, Communication, and Education,* Seventy-Third Yearbook, Part I. Chicago: The University of Chicago Press, 1974.

Wittich, Walter A., and Charles F. Schuller. *Instructional Technology: Its Nature and Use,* 5th ed. New York: Harper and Row, Publishers, 1973.

POST TEST

1. The textbook should not dominate your teaching. How should you use it?

_____

2. In selecting a textbook, what should you look for?

_____

_____

_____

_____

3. How does one conduct a multitext approach?

_____

_____

_____

_____

_____

_____

_____

_____

4. What has been the great advantage of the paperback?

_____

_____

_____

5. In selecting a workbook, what particularly should you look for?

_____

_____

_____

6. What sort of things can you use for springboard material?

_____

_____

7. What is the purpose of a study guide?

_____

_____

8. In speaking of chalkboards and bulletin boards, it is recommended that one leave plenty of white space. What is meant by white space? Why should you leave plenty of it?

_____

_____

9. Flannel boards are supposedly much more effective than chalkboards. Why?

_____

10. How do you make the material to put on a flannel board?

_____

_____

_____

11. How can you get the most benefit out of a bulletin board?

_____

12. How can you make a bulletin board or chart forceful?

_____

_____

_____

_____

13. What is a flip chart?

_____

_____

14. How do you use it?

_____

_____

15. Why use pictures in your teaching? But why not pass them around the room during a class?

_____

_____

_____

16. What is the difference between a linear program and a branching (extrinsic) program?

_____

_____

_____

_____

17. What would you include in a community resource file?

_____

_____

_____

18. Teaching machines and programs should make it possible for teachers to concentrate on higher learning in their teaching. Why?

_____

_____

_____

Becoming a Professional

Leonard H. Clark

Jersey City State College

module 12

Learning to Be a Professional / Analysis of Teaching / Evaluating Specific Teaching Techniques / Pupil Evaluation

RATIONALE

In this module, we shall briefly examine what it means to be a professional, and discuss some ways to examine our own teaching as a means to becoming a "real pro." It is hoped that by studying the module, you will not only learn some techniques for self-examination (we shall point out to you some avenues by which you can reach truly professional status), but that you will reinforce some of the things that it was hoped you would learn in other modules.

SPECIFIC OBJECTIVES

Specifically, it is hoped that at the completion of the module you will be able to do the following:

1. Define what it is to be a truly professional teacher.
2. Describe what is meant by an open style of teaching.
3. List the variables that might be considered when selecting one's teaching strategies and tactics.
4. Explain the practical importance of pedagogical theory to the teacher.
5. Describe how to conduct each of the various methods of analysis and self-evaluation techniques discussed in the module.

MODULE TEXT

In the past few years, rapid changes in values and customs plus the tendency to bind the meaning of words to suit the purposes and prejudices and sometimes ulterior motives of many individuals have greatly diluted the meaning of the word *professional*. In this module, we define a professional as a person who is a master of specialized skills and who has both practical and theoretical knowledge that laymen do not have. Because of these specialized skills and knowledge, he can provide specialized services of a high order and cope with problem situations that are far beyond the abilities of an amateur or artisan.

The professional differs from the artisan in that his expertise is based on scholarship and theoretical considerations rather than simply on empiricism. Artisans can become expert through practice or apprenticeship but a professional must become well versed in theoretical knowledge in addition to the practical knowledge of the artisan. His deep theoretical knowledge and skill make it possible for him to handle difficult matters far beyond the capabilities of the artisan. An example of the difference between the artisan and the professional is the difference between a midwife and an obstetrician. The midwife is sufficient for most births, but when there is a great problem, the know-how and know-why of the obstetrician is what is needed. Another example is the difference between the carpenter and the architect.

Perhaps the example used by Harry Broudy in a speech at the 1967 convention of the American Association of Colleges of Teacher Education is more suitable for our use, because it describes the difference between a professional and an artisan teacher. In his example, Broudy compared three teachers who taught equally well. Of these three, Teacher A taught as she did in various situations as a result of intuition; Teacher B taught as she did because she followed the rule: in such a situation do thus and so; but Teacher C taught as she did because of theoretical reasons. She was the only one who knew why she took the various steps that she took. In this example, Teacher C, who knew why, was a professional; Teacher B, who blindly followed the rule, was a craftsman; and Teacher A, who taught well by following her impulses, was a miracle.[1] When the chips are down, the teacher you would want for your child would be Teacher C, the professional.

Perhaps the connotation of professional that we are trying to describe is best expressed by the slang expression a "real pro." As we pointed out in another context, in our estimation a "real pro" is truly competent in what he does. He is well prepared in the three essentials for teaching—he knows his pupils, his subject, and how to teach. He has mastered a vast repertoire of techniques and strategies and can adapt them skillfully to whatever type of teaching situation he faces. He has learned how to get the most out of his pupils and to adapt the curriculum to their needs and abilities. In short, he is a master teacher.[2] You should try to become a real pro just as soon as you can.

Learning to Be a Professional

Developing a Teaching Style. Every teacher develops a style of teaching that is his own and with which he feels most comfortable. This teaching style is a combination of his personality, plus the amount of expertise he has in teaching technology (methods, etc.), his subject matter, and pedagogical theory. As a beginning teacher, it is important to you not to let yourself become committed to a particular style too soon. Evidently, the most effective teachers are those who can vary their styles, or whose styles are so flexible that they encompass a great number of strategies and tactics, and are therefore readily adaptable to the different sorts of teaching-learning situations that may develop. Ned Flanders, for instance, found evidence indicating that indirect teachers are usually more effective than direct teachers, not because indirect teachers never teach in a direct style, but because they can teach both directly and indirectly better than direct teachers. One reason the indirect teachers seemed to be more effective is that they could teach both directly and indirectly, and could select and use the strategy or tactic most appropriate under the circumstances. Another reason is that the use of indirect teaching techniques secures more active pupil involvement. A somewhat oversimplified definition of direct and indirect teaching is that direct teaching is the

[1] Leonard H. Clark, *Strategies and Tactics in Secondary School Teaching* (New York: Macmillan Publishing Co., Inc., 1968), p. 1.

[2] Leonard H. Clark and Irving S. Starr, *Secondary School Teaching Methods,* 3rd ed. (New York: Macmillan Publishing Co., Inc., 1967), pp. 405–406.

type in which teachers tell pupils directly, but indirect is the type in which teachers try to get pupils to find out and think out things themselves. The indirect type of teaching style requires one to develop a feeling for the appropriateness of various techniques and methods for various kinds of learning situations, and expertise in a large variety of methods, as well as a good command of one's subject matter and an understanding of pupils one is teaching. This sounds like a large order, but many beginning teachers become adept at all of its facets surprisingly soon.

The point of all this is, of course, that you should try to develop an open style of teaching that allows you to be flexible and adaptable. To do so, you must master as many different techniques as you can. It is not too soon to start now. Do not let yourself become handicapped by having only a limited repertory of teaching techniques and methods to work with.

Which of the following techniques are you proficient in? Discussion; small group work; guided (controlled) discussion; committee; formal discussion, such as debate, jury, british debate; inquiry, including controlled discussion, Socratic discussion, springboard, and project; questioning, including probing, divergent, evaluative, and convergent; role playing such as simulation or dramatization.

Observe the teaching of a number of different teachers. What differences in style do you note? What qualities would you like to study?

Building a Teaching Repertory. To master teaching techniques, one must learn how to conduct them and when to use them. Learning how to use them implies that one must practice using them. As a new teacher, you should try out and master new techniques. Too many methods too fast may confuse both the pupils and you. So you should make haste slowly as you introduce new techniques to your methodological repertory, but you should try them.

Sometimes the methods you introduce may fail. If that happens, do not be discouraged and do not give up on the method. When a strategy or tactic fails, it is seldom the fault of the technique but of the human being who used it. Methods and techniques, strategies and tactics in themselves are neither bad nor good. It is how they are used that makes the difference. If you use a method inappropriate for the type of pupils, or the goals, or content, or other factors in the teaching-learning situation, you can expect the method to fail, but it is not the fault of the method. Similarly, if you have not developed skill in the use of the method or if you have not laid sufficient groundwork for it, the method may fail. Again, the fault is not in the method or technique, but in its use. So if at first a method does not succeed, try to determine why it failed, and then try it again.

Selecting the Right Strategies. The success of the methods you use depends not only on your skill, but also on your ability to select the right method or technique for your teaching objectives and subject matter. The tactics and strategies one uses for teaching information are not necessarily the tactics that one should use to teach concepts, or appreciations, attitudes, ideals, or skills. Pupils can and do learn information from teacher presentations, but concepts must be developed by allowing the pupil to look at, feel, handle, and otherwise consider the idea and examples of the idea in a number of contexts. Skills are developed by practice, preferably guided practice, and attitudes are developed slowly by providing models and techniques that enhance their desirability. Among the many tactics and techniques available

Use this form to analyze the class you thought went best this day.

1. Do you feel good about this class? Why, or why not?

2. In what way was the lesson most successful?

3. If you were to teach this lesson again, what would you do differently? Why?

4. Was your plan adequate? In what ways would you change it?

5. Did you achieve your major objectives?

6. Was the class atmosphere pleasant, productive, and supportive?

7. Were there signs of strain or misbehavior? If so, what do you think was the cause?

8. How much class participation was there?

9. Which pupils did extremely well?

10. Were there pupils who did not learn? How might you help them?

11. Were the provisions for motivation adequate?

12. Was the lesson individualized so that pupils had opportunities to learn according to their abilities, interests, and needs?

13. Did the pupils have any opportunities to think?

Figure 12-1 *Self-analysis of a Lesson.*

to you, some are best suited for clarifying ideas, presenting new information, showing pupils how to do things, influencing attitudes, ideals, or appreciations, motivating pupils, evaluating, guiding work in progress, or arousing emotions.

The chart in Figure 12-1 sets forth some examples of the types of goals for which some methods seem most useful.

One needs also to adapt tactics to the pupils. The approaches we use should be interesting to them, neither too difficult nor too easy, and, of course, relevant to their lives. It is necessary to become skilled in methods of diagnosis and techniques for learning about pupils.

Route to Professionalism. To master this type of know-how, it will be necessary to learn much more of the theory behind the various methods than we have been able to discuss in these modules. To become more proficient, teachers take many different routes, such as graduate study, workshops, independent study, curriculum committee work, action research, and professional conferences. The essential point is that all of them are working to improve teaching competencies. One is never too old to learn in the teaching profession. And one is never old enough to let himself become locked into a rigid teaching style. You should always be ready to renew and revamp your style. Who knows, you may find a revised style more comfortable, and new strategies and tactics may make you more interesting. While you are still in training, it would be helpful for you to observe as many different teachers as you can to observe many different styles and strategies in action. You should also avail yourself of every chance you can to try out various techniques and examine your performance in them. Minilessons are excellent for this.

Analysis of Teaching

The examined life is always better than the unexamined life, philosophers tell us. If one knows himself, there is little doubt that the knowledge is beneficial to him as a teacher. Therefore, those who wish to become really professional should examine themselves and their teaching every once in a while. By so doing, it may be possible to detect weaknesses in our classroom behavior and teaching techniques that we can remedy and to discover unrealized strengths on which we can capitalize. In this section of the module, we shall discuss a number of methods by which to examine our own teaching behavior in the classroom. We should like you to learn to examine yourself and your personality in other ways as well, but that would be far beyond the scope of this short module. Neither shall we have the

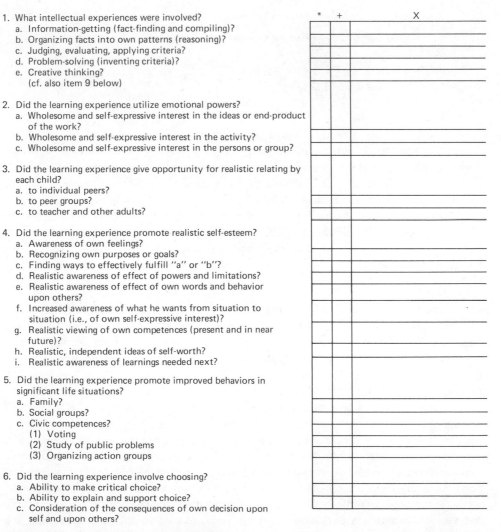

1. What intellectual experiences were involved?
   a. Information-getting (fact-finding and compiling)?
   b. Organizing facts into own patterns (reasoning)?
   c. Judging, evaluating, applying criteria?
   d. Problem-solving (inventing criteria)?
   e. Creative thinking?
      (cf. also item 9 below)

2. Did the learning experience utilize emotional powers?
   a. Wholesome and self-expressive interest in the ideas or end-product of the work?
   b. Wholesome and self-expressive interest in the activity?
   c. Wholesome and self-expressive interest in the persons or group?

3. Did the learning experience give opportunity for realistic relating by each child?
   a. to individual peers?
   b. to peer groups?
   c. to teacher and other adults?

4. Did the learning experience promote realistic self-esteem?
   a. Awareness of own feelings?
   b. Recognizing own purposes or goals?
   c. Finding ways to effectively fulfill "a" or "b"?
   d. Realistic awareness of effect of powers and limitations?
   e. Realistic awareness of effect of own words and behavior upon others?
   f. Increased awareness of what he wants from situation to situation (i.e., of own self-expressive interest)?
   g. Realistic viewing of own competences (present and in near future)?
   h. Realistic, independent ideas of self-worth?
   i. Realistic awareness of learnings needed next?

5. Did the learning experience promote improved behaviors in significant life situations?
   a. Family?
   b. Social groups?
   c. Civic competences?
      (1) Voting
      (2) Study of public problems
      (3) Organizing action groups

6. Did the learning experience involve choosing?
   a. Ability to make critical choice?
   b. Ability to explain and support choice?
   c. Consideration of the consequences of own decision upon self and upon others?

Figure 12-2 *Criteria for an Educational Experience.* [*Source:* J. A. Vanderpol, Jersey City State College, Unpublished Manuscript.]

7. Did the learning experience improve understanding of how own mind works?
   a. Such mind-needs as 'who, how, what, why, when, where, so what'?
   b. Basic outlines or structures of ideas (peg ideas) into which many future ideas will be organized?
   c. Logical reasoning patterns such as 'if. . ., then. . .' thinking; or of 'Are there any alternative answers?'
   d. Examining evidence or making careful generalizations or asking for needed 'date'?
   e. Recognizing own bias or error or mistaken idea?
   f. Considering what thoughts, feelings, and actions will be changed in the future?
   g. Applying the new learning or idea to many situations or kinds of ideas?
   h. Increased readiness for 'more of same' ideas or activities

8. Did the learning experience promote realistic concepts of others?
   a. Awareness of others' feelings?
   b. Recognizing others' purposes or goals?
   c. Finding ways to effectively fulfill 'a' or 'b'?
   d. Realistic awareness and acceptance of others' powers and limitations?
   e. Realistic expectations from others?
   f. Realistic awareness of effect on own words and behaviors upon others?
   q. Increased awareness of what he 'wants' from situation to situation?

9. What intellectual skills or competences have been forwarded?
   a. Speaking skills?
   b. Writing skills?
   c. Reading skills?
   d. Arithmetical skills?
   e. Eye-hand muscular coordination?
   f. Discriminating discussion skills?

10. Did each child experience a feeling of achievement?

11. Did the experience provide for teacher-pupil conferences and constant re-evaluations?

*	+	X

* Insert M for much; or S for some; or L for little; or N for none.

+ Insert A for all children; M for most children; F for few children; N for no children;

X List specific next steps the teacher will take to improve the learning experience.

Figure 12-2 *(Continued)*

time and space to look at the more sophisticated means by which to examine one's teaching. Most of the procedures you will study here are rather simple methods of analyzing or evaluating teaching. It is hoped that they will not only give you a basis for examining your own teaching, but will also serve as a means for reviewing some of the strategies and tactics discussed in earlier modules.

Analyzing Your Lessons. In order to keep out of ruts, you should occasionally stop to examine your lessons. The simplest way to do this is to stop and think back over a lesson and ask yourself how it went and why. Usually, it is best to pick good lessons to examine so that you can see what you are doing well. The practice is good for the ego and tends to reinforce your good traits. From time to time, you will want to examine classes that failed, to see if you can figure out why they did not go well. If you are having trouble with a class, such an analysis may help you spot the difficulty and correct the errors that you may have been making.

Rate yourself   5, 4, 3, 2, 1   5 is best

1. Did I look O.K.?

2. Did I sound O.K.?

3. Did I make my point?

4. Was I clear?

5. Did I make them think?

6. Is my questioning technique O.K.?

7. Is my blackboard work O.K.?

8. Is my audio-visual O.K.?

9. Did the lesson develop logically?

10. Overall rating

Figure 12-3 *Rating Scale Designed by Teaching Internes.*

In this type of analysis, as you review your lesson, ask yourself such questions as What went well? What went badly? Why? What could I have done to improve the lesson? Next time, how should I handle this type of class? A questionnaire, such as that portrayed in Figure 12-1, should prove very helpful in this reviewing of your procedures. Rating scales and check lists are also useful, but probably not as useful as the open-ended questionnaire. Figure 12-2 is an example of a rating scale used in rating the teaching experiences of teaching internes and student teachers. Figure 12-3 is a rating scale devised by a group of prospective student

Level   Performance

I.   Imitating, duplicating, repeating.

      This is the level of initial contact. Student can repeat or duplicate what has just been said, done, or read. Indicates that student is at least conscious or aware of contact with a particular concept or process.

II.   Level I, plus recognizing, identifying, remembering, recalling, classifying.

      To perform on this level, the student must be able to recognize or identify the concept or process when encountered later, or to remember or recall the essential features of the concept or process.

III. Levels I and II, plus comparing, relating, discriminating, reformulating, illustrating.

      Here the student can compare and relate this concept or process with other concepts or processes and make discriminations. He can formulate in his own words a definition, and he can illustrate or give examples.

IV.   Levels I, II, and III, plus explaining, justifying, predicting, estimating, interpreting, making critical judgments, drawing inferences.

      On the basis of his understanding of a concept or process, he can make explanations, give reasons, make predictions, interpret, estimate, or make critical judgments. This performance represents a high level of understanding.

V.   Levels I, II, III, and IV, plus creating, discovering, reorganizing, formulating new hypotheses, new questions, and problems.

      This is the level of original and productive thinking. The student's understanding has developed to such a point that he can make discoveries that are new to him and can restructure and reorganize his knowledge on the basis of his new discoveries and new insights.

Figure 12-4 *Levels of Performance.* [*Source:* James M. Bradfield and H. Stewart More-dock, *Measurement and Evaluation in Education* (New York: Macmillan Publishing Co., Inc., 1957), p. 204.]

1. The Objective

    a. The objective is clearly stated.

    b. The objective is measurable.

    c. The objective is pertinent to the unit and course.

    d. The objective is worthwhile.

    e. The objective is suitable to the pupils' age and grade level.

    f. The objective can be achieved in the time alloted.

    g. The objective can be attained in different degrees and/or amounts.

    h. The objective is relevant to the pupils' lives.

2. The Procedure or Suggested Activities

    a. The suggested activities will stimulate pupils' thinking.

    b. The suggested activities will produce the objectives.

    c. The procedure is outlined in sufficient detail to be followed easily.

    d. The procedure allows for individual differences.
       (1) choice in required work
       (2) optional work for enrichment
       (3) encouragement of initiative

    e. The activities in the procedure are interesting and appealing enough to arouse pupil motivation.

    f. The activites relate to
       (1) the aims of the pupils
       (2) the needs of the pupils
       (3) work in other courses
       (4) extracurricular life
       (5) out-of-school life
       (6) community needs and expectancies.

Figure 12-5 *Form for Evaluating Lesson Plans.*

teachers as a means of rating their teaching during student teaching. Perhaps you could develop a better one yourself.

Another way to check on your teaching is to consider at what level your pupils have learned. According to Bradfield and Moredock, there are five levels of performance. These levels are set forth in Figure 12-4. Ideally, the pupils should attain the highest levels of learning in your units. Examine your teaching. Is it the type that should bring pupils to this high level of learning? Or does it handcuff them to the lower levels?

Another way to upgrade your teaching is to examine your lesson plans. Presumably, the better your lesson plans, the better your teaching will be. Perhaps the form included as Figure 12-5 will help you to evaluate your plans. With a little adjustment, it could be used to evaluate unit and course plans. When using this form, remember that all of the characteristics may not be necessary for every lesson plan, but that in the long run teachers whose lessons do not meet these criteria cannot be fully effective.

Audio and Video Feedback. Both audio- and video-tapes of your classes can be a great help to you as you examine your teaching and personality. Although at first the presence of the tape recorder or camera may make you nervous and self-conscious, the feeling will soon wear off. Then the camera or recorder can get a good record of what you look like and sound like as you teach. You can and should use this record as a basis for detailed analysis of your teaching, but just

Motivating

Planning

Informing

Leading discussion

Disciplining

Counseling

Evaluating

Other

Figure 12-6   *Types of Teaching Activities (Five-second Interval Tallies).*

listening to and seeing yourself may give you important insights into your own teaching behavior. If your self-observation is done thoughtfully and critically, it will, of course, be more rewarding than if it is superficial. Using a simple questionnaire in which you ask yourself such questions as the following may make your self-observation more useful: What are my best points? What points are fairly good? What points are not so good? Are my explanations clear? Do I speak well and clearly? Do I speak in a monotone? Do I slur my words? Do my sentences drop off so that ends are difficult to hear? Do I involve everyone in the class or do I direct my teaching only to a few? Are my questions clear and unambiguous? Do I use broad or narrow questions? Do I dominate class discussion? Do I allow certain pupils to dominate the class?

Make a list of check questions that you might use to evaluate your own teaching.

A usually more profitable use of the recording device is to apply interaction analysis techniques to recording of your own teaching. Such self-evaluation may be more illuminating than simple critical listening to your recordings or hearing the criticisms and comments of an observer.

According to one analysis, there are seven major types of teaching operations: motivating, planning, informing, leading discussion, disciplining, counseling, and evaluating. One way to evaluate your teaching would be to check on a form, such as that shown in Figure 12-6, the type of teaching you were doing every five seconds in one of your classes. In this form an eighth category has been added for operations that do not seem to fit into any of the seven listed.

Interaction Analysis. There are a number of methods by which one can analyze the student-teacher interaction in a class. All of these methods require the services of either an observer or an audio- or video-recorder. Interaction analysis is valuable because it gives one an indication of just who is doing the talking in the class. From it one can learn whether or not the class is teacher-dominated or pupil-dominated, free and open or repressive, and whether the teaching style is direct or indirect—in short, the general tenor of the classroom atmosphere and type of learning that is going on. As a rule of thumb, one can safely assume that when classes are satisfactory, the interaction will show that pupils actively participate at least half of the time. (If the teacher finds himself to be talking more than half of the time, he should check his procedures.)

As far as possible, every pupil participates in some way. (Classes that are dominated by only a few pupils are hardly satisfactory.)

A good share of the classtime is given over to thoughtful, creative activity rather than to mere recitation of information by either teacher or pupils.

Interaction analysis schemes vary from the simple to the complex. The more complex schemes, as one would expect, usually give more dependable information but are more difficult to use. The V.I.C.S. (Verbal Interaction Category System) adaptation of the Flanders system of interaction analysis, for instance, consists of twelve categories and a number of subcategories, as shown in Figure 12-7.

Teacher-Initiated Talk	1. Gives Information or Opinion: presents content or own ideas, explains, orients, asks rhetorical questions. May be short statements or extended lecture.
	2. Gives Direction: tells pupil to take some specific action; gives orders; commands.
	3. Asks Narrow Question: asks drill questions, questions requiring one or two word replies or yes-or-no answers; questions to which the specific nature of the response can be predicted.
	4. Asks Broad Question: asks relatively open-ended questions which call for unpredictable responses; questions which are thought-provoking. Apt to elicit a longer response than 3.
Teacher Response	5. Accepts: (5a) Ideas: reflects, clarifies, encourages or praises ideas of pupils. Summarizes, or comments without rejection.
	(5b) Behavior: responds in ways which commend or encourage pupil behavior.
	(5c) Feeling: responds in ways which reflect or encourage expression of pupil feeling.
	6. Rejects: (6a) Ideas: criticizes, ignores or discourages pupil ideas.
	(6b) Behavior: discourages or criticizes pupil behavior. Designed to stop undesirable behavior. May be stated in question form, but differentiated from category 3 or 4, and from category 2, Gives Direction, by tone of voice and resultant effect on pupils.
	(6c) Feeling: ignores, discourages or rejects pupil expression of feeling.
Pupil Response	7. Responds to Teacher: (7a) Predictably: relatively short replies, usually, which follow category 3. May also follow category 2, i.e. "David, you may read next."
	(7b) Unpredictably: replies which usually follow category 4.
	8. Responds to Another Pupil: replies occurring in conversation between pupils.
Pupil-Initiated Talk	9. Initiates Talk to Teacher: statements which pupils direct to teacher without solicitation from teacher.
	10. Initiates Talk to Another Pupil: statements which pupils direct to another pupil which are not solicited.
Other	11. Silence: pauses or short periods of silence during a time of classroom conversation.
	Z. Confusion: considerable noise which disrupts planned activities. This category may accompany other categories or may totally preclude the use of other categories.

Figure 12-7 *The Verbal Interaction Category System (VICS).* [*Source:* Edmund Amidon and Elizabeth Hunter, *Improving Teaching.* (New York: Holt, Rinehart and Winston, Inc., 1966), p. 11.]

Those such as the V.I.C.S. and the Flanders systems usually require that the observation be done by trained observers. In the V.I.C.S. system, for instance, the observer notes what type of action is happening. Upon completing the observation, he arranges his findings into a matrix from which he can tell not only what happened but what the atmosphere of the class was. This system and the Flanders system from which it was adapted can give you an excellent picture of the interaction in the classroom that may lead to important insights into your own teaching. If you tape record the class, it is possible to apply the analysis to the class without the use of an outside observer. Therefore, it would be very advantageous for you to learn how to use this system of interaction analysis. Unfortunately, we do not have the space to go into the procedure in detail in this module.

Even though they are not so useful as the more sophisticated method, simple interaction analysis techniques can be truly helpful. The picture they give is not as clear, but it will show up glaring faults and give indications of more subtle elements of the classroom interaction and atmosphere.

Probably the simplest type of classroom interaction analysis is for an observer to mark down on a sheet of paper every time the teacher talks and every time a pupil talks, as T P T T T P T T T P P T T. This record shows how much the teacher talks as compared to how much the pupils talk, although it will not show how long they talk.

If a classroom analysis of one of your typical classes consists almost entirely of T's, what would it show about your teaching? Does this analysis indicate that perhaps you should consider changing your style?

A more complex refinement of this technique is for an observer to sit at the back of the class and to record the number of times each person speaks. This technique gives you a much clearer picture of what is happening in the class. The disadvantage of this technique is that it requires an outside observer. Neither audio- nor video-tapes of the type we could procure in the ordinary classroom situation would be usable for such an analysis. Figure 12-9 is an illustration of

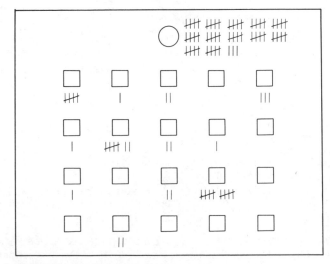

Figure 12-8 *A Form of Interaction Analysis.*

the tallying by this method of interaction analysis. In this figure, the teacher is represented by a circle, and the pupils by squares.

Do the tallies in Figure 12-8 give you any inkling about the style of the teacher in this class? How about the class participation? In general, what does the chart tell you about this class?

Another version of the form of analysis just described is for the observer to record who is talking every five seconds. This variation of the tallying approach has the advantage of showing what persons are interacting and how much they talk, although it does not give as complete a picture as the V.I.C.S. or Flanders analysis system.

Some supervisors use a simplified version of the Flanders system for analyzing interaction. In this version, the observer records the type of interaction going on in the class at regular intervals, but does not convert the tallies into a matrix. This simplified process does not give one as clear an analysis as the complete system does, but it is very useful for a quick rundown of what is going on in the classroom. The categories in the Flanders system are noted in Figure 12-9.

Teacher Talk	Indirect Influence	1. ACCEPTS FEELING: accepts and clarifies the feeling tone of the students in a nonthreatening manner. Feelings may be positive or negative. Predicting and recalling feelings are included. 2. PRAISES OR ENCOURAGES: praises or encourages student action or behavior. Jokes that release tension, not at the expense of another individual, nodding head or saying "uhhuh?" or "go on" are included. 3. ACCEPTS OR USES IDEAS OF STUDENT: clarifying, building, or developing ideas or suggestions by a student. As teacher brings more of his own ideas into play, shift to category five. 4. ASKS QUESTIONS: asking a question about content or procedure with the intent that a student answer.
	Direct Influence	5. LECTURES: giving facts or opinions about content or procedure; expressing his own idea; asking rhetorical questions. 6. GIVES DIRECTIONS: directions, commands, or orders with which a student is expected to comply. 7. CRITICIZES OR JUSTIFIES AUTHORITY: statements intended to change student behavior from nonacceptable to acceptable pattern; bawling someone out; stating why the teacher is doing what he is doing, extreme self-reference.
Student Talk		8. STUDENT TALK-RESPONSE: talk by students in response to teacher. Teacher initiates the contact or solicits student statement. 9. STUDENT TALK-INITIATION: talk by students, which they initiate. If "calling on" student is only to indicate who may talk next, observer must decide whether student wanted to talk. If he did, use this category.
		10. SILENCE OR CONFUSION: pauses, short periods of silence, and periods of confusion in which communication cannot be understood by the observer.

Figure 12-9 *Summary of Categories for Interaction Analysis.* [*Source:* Edmund J. Amidon, and Ned A. Flanders, *The Role of the Teacher in the Classroom.* (Minneapolis, Minn.: Paul S. Amidon and Associates, 1963), p. 15.]

Evaluating Specific Teaching Techniques

Evaluating One's Discussions. To improve your skill in using class discussions, you analyze the discussions that you lead. It is possible to do this in armchair fashion, but it would be more productive to react to a tape recording of the discussion. A self-evaluation form, similar to the one presented as Figure 12-10, should be very helpful for spotting one's weaknesses and building one's strengths in leading discussions.

Interaction analyses can also be used to study one's skill in conducting discussions. Any system that shows who is carrying the load of the discussion would be helpful. Flow charts that depict the course of the discussion are even more useful. Preparing the flow chart can be entrusted to a pupil observer since the technique for preparing one is so simple.

If the class is arranged in a circle, preparing the flow chart is easier; it is slightly less so if the class is arranged as a hollow square; but when the class is arranged in rows, making the chart becomes quite difficult. (Discussions are difficult to conduct when the pupils are in rows, too.) All the observer does is to make an arrow from the speaker to the person to whom he is speaking each time anyone speaks. A direct reply to a speaker can be noted by a double-headed arrow. Comments or questions that are directed to the group rather than to an individual are indicated by arrows that point to the center of the circle or square. An example of a flow chart showing a portion of a class discussion appears as Figure 12-11.

Figure 12-12 shows another device used to analyze class discussions. In this technique, a recorder simply tallies the number of times each person talks. There

A.

    1.   Did I have a legitimate objective?

    2.   Were the objectives suitable for the discussion technique?

    3.   Did I get good participation?

    4.   Did I encourage participation or did I tend to cut people off?

    5.   Did I keep from letting people dominate?

    6.   Did I encourage the shy, timid, etc.?

    7.   Did I keep the group to the subject?

    8.   Did I domineer or dominate?

    9.   In what did I best succeed?

   10.   In what was I least successful?

   11.   Did I solicit evocative questions and tentative solutions?

   12.   Did I summarize conclusions or positions so as to follow through and tie the discussion together?

B.

    1.   Identify the techniques that seemed to make the discussion effective.

    2.   Identify the techniques that seemed to detract from the effectiveness of the discussion.

Figure 12-10 *Self-evaluation Form for Discussion Leaders.*

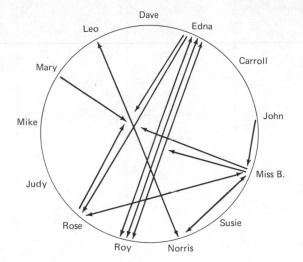

Figure 12-11

is no indication of the conversational interchanges so this type of record does not give one as complete a picture as the flow chart does. Essentially, this is the same technique illustrated by Figure 12-8.

Questions. Questions are among the teacher's most important tools; it is important to learn how to use them well. To check on your questioning technique, you might record and observe yourself. Among the things you might observe are the following:

1. What sorts of questions do I use?
2. Are my questions clear?
3. Do I ask one question at a time or do I confuse pupils by asking two or more questions as one?

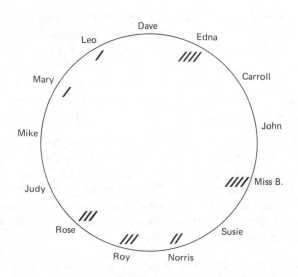

Figure 12-12

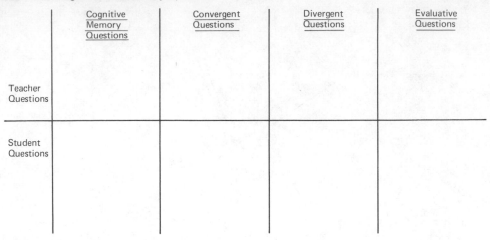

	Cognitive Memory Questions	Convergent Questions	Divergent Questions	Evaluative Questions
Teacher Questions				
Student Questions				

Figure 12-13 *A Form for Analyzing Questions.*

4. Do I ask real questions, or are my questions whiplash questions that start out as statements and then suddenly convert into questions, such as the point that the author was trying to get across is what? Whiplash questions are not really fair because they give pupils the wrong set.
5. Do my questions require pupils to use their knowledge, information, and ideas?
6. Do I direct my questions to pupils or to the class as a whole?
7. Do I wait until I have finished asking my question before calling on someone to answer it?
8. Do I follow up my question with probing questions to ferret out ideas, understandings, and thinking?

List other questions you might use to check your questioning technique. Refer to Module 3.

Construct a questionnaire and use it to analyze the use of questions in one of your own lessons or a lesson you observe.

Most questions in a typical class are aimed at eliciting memorized facts and information. When teachers do ask higher-order questions, the questions are likely to be convergent questions rather than divergent or evaluative questions. See Module 3 if you cannot remember what these are. To find out what type of questions you and your pupils use, a form similar to that presented as Figure 12-13 can be helpful. To use the form, an observer simply checks the appropriate column each time the teacher asks a question.

Probing Questions. Probing questions are used to follow up questions that originally elicit only superficial answers. According to Dwight Allen and his associates, this can be done in five ways: (1) asking pupils for more information or more meaning; (2) requiring the pupil to rationally justify his response; (3) refocusing the pupil's or class's attention on a related issue; (4) prompting the pupil or giving him hints; and (5) bringing other students into the discussion by getting them to respond to the first student's answer.[3]

---

[3] Dwight W. Allen, et al., *Technical Skills of Teaching*, rough draft proposal, Stanford University School of Education, July 24, 1967. (Mimeographed).

Objective	Item	Joe	Julia	Jim	Jane	Jean	Josie
1.	1	+	+	+	+	+	+
	2	+	0	+	+	+	+
	3	+	0	0	+	+	+
2.	4	+	0	0	0	0	+
	5	+	+	+	0	0	0
	6	0	+	0	+	0	0

+ correct answer
0 incorrect answer

Figure 12-14   *Example of Test Item Analysis Form.*

To check your use of probing questions, listen to a tape of one of your classes to observe whether or not you actually do follow up and what type of probing tactics you use. Ask yourself if these tactics were the best under the circumstances. Why, or why not?

Analysis of Test Results.   Analysis of pupils' test results can give one an inkling of the success of one's teaching, providing the tests are properly designed and written. For test results to be of value for the analysis of one's teaching success, the teaching objectives must be carefully defined and each test item must be aimed at a teaching objective. Once you have given and corrected the test, to analyze the test you must set up a chart which indicates what objective each test item tests, and what items each pupil got right ,as in Figure 12-14. Such a chart would show you how effectively you taught by indicating how well you achieved each of your objectives. In the example, for instance (Figure 12-14), if our small sample is any indicator, the teacher evidently was quiet successful with objective 1; not so successful with objective 2. This type of analysis is also an excellent tool by which to diagnose the progress of the various pupils in the class.

Key: + = correct response; 0 = incorrect response.

Pupil	Total score	1	2	3	4	5	6	7	8	9	10	11	12	13	14	15	16	17	18	19	20	21	22	23
Pat	95	+	+	+	+	+	+	0	0	+	+	+	0	+	+	+	+	+	0	0	0	+	+	+
Al	93	+	+	0	0	+	0	0	+	+	+	0	+	+	+	+	+	0	0	+	0	+	+	+
Carol	88	+	+	+	0	+	+	0	+	+	+	+	+	+	+	+	+	+	0	+	0	+	+	+
Lee	85	+	+	0	0	+	0	0	+	+	+	+	0	+	+	+	+	+	0	0	+	0	+	+
Tina	83	+	+	0	0	+	+	0	0	+	+	+	0	+	+	+	+	+	0	0	0	+	+	+
Linda G.	83	+	+	0	0	+	+	0	0	+	+	0	0	+	+	+	+	+	0	0	+	+	+	+
Tom	81	+	+	0	0	+	+	0	+	0	+	+	+	+	+	+	+	+	0	0	0	+	+	+
Ed	80	+	0	0	+	+	0	0	0	+	+	+	0	+	0	+	0	+	+	+	+	+	+	+
Barbara	80	+	+	0	0	+	0	0	0	+	+	0	+	0	0	0	0	+	0	0	0	+	+	+
Alfred	80	+	+	0	0	+	+	0	0	+	+	0	+	+	+	+	+	+	0	0	+	+	+	+
Linda B.	79	+	+	+	0	0	0	+	+	+	0	0	+	+	+	+	+	+	0	+	0	+	+	+
Mary	77	+	0	+	0	0	+	0	0	+	0	+	+	+	+	+	+	0	0	0	0	+	+	+
Vance	77	+	+	0	+	+	+	0	0	0	0	+	+	+	+	+	+	0	0	+	0	+	+	0
Mike	77	+	+	0	0	+	+	0	0	+	+	+	+	+	+	+	+	0	+	0	+	+	+	+
Fred	74	+	0	0	0	+	0	0	0	0	0	0	+	+	0	0	+	+	+	+	0	+	+	+
Bill	73	0	+	0	0	+	0	+	+	0	0	+	0	+	+	+	+	+	0	0	+	+	+	+
Joe	72	+	+	+	+	0	0	0	0	+	+	+	0	+	+	+	+	+	0	+	0	+	+	+
Tim	72	+	+	0	+	+	+	0	0	+	0	0	+	0	+	0	+	0	+	0	0	+	+	+
Steve	71	0	0	0	+	+	+	+	+	+	+	+	+	+	+	+	0	0	+	0	+	+	+
Bea	65	+	+	0	+	+	0	0	0	+	0	+	+	+	+	+	0	0	+	0	+	+	+
Joe	64	+	0	0	+	0	+	0	+	0	+	+	+	+	0	+	0	+	0	0	0	+	+	+
Carl	63	+	+	0	0	+	0	0	0	0	+	0	+	+	0	+	+	0	0	0	0	+	+	+

Figure 12-15   *Test Item Analysis.*

Problem: A test was given to a 10th grade class. Figure 12-15 shows the results for items 1 to 23. In this test items 1, 2, 21, 22, 23 test objective A; items 3, 4, 7, 18, 20 test objective B; items 5, 6, 8, 9, 13 test objective C; items 10, 11, 14, 15, 16 test objective D; items 12, 17, 19 test objective E. Interpret the test results

Pupil Evaluation

You can learn much from the pupils' opinions of your teaching. Just watching their reactions will be enlightening. An eager, enthusiastic, attentive class is a good sign; an apathetic, inattentive, antagonistic class is not. Another method by which to gather pupil evaluations is to use a simple questionnaire or opinion sampling. Some teachers make a practice of collecting such data at the end of the school year, but if you are to capitalize on the information, perhaps it would be better to collect it earlier in the year. Whenever you do it, make sure that the evaluations are entirely anonymous. To preserve anonymity, use check sheets rather than handwritten comments. Sometimes, however, pupils will react well to open-ended, free response questions if the questions ask for constructive criticism concerning ways to make the course more effective.

SUGGESTED READING

Allen, Paul, et al. *Teacher Self-Appraisal*. Worthington, Ohio: Charles A. Jones Publishing Co., 1970.

Amidon, Edmund J., and Elizabeth Hunter. *Improving Teaching*. New York: Holt, Rinehart & Winston, Inc., 1966.

Amidon, Edmund J., and Ned A. Flanders. *The Role of the Teacher in the Classroom*. Minneapolis: Paul S. Amidon and Associates, 1963.

Andrew, Michael D. *Teachers Should Be Human Too*. Washington, D.C.: Association of Teacher Educators, 1972.

Beegle, Charles W., and Richard M. Brandt, eds. *Observational Methods in the Classroom*. Washington, D.C.: Association for Supervision and Curriculum Development, 1973.

Sharp, D. Louise. *Why Teach?* New York: Holt, Rinehart & Winston, Inc., 1957.

Stinnett, T. M., and Albert J. Huggett. *Professional Problems of Teachers*, 2nd ed. New York: Macmillan Publishing Co., Inc., 1963.

Stuart, Jesse. *To Teach, To Love*. New York: Penguin Books, Inc., 1973.

Wilson, Charles H. *A Teacher Is a Person*. New York: Holt, Rinehart & Winston, Inc., 1956.

Wilson, Elizabeth C. *Needed: A New Kind of Teacher*. Bloomington, Ind.: The Phi Delta Kappa Educational Foundation, 1973.

POST TEST

1. What seems to be the principal difference between a professional teacher and an artisan teacher, according to Broudy?

_____

_____

2. Why does the indirect teacher seem to be more effective than the direct teacher?

_____

_____

3. Which seems to be preferable, a flexible or rigid teaching style?

_____

_____

4. Suppose you should try out a new teaching technique and it fails miserably for you. What should you do, according to this module?

_____

_____

5. Why is theoretical pedagogical knowledge important for the teacher?

_____

_____

6. According to Bradfield and Moredock, what is the highest level of teaching?

_____

_____

_____

7. List four of the eight criteria included in the forms for evaluating lesson plans.

_____

_____

_____

8. What is the purpose of recording and playing back your lessons?

_____

_____

9. An interaction analysis shows that most of the class consisted of teacher-initiated talk in which the teacher gave pupils information and asked narrow memory questions. If this class is typical of this teacher's style
  a. is she a direct or indirect teacher?
  b. is her style a most effective one?

_____

_____

_____

10. A simple interaction analysis tally shows the following: T T T T T P T P T
    P T T T T P T T P T T P T P T P T P.
    a. What does this show about the class?
    b. Is the class good or bad?

    _____

    _____

11. List six things you would look for in evaluating a discussion.

    _____

    _____

    _____

    _____

    _____

12. The flow chart of a discussion shows that there are only a few arrows from
    the teacher's position and all of these point to the center of the diagram. How
    would you interpret this phenomenon?

    _____

    _____

13. Why should you avoid using whiplash questions?

    _____

    _____

    _____

14. In what ways are cognitive memory questions, convergent questions, and
    divergent questions different?

    _____

    _____

    _____

    _____

    _____

    _____

15. In an item analysis, we find the following:

Objective	Item	Pupil					
		A	B	C	D	E	F
	1	+	+	+	+	+	+
1	2	+	+	+	+	+	+
	3	+	+	0	+	+	0
	4	0	0	+	0	0	0
2	5	0	0	0	0	0	0
	6	+	0	+	0	+	0

Assuming that this excerpt is typical of the entire test item analysis, what does it tell you?

_____

_____

_____

Post Test Answer Key

Module 1.1

1. a. Teachers have not really thought through what they are trying to do.
    b. Teachers have not thought about how they ought to do it so their teaching becomes inconsequential, irrelevant, and dull.
2. a. What should my objectives be?
    b. How should I try to achieve these objectives?
3. Select any four from this list:
    a. What do I want to accomplish?
    b. How can I accomplish it?
    c. Who is to do what?
    d. When and in what order should things be done?
    e. When will things be done?
    f. What materials and equipment will I need?
    g. How will I get things started?
    h. How shall I follow up?
    i. How can I tell how well I have accomplished my goals?
    j. Why?
4. Teachers do not ask themselves: why should the pupils have to study and learn this?
5. Pick your answers from this list:
    a. The curriculum
    b. Nature of the learners
    c. What do you have to work with?
    d. Nature of the community
    e. What the community expects
    f. The nature of the subject matter
6. Will it contribute to the achievement of the objectives?
7. General.
8. You should not.
9. The statement is preferred. A statement describing the terminal behavior of the learner (a behavioral objective) is considered best by many authorities.

10. Does it contribute to the objectives?
11. **a.** Suggested objectives.
    b. Suggested content.
    c. Suggested learning activities.
    d. Suggested reading.
    e. Suggested audio-visual and other materials of instruction for a course or curriculum.
12. It makes the coordination of teaching and learning activities easier.

Module 1.2

1. a, b, and h are behavioral objectives; c, d, e, f, and g are not.
2. A criterion-referenced behavioral objective is one that specifies the standards of behavior required.
3. **a.** They provide a clear objective for one's teaching.
   b. They provide definite bases for evaluation. Other objectives are too vague, it is claimed.
4. Terminal behavior is the behavior of the student at the end of and as a result of instruction.
5. A covert objective is a behavioral objective in which behavior cannot be observed directly.
6. Appreciate, comprehend, realize, and understand are covert; define, estimate, identify, organize, predict, recognize, solve, and write are covert.
7. a is quite general; b is very general; c is pretty specific; d is rather general; e is definitely specific; f is also specific; and g is quite general.
8. c and d are overt; a is covert; and b is iffy, but probably observable in most cases and, therefore, overt.
9. e, c, b, a, f, d
10. It gives you a framework by which to structure your teaching so as to ensure that it covers the more important types of learning.
11. **a.** Who?
    b. Does what?
    c. Under what conditions?
    d. How well?
12. **a.** Questionable. How accurate is accurate? But, yes.
    b. Yes
    c. Yes
    d. Yes

Module 1.3

1. You, the teacher.
2. **a.** Determine the objectives.
   b. Determine the course content including topic, sequence, and emphasis.
   c. Decide on the time allotment.
   d. Determine basic strategies, major assignments, and materials.

3. This means to organize the course on the basis of the nature of the learner rather than the nature of the discipline. Both must be considered, but the emphasis must be on the learner. There are several other characteristics of psychological organization that you should know, but they are not called for by the question. Look them up if you do not know them.

4. There are more than three possibilities. Your module text mentions the following. Take your pick.
   a. The value of the learning needs to be pointed out.
   b. The ways the learning can be used needs to be pointed out.
   c. The learning should be thorough. It is better to learn a lesser amount thoroughly than a lot superficially.
   d. The student should have occasion to draw generalizations and apply them.
   e. There should be many opportunities for renewal of the learning.

5. The over-all objective must be quite general although it may include very specific standards.

6. Allow yourself time for conflicts with assemblies or storms, and for units that run overtime. If you finish early, a little review or some good culminating lessons which tie things together will fill out and add to the course.

7. A textbook will give you a carefully thought out organization.

8. Too many teachers marry the text. After a couple of weeks textbook teaching can get very dull.

9. The steps are
   a. Prepare over-all course objectives.
   b. Determine the sequence of modules.
   c. Prepare general and specific objectives for the modules.
   d. Select content and learning procedures for the modules.
   e. Prepare learning packet for the modules.

10. a. Introduce course and planning.
    b. Set up limits.
    c. Set up criteria for topic selection.
    d. Select topics.
    e. Select problems to be studied in each unit.
    f. Make final decisions by discussion and consensus procedures.

Module 1.4

1. a. An ordinary unit made up of a series of lesson plans concentrated around a central topic.
   b. A true unit that consists of laboratory work.
   c. A learning packet or module.
   d. A learning contract.

2. Both.

3. Of course.

4. Yes, if you think it advisable.

5. Either. It's up to you. The trend at the moment is to favor behavioral objectives for everything.

6. Yes. Either approach is acceptable.

7. **a.** It is pertinent to the course.
   b. It centers on some major underlying issue, problem, or theme.
   c. It is not too difficult, too big, or too demanding of time or resources.
   d. It is relevant to pupils' lives and to the community.
   e. It is suitable to pupils' interests and abilities.

8. Pick four from the following:
   a. They really contribute to the larger (general) objectives of the course or unit.
   b. They should be clear to you and to your pupils.
   c. They should be specific enough.
   d. They should be achievable in the time and with the resources available.
   e. They should be worthwhile and seem worthwhile.
   f. They should allow for individual differences, that is, attainable in different amounts and in different ways.

9. **a.** Activities that motivate.
   b. Activities that tie in with past units and other course work.
   c. Planning units.

10. **a.** Introductory: to launch the unit of work, motivate, orient, and plan.
    b. Laboratory: to give pupils a chance to study on their own, both in small groups and as individuals.
    c. Sharing: to give pupils a chance to hear what others learned and to share ideas.
    d. Evaluative: to see how well pupils have progressed and to see how well the unit works.

11. The idea of the unit is for the pupils to learn through problem solving, each in his own way. The study guide should, therefore, present to the pupil problems relevant to the objectives and with directions telling him where he can learn. The pupils do not all have to study the same as long as they find a proper solution.

12. **a.** No. They can schedule themselves during the laboratory sessions.
    b. No. They do not all have to read the same material to solve the problems, for instance.

13. The learning packet is designed more for independent, individual self-study.

14. None, really.

15. Note the requirements for 1, 2, 3, and 4 on the study guide. Then have the pupil indicate which level he intends to shoot for.

16. **a.** Problems to be solved.
    b. Activities to do.
    c. Directions for finding information needed to solve problems and for doing the activities.
    d. Optional, related activities from which to select.
    e. Information concerning readings and materials.

17. **a.** Rationale including over-all objectives and reasons why this learning is worth study.
    b. Specific objectives.
    c. Directions for carrying out the activities to be included in the module.
    d. Materials needed for the module or directions for obtaining them.
    e. Measuring devices, such as pretests, progress tests, and post test.

Module 1.5

1. F. "The best laid plans of mice and men gang aft agley."
2. T. Not necessarily detailed written plans, but plans. Otherwise how do they know what to do and how to do it.
3. F. You must have more than subject matter in your head. The lesson plan outlines what and how to teach. In the beginning you had better have both a written objective and procedure.
4. T. You will develop your own style anyway. It would be nice if it should be appropriate to you.
5. F. Why not?
6. F. Not after several years.
7. T. Bring them up to date and smooth out the wrinkles.
8. F. Not really. There is no single most important element. If your overall conception is no good, the lesson plan will not save it.
9. T. Course or unit goals are usually general. Lesson plans should be specific.
10. F. That is a class period. A lesson begins when you begin it and ends when you end it.
11. F. If it is a good one, why not?
12. T. Use the one that suits you and your purposes best.
13. F. This one is iffy. Probably you could find something better to do as a follow-up, but studying in class under supervision is an excellent thing.
14. T. If you have made a careful plan, it is usually best to stick with it, but one should never marry a set plan until death do you part.
15. T. It may make all the difference.

Module 2

1. All sorts of information. Test scores, academic record, home information, extracurricular activities, and health information.
2. Open-ended.
3. To find out the pupil's interests, of course.
4. Looks like a clique.
5. M. is popular, maybe a natural leader.
6. There are a raft of possibilities. Take your pick from
    a. Provide a supportive atmosphere.
    b. Be sure it seems worthwhile.
    c. Keep things lively.
    d. Be sure they know what to do and how to do it.
    e. Take advantage of their motives.
    f. Try to run a happy ship.
    g. Introduce variety and novelty.
    h. Reinforce desirable activity.
    i. Be enthusiastic about what you teach.
    j. Personalize your teaching.
    k. Try to build trust.
    l. Try to use interesting strategies and tactics.

7. Reward.
8. Immediate.
9. A list of rewards which a person can choose if he does well.
10. Plutarch was pretty modern; his method is still theoretically sound.
11. Classes need order, quiet, and discipline. When anything goes (which is what the French phrase means), discipline, order, quiet, and learning go too.
12. Make the pupils aware of the advantages of high standards and the disadvantages of low standards. Value-clarifying techniques may help.
13. Tiresome, boring, irrelevant teaching and courses.
14. Sounds ridiculous to me. Try to be firm, businesslike, but pleasant.
15. No. Rigid rules may cut down on your options too much. A few simple ones would be much better.
16. It is much easier to relax after being strict than to try to become strict after being relaxed. Start off being quite strict and you will usually do better.
17. Making life miserable for a student while he is misbehaving and then removing the aversiveness the minute his behavior improves.
18. You set up an alternative behavior that is so rewarding the pupil gives up his misbehavior.

Module 3

What follows are suggested answers to Part I. Compare them to your own answers and consider the reasons for whatever differences may exist.

Questions	Poor	Fair	Good	Why?
1. In what region are major earthquakes located?		X		B
2. According to the theory of isostasy, how would you describe our mountainous regions?			X	C
3. What mineral will react with HCl to produce carbon dioxide?		X		B
4. What kind of rock is highly resistant to weathering?		X		B
5. Will the continents look different in the future and why?			X	C
6. Who can describe a continental shelf?	X			A
7. What caused The Industrial Revolution?			X	C
8. What political scandal involved President Harding?		X		B
9. This is a parallelogram, isn't it?	X			A
10. Wouldn't you agree that the base angles of an isosocles triangle are congruent?	X			A
11. In trying to determine the proof of this exercise, what would you suggest we examine at the outset?			X	C
12. What conclusion can be drawn concerning the points of intersection of two graphs?			X	C

Questions	Poor	Fair	Good	Why?
13. Why is pure water a poor conductor of electricity?		X		B
14. How do fossils help explain the theory of continental drift?			X	C
15. If Macbeth told you about his encounter with the apparitions, what advice would you have offered?			X	C
16. Who said, "if it were done when 'tis done, then 'twere well if it were done quickly"?		X		B
17. In the poem, "The Sick Rose," what do you think Blake means by "the invisible worm"?			X	C
18. Should teachers censor the books which students read?			X	C
19. Explain the phrase, "Ontogeny recapitulates Philogeny."			X	C
20. What are the ten life functions?	X			B
21. What living thing can live without air?	X			B
22. What is chlorophyll?	X			B
23. Explain the difference between RNA and DNA.			X	C
24. Who developed the periodic table based on the fact that elements are functions of their atomic weight?		X		B

II.

1. For several reasons (check the module), but principally because pupils are receivers rather than doers and, as a result, seldom learn as well by this method as by others.

2. The module suggests the following:
   a. State purpose.
   b. Be logical.
   c. Include clues to development.
   d. Avoid attempting too much.
   e. Begin with an interest catcher.
   f. Provide for repetition.
   g. Provide for real and rhetorical questions.
   h. Be as short as reasonably possible.
   i. Include humor.
   j. Give examples.
   k. Summarize at end.
   l. Tell what you are going to tell them, tell them, and tell them what you told them.

3. Give pupils a chance to think before you give the answers. Use questions.

4. The module mentions the following:
   a. Establish a general point of view.
   b. Present facts quickly.
   c. Arouse interest.

    d. Fill in background information.

    e. Introduce new units.

    f. Summarize.

    g. Provide information.

5. Cognitive memory questions are those that test one's memory for facts or information; convergent questions are narrow-range questions that require a correct answer; divergent questions are open-ended, broad questions that have no correct answer; evaluative questions are divergent questions that ask one to put a value on something.

6. Reword, rephrase, come back again.

7. Of course.

8. To lead the pupil to discover the desired answers or come to the desired conclusions.

9. Of course. The open-text recitation is one of the best techniques.

10. Ordinarily, if we can use the regular materials, the pupils' learning will be more beneficial.

Module 4

1. d	**4.** c	**7.** c	**10.** b
2. d	**5.** a	**8.** a	**11.** a
3. b	**6.** d	**9.** c	**12.** b

Module 5

1. **a.** Good motivating qualities.
   b. Teaches and offers practice in intellectual skills.
   c. Results in more thorough learning.
   d. Involves pupils.
2. **a.** Costly in time.
   b. Costly in effort.
   c. Sometimes lead to mislearning.
   d. Not very efficient.
3. Of course.
4. Why not?
5. Check back to the text for the answer. Basically, the steps are as follows:
   a. Become aware of a problem.
   b. Look for a solution.
   c. Test out solution to see if it will work.
6. **a.** Is it pertinent to course objectives?
   b. Is it relevant to pupils' lives?
   c. Is it feasible (time, materials, abilities)?
   d. Is it worthwhile?
7. **a.** Provide lists.
   b. Class discussion.
   c. Describe past projects.
   d. Bring in former pupils.

8. No.
9. **a.** Rating scales.
   b. Checklists.
   c. Standardized directions for observing.
10. **a.** Set procedure required of all interviews.
    b. Standard list of exactly worded questions used by all interviewers.
11. Turn back to module and check your answer against the explanation.
12. Turn back again. Socratic dialogue is mostly a matter of asking leading questions until you get the pupil to arrive at the conclusion you wanted him to reach.
13. Basically that it is controlled by the teacher and so teacher-dominated. True discussions are free and open ended.
14. Value-clarifying discussions are very open, free from leading questions, preaching, or teacher judgments.
15. Refer to module text to see if your answer checks with it.
16. They are fun. They make clear difficult concepts and procedures. They give practice.
17. See the section in the module text.
18. **a.** Assign note taking.
    b. Ask for pupil summaries.
    c. Give quizzes.
    d. Ask pupils to criticize presentation.
19. Again, see the module text, and compare your answer with it.
20. The pupil arrives at the conclusion or generalization himself rather than having it told to him.

Module 6

The most accurate statements are as follows:

1. b	**4.** d	**7.** a	**10.** a
2. c	**5.** b	**8.** b	**11.** d
3. b	**6.** a	**9.** d	**12.** b

For supporting reasons and for explanations of the limitations or inaccuracy of the other statements, reexamine the module at appropriate points.

Module 7

1. True individualization entails a tailor-made curriculum for each pupil, not just a change of pace or varying amount of content to be covered.
2. Theoretically, it makes it easier to pick content and methods suitable for everyone.
3. There is always a spread of characteristics in a homogeneously grouped class. Besides, all the characteristics, other than those reduced by the grouping process, run the entire gamut found in the population.
4. They tend to be written off. Teachers give up on them. Teachers concentrate on the uninteresting and unchallenging content and presentation.
5. Everyone can move through the curriculum at his own pace. No one is forced to move on before he is ready or to wait for others to catch up.

6. To provide for more variety.
7. It provides a place for pupils to work on their own with all the materials they need readily available.
8. **a.** Give some pupils more work, and others, less.
   b. Give some pupils more difficult work, and others, easier.
   c. Use committees and small group work.
   d. Individualize.
   e. Give totally different assignments.
9. A classroom laboratory is arranged so that the materials and equipment are readily available for pupils to work individually and in groups, or on a variety of assignments or projects, under guidance.
10. The bulk of the work is done in a laboratory situation in the true unit. Not everyone does the same thing in the same way.
11. It allows pupils to work individually on different units at the same time as well as allowing for laboratory-type procedures.
12. The feature of *quid pro quo*.
13. They give the pupil direction and structure so that he can work without constant recourse to the teacher for direction.
14. Practice, diagnosis, and study, but not for marks.
15. Focus it on a small sheet of paper or into a box. Attach earphones if it is a sound program.
16. Same way. Arrange it so that pupils do not run out the film, but reverse it for the next pupil or group of pupils.
17. Use study guides, self-correcting materials, student tutors and proctors, and laboratory teaching.
18. Not much, just that you adapt the content, materials, and methods to the group. The basic approach should be about the same, but adapted to pupils' talents, interests, abilities, and goals.

Module 8

1. a	**6.** f	**11.** O	**16.**	**21.** h
2. b	**7.** c	**12.** L	**17.**	**22.** g
3. a	**8.** d	**13.** R or Q	**18.** √	**23.** f
4. d	**9.** A or D	**14.** √	**19.** √	**24.** c
5. b	**10.** K	**15.** √	**20.**	**25.** e

Module 9

1. b	**4.** c	**7.** b	**10.** b	**13.** √
2. c	**5.** a	**8.** d	**11.**	**14.**
3. a	**6.** d	**9.** c	**12.** √	**15.** √

16. 5 ⎫
17. 2 ⎬ any other numbers in same relationship, such as
18. 2 ⎪
19. 1 ⎭

⎧ 10
⎨ 4
⎪ 4
⎩ 2

or

⎧ 50
⎨ 20
⎪ 20
⎩ 10

20. a   **22.** b   **24.** d
21. d   **23.** b   **25.** a

Module 10

1. By showing pupils the real thing or representation of the real thing, the pupils see or hear it rather than words about it.
2. Is it suitable to do the job you want it to do? Other considerations pale before this one.
3. The distance between the lens and light source must be properly adjusted.
4. Use the opaque projector. With it you can blow up the pictures so all can see and study them.
5. You can show the material on the screen or board while pupils work with copies at their seat.
6. Of course.
7. Overhead projectors project only transparent (translucent) material. An opaque projector projects the image of opaque materials.
8. It is versatile, can be used in a lighted room, takes only a second to prepare, can be used as a chalkboard, and for many things.
9. That depends upon how fancy one wants to make it. A quick, temporary transparency can be made by drawing on the frosted plastic with a grease pencil or felt-tipped pen. To draw a more finished project, follow the procedure outlined in the module text.
10. Lay it on top of the basic transparency to add new information, or take it off to subtract information.
11. It blocks out part of the transparency you do not want pupils to see now.
12. Run it on a small screen or box. Use earphones if it is a sound program.
13. To do a good job is quite a lengthy process. Check your answer against the module text.
14. Wrap the film around the take-up reel a few times, mark the break with a slip of paper, and continue with the show. *Do not* try to tape or pin the film together.
15. Lots of things. Require notes, give quizzes, introduce it well, use study guide, follow-up, discussion, and assignments, for example.
16. Some movies are pretty awful—boring, irrelevant, or incorrect. Pupils tend to think of them as entertainment. Movies may emphasize what you would rather not emphasize. They are not very adaptable. They require special arrangements and are generally awkward to use. They are expensive and often difficult to get when you need them.
17. Follow up. What else?
18. See special films. Use them as optional activities, assign activities for theater parties, bases for committees, or individual reports.
19. Introduce. Explain. List key words, use a handout (study guide). Be sure pupils know what is expected of them.
20. Music plus pictures, maps plus pictures, tape plus pictures, board plus screen, or two screens. Or any other combination you think of.

Module 11

1. The textbook should be just one of many tools.
2. The module lists eighteen items. Basically, it should present the relevant content interestingly, logically, and accurately at a reading level that is compatible with that of the pupils.
3. Select a number of readings that will lead to the instructional goals. Let the pupils under guidance read those things that will best suit them. Although they read different things, since the readings all lead to the goals, the pupils should emerge with the concepts. A study guide will help the pupils in their study. The readings should have as much spread in interest and reading level and so on as feasible to provide for the pupils' differences.
4. The greatest advantage has been their inexpensiveness which allows one to use multitexts, introduce original pieces, and mark up books, and so on.
5. Most important, try to find something that encourages thinking. Avoid workbooks that are cut and dried. Otherwise, use the same criteria as for other books and materials.
6. Almost anything, including anecdotes, stories, case studies, pictures, films, filmstrips, histories.
7. To guide pupils so that they can study alone without being tied to the teacher's apron strings.
8. White space is blank space. Leave white space so what you want to stress will stand out.
9. They are more dramatic.
10. Attach sandpaper, felt, or flannel, or Velcro fasteners to light material e.g. paper. See the module text for the details.
11. Use it as a teaching tool.
12. Have a central focus without clutter which draws the eye toward what you want to show off. Use eye catchers and lines to draw the attention to the center of interest. There should be plenty of white space and no clutter.
13. A flip chart is a big pad of charts that one can flip back and forth as needed.
14. You flip the pages to the proper place, talk about it, and then flip to the next page.
15. Pictures give life to dull classes and reality to abstract descriptions, but when you pass them around the room, they distract the pupils from the lesson.
16. In a linear program, the pupils all progress in order through the program in small steps. In a branching program, the pupils take large steps. If they make mistakes, the program branches to reteach them.
17. People, places, things, directions, persons to contact, and any other information on local resource persons, materials, and places to visit.
18. Theoretically, the machine can teach the facts and leave the teacher free to individualize, give additional help, and teach the higher mental skills and processes.

Module 12

1. The professional is strongly based in theoretical knowledge and therefore understands why.
2. He uses methods that involve the student more actively and has a broader repertory and more open style.
3. Flexible style is usually better because it allows one to suit the tactics to the situation.
4. Examine the incident to see what went wrong and then try again.
5. Because it shows why and gives one a base for solving unusual or difficult problem situations.
6. One that includes all the lower levels plus creating, discovering, reorganizing, and formulating new hypotheses, new questions and problems; in short, the level of original and productive thinking.
7. The objective should be clearly stated, measurable, pertinent to unit and course, worthwhile, suitable to age and grade level, achievable, attainable in different degrees and/or amounts, and relevant to the pupils' lives.
8. So you can get a picture of what you and your teaching are like.
9. **a.** Direct.
   b. Probably not as effective as it would be if it were more indirect.
10. **a.** Teacher did most of the talking.
    b. Can't tell. Probably the teacher talks too much.
11. Select from good objectives, objectives obtainable by discussion techniques, good participation, teacher drew pupils out, teacher did not let anyone dominate, teacher kept group on the topic, teacher did not dominate, teacher used evocative questions and tentative solutions, teacher summarized well when needed, and teacher tied the discussion together in summary.
12. Teacher runs a good discussion, does not dominate, and draws out the class.
13. Whiplash questions are really incomplete sentences. They tend to confuse. They do not induce the proper set for answering questions.
14. Cognitive memory questions are narrow memory questions calling only for recall of information. Convergent questions are narrow thought questions which call for coming to a correct solution. Divergent questions are broad, open-ended thought questions for which there are probably no single correct answers.
15. The pupils seem to have achieved objective 1, but missed objective 2. If objective 2 is important, it probably should be retaught.

NOTES

NOTES

NOTES

NOTES

NOTES

NOTES

NOTES